Nineteenth-Century Opera and the Scientific Imagination

Scientific thinking has long been linked to music theory and instrument making, yet the profound and often surprising intersections between the sciences and opera during the long nineteenth century are here explored for the first time. These touch on a wide variety of topics, including vocal physiology, theories of listening and sensory communication, technologies of theatrical machinery and discourses of biological degeneration. Taken together, the chapters reveal an intertwined cultural history that extends from backstage hydraulics to drawing-room hypnotism, and from laryngoscopy to theatrical aeronautics. Situated at the intersection of opera studies and the history of science, the book therefore offers a novel and illuminating set of case studies of a kind that will appeal to historians of both science and opera, as well as European culture more generally from the French Revolution to the end of the Victorian period.

DAVID TRIPPETT is University Senior Lecturer at the University of Cambridge and a Fellow of Christ's College. His first monograph, *Wagner's Melodies* (Cambridge, 2013), examines the cultural and scientific history of melodic theory in relation to Wagner's writings and music. He recently co-edited *The Companion to Music in Digital Culture* (Cambridge, 2019) and produced critical and performing editions of Liszt's mature opera, *Sardanapalo* (NLA, 2019). His research has received the Einstein and Lockwood Prizes (American Musicological Society), and the Nettl Prize (Society for Ethnomusicology).

BENJAMIN WALTON is University Senior Lecturer at the University of Cambridge and a Fellow of Jesus College. His monograph *Rossini in Restoration Paris: The Sound of Modern Life* was published by Cambridge University Press in 2007, and a collection of essays entitled *The Invention of Beethoven and Rossini*, co-edited with Nicholas Mathew, appeared in 2013. From 2014 to 2018 he was co-editor of *Cambridge Opera Journal*.

Nineteenth-Century Opera and the Scientific Imagination

Edited by

DAVID TRIPPETT
University of Cambridge

BENJAMIN WALTON
University of Cambridge

CAMBRIDGE
UNIVERSITY PRESS

University Printing House, Cambridge CB2 8BS, United Kingdom

One Liberty Plaza, 20th Floor, New York, NY 10006, USA

477 Williamstown Road, Port Melbourne, VIC 3207, Australia

314-321, 3rd Floor, Plot 3, Splendor Forum, Jasola District Centre, New Delhi - 110025, India

79 Anson Road, #06-04/06, Singapore 079906

Cambridge University Press is part of the University of Cambridge.

It furthers the University's mission by disseminating knowledge in the pursuit of
education, learning and research at the highest international levels of excellence.

www.cambridge.org
Information on this title: www.cambridge.org/9781107529021
DOI: 10.1017/9781316275863

© Cambridge University Press 2019

This publication is in copyright. Subject to statutory exception
and to the provisions of relevant collective licensing agreements,
no reproduction of any part may take place without the written
permission of Cambridge University Press.

First published 2019
First paperback edition 2021

A catalogue record for this publication is available from the British Library

Library of Congress Cataloging in Publication data
Names: Trippett, David, 1980– | Walton, Benjamin, 1972–
Title: Nineteenth-century opera and the scientific imagination / edited by David Trippett,
Benjamin Walton.
Other titles: 19th-century opera and the scientific imagination
Description: Cambridge, United Kingdom ; New York, NY : Cambridge University Press,
2019. | Includes bibliographical references and index.
Identifiers: LCCN 2019007845 | ISBN 9781107111257 (alk. paper)
Subjects: LCSH: Opera – 19th century. | Music and science – History – 19th century.
Classification: LCC ML1705 N56 2019 | DDC 782.109/034–dc23
LC record available at https://lccn.loc.gov/2019007845

ISBN 978-1-107-11125-7 Hardback
ISBN 978-1-107-52902-1 Paperback

Cambridge University Press has no responsibility for the persistence or
accuracy of URLs for external or third-party internet websites referred to in
this publication, and does not guarantee that any content on such websites is,
or will remain, accurate or appropriate.

Contents

List of Figures   [*page* vii]
List of Tables   [ix]
List of Music Examples   [x]
List of Contributors   [xi]
Acknowledgements   [xv]

Introduction: The Laboratory and the Stage   [1]
DAVID TRIPPETT AND BENJAMIN WALTON

PART I   VOICES   [19]

1 Pneumotypes: Jean de Reszke's High Pianissimos and the
   Occult Sciences of Breathing   [21]
   JAMES Q. DAVIES

2 Vocal Culture in the Age of Laryngoscopy   [44]
   BENJAMIN STEEGE

3 Operatic Fantasies in Early Nineteenth-Century Psychiatry   [63]
   CARMEL RAZ

4 Opera and Hypnosis: Victor Maurel's Experiments with
   Verdi's *Otello*   [84]
   CÉLINE FRIGAU MANNING

PART II   EARS   [107]

5 Hearing in the Music of Hector Berlioz   [109]
   JULIA KURSELL

6 From Distant Sounds to Aeolian Ears: Ernst Kapp's Auditory
   Prosthesis   [134]
   DAVID TRIPPETT

vi *Contents*

7 Wagner, Hearing Loss and the Urban Soundscape of Late
Nineteenth-Century Germany [155]
JAMES DEAVILLE

PART III TECHNOLOGIES [173]

8 Science, Technology and Love in Late Eighteenth-Century
Opera [175]
DEIRDRE LOUGHRIDGE

9 Technological Phantoms of the Opéra [199]
BENJAMIN WALTON

10 Circuit Listening [227]
ELLEN LOCKHART

PART IV BODIES [249]

11 *Excelsior* as Mass Ornament: The Reproduction
of Gesture [251]
GAVIN WILLIAMS

12 Automata, Physiology and Opera in the Nineteenth
Century [269]
MYLES W. JACKSON

13 Wagnerian Manipulation: Bayreuth and Nineteenth-Century
Sciences of the Mind [287]
JAMES KENNAWAY

14 Unsound Seeds [303]
ALEXANDER REHDING

Bibliography [335]
Index [375]

Figures

I.1 A demonstration of Charles Wheatstone's 'Enchanted Lyre' [*page* 11]

1.1 Thomas J. Mays, 'Tracings taken from chests of Indian girls' [36]

1.2 Holbrook Curtis, 'The Tonograph' [40]

1.3 Watts-Hughes's voice-figures in Holbrook Curtis, *Voice Building and Tone Placing* [42]

2.1 'Ammoniaphone', *Life*, 7, 159 (14 January 1886) [45]

2.2 Ammoniaphone users in *Health*, 3, 74 (5 September 1884) [46]

2.3 'Laryngoscope', Johann Nepomuk Czermak, *Der Kehlkopfspiegel und seine Verwerthung für Physiologie und Medizin* (1860) [52]

2.4 Image of the laryngoscope in use from Lennox Browne, *The Throat and Its Diseases* (1887) [53]

2.5 Laryngoscopic views in Morell Mackenzie, *Hygiene of the Vocal Organs* (1886) [53]

4.1 Cover illustration for Albert de Rochas, *Les Sentiments, la musique et le geste* [90]

4.2 *Un Vieux menuet dansé par Lina* in Rochas, *Les Sentiments* [94]

4.3 *Le 'Miserere' du* Trouvère in Rochas, *Les Sentiments* [95]

7.1 André Gill, 'Richard Wagner' (1869) [170]

8.1 Christoph Friedrich Bretzner, *Die Luftbälle, oder der Liebhaber à la Montgolfier* (1786), title page [187]

8.2 'Drei Knaben', from *Die Zauberflöte*, Neubrandenberg/Neustrelitz, 2013 [195]

10.1 'The Magnetic Rope', from Andrew Jackson Davis, *The Present Age and Inner Life* (1853) [239]

10.2 Carlo Matteucci, 'Piano dei telegrafi elettrici in Toscana' (1861) [245]

11.1 Front cover of *Il teatro illustrato* (March 1881) [254]

11.2 Costume design for 'Il telefono' in *Excelsior* [261]

14.1 Tovey's evolutionary model of music, from a modal turn of phrase to the *Tristan* chord [314]

viii *List of Figures*

14.2   Ernst Haeckel, Parallel evolution of embryos from various species (1874) [315]
14.3   J. J. Grandville, 'L'homme descend vers le brute' (1843) [320]
14.4a Johann Kasper Lavater, 'Vom Frosch zum Apollo Belvedere' (1775–78) [323]
14.4b J. J. Grandville, 'L'homme descend vers la grenouille' (1844) [325]
14.5   Ernst Kurth's analysis of the opening bars of *Salome* (1913) [330]

Tables

3.1   A comparison of de Ernst de Valenti's and Peter Schneider's
      reports of the patient's speech   [*page 75*]
7.1   Key nineteenth-century texts on the ear and its diseases
      and injuries   [161]

Music Examples

5.1 Berlioz, *Symphonie fantastique*, arr. F. Liszt, IV: March to the Scaffold, bb. 17–25   [*page* 117]

5.2 Berlioz, *Symphonie fantastique*, arr. F. Liszt, IV: March to the Scaffold, bb. 62–71   [118]

5.3 Berlioz, *Symphonie fantastique*, arr. F. Liszt, IV: March to the Scaffold, bb. 78–86   [120]

6.1 Richard Wagner, *Lohengrin*, Act I scene 2, bb. 551–575   [135]

6.2 Franz Schreker, *Der ferne Klang*, Act I scene 1   [151]

8.1 Haydn, *Il mondo della luna*, Act II, Sinfonia, bb. 1–10   [181]

8.2 Haydn, *Il mondo della luna*, Act II, 'tree symphony', bb. 1–14   [182]

8.3 Haydn, *Il mondo della luna*, Act II, 'Che mondo amabile', bb. 44–49   [183]

8.4 Paisiello, *Il mondo della luna*, Act II, 'air', bb. 1–21. Österreichische Nationalbibliothek Musiksammlung, Mus.Hs.17806/2   [184]

8.5 Ferdinand Fränzl, *Die Luftbälle, oder Der Liebhaber à la Montgolfier* (1785), Act II finale: instrumental ritornello while the balloons ascend   [191]

8.6 Mozart, *Die Zauberflöte*, Act II finale, 'Bald prangt, den Morgen zu verkünden'   [197]

10.1 Puccini, *La scossa elettrica*, bb. 1–12   [230]

10.2 Romualdo Marenco, 'I fattorini del telegrafo. Galop', from *Excelsior* (1881), piano reduction   [247]

11.1 Romualdo Marenco, 'Galop', preceded by a waltz, from *Excelsior* (1881), piano reduction   [264]

12.1 Richard Wagner, *Parsifal*, Act II, bb. 1025–1034   [283]

Contributors

JAMES Q. DAVIES is Associate Professor of Music at the University of California, Berkeley. He is author of *Romantic Anatomies of Performance* (2014) and co-editor of *Sound Knowledge: Music and Science in London, 1789–1851* (2016). He is also co-editor of *New Material Histories of Music*. He is working on *Creatures of the Air*, a project about aero-technologies and aero-techniques. The book will explore nineteenth-century ideas about breath control, ideas for air-conditioning systems in buildings, and ideas about how musical civilisations form in relation to the aerial effects of different climates.

JAMES DEAVILLE teaches in the School for Studies in Art and Culture at Carleton University, Ottawa. He edited *Music in Television* (2010), co-edited *Music and the Broadcast Experience* (2016) and is editing *The Oxford Handbook on Music and Advertising*. He has published in *Journal of the American Musicological Society, Journal of the Society for American Music* and *Nineteenth-Century Music Review*, and has contributed to books published by Oxford, Cambridge and Routledge, among others. In particular, he published 'Negotiating the "Absolute": Hanslick's Path through Musical History', in *Rethinking Hanslick: Music, Formalism, and Expression*, edited by Nicole Grimes, Siobhan Donovan and Wolfgang Marx (2013), 15–37.

CÉLINE FRIGAU MANNING is Associate Professor in Performance Studies and Italian at Université Paris 8 and a member of the Institut Universitaire de France. A graduate of the École Normale Supérieure, she was a resident scholar at the Villa Medici in 2011. She is the author of *Chanteurs en scène: L'œil du spectateur au Théâtre-Italien* (2014), editor of *La Scène en miroir : Métathéâtres italiens* (2016) and of a special issue of *Laboratoire italien* on 'Italian Music and Medicine in the 19th Century' (2017). She is the recipient of a five-year grant from the Institut universitaire de France, which includes her current book project on music and hypnosis entitled *Spectacles de l'esprit: Hypnose, musique et sciences au XIXe siècle*.

MYLES W. JACKSON is Professor of the History of Science at the Institute for Advanced Study in Princeton, New Jersey. He is the author of *Spectrum Belief: Joseph von Fraunhofer and the Craft of Precision Optics* (2000), *Harmonious Triads: Physicists, Musicians, and Natural Philosophers in Nineteenth-Century Germany* (2006) and *The Genealogy of a Gene: Patents, Race, and HIV/AIDS* (2015).

JAMES KENNAWAY is a Senior Research Fellow at the University of Roehampton in London. He has previously worked at Oxford, Stanford, Vienna, Durham, Newcastle and Groningen. He has written extensively about topics related to music and medicine, notably in his monograph *Bad Vibrations: The History of the Idea of Music as a Cause of Disease* (2012). His other interests include the history of emotions and the history of surgery.

JULIA KURSELL is professor and chair of the Institute of Musicology at the University of Amsterdam. She studied musicology, Slavic philology and comparative literature in Munich, Moscow and Los Angeles, and completed her doctoral studies at Munich University with a thesis on music in the early Russian avant-garde. In 2013, she received the Habilitation (professorial degree) in musicology and history of science from Technical University, Berlin, for her thesis 'Ohr und Instrument: zu Hermann von Helmholtz' physiologischer Grundlegung der Musiktheorie'. Her research interests include twentieth- and twenty-first-century composition, the history of musicology and the relation between music and science. She is co-director of the University of Amsterdam's Vossius Center for the History of Humanities and Sciences and editor of the journal *History of Humanities*.

ELLEN LOCKHART is Assistant Professor of Musicology at the University of Toronto, following a postdoctoral fellowship at the Society of Fellows in the Liberal Arts at Princeton University. Her book *Animation, Plasticity and Music in Italy, 1770–1830*, was published in the autumn of 2017, and she has co-edited, with James Davies, a volume on the history of music and science in London in the period 1789–1851. Her critical edition of Puccini's *La fanciulla del West* had its debut at La Scala in 2016 under the direction of Riccardo Chailly.

DEIRDRE LOUGHRIDGE is Assistant Professor of Music at Northeastern University. Her first book, *Haydn's Sunrise, Beethoven's Shadow: Audiovisual Culture and the Emergence of Musical Romanticism* (2016), won the 2017 Kenshur Prize for outstanding monograph in eighteenth-century studies. Her research has also appeared in such publications as the *Journal of the Royal Musical Association*, *Early Music* and *Journal of Musicology*. Her current book project, 'Sounding Human', explores how music has been used to define the nature of, and relationships between humans and machines from the eighteenth century to today.

CARMEL RAZ is a Research Group Leader at the Max Planck Institute for Empirical Aesthetics in Frankfurt, where she directs the group 'Histories of Music, Mind, and Body'. She received her PhD in music theory from Yale in 2015, and also holds a master's degree in composition from the University of Chicago and a Diplom in violin performance from the Hochschule für Musik 'Hanns Eisler' in Berlin. From 2015 to 2018 she was a postdoctoral research fellow at the Columbia Society of Fellows.

ALEXANDER REHDING is Fanny Peabody Professor of Music at Harvard University. His research is located at the intersection between the history of music theory and cultural history. His books include *Hugo Riemann and the Birth of Modern Musical Thought* (2003), *Music and Monumentality* (2009) and *Beethoven's Symphony no. 9* (2017). A former editor of *Acta musicologica*, he is editor-in-chief of the Oxford Handbook Online series for music, and a series editor for Bloomsbury's *Cultural History of Music*. His contributions have been recognised with such awards as a Guggenheim Fellowship and the Dent Medal.

BENJAMIN STEEGE is Associate Professor of Music at Columbia University. He studies theoretical discourses around music in the nineteenth and twentieth centuries, with particular attention to intersections with the history of science. His first book, *Helmholtz and the Modern Listener* (2012), thematised the collision between orthodox music-theoretical knowledge and experimental modes of observation developed in laboratory environments. He is currently writing a second book, *Music and the Limits of Psychology, 1910–1960*, which asks what it meant to adopt a sceptical stance toward the ascendant authority of psychological knowledge, especially in the context of the Weimar Republic and its legacy.

DAVID TRIPPETT is University Senior Lecturer at the University of Cambridge. His research interests focus on nineteenth-century cultural and intellectual history, opera, posthumanism and the scene of digital culture. He is author of *Wagner's Melodies: Aesthetics and Materialism in German Musical Identity* (2013), and in 2018 he edited and orchestrated Liszt's mature opera, *Sardanapalo*, for the *Neue Liszt Ausgabe* and Schott Music. He currently runs a research group in Cambridge, funded by a European Research Council starting grant, that examines the dialogue between natural science and music during the nineteenth century.

xiv   *List of Contributors*

BENJAMIN WALTON is University Senior Lecturer in Music at the University of Cambridge, and a Fellow of Jesus College. His previous publications with Cambridge University Press include *Rossini in Restoration Paris: The Sound of Modern Life* and *The Invention of Beethoven and Rossini: Historiography, Analysis, Criticism*, co-edited with Nicholas Mathew. Between 2014 and 2018 he edited *Cambridge Opera Journal* with Stefanie Tcharos; he is currently working on a book about the first Italian opera troupe to go around the world, during the 1820s and 1830s.

GAVIN WILLIAMS is a musicologist and Leverhulme Early Career Research Fellow at King's College London. He wrote a PhD dissertation at Harvard University on sound and media in Milan *c.* 1900, and was then a postdoctoral fellow at Jesus College, Cambridge. He has published articles and book chapters on Futurist music, Italian opera and ballet, and soundscapes in nineteenth-century London, and is currently writing a book on the imperial geographies of recorded sound during the first half of the twentieth century.

Acknowledgements

This book began life as a discussion in The Plough in Fen Ditton. It was a breezy spring day, with a slow-moving river in the distance. Since that time, when the seed of an idea for excavating dialogues between opera and natural science during the nineteenth century was planted, conversations with colleagues and friends, near and far, have nurtured the subject in ways we had neither anticipated nor sought to constrain. For this stimulating engagement, and to all our interlocutors, we are most grateful; the tree of knowledge that resulted from that spring seed has many branches, and offers generous scope for further cultivation. Specifically, we thank the contributors for their intellectual commitment, and on a practical plane, we thank Ariana Phillips-Hutton for invaluable assistance in copyediting, and for helping to draw the editorial threads together in the final stage. We are grateful to Victoria Cooper at Cambridge University Press for believing in the project from the outset, and thank Kate Brett and Eilidh Burrett for seeing it deftly through the production process. We also acknowledge the support of the European Research Council and the Leverhulme Trust, both of whom enabled work on this project to proceed.

Introduction
The Laboratory and the Stage

DAVID TRIPPETT AND BENJAMIN WALTON

At first sight, opera and science would seem to occupy quite separate spaces. The one typically unfolds on the stage of a theatre, the other most often takes place in a laboratory or lecture hall. The one draws on creative inspiration in entwining music, poetry and spectacle, the other on inductive reasoning through observation and experiment; patient activities that, for John Herschel in 1831, constituted the 'fountains of all natural science'.[1] And while the one offers an opportunity for emotional and intellectual engagement through the public gaze, the other cautiously validates the empiricism of verifiable experience through critical acts of witnessing. To yoke the two together, then, may appear arbitrary.

Yet such a view not only risks caricature through its stark oppositions, but also overlooks a scene of rich interconnection within nineteenth-century European social and intellectual life. To start at the biographical level, we find a famous scientist such as Michael Faraday not only regularly attending the opera during the 1830s, but also passing judgment in his correspondence on works such as *Fidelio, Il barbiere di Siviglia, Lucrezia Borgia, Les Huguenots* and *L'Étoile du Nord*, while collaborating with Charles Wheatstone in lectures on acoustics at London's Royal Institution.[2] Or take the Victorian polymath Herbert Spencer, who would voice loud opinions on quantifiable 'originality', arguing, for instance, that Meyerbeer's operas were less 'hackneyed' than Mozart's keyboard sonatas.[3] At the same time, composers such as Berlioz and Borodin undertook significant scientific training, the former (unwillingly) in medicine, the latter (enthusiastically) in chemistry – a field in which, for twenty-five years, he held a chair at the Medical Surgical Academy in St Petersburg.

In the context of institutions, meanwhile, a book published in 1908 by two scientific practitioners, entitled *La Science au théâtre*, justified its subject on the basis that 'the applications of science in the theatre are

---

[1] Herschel 1831, 76.
[2] See Faraday's letters 2835, 2991, 3009, 3448, 3455 in F. James 1991, 4:684, 871, 888, and 5:388, 391.
[3] Spencer 1902, 114.

today so numerous, the scenic reproduction of natural phenomena so perfect, [and] effects of all kinds so ably executed' that a study of procedures, devices and machines seemed worthwhile for the theatre-going public.[4] Such a call echoed the opinions of Gaston Tissandier, editor of the eminent journal *La Nature* (founded in 1873). Having completed recent articles on subjects as diverse as the manufacture of artificial butter and the chemical properties of snowflakes, in early 1875 Tissandier turned his attention to the recently inaugurated Garnier opera house in Paris, on the basis that 'all branches of physics are represented at the new Opéra: heating, lighting, optics, electricity, acoustics [all] play different parts in it'.[5]

The following fourteen essays contained in this book advance many more examples of such intersections, with a large cast of both scientists and musicians, famous and forgotten, and touching on topics from vocal physiology to theories of mental health, and from urbanisation to hypnotism. Yet the separation of the two fields can still seem deep-set, for a variety of reasons that themselves have their roots in the nineteenth century and that deserve further attention. These include an approach to opera centred on composers and their works, rather than on performers and performances, but can also be linked to a scientific understanding of sound that sets it apart from romantic opera's quest for 'the magic force of poetic truth', as E. T. A. Hoffmann put it in 1813.[6] At the same time, as numerous contributors here attest, opera's tendency towards excess – whether in terms of voice or spectacle – has frequently made it an object of scholarly suspicion for scientists and musicologists alike, to the point that even a work as inclusive as Guido Adler's famous musicological manifesto of 1885 hides opera within a small subset of his study of 'basic historical categories'; well away from the study of 'systematic musicology', with its 'auxiliary sciences' of acoustics, mathematics, physiology, psychology, logic, metrics, pedagogics and aesthetics.[7]

Such separations, of course, also fit neatly within the standard divisions between the Humanities and Natural Science, whether figured as 'two

---

[4] 'Les applications de la science au théâtre sont aujourd'hui si nombreuses, la reproduction scénique des phénomènes naturels si parfaite, les trucs de tous genres si habilement exécutés.' Vaulabelle and Hémardinquer 1908, 1. Vaulabelle was a scientific writer, Hémardinquer a physicist.

[5] 'Toutes les branches de la physique sont représentées au nouvel Opéra: la chaleur, la lumière, l'optique, l'électricité, l'acoustique y jouent des rôles différents.' Tissandier 1875, 150. The previous two articles by Tissandier on the same topic addressed 'Ventilation and Heating' and 'Gas and Lighting': a reminder of the ways that the meeting of science and opera also brings us towards aspects of the operatic industry unfamiliar from traditional histories.

[6] Hoffmann 1963, 788.   [7] Adler 1885, 5–20; Eng. trans. Mugglestone 1981, 1–21.

Introduction: The Laboratory and the Stage

cultures' or as a natural result of specialisation, with the result that one might be tempted to rephrase the aim of this book as an integration of two parallel but separate cultural scenes: two tributaries in search of a single river. Yet we argue instead that at this time the river already existed, and that discourses of science and opera already overlapped, only later to be channelled into separate streams. Both, for instance, strove for universals. Some writers on music, such as Giuseppe Carpani in 1821, fantasised about opera itself – here in the form of the melodies of Rossini – as a universal force; spreading beneficently throughout the world, freely floating over the seas, and in a short time 'mak[ing] the circuit of the earth, touch[ing] on every shore, and enter[ing] every port'.[8] Others, like Arthur Schopenhauer – another Rossini fan, though one who would dub opera 'an unmusical invention' – would be unequivocal in labelling music 'a universal language which is understood everywhere, so that it is ceaselessly spoken in all countries and throughout all the centuries with great zeal and earnestness'.[9] Charles Darwin, in similar terms, would argue that a shared biological origin was the guarantor for the universal nature of all human expression and emotion.[10] And some decades earlier John Herschel (keen composer and violinist) spoke of 'those universal axioms which we aim at discovering', and cited the law of gravitation as the 'most universal truth' at which human reason has yet arrived, in permitting the most precise quantitative statement: 'not merely the vague statement that its influence decreases as the distance increases, but the exact numerical rate at which that decrease takes place'.[11] Leaving aside the philosophical distinction between what is given (discovered) and what is made (invented), we argue that such parallelism exceeds mere semblance. Instead it bears witness to a shared universalising impulse with its roots in the eighteenth century that would be simultaneously discharged in different directions in the nineteenth: through the urge to communicate on the one hand, and a desire for knowledge of natural laws on the other.

Not that 'opera' and 'science' were themselves in any way stable categories in this period, of course. The operatic long nineteenth century – stretching from Mozart and Rossini via Verdi and Wagner all the way to Puccini and Strauss – can give an illusion of uniformity in its position as the backbone of the twenty-first-century operatic canon. Yet in its course,

---

[8] 'fa ben tosto il giro della terra, abborda a tutt'i lidi; entra in tutt'i porti'. Carpani 1822, 302–3.

[9] Schopenhauer 2004, 162. His proof was far from empirical: the ready comprehensibility of a 'significant melody which says a great deal . . . [proving] that the content of a melody is very well understandable'.

[10] Darwin 2009, 329ff.   [11] Herschel 1831, 123.

this is a history that encompasses not just a variety of genres – including *opéra comique*, operetta, grand opéra and music drama – but that also saw an explosion of operatic performance inside and outside the opera house across Europe and around the world.[12] And the conception of science remained equally in flux: in 1824, for example, when the term 'Naturwissenschaft' appeared for the first time in Brockhaus's lexicon it received the following pithy definition: 'Nature is mirrored in the spirit of the cultivated person, and this reflection, this ideal image of nature, is natural science.'[13] The combination of nature, her beauty and lawfulness mirrored in cultivated human nature created a triad of contemporary values that were embodied in the emergent persona of the *Naturforscher* ('physicien' and 'naturaliste'/'natural philosopher'), someone who in learning and specificity of purpose exceeded the dilettante butterfly collectors and brilliant amateur polymaths of earlier generations. But as Denise Phillips has shown, while the word 'science'/'Wissenschaft' took on its modern meaning during the course of the nineteenth century, and while ideas of a unified science became associated with mid-century figures such as Du Bois Reymond, Helmholtz and the students of Johannes Müller, 'the power of the term came in part from its continued ambiguity'.[14]

This ambiguity is to some extent a fact of continuous development. As is well known, it is precisely during the nineteenth century that the scientific enterprise underwent unprecedented intellectual and social changes. This is partly reflected in the emergence and professionalisation of the differing disciplines of chemistry, biology, physics, medicine, physiology and the earth sciences, whose public presence became manifest in the formation of national institutions (such as the Royal Institution in London, established in 1799, the Schweizerische Naturforschende Gesellschaft in Geneva, established in 1815, the Kaiserliche Akademie der Wissenschaften in Vienna and the Real Academia de Ciencias Exactas, Físicas y Naturales in Madrid, both established in 1847, as well as the American National Academy of Sciences, established in 1863) and university curricula, and partly through the vast efforts made at disseminating knowledge through popular lectures and a wide range of non-specialist publications. Everything from natural philosophy, literature and educational methods, to military strategy – and, of course, music – became implicated within the scientific enterprise. And so did their agents. Singers seeking vocal enhancement or a cure for loss of voice turned to chemical treatments and physiological experiments; composers experimented with new

---

[12] See Osterhammel 2014, 5–7.   [13] [unsigned] 1824, 6:740–7.   [14] Richards 2012, 9.

instruments; machinists sought out new scenic effects. In daily life, meanwhile, composers and performers came to rely on developments in medicine and applied science as much as any other sector of society. Berlioz and Wagner, for instance, both underwent 'galvanic' treatment for ailments; Wagner also reluctantly recommended train travel and steamers to friends as the fastest means of getting around, just as opera houses newly linked through networks of rail lines advertised for wider audiences, and steam-powered seafaring facilitated touring companies in travelling further afield.[15]

Our concern here, however, is not just a matter of opera and its personnel interacting with and responding to claims for scientific universalities and technological developments. Instead, we argue for a more complex reciprocity, in which operatic production and performance is transformed and reframed by its contact with a variety of scientific (and pseudo-scientific) thought, and where different branches of science are informed and shaped by their contact with opera, broadly conceived. For our purposes, that breadth supports a definition of opera easily encompassing vocal pedagogy, opera house architecture and stage machinery as much as music and drama. It also, in several of the chapters here, conjures a real of the 'operatic' that extends on the one hand towards dramatic instrumental music (such as Berlioz's *Symphonie fantastique*), and on the other the sorts of spectacular allegorical dances that shared the stages with sung drama on many of Europe's great opera houses during the period.

Underlying such variety, the broad questions in pursuit of universals gained urgency as the century wore on. 'Light and tone are the building blocks of art,' explained Eugen Dreher in his 1875 reflections on the relationship between art and natural science. 'In order to understand artistic works philosophically, though, we must unavoidably turn to the physical part of light and tone, and see whether we can use the laws of optics and acoustics to conceive a theory of art with their assistance.'[16] And if such a statement emerges somewhat flat-footed, in a rational tract, it mirrors earlier, flightier forays in the form of fiction. In 1837, for example, one of Balzac's most musical short stories, 'Gambara', depicts an aging composer and instrument builder whose unperformed opera sounds radiant on his new, retuned instruments, but cacophonous on those in common usage. 'Music is at once a science and an art,' Gambara tells his

---

[15] Walter 2016, 51–2.

[16] 'Licht und Ton sind somit das Baumaterial der Kunst. Um aber die Kunstschöpfungen philosophisch zu verstehen, müssen wir nöthgedrungen auf den physikalischen Theil von Licht und Ton eingehen und sehen, ob wir die Gesetze der Optik und Akustik gebrauchen können, um mit ihrer Hilfe eine Theorie der Kunst zu entwerfen.' Dreher 1875, 23.

curious Italian patron. 'Its roots in physics and mathematics make it a science; it becomes an art by inspiration which unconsciously employs the theorems of science. It derives from physics by the very essence of the substance it employs: *sound is air modified.*'[17] Such a potted definition of the mechanical propagation of acoustic waves chimes with experiments by the likes of Chladni and Wheatstone, and pre-empts those of Helmholtz, John Tyndall and Alexander Ellis.[18] Yet Balzac's optimism for the potential of acoustic science would prove more speculative than that of his scientist counterparts:

> What heights could we not attain if we were to find the physical laws by virtue of which – consider this! – we collect . . . a certain ethereal substance, diffused within the air, which affords us music as well as light, the phenomena of vegetation as well as those of zoology! . . . Those new laws would arm the composer with new powers, offering him instruments superior to those he has now, and perhaps a more wondrous harmony compared to the one which governs music today.[19]

A smattering of orphan music technologies emerged under the auspices of such rhetoric. These included real new instruments, from melographs and the melodium, to orchestrions such as Johann Nepomuk Mälzel's panharmonicon (a large mechanical orchestral organ), Dietrich Niklaus Winkel's Componium (an algorithmic generator of melodic variations), Johann Jakob Schnell's *anémocorde* (an elongated keyboard whose strings were vibrated by compressed air), and Angelo Barbieri's automatic organs intended for churches unable to afford an organist.[20]

To be sure, such new instruments rarely if ever established themselves in the opera house pit (though they may well have been put to the task of performing operatic arrangements). Instead we have unsuccessful attempts like the glass harmonica intended for *Lucia di Lammermoor* (1835) that had to be rescored for two flutes in Donizetti's autograph manuscript, for

---

[17] 'La musique est tout à la fois une science et un art: les racines qu'elle a dans la physique et les mathématiques en font une science; elle devient un art par l'inspiration qui emploie à son insu les théorèmes de la science. Elle tient à la physique par l'essence même de la substance qu'elle emploie, car le son est de l'air modifié'. Balzac 1837, 359; Eng. trans. 2001, 77; emphasis added.

[18] See, for instance, Chladni 1787; Tyndall 1867; Ellis 1885; Helmholtz 1954; and Wheatstone 2011b.

[19] 'où n'irions-nous pas si nous trouvions les lois physiques en vertu desquelles (saisissez bien ceci) nous rassemblons . . . une certaine substance éthérée, répandue dans l'air, et qui nous donne la musique aussi bien que la lumière, les phénomènes de la végétation et de la zoologie! . . . Ces lois nouvelles armeraient le compositeur de pouvoirs nouveaux en lui offrant des instruments supérieurs aux instruments actuels, et peut-être une harmonie grandiose comparée à celle quie régit aujourd'hui la musique.' Balzac 1837, 359; Eng. trans. 2001, 78.

[20] See Dolan 2008, 11–12; Trippett 2013, 96–100; Farabegoli 2016, 59–71.

instance.[21] And when Meyerbeer first incorporated a church organ into *Robert le Diable* (1831), *Le Figaro* branded it a 'sublime invasion of the domain of the Opéra', where the shock arose more from cultural disorientation, from repurposing the soundtrack of ecclesiastical worship, rather than from scientific novelty per se.[22]

Yet Balzac's original conception of Gambara's super-instrument leads us beyond such specifics, expanding in Balzac's freewheeling text not only to include voices as well as multiple instrumental parts, but also reaching towards the idea of Meyerbeerian grand opéra as itself 'a gigantic, unified machine', as Emily Dolan and John Tresch have suggested.[23] Such a view accords with Tresch's broader image, developed in his monograph *The Romantic Machine*, of a transformed post-Napoleonic understanding of machines as 'flexible, active, and inextricably woven into circuits of both living and inanimate elements'.[24]

This line of research, with its close imbrication of romanticism and industrialisation, and its insistence on breaking down boundaries not only between art and science, but also between opera and other artistic and technological developments (the daguerreotype, the automaton and so on), forms a key precursor to the sort of approach that we pursue here. But it is not the only one: Wagner scholarship, after all, had been switched onto technological questions at least since Adorno's *In Search of Wagner* (drafted, in part, during 1937–8), with its analysis of the Bayreuthian concealment of technology and labour through novel instrumentation as well as the hidden orchestra, the loss – for Adorno – of individual identity in the body's physiological response to mediatised sounds – sounds studded by leitmotifs, repeated advert-like, for the purpose of dulling critical faculties (i.e. mirroring – for Adorno in 1938 – the propaganda mechanisms of National Socialism), the darkened auditorium and the pursuit of a controlling, proto-cinematic illusion. Hence when Friedrich Kittler sketched out both a history of operatic lighting and an argument for the analogue orchestra modelling electronic amplification, Wagner remained at the centre, as he would in Carolyn Abbate's second book, whose title pays homage to Adorno's example and follows Kittler's provocative analysis of moments of Wagnerian sonic climax vis-à-vis media, from rock amplification to Zeppelin bombers.[25] Yet while Abbate's *In Search of Opera* remains perhaps the richest and most

---

[21] See Smart 1992, 129.

[22] 'L'Orgue qui a fait une sublime invasion dans le domaine de l'Opéra.' [unsigned] 1831, 2–3; cf. Coudroy-Saghaï 1988, 62.

[23] Dolan and Tresch 2011, 9.   [24] Tresch 2012, xi.   [25] Abbate 2001; Kittler 2013.

suggestive study of nineteenth-century opera and technology to appear in recent years, it nevertheless leaves a gap between *Die Zauberflöte* and Wagner's music dramas that Tresch and others have only recently begun to fill.[26] More generally, although both Adorno and Abbate proceed from a desire to demystify Wagner in a way that from one perspective harks back to the sort of unveiling of stage trickery found in earlier books like *La Science au théâtre*, the familiar orbit around Bayreuth and its associated dramatic innovations risks overlooking not just the wider operatic histories of the period, but also the intersections of those histories with a wide variety of both technologies and theories outside the Wagnerian purview.

Wagner is not neglected in the present study. But across the essays we have tried to bring together a variety of different kinds of approach to the study of opera and science that both reflect the variety of recent work in what is a fast-growing field, and that also seek to indicate future directions. Given the diversity of our topic, moreover, we make no claims here either to full chronological or geographical coverage. Instead, we have sought a selection of case studies that engage with – or else offer alternatives to – existing narratives whose key events are by now well established. One such narrative, outlined by Kittler and others, is the history of operatic technology (specifically lighting), with a special place reserved for the inauguration of dimmable gaslight at the Paris Opéra for Nicolas Isouard's *Aladin ou La Lampe merveilleuse* (1822), thereby permitting a darkened auditorium that refocused onlookers' sensoria, and demanded a new sensory engagement with the unfolding production, as though the magical lamp doubled as a quasi-Promethean gift. (It is indicative of applied science's transformative impact on daily life that, prior to the invention of yellow phosphorus matches in 1805, fires and lamps were still lit by flint, steel and tinder, a method dating back millennia.) By the mid-century, carbon electric arc lamps allowed for an unprecedented intensity of illumination that rendered naked flame passé. The spectacular electric sunrise in the third act of Meyerbeer's *Le Prophète* (1850) then 'doomed' to inadequacy earlier candle- and gas-powered effects in the prologue to Verdi's *Atilla* or in the ode-symphonie to Félicien David's *Le Désert*, as Anselm Gerhard and others have noted.[27]

---

[26] A representative sample of such works includes Jackson 2006; Smocovitis 2009; Hui 2012; Steege 2012; Tresch 2012; Hui, Kursell and Jackson 2013; Pesic 2014; Davies and Lockhart 2016; Henson 2016.

[27] Gerhard 2000, 299. Cf. Loughridge 2016, 11ff.

Introduction: The Laboratory and the Stage   9

If staged optical illusions proliferated from the possibilities of controllable lighting technologies, from realist dioramas (including shimmering clouds in Meyerbeer's *L'Africaine*[28]) to panoramas, magic lantern shows and the two locomotive boilers that created steam effects for the *Ring* at Bayreuth,[29] another, more concealed operatic history of hallucination and hypnotism had a less deterministic influence. This might draw a tentative connection between depictions of ghosts and spirits (*Der Freischütz, Undine*), visitations (*Les Troyens, Palestrina*) and – somewhat later – séance (*The Medium*), merging audience association of occult practices offstage with their sometimes all-too-material aesthetic representation onstage, all amid the cult of visual phantasmagoria that had become intrinsic to the reinvention of grand opéra during the 1830s.[30] Later in the century, we might look for another shadow history in the use of novel acoustic effects in Wagner's depiction of three-dimensional soundscapes (*Lohengrin, Die Meistersinger, Parsifal*), and artificially enhanced auditory communication implied at the close of Schreker's *Der ferne Klang* (1903), for moments of interchange between scientific knowledge and operatic production.

If these each represent stories yet to be fully pieced together, it is also important to stress that the thematic interrelation between opera and science could also on occasion be disarmingly explicit, as explored here in Deirdre Loughridge's chapter on late eighteenth-century 'scientific' operas. A further notable instance occurs in *The Devil's Opera* (1838), George A. Macfarren's first musical drama, whose commercial success was credited with saving the fortunes of London's ailing Lyceum Theatre. Midway through Act I, the bass Posillipo, a Venetian noble, is planning an occult experiment for the evening, which he anticipates will bring him immortality. Sitting at his desk amid the accoutrements of scientific learning – 'books, globes, telescopes, chemical apparatus, skeletons ... skull, hourglass' – it is his dark pact with 'science' that paves the way:

---

[28] A handwritten addition to Meyerbeer's manuscript for *L'Africaine* reads: 'At this moment the branches of the manchineel open and one sees through transparent foliage the dream of Sélika in action: from the two opposing sides of the theatre, one sees two group of shimmering clouds, one over the top where Sélika is set, the other on the bottom where Vasco is set. The cloud supporting Vasco rises while Sélika's lowers (on a diagonal line), and they become one as they meet.' Cited in Cruz 1999, 46–7.

[29] See Kreuzer 2011.

[30] On the problematic materiality of the effects in Weber's *Der Freischütz*, see Newcomb 1995.

Hail science! Potentate sublime!
Schoolmistress, that all knowledge teaches!
Freeholder of all space and time,
And banker of all wisdom's riches!
Inspired, and cherished by thine aid,
To seek what ne'er was sought before,
A weary pilgrimage I've made
Through all the realms of learned lore:
> Mathematics – hydrostatics –
> Pyrotechnics and pneumatics –
> Metaphysics – economics –
> Necromancy and mnemonics –
>> Necrology –
>> Astrology –
>> Meteorology –
>> Demonology! –

At length I reached the happy goal;
At length, by my endeavor,
Stern Death shall have no more control,
And life shall last for ever!

When this premiered on 13 August 1838, its gesture towards the wonders of science was evidently plausible. The first season ran for fifty nights, and its second for thirty.[31] Posillipo's eulogy is consistent, perhaps even repetitive (in the second act, we find 'Science! Thou queen of mysteries! Let thy phosphoric lantern penetrate this double darkness . . . Science pays all, and ennobles the world.'[32]), though at least one critic dismissed the libretto as so much hocus-pocus, 'a succession of pantomime tricks', and advised the composer to seek a better poet (it was his father).[33]

Scientists, though, were not immune from the power of theatre and the well-timed pantomimic revelation, as can be seen in the growth through the century of public scientific demonstrations and public lectures. 'Science lecturing was a competitive business', as Bernard Lightman has pointed out. 'Not only were lecturers competing with one another to draw audiences, they were also vying with the theater, the panorama, the exhibition, museums, and other forms of popular entertainment.'[34] Naturally, such

---

[31] Bennett 1897, 454. [32] Macfarren 1838, 23–4. [33] [unsigned] 1838, 197.
[34] Lightman 2007, 125.

Figure I.1 A demonstration of Charles Wheatstone's 'Enchanted Lyre', The frontispiece to John Pepper, *Boy's Playbook of Science*, 2nd edn. (London: George Routledge and Sons, 1866), Whipple Library, University of Cambridge.

lectures included those on acoustic science. A well known example, shown in Figure I.1, is Charles Wheatstone's 'Enchanted Lyre' that appeared to play itself when suspended by strings from the ceiling, but was in fact stimulated into sonorous resonance by concealed, interlocking metal rods that conducted vibrations produced in an adjacent room. John Henry Pepper's illustration of this illusion – with four harps – formed the frontispiece for his best-selling primer *Boy's Playbook of Science* (1860), where he wrote of Wheatstone's 'telephone concert ... in which the sounds and vibrations pass *inaudible* through an intermediate hall, and are reproduced in the lecture-room unchanged in their qualities and intensities'.[35] Such demonstrations of acoustic illusion could claim separation from straightforward scientific fraud (such as Wolfgang von Kempelen's famous chess-playing Turk), in that the rational basis of the illusion remained; the one used ingenuity to apply uncommon knowledge for dazzling effect, the other did the same without any claim for scientific truth. Yet the parallels remained, and were foregrounded in cities in possession of fewer theatres than London or Paris, where a single institution might stage an opera one night, a spoken play the next and an exhibition of scientific experiments the third.[36]

Back in the vast metropolis of London, Wheatstone's spectacle entertained street audiences in London's Pall Mall district as well as professional scientists at the Royal Institution, and a general public at the Royal Polytechnic Institution's lecture theatre. Founded in 1838, the Polytechnic (later the University of Westminster) was a commercial enterprise specifically for displaying novel invention and eye-catching demonstrations. Located at 309 Regent Street in the heart of London's commercial district, its mixture of authoritative scientists, such as Faraday, and showmen, such as Pepper, meant that it trod a delicate line between theatrical display and didactic demonstration.

Perhaps the most salient phenomenon to dovetail demonstration with operatic spectacle was the so-called 'Pepper's ghost'. Pepper, whom we met above, popularised an illusion (invented by Henry Dircks) in which a large piece of plate glass placed at forty-five degrees to an audience gave the illusory appearance of a ghost when lighting for a concealed second actor was closely controlled. This device was first used in stage plays (Charles Dickens's *The Haunted Man*, 1862, and later, adaptations of *A Christmas Carol* and Goethe's *Faust*) but also migrated to operas, including canonical works such as *Der fliegende Holländer* and *Der Freischütz*, as well as once-familiar hits such as John Barnett's *The Mountain Sylph* and Michael William Balfe's *Satanella*, based on a female demon.[37] There was even

---

[35] Pepper 1866, frontispiece.

[36] This was the case, for instance, in various port cities of the Americas during the 1820s, when Italian opera was being performed for the first time.

[37] Burdekin 2015, 158.

a dedicated touring company formed in 1869 entitled The Original Pepper's Ghost and Spectral Opera Company, whose performers travelled widely in Great Britain and Ireland.[38] It is indicative of both public expectation and the appeal of such effects that Wagner's seafaring tale was explicitly advertised in Exeter as having 'great scope for the introduction of Optical illusions, Scenic and Mechanical Effects'.[39] And that, thirteen years after Meyerbeer's electric sunrise, Pepper would deploy a modified arc lamp technology to illuminate Trafalgar Square and St Paul's Cathedral for the wedding of Edward Albert, Prince of Wales, and Alexandra of Denmark.

The closer the investigation of the interactions between science and opera, in other words, the more intertwined the two become, to the point that any distinction between public scientific demonstrations and operatic or theatrical performance becomes blurred. Just as scientists reached for the revelatory tricks of the theatre to hold their audiences entranced (or else, like Charles Darwin, described the wonders of tropical scenery through comparison with the opera[40]), so books like *La Science au théâtre* sought to explain the mechanics of the theatre as a way to replace one form of enchantment (based on aesthetic appreciation) with another (based on the technological sublime).

Faced with such enchantment, there is a temptation for the twenty-first-century historian to treat the intersection of science and opera as an invitation to bask in the wonder of once-novel technologies, in pursuit of a time before opera irreversibly lost its place to cinema as the most visually (and sonically?) spectacular of artforms. And sure enough, in the course of this book we invite the reader to marvel at the union of dance, technology and scientific technology in Manzotti and Marenco's 1881 ballet *Excelsior*; to imagine operatic performances designed to alleviate mental disorders, or as part of experiments in hypnosis; to rehear Wagner's music through the novel science of otology as literally deafening; or to rediscover the initial potential of technologies now invisible through their ubiquity, such as electric circuits, or long obsolete, like the original laryngoscopes. Counterbalancing all such invitations to wonder, though, is an underlying insistence on the fundamentally unremarkable nature of all these stories as part of the larger cultural life of the time; a quality that can help to counteract the 'quirky' potential so often lurking within attempts to

---

[38] Burdekin 2015, 156.

[39] [unsigned] 1882, 1. On the English phantasmagoric nautical predecessors of Wagner's opera, see Cruz 2017.

[40] See Keynes 1988, 69–70; cf. Walton 2018.

combine the histories of music and science by grounding each chapter within a cultural sphere in which the intersection of opera and science becomes in itself unremarkable.[41]

***

There would have been many ways to group the individual chapters here, and we hope and expect that readers will find fruitful connections within and beyond our four broad thematic categories: 'Voices', 'Ears', 'Technologies' and 'Bodies'. Each part privileges thematic congruence over strict chronology, yet some themes (such as hypnosis or degeneration) intentionally resurface in new contexts from one part to another. Taken as a whole, the chapters represent a geographical spread across the main operatic centres of Europe (which for the most part map onto the main centres of scientific research), with occasional forays over the North Atlantic.

We open the first part, on 'Voices', with two chapters exploring the direct influence of science and new technology on the art of operatic singing. Benjamin Steege describes the decades around 1870 as 'a particularly anxious moment in the history of the voice'; a period in which opera's perennial preoccupation with a lost golden age manifested itself in an attempt to transform vocal pedagogy through anatomical and physiological understanding. The adoption of the laryngoscope by the likes of Manuel García *fils* and Emma Seiler opened up the pursuit of correct singing aided by laryngeal observation, with a view to returning to the supposedly lost art of Italian vocal virtuosity, yet at the same time hinting at modernist concerns to come.

Within a similar pan-European (and increasingly transatlantic) context of scientific enquiry, James Q. Davies uses the voice of the great tenor Jean de Reszke to explore the preoccupation towards the end of the nineteenth century with various forms of breath control, and to argue for a history of sound recording that establishes a continuum between the new technologies of reproduction and earlier interests in extracting vocal sounds from the air. In Davies's telling, Reszke's novel breathing method, achieved with the help of medical science, represented a break with techniques of earlier decades, leading to accusations that the singer had wilfully ignored the still-recent revelations of laryngoscopy. This set the stage for a scientific dispute over techniques of vocal production that drew on contemporary racial theory and ultimately spilled over into the

---

[41] On the risks of quirky histories, see Mathew and Smart 2015.

advocacy of mass adenoidectomies among the schoolchildren of early twentieth-century New York.

The chapters by Carmel Raz and Céline Frigau Manning turn from attempts to understand and shape the operatic voice scientifically to the uses of the operatic voice as part of scientific research. Raz focuses on the connections between opera and psychiatry by looking at the theatrical productions staged at Charenton in the early nineteenth century, which contributed to a debate among doctors over the benefits of such therapy. In this light, she interrogates two case histories from the 1830s that illustrate contemporary medical ambivalence over the operatic voice as either therapeutic or pathological. Frigau Manning excavates another case history from the other end of the century, in which one of the most renowned baritones of the age, Victor Maurel, explored the connections between voice and gesture through hypnosis. Maurel's experiments, Frigau Manning suggests, reveal some of the ways that the culture of hypnosis exploited the often porous boundaries between experiment and entertainment, science and spectacle, while also shedding new light on Maurel's own psychology of acting.

In the second section, 'Ears', we turn from singing to hearing, and from performers to composers. Julia Kursell explores the role of aural perception in the music of Hector Berlioz, in the context of contemporary physiological theory. In a movement like the famous 'March to the Scaffold' of the *Symphonie fantastique* (an early example of the many operatically saturated non-operatic works that Berlioz would go on to produce), Kursell argues that Berlioz creates the aural effect of a moving band, an acoustic image that challenges the boundaries between the realms of the real and the fantastic, by playing with the boundaries between aural perception and the romantic fascination with supernatural sounds. Similarly, the appearance of ghosts in his grand opera *Les Troyens* can be read as a compositional exploration of sound intensity and timbral expression. Scientific ideas of perception become entwined with a compositional desire to create music from an unreal and imagined world.

David Trippett takes up this interplay between scientific theory and aural effect to explore how acts of listening can be depicted beyond passive silence. The study of auditory mechanisms by Wheatstone, Helmholtz and Tyndall et al. gave rise to mid-nineteenth-century comparisons between the ear and the Aeolian harp – the romantic-automatic instrument par excellence – thereby inviting us to reconsider the many moments in contemporary opera when acts of listening are foregrounded. In this way, the harp becomes not simply the voice of nature, but signifies instead a way of relating to nature without reflexive thought, amounting to a kind of automatic audition.

Finally, James Deaville turns to the later nineteenth-century exploration of ear disease and injury to explore how a growing concern with levels of urban noise became enmeshed with complaints about the aural excess of the music of Richard Wagner. Viewed in this light, Deaville suggests, the many representations of Wagner's works as deafening go beyond the realm of comic hyperbole, and instead fit with live concerns about the risks of the excessive volume of modern life, and Wagner's role in contributing to it (a subject given recent topicality by the UK court case in which a viola player at the Royal Opera House, Covent Garden, won damages for the irreversible hearing loss stemming from his participation in the opera house's 2012 *Ring* cycle).[42]

In the third section, we move from modes of perception to the relationships of opera with technology. For Deirdre Loughridge, this involves the exploration of a period in the late eighteenth century during which various operas thematised contemporary scientific fascination with lunar astronomy and balloon flight. For a brief time, Loughridge suggests, science and fantasy could come together on the operatic stage and inform each other, before the magical realms of romantic opera relegated technology back to the wings.

It is here, offstage, that Benjamin Walton's chapter focuses, in seeking to reconstruct the attempts to develop a revolutionary new type of stage machinery for Charles Garnier's grand new Paris Opéra during the decade and more of construction leading up to its inauguration in 1875. The eventual adoption of a machinery system almost identical to that employed for many years in the previous opera house, Walton suggests, invites us to consider the role of failure in the history of operatic technology, and its potential to expand our understanding of opera's material history.

Ellen Lockhart then turns to another hidden story, with ramifications that spill out well beyond the world of opera. She begins, though, with Giacomo Puccini, and his fascination with electricity. While his brief and long-forgotten squib for piano *La scossa elettrica* ('Electric shock'), written for an international convention of telegraph operators, offers few revelations to anyone in pursuit of rich connections between opera and science, it nevertheless points towards what Lockhart terms 'a shared history of music and electricity' running through much of the nineteenth century, and

---

[42] The judgment on this case, given by Mrs Justice Nicola Davies on 28 March 2018, is recorded here: www.judiciary.uk/wp-content/uploads/2018/03/goldscheider-v-roh-judgmentL.pdf.

spreading from scientifically inflected Italian aesthetic theories in which music becomes the purveyor of electric effect to descriptions of shared musical listening akin to a séance. Finally, the creation of 'electrical music' was realised in the production of two Italian ballets which thematise scientific discoveries in a way akin to the operas described by Loughridge almost a century before.

The second of Lockhart's ballets, Luigi Manzotti's *Excelsior*, premiered at Milan's La Scala in 1881, also forms the focus of Gavin Williams's chapter, which opens our final section, on 'Bodies'. An entire act of this work is devoted to the subject of electricity, divided into 'The Genius of Electricity' and 'The Effects of Electricity' and concluding with a grand 'Dance of the Telegraph Operators', complete with scoring for a telegraph machine alongside the normal orchestra. Williams's interest, however, is less in the grand narrative of scientific progress enacted on stage (including the invention of the steam engine, the opening of the Suez Canal, and the construction of the Mont Cenis tunnel under the Alps), than in the status of such a work as 'proto-robotic' in its choreography, thereby linking the ballet to the celebration of industry at the 1881 Milan Exposition. In this context, Williams suggests, we can see an exploration of balletic bodies as automata stretching back well before such totemic modernist works as Erik Satie's *Parade* (1917), and can instead reopen an investigation of connections between choreographed (and, by extension, operatic) gesture and a wider range of nineteenth-century urban experiences.

The figure of the automaton similarly forms the focus of Myles Jackson's chapter, which revisits the history of operatic androids, in placing the uncanny fascination of Offenbach's Olympia, in *Les Contes d'Hoffmann*, in the context of nineteenth-century studies in physiology and physiognomy. Where early nineteenth-century anatomists like Sir Charles Bell sought to demonstrate the links between mind and body via the workings of the nerves, later researchers such as Guillaume Duchenne sought to replicate the nervous gestures of emotion through artificial stimulation (electricity again), thereby turning pliant – typically female – medical subjects into Olympia-like mannequins, able to mimic emotions through the application of electrodes.

The last two chapters of the book turn to late nineteenth-century fears of the effects of musical degeneracy. First, James Kennaway echoes James Deaville's attention to the perceived dangers of Wagner's music on its first audiences. But where Deaville addresses the volume of the Wagnerian orchestra, Kennaway turns to the neurasthenic effects of Wagner's music on the brain, and the threat of a resulting loss of willpower. By revisiting the novelty of the Bayreuth experience, Kennaway suggests, with its darkened auditorium, we can understand its connections to long-standing preoccupations with hypnotism and other trance states, including the sorts of sensory experiments performed on hysterics at institutions such as Paris's Salpêtrière hospital also mentioned by Jackson. Music, in these terms, became a trigger for a neurological reflex that could lead to mental derangement. And the best escape from such a condition was the successful (and masculine) exercise of willpower to escape the drug-like threat of the Bayreuth experience.

By 1905, the premiere of Richard Strauss's *Salome* only intensified such fears. And as Alexander Rehding argues in the final chapter, critics reached for a language of degeneration grounded in what he terms 'the unholy trinity of nineteenth-century criminal pathology, evolutionary biology and social Darwinism'. What started out as a description of hereditary organic abonormalities, then, turned quickly into a discourse designed to exclude and to vilify. An opera, in these terms, has the potential to itself become a diseased body, subject to dissection from critics determined to reveal all its unhealthy impurities, and brought to life by a composer who has turned away from the romantic imperative to produce truth and beauty, and has instead produced something decayed and degenerate, with the risk of further artistic development along socially damaging lines of a kind that would resurface in the reception of operatic compositions through the early decades of the twentieth century.

Across all the chapters, then, familiar operatic objects, rooted in reception and cultural histories, encounter a newer rhetoric; whether of sonic epistemologies, the complex interfaces of a listening subject, or the agentic capacities of instruments – scientific and musical. The potential unease of classification for such work, we argue, indicates a mutation underway, and we are reminded of Barthes's 'epistemological slide'; his observation that work within the interstices of disciplines eschews the calm of an easy security: 'it begins *effectively* ... when the solidarity of the old discipline breaks down, perhaps even violently' by ushering in new, contested objects, and a language without a recognisable home.[43] By scrutinising the kind of cultural work that underlies Macfarren's forgotten operatic bass when he cries: 'Science! Potentate Sublime!' we aim to establish new ways for others to pursue an ever more holistic approach to the eddying currents of nineteenth-century operatic and scientific culture.

---

[43] Barthes 1977, 155; on the challenges and possibilities of musicological interdisciplinarity, see Born 2010.

PART I

Voices

1 | Pneumotypes
Jean de Reszke's High Pianissimos and the Occult Sciences of Breathing

JAMES Q. DAVIES

Aesthetic Capture

On the threshold of our modernity, on 29 March 1901, Lionel Mapleson made two artful cylinder phonautograms of the air.[1] It was no ordinary air. His wax tracings captured for posterity the legendary vocal tones of the fifty-year-old Jean de Reszke and the chorus of the old Metropolitan Opera House in Richard Wagner's *Lohengrin*. The atmosphere was thick with anticipation for this final gala performance of the first twentieth-century season, an event that had been offered as an extra night to subscribers, and the last time that Reszke would appear in New York in a complete opera. The newspapers reported a crush as never before in the lobby and outside on the street for 'the strongest cast which can be brought together', including Jean's younger brother Édouard, David Bispham, Adolph Mühlmann, soprano Milka Ternina and Bohemian–German contralto Ernestine Schumann-Heink.[2]

Onstage, an 'Edison Home Phonograph', purchased a year earlier and affixed with a giant recording horn, lurked beneath the hood of the prompter's box.[3] The librarian of the Metropolitan Opera was determined to capture a sound image of the evening's performance. His idea was to seize the moment – to arrest an enigmatic tone picture of a season for the centuries.

The air itself seemed to still for the last scene of the final act. Critics marvelled at 'the attitude of the audience which hangs breathless on every

---

[1] I have used the term 'phonautogram' to suggest that Mapleson manufactured the record more for storage than playback. Around 1900, the word was often a synonym for Emile Berliner's 'gramophone', though it is today more associated with Édouard-Léon Scott de Martinville's 'phonautographe' and his *Fixation graphique de la voix* (1857).

[2] [unsigned] 1901e, 8.

[3] Late the following year, general complaint would compel Mapleson to remove his 'obtruding contraption' (with its peculiarly outsized giant recording horn) to the catwalk in the rigging above the stage; see Thompson 1938, 28.

note of Jean de Reszke'.[4] Time stopped. Or rather, the urgent cultural imperative was to *arrest time* both technologically and vocally. Reszke appeared breathless. For Lohengrin's farewell, the 'Polish Apollo' sang his high pianissimos in myriad shades and colours, displaying patented vocal techniques over which he reputedly reigned supreme. In the terms of his system, he 'drank in tones', which is to say that Reszke 'formed voice', not by projecting tone outwardly, but by cultivating a sense of holding breath in or of generating vibration inwardly – by colouring tone, as he put it, *dans le masque*.[5] These resonant tones were allied to a style of aesthetic capture and 'vocal compression' founded upon a 'fixed high-chest method' (or 'inferior costal and diaphragmatic respiration').[6] By this, as we shall see, Reszke was transported ecstatically to an at once rarefied and reified realm of absolute art, his monologue elevated to a space of permanent airless purity.

The most acclaimed vocal sounds of a golden epoch thus brought the curtain down on what Mark Twain famously called the Gilded Age. The pre-phonographic era was ending, an era that would be recalled by many as a time of sovereign vocalism. Since the 1880s, Jean de Reszke had been *Lohengrin*'s chief publicist in Europe, an opera by then firmly fixed in the repertory, though mostly in French and Italian translation. In New York, the fashion was for eclecticism. Reszke sang Wagner's 'bel canto opera' – as he had since 1896 – in the original German, whilst the chorus of the Met sang back in Italian.[7] This was a magical night, one made more legendary still by the atmospherics of Mapleson's eerie records of a distant universe of nineteenth-century song.

That distance is the focus of this chapter. Or rather, I will eschew nostalgia for the terra incognita of lost vocalism, in favour of documenting the twentieth-century struggle to project that aesthetic distance vocally. My subject is breath control, and the cultural effort (at the purported dawn of the age of mechanical sound reproduction) to discipline breath – to

---

[4] Henderson 1901a, 20.

[5] Walter Johnstone Douglas, Reszke's long-time accompanist and friend, reported that 'to get the maximum amount of "forward" tone to the voice, which [Reszke] deemed "essential", it was his plan to imagine that you were drinking in the tone, rather than pushing it out. This idea encouraged the palate to draw back and give *timbre* to the voice, while it helped the tone to find its way into the true mask.' Douglas 1925, 207.

[6] Curtis 1896, 63–6.

[7] Reviewing the season as a whole in May that year, Esther Singleton (1901, 252) claimed that '*Lohengrin* is the most popular opera in the Grau repertory'. Several reviewers lamented the Italian chorus throughout the season. 'It is a pity', said a *New York Times* review of the farewell Reszke *Lohengrin* in March, 'that the chorus still sings in a mixture of German and Italian. That, however, must be endured while an Italian chorus is employed' [unsigned] 1901e, 8.

regulate or stay the flow of air. In question here are not only phonographic technologies, but wider social apparatuses, air-conditioning, storage and management systems. With Reszke in view, I am interested in airless song and the kinds of vacuum-packed purity required of his vocal style. I want to know what it means to sing without the emission of air, according to modern theories of standing resonance, instead of age-old vocal manners involving 'streams of sound' or 'threads of breath'.

The chapter, in other words, reflects upon modern vocal knowledge, and 'extraction': the purported extraction of voice from the body so-called, as much as voice's extraction from air. If 'modernity' rears its head here, it is only as a 'process of atmosphere-explication' in ways redolent of Heidegger's writing on technology (though I will avoid equating air-conditioning systems with smog, air raids, chemical weapons, virtual reality, gas chambers, drone strikes or other such twentieth-century atmospheric terrors).[8] 'Modern' vocal knowledge, I will suggest, formed not merely because voice was suddenly fixed as a graphic or visible matter of concern. In my account, the origin story told of mechanical sound reproduction is not a story belonging to the history of technology. Rather, it is a tale beholden to the history of cultural techniques. Technologies, as I understand them, are mere crudescences of consolidated cultural behaviours; vocal technologies are the mere accoutrements of wider techniques for projecting voice.

I will not be telling a modernist story about the voice's severance or rupture from the body so-called. Nor will I be claiming that phonographic technology somehow 'wrenched the voice from the throat and out of time'.[9] At issue here are the vocal freedoms afforded – according to technological determinists – by scientific advances in sound reproduction. My provocation is to resituate accounts of that modernist break in view of embodied vocal techniques that made a fetish of visible sound – that conjured fantastical sound-images from voice. I will argue that such fetishisations served aesthetic imperatives attuned less to the physiological sciences than to acoustic research and such voice-imaging instruments as Edison's 'talking machine', routinely hailed in this period for its ability to speak the sounds of every international language. The task of this chapter is first to link the purported internationalism of Reszke's style with the transnational project to make icons of vocal sound. It is then to detail the finer workings of Reszke's pianissimo techniques, before allying these workings to the efforts of voice scientists that debated the Reszkeian art

[8] See Sloterdijk 2002.   [9] Kahn 1999, 9.

and science of breathing. My aim, in short, is to enfold questions of technology into deeper issues of technique, and to record the kinds of suffocation necessary to the invocation of Art.

The Incorporation of Opera

Jan Mieczysław Reszke could speak little German and even less English. Yet he was at the forefront of the movement for 'Polyglot Opera' or what he himself called 'Russian Salad'.[10] 'Polyglot Opera' was a phrase popularised in London by Augustus Harris, the celebrated operatic impresario, who used it most during his 1889 season, when Reszke persuaded him to produce Charles Gounod's *Romeo* in French at the 'Royal Italian Opera', Covent Garden.[11] The 'polyglot' singer himself had made his debut as an Italian baritone in Venice by the name of Jan de Reschi. He then gathered a formidable French reputation in Paris, during a five-season stint (1884–9), as the 'tenorised' Jean de Reszké. This was the same Reszké for whom Jules Massenet had composed the picturesque tableaux of *Le Cid* (Théâtre National de l'Opéra, 1885). By 1889, the dream of three great schools of opera (Italian, French and German) exploited by a single company still seemed far off. Progress would be made five years later, however, in the summer of 1894, when Jean, his brother Édouard and Harris were all induced to make the pilgrimage to Bayreuth, following in the footsteps of dramatic soprano Lillian Nordica, who on 20 July that year sang Elsa in the first ever *Lohengrin* to be staged at the Festspielhaus. The success of this Milanese-trained American in this landmark production 'as the author conceived it' was such that critic William James Henderson, at the *New York Times*, could proclaim that 'the twilight of the so-called Wagner singer is at hand'. Nordica's supporters crooned that this was the first time Wagner had been 'actually sung', rather than barked in the usual guttural Teutonic tone-speech.[12] Wagnerphiles meanwhile lamented 'the downfall of Bayreuth', which had become just another 'holiday resort for rich Americans'.[13]

The toast to victory was made in New York on 27 November 1895. At a celebratory dinner in mock medieval style, Reszke raised his drinking horn to 'International Opera' after a triumphant all-German performance with Nordica (the Italian chorus excepted) of *Tristan und Isolde* at the

---

[10] Mawson 1891, 917. [11] Harris 1889, 605. [12] Henderson 1894, 207–8.
[13] [unsigned] 1894b, 79–80.

Metropolitan Opera.[14] The Pole spoke in four languages that night –
English, German, Italian and French – though he showed little interest in
the Anglo-American dream of a permanent native-language tradition on
home soil.[15] The previous May, Henderson had already caught wind of
a future 'Opera in Three Tongues' at the Metropolitan Opera House: '"The
French operas in French, the Italian operas in Italian, and the German in
German" has been the De Reszke war cry all Winter.' Reszke's German-
language *Tristan*, according to Henderson, was a 'genuine musical event'
and 'a triumphant demonstration of the universality of Wagner's genius'.[16]
Gone were the usual 'discordant shouts and ejaculations' of an Ernest van
Dyck, Max Alvary or Albert Niemann. Instead, Reszke preferred a dreamy
fusion of the best of three sound worlds: French tone-colour, Italian
cantilena and German sublimity. The battle against the frenzied *'voix
blanches'* of such singers as van Dyck or Lola Bleeth was won, their
'eiffelesco-babelesco-pyramidal grunts' supplanted by Reszke's own
matchless timbral shadings and commanding 'breadth of style, perfect
intonation, and deep emotion'.[17] The project in view, for the invited dinner
guests, was the crystallisation of an absolute twentieth-century art and an
international standard of vocal prowess.

In preparation for his debut at Bayreuth, Reszke had reportedly taken
twenty days off during the summer of 1894 to work with Cosima Wagner's
musical advisor, Julius Kniese, in the resort town of Karlsbad. For five
hours a day, the cultured Pole trained with Kniese, though in the end the
singer still expressed himself positively opposed to German 'naturalism'
and such antipathetic tenors as Niemann who failed to 'give the words their
proper softness in singing'.[18] Only a month after toasting 'Opera in Three
Tongues' in New York, Reszke advanced the internationalist cause by
singing his first German Lohengrin opposite Nordica on 2 January 1896.
The New York press lauded his 'strange and potent' Wagnerian speech-
song. 'Spectral, magical and the wonder of another world', he 'poured
forth', in the words of one writer, 'singing for the first time the part as it
should be sung, without soft Tuscan "cignos" and saccharine "io t'amos"'.[19]
The old toyshop Italian figure, they swooned, had been exchanged for
a creature of universal power: 'no longer a sentimental chevalier, but

---

[14] For more on Reszke's internationalism, see Karen Henson's (2015, 122–53) excellent chapter
on Reszke.
[15] For more on this dream, see Horowitz 2005, 145–7.   [16] Henderson 1895, 13.
[17] Henderson 1895, 13; for the 'eiffelesco-babelesco-pyramidal grunts', see [unsigned] 1894c,
661–2.
[18] [unsigned] 1895, 37.   [19] [unsigned] 1896, 7.

a devoted hero'.[20] The French–German–Italian merger on English-speaking terms, many agreed, had 'opened a new era in the style of Wagnerian performance', and illuminated a modern status quo.[21]

Reszke appeared both in London and New York under the auspices of the Maurice Grau Opera Company: a multinational conglomerate managed by a French-based, Austrian-born 'monarch of the operatic world' with signatories including Edward Lauterbach, chairman of the Republican County Committee in New York, railway magnate Frederick W. Sanger, and 'Bonanza King' industrialist John William Mackay, who had amassed obscene wealth in transatlantic telecommunications and silver mines in the American west. From 1896 to 1902–3, Grau oversaw an operatic plutocracy under the autocratic thumb of Jean de Reszke and his equally authoritative sibling Édouard, a bass of giant stature who had first made his mark singing the King of Egypt in the first Paris performance of Giuseppe Verdi's *Aida* under the composer's baton.[22] The company product was international grand opera on an impossibly lavish scale, it being 'the most brilliant operatic government that the world has ever known from a financial point of view', with Jean commanding stipends in excess of $3,000 a night.[23]

Grau's scheme functioned according to a lucrative 'star system' according to which, in the words of Hermann Klein in 1903, 'what Covent Garden does this year, New York does the next', though he qualified this by saying that in matters Wagnerian it was the American city that led the way.[24] In London, over every summer, the smooth-operating businessman ('with heavy-lidded eyes that seem lost in reverie') was managing director of Covent Garden's Grand Opera Syndicate Ltd, a corporation bankrolled by the aristocratic investments of the Marchioness of Ripon, Lord Esher, Lord Wittenham and (of course) the Reszkes.[25] In New York, late every following winter, Grau leased the rebuilt opera house from its property owners: the Metropolitan Opera and Real Estate Company. The 'real estate' in question here was the thirty-five parterre boxes of the Met's so-called Diamond Circle, bejewelled by an oligarchy of shareholders of unspeakable wealth who had rebuilt their playhouse after the disastrous fire of

---

[20] Henderson 1896, 8.   [21] Krehbiel 1908, 266.

[22] The first Paris performance of *Aida* occurred on 22 April 1876. As for Édouard, although it is difficult to distinguish him from the Italian chorus on Mapleson's *Lohengrin* cylinders, he is detectable somewhere amidst the phonographic fog, singing the part of King Henry.

[23] Krehbiel 1908, 277. Hillary Bell, of the *New York Press*, quoted in [unsigned] 1901b, 11. For Jean's fee, see Finck 1909, 12.

[24] Klein 1903, 467.   [25] Samson 1900, 601.

August 1892. In the remodelling, as if to reflect newly obscene inequities in American wealth and new concentrations of corporate prosperity, the number of boxes was reduced to accommodate only the richest patrons, while space for standing room was increased.

The fumes and stifling heat of the old gas burners were gone. Instead, the 'plenum ventilation' system of Frederic Tudor, which air-conditioned the original building, was expanded, with the additional installation of myriad personalised vents through the parterre floor and chair legs from below. (Tudor was the son of the 'Ice King' of the same name, who made his fortune shipping New England ice to the Caribbean, Europe and India.) The object was compression: to 'have an excess of air entering the building beyond that escaping by the regularly provided foul-air outlets, thus insuring an internal atmosphere pressure slightly in excess of the air without the building'.[26] Many still found the system suffocating – though not nearly so much as the notoriously oppressive Festspielhaus in Bayreuth, where Carl Brandt's steam-generating boilers and Wagner's so-called 'endless' (or airless) melodies seemed fixed to entirely smother the intoxicated audience.[27] In the 1890s, New York saw a veritable explosion in proto-airconditioning or 'refrigeration' techniques as an addendum to the smoke and noise abatement campaigns and the struggle for rarefied air. This 'airscaping' of the environment was engineered such as to keep the increasing nuisance of foul gases, smoke, and cinders in midtown Manhattan where they belonged – on the streets, and in the lungs of the working poor. The luxuriant ambiance of the playhouse's fantastical interior, meanwhile, was enriched, not only by pressurised conditioning, but also by the fragrant fumes of Turkish tobacco and ivory-tipped De Reszkes, the patented 'Aristocrat of Cigarettes'.

Remembering 'the Greatest Tenor of the Nineteenth Century'

'Jean de Reszke's voice is dead', or so the newspapers announced five months before his comeback on 31 December 1900, the last night of the nineteenth century. In the days leading up to the event, the 'bull-baiting' subscribers anticipated a fracas.[28] Word had it that the fifty-year-old had lost his mojo in London, notwithstanding his high-profile arrival along

---

[26] Kidder 1886, 471.   [27] For more on Brandt, see Kreuzer 2011.
[28] This is Franklyn Fyles's phrase from the *New York Sun*, quoted in [unsigned] 1901b, 11.

with the rest of the Metropolitan company (Italian chorus included) two weeks earlier aboard an immense four-funnelled luxury transatlantic cruise liner, the *Kaiser Wilhelm der Große*. Reszke's cancellations in London had been mercilessly publicised. *The Times* reported of his isolated 12 June appearance at Covent Garden as Gounod's Romeo that he saved himself only for the famous 'duo de l'alouette' and the duel scene.[29] One rumour held that Reszke had broken down in mid-performance; the Australian diva Nellie Melba, who sang Juliette in French alongside him, was reportedly 'so affected by the sudden loss of voice that she burst into tears on the stage'.[30] The tenor's only other engagement that season, again according to the London *Times*, involved an over-poetic impersonation of Walther in Wagner's *Meistersinger* where Reszke battled on bravely in German even though his voice had run aground. 'The wreck is beautiful', the critic wrote, 'but a wreck it is, and the performance could not but excite painful memories'.[31]

Other critics knew that fans would applaud even 'if he but moved across the canvas, a fascinating though voiceless apparition'. And at precisely 8.26 p.m. on New Year's Eve, Reszke was 'greeted by an immense audience'. Floating mystically into the third scene on the Metropolitan swan, Lohengrin competed, as Henderson of *The New York Times* put it, with 'a burst of applause which was with difficulty stilled soon enough to permit his adieu to the bird of transportation to be heard'.[32] 'He began his farewell to the swan', according to the *New York Evening Post*, 'and ere he had sung six bars the fact was established that the London rumors were once more proven false.' His voice was 'a trifle thinner', in the words of the *New York Sun*, but he still sang with 'the voice of a healthy, mature man, the voice of an impregnable artist'. For Hearst's *New York World*, there was an audible sigh of relief when Jean's first 'few notes confounded his detractors and revealed the fact that his voice still possesses ... its indescribable spirituality, its dignity and its pathos'. The *Morning Telegraph* spoke of Reszke's patented 'mystic, almost divine suggestion'.[33] 'When the opera was over, at 11:30,' another critic concluded, 'the fact was clear that Jean de Reszke had remained to the end the greatest tenor of the nineteenth century, and that he would set a standard for the twentieth which coming generations will find it difficult to live up to.'[34]

---

[29] [unsigned] 1900b, 6.   [30] As recounted in Kobbé 1901, 390.
[31] [unsigned] 1900c, 6; [unsigned] 1900a, 10.   [32] Henderson 1901b, 6.
[33] The extract from the *New York Evening Post* is quoted in [unsigned] 1901b, 11; [unsigned] 1901c, 3; [unsigned] 1901a; [unsigned] 1901d, 3.
[34] Franklyn Fyles quoted in [unsigned] 1901b, 11.

Rarefied Air

Mapleson's cylinders are ill-equipped to recover that standard, if historical recovery is your scholarly game. When played back on modern equipment today, the haunting vocal traces still etched into the wax are heard as if competing with what sounds like the passing of one of Manhattan's *c.*1900 elevated trains, or a ferocious *c.*2000 popcorn machine. And yet both two-minute records of the Reszke-Lohengrin final act, I think, are documents of perfect fidelity. The achievement of the librarian was to capture the atmospheric charge of an epochal farewell performance. It was to vacuum-pack the dying vocal throes of the expiring century for sentimental enclosure in two sealed cardboard canisters.

Mapleson's souvenirs, in other words, were crystallised less for playback than as mystic keepsakes for archival storage, since every replaying of the cylinders modified the soft waxen image. As many historians of twentieth-century 'sound' – that newly sacred matter – have noted, before commercial consolidation, talking machines served a bewildering variety of functions: as proto-dictaphones, entertaining parlour instruments, music boxes, medical devices for diagnosing vocal health, tools for teaching elocution, apparatuses for learning foreign languages, objects of public instruction and so on. The Edison phonograph came with a shaving tool to smooth away old wax tracings, horns could be exchanged to suit individual situations, and the diaphragm was designed for continual resetting. It was, as Patrick Feaster has written, usual for 'sounds' to be educed 'at different speeds or backwards, layered one over the other into elaborate montages, and otherwise manipulated to create novel effects'.[35] Mapleson, in other words, did not necessarily freeze the air, so to speak, for the purposes of future thawings. He certainly could not have imagined that his rare impressions would be 'reproduced' over and over again in the way that they were after their first transference to disc in the 1930s. His purposes were hardly that democratic.

Mapleson began his Reszke-Lohengrin recording at the tragic dissolution of the bridal chamber scene, the penultimate of the opera. A failed Italianate love duet has preceded this moment ('Fühl'ich zu dir so süss mein Herz entbrennem, atme ich Wonnen, die nur Gott verleiht'). In an extended slow movement, the divine knight presses Elsa (here sung by Croatian–Slavonian diva Milka Ternina) to follow his long-breathed phrases, to breathe in the rarefied air wafted in from afar ('Atmest du

---

[35] Feaster 2007, 57.

nicht mit mir die süssen Düfte?'). 'When [Lohengrin] led Elsa to the window,' novelist Willa Cather had written when she saw Reszke and Nordica perform the scene in Italian a year earlier, 'I assure you he brought the stillness and beauty of the summer night into the hot air of the playhouse.'[36] Elsa, by her gasping failure to respond, has proved herself unworthy of her breathless hero's love. The lovers do not breathe the same air, a fact made clear by Elsa's fitful and distorted cabaletta where she pesters her husband to reveal his secret identity ('Hilf Gott, was muss ich hören!'). She demands to know his name. And this forbidden question precipitates catastrophe: the duet's formal structure crumbles to the extent of admitting the worldly intrusion of the evil Telramund (played here by American baritone David Bispham) and four knights, swords drawn. Here, the cylinder seized a snatch of a controversial moment for Reszke, who, rather than striking Telramund to the ground as directed in the score, would customarily raise his sword in a magic gesture as if to compel his foe 'by some supernatural power to fall to the ground vanquished'.[37]

Reszke, in other words, played Lohengrin as a kind of spellbinding sorcerer. The frozen silence that attended his every appearance was dependent, in the description by Cather, on a singer 'whose tenderness is wholly without effeminacy, or whose voice can rise clear, melodious and true, to the full measure of tragedy, and then there is, undeniably, a deep sentimental quality, that baffling minor tinge that is in the acting of Modjeska and the music of Chopin'.[38] After only a few seconds, Mapleson stopped the cylinder in order to skip ahead and render the spectral sounds of Reszke, doubled by a distant oboe, weeping the second half of the so-called *Frageverbot* motif at his characteristically slow tempo ('Dort will ich Antwort ihr bereiten'). The first cylinder, in other words, ends with Lohengrin looking outward toward the final scene where he will reveal himself before Elsa and the assembled court.

Mapleson engineered the second cylinder similarly – to gesture toward this hallowed moment of truth. The needle was dropped deep into the finale after the grand arrival of the assembled Brabantine armies. Mapleson began this record, then, with the Italian chorus, who sang out of tune 'with dogged persistence', proclaiming Lohengrin's final entrance in full.[39] Reszke's opinion that Wagner's scores were always best reworked with heavy cuts (to alleviate tedium) is borne out in what follows, the hero's

---

[36] Willa Cather's words (in the *Courier* (10 June 1899), 3) were reprinted as 'Lohengrin and Walküre', in Cather 1970, 2:622.

[37] Moffatt 1896, 32. [38] Cather 1970, 2:622. [39] Henderson 1896, 8.

Pneumotypes: Reszke's High Pianissimos   31

instigation of a vicious choral denunciation of Elsa's 'betrayal' edited out to speed the dramatic flow.[40] Thus the hero's request to be exempt from guilt for Telramund's murder skips to the grand set-up: 'So hort!' and the chorus's expectant 'what mystery must I now hear?' Which is where the cylinder leaves off ... but for Mapleson sealing his creation by shouting into the horn the following day: 'De Reske! Last night! March the 29th 1901! At the Metropolitan Opera House! New York!'

Stop the Breath!

That moment of truth – which Mapleson left artfully to the beyond – was the so-called Grail Narration, a scene where Reszke was reputedly supreme as at no other. To paraphrase Friedrich Nietzsche on Wagner, this would be the moment when 'the musician himself suddenly grew in value to an unheard-of extent: from now on he would be an oracle, a priest, even more than a priest, a kind of mouthpiece of the "essence" of things, a telephone from the world beyond us'.[41] It was here that the mystical visitant show-cased his highly cultivated pianissimos and superhuman control of breath. This vision of a far-away eternity seemed to bring into the opera house the more precious air of a distant heaven. And it would end with Elsa's gasping for air – 'O Luft! Luft der Unglücksel'gen!' – as she realises that she can no longer breathe on Lohengrin's level. One is again reminded of Nietzsche: 'I should like to open the window a little,' he protested in *Der Fall Wagner* (1888). 'Air! More air!'[42]

Lohengrin's dramatic transubstantiation, Wagner's score shows, was introduced by the brightly coloured return of the shimmering high strings of the hushed opening of the opera's Prelude. The radiant A-major sono-rities, as ever, were conjured first by the divisi first and second violins, their incandescent pianissimos morphing first into high flutes and oboes before evaporating into four solo violins playing harmonics high on the bridge. Here, as Theodor Adorno would have it, Lohengrin's rapt vocal pianissi-mos were allied with a coeval transmogrification of orchestral instruments, achieved, apparently, by obscuring their timbral individuality one from another. Wagner's ideal, Adorno argued, was a sacralised sound-image from which all trace of the technical means of production and instrumental

---

[40] 'I confess it bores me to hear the same narrative repeated and repeated in his music dramas', said Reszke in a 1908 interview, adding: 'It is right to cut Wagner.' Moltzor 1902, 3.

[41] Nietzsche 1994, 77–8.   [42] Nietzsche 1969, VI. 3§5.

labour had been removed.[43] Verdi, having witnessed the Italian premiere of *Lohengrin* at Bologna in 1871, used these same high suffocating strings for the prelude and final scene of *Aida*, with Radames (another of Reszke's favoured roles) buried alive with his Ethiopian lover in an airless Egyptian tomb. Airlessness, of course, was conceived differently by Wagner: scarcity of breath symbolised vacuum-sealed purity, rather than asphyxiation under oppressive Pharaonic power. The 'vaporous ether', that Franz Liszt heard conjured by the returning music of the prelude, 'extends outward, in order that the sacred tableau may be painted before our profane eyes', the colours, overtones and resonance of sacred delirium roused by 'indescribable perfumes' wafted in 'from the dwellings of the Just'.[44]

For one pupil of Reszke, who studied the scene in detail, Lohengrin's recitation had always seemed 'rather dull, another of Wagner's interminable sermons'. This was until he heard Reszke invoke the sacred courts of Montsalvat. 'As soon as he began "In fernem Land unnahbar euren Schritten",' wrote the pupil, 'I realised that there was an other-worldliness about it all that had been hidden from me.'[45] The invocation of the temple, his acolyte reported, was beholden to the practice of so-called *appoggio*, a technique of 'fixing the voice' or 'leaning on the breath' promulgated famously by Francesco Lamperti in Milan. The art of 'drinking the tone', as Lamperti put it in 1864, involved supporting 'a column of air over which the singer has perfect command, by holding back the breath, and not permitting more air than is absolutely necessary for the formation of the note to escape from the lungs'.[46] 'The breath,' as a pupil would explain, 'though vigorously pressed out, still remains inside the body,' in line with Lamperti's belief in making his disciples sing in front of lighted candles, the non-flickering flame being confirmation of ideal breath management.[47]

To Lamperti's system of pressurised containment, Reszke added his own brand of vocal hypostatisation, by fostering sensations of 'placing', 'focusing' or 'directing' compressed regions of air to various parts of the head,

---

[43] See Adorno 2005, 71–84.

[44] Liszt 1851, 49. These words imply a genealogy of *Lohengrin* reception extending through Baudelaire, whose account of the 'light' of the prelude music was famously influenced by Liszt, and probably later absorbed by Reszke. Baudelaire famously described 'a delectable state . . . [of] solitude with *vast horizons* and *bathed in a diffused light*. . . . I became aware of a heightened *brightness*, of a *light growing in intensity* so quickly that the shades of meaning provided by a dictionary would not suffice to express this *constant increase of burning whiteness*. Then I achieved a full apprehension of a soul floating in light.' See Baudelaire 1972, 331. I am indebted to David Trippett for this observation.

[45] W. 1925, 211.   [46] Lamperti 1864, 16.   [47] Shakespeare 1898, 519.

nose, cheekbones, teeth and soft or hard palate. Thus at the opening phrase of the narration – 'In fernem Land', which continued the orchestral invocation of the harmonic series – Reszke instructed his pupil to 'draw back the uvula, pinch the tonsils, [and] push the diaphragm', in order to achieve sounds devoid of head and chest resonance. This was a version of what Reszke elsewhere called *la voix écrasée*, the indication to 'appuyer la poitrine' supplemented here by the recommendation to focus vibration behind the soft palate, such that the singer physically embodies Lohengrin's ecstatic detachment from earth.

'Plus loin, plus loin', Reszke would exhort at the second phrase: 'liegt eine Burg, die Montsalvat genannt'. 'How hopeless to try to get the sort of passionate reverence he got into the word *Monsalvat!*' his pupils lamented, 'a sort of *ripæ ulterioris amor*, very simple, very personal, but all accomplished by a definite technique: a tiny upward *portamento*, a half-smothered M, a sudden piano, his marvelous *voix étouffée*; it was like a recipe, shake the bottle and apply the Elixir of Life.' The *voix étoufée* or 'crushed voice' was yet another Reszke pianissimo technique, achieved, according to reports, with an 'almost closed mouth and low palate, the larynx being rather high, but the support [*appoggio*] as deep and strong as possible'.[48] There were a myriad of other soft Reszke placements, such as his patented 'echo voice' or 'piano tone', the latter used at 'Ein lichter Tempel stehet dort inmitten', where the instruction was to 'throw light into the voice, strike right above the uvula'. 'Take your time,' Reszke directed throughout the narration, and at its climax – 'es heist der Gral!' – he drew back even further: 'Get your support on the note preceding the high note, and just carry the resonance of the high note further up by drawing back the uvula as far as possible, and when on the note itself, expand the ribs to support it "like the pinions of a bird".'[49]

A True Picture of Voice

No critics disdained Reszke's 'crushed' aestheticism more than exponents of traditional voice science, though singers – to this day – have never stopped singing 'into the mask', 'making' or 'placing' voice, or singing by sensations or images. 'What "goes on" above the throat are illusions no

[48] Reszke also recommended *la voix étouffée* for 'Nun sei bedankt mein lieber Schwan', the hero's farewell to the swan in Act I; Douglas 1925, 202–9.

[49] W. 1925, 212–13.

matter how real they may feel or sound', wrote W. E. Brown in the 1950s, professing to speak for Giovanni Lamperti.[50] 'I do not believe in teaching by means of sensations of tone', agreed a spokesperson for the eighty-nine-year-old Manuel García in 1894, apparently in direct response to 'modern theories' of Reszkeian breath control. The views of the great ageing Franco-Italian pedagogue and laryngologist had narrowed; García was quoted complaining that, earlier in his career, he 'used to direct the tone into the head, and do peculiar things with the breathing, and so on, but as years passed by I discarded them as useless, and I now speak only of actual things and not mere appearances'. 'All control of breath is lost the moment it is turned into vibrations [at the glottis],' García was made to protest in an 1894 article, 'and the idea is absurd that a current of air can be thrown against the hard palate for one kind of tone, the soft palate for another, and reflected hither and thither.'[51] The singer, as far as old-hat physiology was concerned, had no business 'making timbre', since timbre was not within his power to control. Timbre was a property of brute pharyngeal fact, a quality to be observed by science rather than confected by art. The colour and beauty of various sounds, they insisted, had nothing to do with Byzantine internal patternings of air. For García's twentieth-century apostles – most prominent among them French mezzo Blanche Marchesi (daughter of Mathilde) – the naïve mysticism of 'the sensation school' was dangerous, since it decried basic physiological realities.

At the head of the movement of 'The Nasal Method', meanwhile, stood 'The Triumvirate': Jean and Édouard de Reszke, and as their personal physician and intimate friend, the prominent New York socialite and medical doctor, Henry Holbrook Curtis. These 'ignoramuses' of the 1890s – as Marchesi called them – failed to locate voice in Nature, which is to say that their eyes had wondered from the true source. That source was the glottis, the 'tongue' (after the Greek *glôttís*) or 'inner mouth' that García had famously first seen 'live' through his patented laryngoscope some forty years earlier.[52] The reality of vocal folds and glottal strokes, she explained, could never be wished away as the Reszkes dreamed, merely by cultivating such obscure vocal onsets as would 'mouth' every tone with a consonant 'h' or the consonant 'm'. (Reszke developed an influential set of daily exercises that softened plosive attacks.) The clouding of laryngoscopic objectivity, Marchesi lamented, had led to 'the foundation of a New Religion', a 'new gospel'

[50] Stark 1999, 53.   [51] [unsigned] 1894a, 229.   [52] For more, see Davies 2014, 126–9.

which, having declared war on science, 'spread like a prairie fire' 'from the North Pole to the South'. The metaphysical speculations of The Triumvirate, she bristled, wreaked 'havoc in the singing profession'.[53]

Reszke had in fact enlisted the assistance of two specialists in the emerging field of oto-rhino-laryngology in order to defend his occult theory of voice. The first was Joseph Joal, an amateur musician and doctor at the bathhouses of Le Mont-Dore, a high-altitude spa in the Massif Central frequented by famous European singers and other fashionables over the summer. Joal was an expert in 'thermal therapies' and inventor of the 'pulvérisateur', an improved spirometer, and a device for the inhalation of carbonic acid. His position allowed him unparalleled access to the finest singers in Europe – Emma Albani, Rose Caron, Josephine de Reszke, Victor Capoul, Jean Lassalle, Léon Melchissédec, Jean-Alexandre Talazac and François-Pierre Villaret among them, who featured in the publication of his spirometric readings. In 1888, Jean de Reszke attended the mountain retreat. According to Joal, Reszke was a fellow self-experimenter and the inspiration for the doctor's 'On Forms of Breathing in Singing' that appeared in a specialist French journal four years later.[54] Joal's publication was a blistering attack, 'telephoned in' from the Monsalvat of mainstream French medicine, on the violent encroachment of mainstream medical science into matters of artful song.[55]

The main target of Joal's scorn was not so much García as Louis Mandl, the Parisian doctor of Hungarian origin whose long-standing insistence on the supremacy of 'abdominal breathing' had been folded into the vocal curriculum of the Conservatoire since 1866. According to Joal, Reszke, *pace* Mandl, was a 'resolute defender' of the refinements of 'costal', ribcage or 'clavicular' respiration. He also cited recent research that used his favoured graphic method (rather than laryngoscopic probes) to illustrate the vulgarity of Mandl's 'low' methods. It is true that Mandl had been concerned with identification and classification of *types respiratoires*. (Here, he followed Beau and Maissiat, who, as far back as 1842, had given the first scientific descriptions of the 'superior costal type', 'inferior clavicular type' and 'lower abdominal type'.)[56] Experiment showed that such typologies were useful to science, since any subject's 'vital capacity' and level of civilisation (thanks to the pulvérisateur) could be measured with unprecedented accuracy.

---

[53] Marchesi 1932, 91–8.   [54] Joal 1892, 225–49.

[55] For imaginary telephones after Nietzsche in *Lohengrin*, see Abbate 2001, 30.

[56] To get a sense of Mandl's methods, one could enter the search terms 'breathing' and 'Montserrat Caballé' on YouTube.

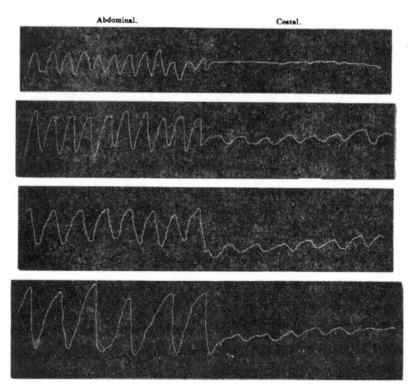

Figure 1.1 'Tracings taken from chests of Indian girls', in Thomas J. Mays, 'An Experimental Inquiry into the Chest Movements of the Indian Female', *The Therapeutic Gazette* 3/5 (16 May 1887), 298.

In 1890, as Joal pointed out, Dr Thomas Jefferson Mays of the Philadelphia Polyclinic racialised breathing by applying pneumographs to the chests of eighty-two Native American girls between ten and twenty-two years of age, thirty-three 'Indian of pure breed' and thirty-five 'half-breeds'. As Figure 1.1 shows, the majority of these 'savages', his pneumographic results verified, breathed according to Mandl's vulgar abdominal descent. Only a few girls from 'tribes comparatively civilized, such as the Mohawks and Chippawas', were found to be of 'costal type'.[57] Similarly, Dr John Harvey Kellogg – eugenicist, future founder of the 'Race Betterment Foundation' and originator of Kellogg's Cornflakes – conducted research on forty women, again divided equally and racially: twenty Chinese and twenty Native Americans. As Joal reported, all such primitives proved to be of the same abdominal type. European women, on the other

[57] Mays 1887, 297–9.

hand, more usually sported the 'costal' variety. For that fairer sex, apparently, this type of respiration constituted 'a true secondary sexual characteristic', one that circumvented impediments to genital and uterine function. This was at least according to the research of such men as Albrecht von Haller, Hermann Boerhaave, Jean-Baptiste Bérard, François-Achille Longet, John Hutchinson, Emile Küss and Mathias Duval. Feminists such as Elizabeth Chamberlayne, English composer and member of the Royal Musical Association, disagreed. 'I have by nature, and always, as far as I know', Chamberlayne protested, 'breathed from the abdomen.'[58] Joal countered that, of the thirty-three he had tested pneumographically, not a single chanteuse of value was a stomach breather. Higher forms, he insisted, used higher breathing.

An even greater proselytiser for Reszkeian breathing was Holbrook Curtis, a doctor key to the international dissemination of the laws of sound imagery, nasal resonance, timbral shifting and 'forward tone'. Like Joal, Curtis was the intimate friend and a personal physician of Reszke, who after the singer's New York debut was invited to his gigantic estates and stud farm near Klomnice in Russian Poland. Curtis – a specialist rhinologist-surgeon at the New York Throat, Nose and Lung Hospital – had made his name in the operatic world in December 1889 after performing a notable operation on the tumour on the vocal cords of Italo Campanini, pupil of Lamperti in Milan, notable early exponent of Radames, and the original Italian Lohengrin (in the version seen by Verdi). Curtis was a powerful advocate of 'voice culture', a social and artistic movement for the purification of elocutionary and singing practice for the improvement of the nation's cultural, economic and political well-being.[59] He was also a physician to the stars, with a clientele that by the end of his career included Enrico Caruso, Ignacy Jan Paderewski, Ellen Terry, William Faversham, Antonio Scotti, Emma Calvé, Johanna Gadski, Luisa Tetrazzini, Pol Plançon and Teddy Roosevelt. In 1906, he would become embroiled in the celebrated 'adenoid riots', when massed adenoidectomies began to be rolled out in the New York public school system, and parents in the Lower East Side and Brooklyn revolted. Throughout, Curtis stood firm in his diagnosis that congested nasal passages prevented some 75,000 children from breathing properly, which explained the cultural ubiquity of poor voice tone, speech defects, retarded intellectual development and 'depraved and ungovernable' behaviour.[60]

[58] Chamberlayne 1895, 277.   [59] Carter 2013, 11–34.   [60] [unsigned] 1908b, 6.

In a paper read to New York State Teachers' Association in Rochester in 1893, Curtis introduced Joal's findings to an American audience, adding that in his laryngological work with singers he had been struck by the deleterious effects of different schools of training on the vocal folds. (Those schooled in García's notorious 'glottal attack', for example, presented cords with disfigured convex bulges, 'the centre showing the result of attrition'.) Instead of inspiring with Mandl's 'advancing abdomen', Curtis recommended 'girding the loins'. Reszke's system was to flatten the stomach, fortify the lower regions and expand laterally. His recommendation was to harness the mysteries of compound vibration by use of his so-called 'high-chest method', 'a clever trick which maintains great resonance even when the lung is nearly exhausted of air'.[61] That is, Curtis recommended that singers fix their chests high in the puffed-out manner familiar from Reskze's portrait photographs of the period. The elevated ribcage worked to add 'secondary resonance to the voice from below – a sort of complementary timbre – the fixed upper thorax allowing of the least possible change of colour during tone production'.[62] To assist in the production of resonance, the use of a 'Sbriglia belt' was recommended (named after Reszke's teacher, Giovanni Sbriglia), strapped tight around the waist in order to 'cure [oneself] of the bad habit of so-called abdominal respiration'.[63] In modern times, such singers as Franco Corelli, Plácido Domingo and Lauritz Melchior forced air against the higher chest using similar reinforcement, abdominal braces being yet another means to envelop oneself in a sonic haze and hold breath within.

In addition, Curtis preached that there was far more to singing than García's tiny vocal folds, urging singers to study the 'ingenious mingling of pure spectrum colours', and 'colour harmonics in music in the same way that they must be studied in painting'. The idea, following Reszke, was to 'cultivate tone harmonies and sympatica in the voice at the expense of brilliancy of execution'. This was possibly the most painterly conception of singing ever conceived. 'There is no rule [other than the magic rule of feeling]', wrote Curtis in reference to a painter who was also a regular at bathhouses of Le Mont-Dore, 'for the palpitating sunlight effects and prismatic play of colours in the school of Claude Monet.'[64] Adapting enigmatic Helmholtzian notions of sympathetic vibration, Curtis imagined singers building tone by the addition or subtraction of 'those harmonics, which are added to the original tone by intervibrations within the accessory

---

[61] Curtis 1894b, 389; see also Curtis 1894a. [62] Curtis 1894a, 73. [63] Curtis 1896, 192.
[64] Curtis 1894a, 73.

cavities of the nasal passages'.[65] Rather than zeroing in on the glottis, in other words, Curtis directed attention upward and outward toward the facial resonators. The glottis, after all, was only a void, an 'orifice glottique' in the words of Mandl, a reverberant space that (in Curtis's conception) was activated as much by secondary vibration from above as direct air-pressure from below. 'I find that the great question of the singer's art becomes narrower and narrower all the time,' Reszke (who famously sniffed cocaine to open the airways before performance) declared in an interview with Curtis, 'until I can truly say that the great question of singing becomes a question of the nose – *la grande question du chant devient une question du nez.*'[66]

The most auratic vocal sounds, for Reszke, were to be found in 'forward placement'. This was the point of Curtis's aptly named treatise *Voice Building and Tone Placing, Showing a New Method of Relieving Injured Vocal Cords by Tone Exercises*, first published in 1896. It was to project a graven image against the 'sounding boards' of the palate. In Curtis's active vision of 'forward placement' and 'timbrated sounds', the idea was literally to paint a sound image 'against the mask'. It was to 'put on' tone, or give vocal sound 'a face'. Lilli Lehmann, alongside Reszke the prime exponent of 'international opera' (who in 1899 sang opposite him in 'the ideal *Tristan* performance of [her] life'), agreed. In her famous vocal tutor of 1902 she spoke of the cultivation of living tones, 'perfect tones' forged from 'continuous streams' and 'whirling currents and vibrations', which filled the spaces artfully prepared for them by the raised soft palate. She wrote of 'soaring inner sounds' vivified by directing breath toward focal points on the palate, and sensations of a 'very elastic rubber ball' above and behind the nose and toward the cavities of the head, an imaginary shape or 'balloon' which she could shape to suit the sound form desired. 'In order to bring out the colour of the tone the whirling currents must vivify all the vowel sounds that enter into it,' the high priestess explained, 'and draw them into their circles with an ever-increasing, soaring tide of sound.'[67] These animated tides of sound circulated 'in unbroken completeness of form' as swirling arabesques or overtone patterns resonating ecstatically in the region of the brain. Hers was a vision of singers generating tones from nothing, of miraculously incanting breath to life.

Her ideal of 'tonal life' achieved its fullest graphic expression in such voice-printing technologies of the era as the Curtis tonograph, shown in

---

[65] Curtis 1894a, 73.   [66] See Favia-Artsay 1991, 44–61; Curtis 1896, 160.
[67] Lehmann 1902, 69–70.

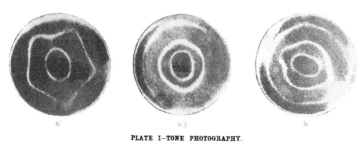

Figure 1.2 Holbrook Curtis, 'The Tonograph', *Scientific American* 76/22 (1897), 345.

Figure 1.2. The tonograph was an instrument invented in 1897 by Curtis for photographing 'tone forms', and for observing the coming-into-being of 'ravishing beauty of sound'.[68] This means of 'recording in geometrical figures the vibrations of the voice' consisted of a circular turntable-sized membrane stretched over a metal tube and covered in a mixture of salt and emery. When activated by the standing vibration of a singer's vocal sound, the tonograph produced phantasmic tone-figures or, to put this in Wagnerian terms, 'deeds of music made visible'. By means of his invention, Curtis published vocal records of such illustrious singers as Calvé, Caruso, Plançon and (of course) both Reszkes. These 'copies of the will', which looked remarkably like Berliner's latest gramophone records, were the products of just another of a new breed

---

[68] Curtis 1897, 345–6.

of next-generation voice-imaging technologies. Curtis explained how the tonograph assisted tone building:

A tone, to make a perfect geometric figure, must be sung well forward, with no forcing or tension, and with absence of shock or breathiness of tone. In other words, perfect production must be employed to make a harmonious figure, in the same way that it must be studied to make an agreeable impression upon our ear; and, for the same analogy, may we not reason that the little membrane of our ear drum may be divided up in the same exquisite arrangement of nodal lines by audible tones, and thus communicate to the brain, by means of the auditory nerve, the impression of agreeable quality in tone.[69]

The most influential precedent for bringing tone to visual life, Curtis admitted, was the 'eidophone', as developed by the remarkable British soprano Margaret Watts-Hughes. Exhibited at the Arts and Crafts Exposition in London in 1889, the eidophone deployed standing wave patterns and colour pigments on glass, in order to animate strange 'voice flowers', 'tree forms', 'serpent forms', a myriad of strange organic forms come to life. According to Curtis, the eidophone opened up a new world of voice, one where the resonant cavities of the head were analogous to 'weird caverns at the bottom of the sea, full of beautiful coloured sea anemones and mussel shells, headless snakes, entanglements of flower and leaflike forms, all seemingly vital with the same laws of growth as those which inspired the creation of the designs in Nature which they suggest'. These self-organising forms, produced by the magic of cross-vibration, made immortal records of vocal psychophysiology and vocal personality. They could be imprinted visually: either upon the roof of the mouth, the diaphragm of the ear, as well as on membranes of glass or wax, as shown in Figure 1.3.

This was an international and absolute art. At once French, German, Italian, English, American and Polish, the nebulous sound-forms that Reszke divined were never fully localisable to particular organs or particular environments. Expression, ideally, was placed in the mystical realms of resonance or in 'breath' broadly conceived. The organ of voice, in other words, was remote; or at least the source of voice was located as much at the ear or mouth as it was located atmospherically. The implication of Reszke's work, then, was that vocal tones were airborne and spectral. While they occurred in nature, these enchanting entities could be summoned into visible being via highly sophisticated rituals of sonic capture.

---

[69] Curtis 1897, 346.

Fig. 56.—Fern form.

Fig. 57.—Serpent form.

Fig. 58.—Cross-vibration figure.

Fig. 59.—Tree form.

Figure 1.3 Watts-Hughes's voice-figures in Holbrook Curtis, *Voice Building and Tone Placing, Showing a New Method of Relieving Injured Vocal Cords by Tone Exercises* (New York: D. Appleton, 1896), 227–31.

Their cultural production depended on highly rarefied, in fact 'aristocratic', levels of technical and technological expertise, which is why it mattered little that Reszke arrived in New York with no voice. 'Jean de Reszke is more than an artist,' Gounod reportedly agreed. 'His is the richest and most marvellously colourful of palettes.'[70]

It remains to point out that, all this talk of suffocation notwithstanding, this was not a period in which singers lost control and gave their voices away. Nor was it one in which we can properly speak of the decline of the singer or lament his or her replacement by technology. It was merely a time

---

[70] Barrington 1890, 79. Curtis 1896, 205. Gounod's words appear in [unsigned] 1894c, 661.

when vocal practice revelled in that quiet and yet ecstatic asphyxiation that made an art and science of breathing. The capture of vibration through projection and preservation, as we have seen, was the common goal of a range of nascent cultural technologies and techniques in this period. When Mapleson seized that small portion of the vibrating world on 29 March 1901, he was invested in far more than the modernist production of historical distance, in recording the last vocal tones of 'the greatest tenor of the nineteenth century'. The librarian was also devoted – as much as Reszke was – to a kind of disciplining of the air; in the abstraction, subjugation and imaging of the living atmosphere itself. The achievement of such sacred sound images as modern art required, in other words, necessitated, not only extraordinarily complex forms of breath control, but also a virtual abnegation of the most basic means of human production and reproduction. Modern song, that is, required suspension of the very air.

2 | Vocal Culture in the Age of Laryngoscopy

BENJAMIN STEEGE

For several months beginning in 1884, readers of *Life, Science, Health*, the *Atlantic Monthly* and similar magazines would have encountered half-page advertisements for a newly patented medical device called the 'ammonia-phone' (Figure 2.1). Invented and promoted by a Scottish doctor named Carter Moffat and endorsed by the soprano Adelina Patti, British Prime Minister William Gladstone and the Princess of Wales, the ammoniaphone promised a miraculous transformation in the voices of its users. It was recommended for 'vocalists, clergymen, public speakers, parliamentary men, readers, reciters, lecturers, leaders of psalmody, schoolmasters, amateurs, church choirs, barristers, and all persons who have to use their voices profess-sionally, or who desire to greatly improve their speaking or singing tones'.[1] Some estimates indicated that Moffat sold upwards of 30,000 units, yet the ammoniaphone was a flash in the pan as far as such things go, fading from public view after 1886.[2] If this forgotten object is an apt point of departure for a chapter on what might be described as the moral imagination of Victorian voices, that is because it so effectively draws attention to certain fantasies of the vocal self playing out across a broader public discourse at this time.

The ammoniaphone was elegantly simple in design (and, despite its name, soundless): it was a species of inhaler consisting of 'a tube about 25 inches long, constructed of a specially prepared non-corrosive metal, with handles, having patent spring valves'. The tube was 'charged with a chemical compound, combined so as to resemble in effect that which is produced by the SOFT BALMY air of the Italian Peninsula when inhaled into the lungs, hence the term – ARTIFICIAL ITALIAN AIR'.[3] What one observer referred to as 'the harsh sputterings and cacklings of our Northern throats' might be softened by inhaling its vapour of hydrogen peroxide, a little ammonia and various other chemicals, which were supposed to approximate the soothing and invigorating properties of the atmosphere

---

An earlier version of this chapter was presented at 'Performing Voices: Between Embodiment and Mediation', a conference at the American Academy in Rome in collaboration with the Max Planck Institute for the History of Science, December 2009. I thank David Trippett and Benjamin Walton for their insightful critiques as I prepared the present version.

[1] [unsigned] 1885b, 27. [2] [unsigned] 1899, 1:392. [3] [unsigned] 1885a, viii.

Figure 2.1 'Ammoniaphone', *Life*, 7, 159 (14 January 1886), p. 43.

Figure 2.2 *Health*, 3, 74 (5 September 1884), p. 351.

breathed by so many prominent Italian singers and, before them, Roman orators.[4] Figure 2.2 shows an advertisement depicting two people in evening dress putting the instrument to their lips as if playing a piccolo, while in fact the airflow went in the reverse direction. 'Thus, by means of chemical science we are brought into a fairy land of which no one knows the extent. We can have as it were Italian air laid on at our own doors.'[5]

---

[4] Mackenzie [1886] 1891, 157; but note that Mackenzie, a respected laryngologist, judged the apparatus in the negative: 'Any real effect which it may have is of a highly stimulant nature; of its powerful influence on the imagination, however, there can be no doubt' (159). That ammonia is a corrosive chemical with considerable potential for damage to the internal organs was evidently unknown at the time.

[5] Bowick 1884, 123.

The ammoniaphone's working principle suggests more than just a belief in environmental determinism – the conceit that the superiority of Italian vocal art was due principally to climatic factors – but also a sense that one's voice might be transposed from another place, 'inspired' according to the literal etymology of the term. Inhaling the ammonia vapour was like taking breath from elsewhere into one's own person, conjuring a sense of vocal self out of thin air. Furthermore, it suggests that by laying claim to this foreign breath – 'Italianising' the voice, as it was said – one might not simply become a better vocalist but in fact be healed and made whole. Hygiene and musicality overlap here in a convergence characteristic of the era. The ammoniaphone typifies a generational fever for a wide variety of self-administered techniques of bodily care, attesting to a morality that might be described as equally self-glorifying and self-denying: self-glorifying because it encouraged absorption in one's own aesthetic self, self-denying because the instrument's conception derogated the sensation of the user's own personhood in relation to some projected space or thing beyond the person. The ammoniaphone capitalised on the suspicion that value comes from a fantasised attachment to a 'not here', a certain dimly imagined spatial dislocation. In facilitating a fascination with the inward vocal self only through an intermediary external element, the device set up a dynamic in which the self is made by being made strange.

The ammoniaphone is thus an emblem of a particularly anxious moment in the history of the voice. The Victorian nineteenth century, and especially the decades after 1870, witnessed a marked surge in amateur obsession with various acts of vocalising (and not only, or even primarily, in the performance contexts most familiar to music historians).[6] Faced with the burgeoning market for instruction manuals on what was called 'vocal culture', it is not difficult to assent to Steven Connor's comment on the period that 'a generalised cultural engorgement of the idea of the voice suggested and produced as much nervousness as it did exultation'.[7]

Nor is it difficult to sympathise with George Bernard Shaw's condescension toward this phenomenon in an 1886 sketch of the relevant cultural milieu:

---

[6] The culture of domestic theatre is relevant here; see Cobrin 2006 and Meeuwis 2012.

[7] Connor 2000, 332. The steady stream of such manuals would include Urling 1857, Atwell 1868, Monroe 1869, Barnes 1874, Lunn [1874] 1900, E. Seiler 1875, 1884, Barraclough 1876, Thwing 1876, Holmes 1879, Sandlands 1886, Mackenzie [1886] 1891, Myer 1891 and Aikin 1900.

Though there must by this time be in existence almost as many handbooks for singers and speakers as a fast reader could skip through in a lifetime or so, publishers still find them safe investments. Young people who are born into the fringe of the musical and theatrical professions from which we draw our great stock of deadheads are generally much at a loss when the question of earning a living comes home to them ... Their ineptly stagy manners and appearance, like their morals, are the impress of an environment of bismuth and rouge, overcoats with Astrakhan collars, moustaches, sham concerts for the benefit of sham singers out of engagement, and an atmosphere which creates an unquenchable craving for admission without payment to all sorts of public entertainments, especially to the Opera. ... Unsuspicious of their own futility, they have some distorted ideas of practice, but none of study. They are always in search of a method – especially the old Italian one of [Nicola] Porpora; and they will even pay cash for a handbook of singing, a set of unintelligible photographs of the larynx, or an ammoniaphone from which to suck a ready-made compass of three octaves with the usual fortune attached.[8]

Harping on a commercialism targeting dilettantes, Shaw reacts to the emergence of cultural forces – the market and the popular, in an adolescent phase of what would later come to be known derogatorily as the 'culture industry' – which still bore the added threat of a relative novelty that has long since worn off. His immediate concern is with the easily discreditable notion of a short cut to artistry. It is the extreme temporality of the market, exemplified by the scarcely two-year lifespan of the ammoniaphone itself, that denies the possibility of a more genuine 'practice' and forsakes anything so sustained and invested as 'study'. But it is also worth noticing how thoroughly Shaw's scene is pervaded by an insistent staging of the self, both in the local sense of simply acquiring 'stagy manners', and also in the more expansive sense of seeking techniques for constructing a persona through which one might activate oneself as an agent of public action in the first place. Despite his intentions, Shaw's critical-anthropological impulse does not appear to prepare a principle for drawing the line between appearance and reality, between the superficial activity of acquiring manners and the more durable disposition toward becoming capable of entering vocally into the world at all.

Beyond the optimistic promises of a 'ready-made' substitute for bel canto technique, the ongoing communal project of developing (strengthening, smoothing, curing) the voice was persistently nagged by a set of challenges that might be described as problems of self-observation. The

---

[8] Shaw, in Tyson 1991, 164–5.

voice had so often been described, perhaps most familiarly by Augustine, as that non-object which exemplified the fleeting and the insubstantial.[9] How, then, might one make even one's own voice present to oneself, in order to 'fix' its qualities, both in the sense of improving inadequacies and also in the sense of stabilising, maintaining and, especially, holding-before-oneself for observation? The ammoniaphone answered these questions by short-circuiting them: denying the problem of self-observation by giving the appearance that voice could be acquired from without. At roughly the same historical moment, though, another medical-cultural object approached the problem from a different angle, making the voice in some sense present by making it *visible*. This object was the laryngoscope, originally a clinical instrument, which came to occupy a central, if disputed, place in vocal pedagogy by 1870. Its story, along with that of one of its most fervent devotees, follows. What this episode demonstrates, I suggest, is simply how that initial orientation toward fixity or stability in the voice is increasingly frustrated by the very techniques adopted to accomplish it. Put somewhat differently (and more theoretically), the episode turns out to be an instance where efforts at naturalisation invert into a kind of defamiliarisation that arguably affiliates these practices with an experience of modernism more broadly conceived.

Even in more respectable niches of vocal pedagogy and clinical practice, the force exerted by Dr Moffat's Italian fantasy was strongly felt. In many Northern European accounts of vocal culture, narratives of cultural–historical decline spurred the ambition of returning the voice to a supposedly more natural state associated with Italy in the eighteenth century. This impulse overwhelmingly determined the rhetorical trajectory of writing by Emma Seiler (1821–1886), a German voice teacher later active in North America, who rehearsed the declinist motif with a sense of personal urgency informed by her experiences as a vocal student in Dresden in the 1850s. Finding her own voice ruined at the age of thirty by the harsh pedagogy of an unnamed teacher, Seiler sought to ameliorate the crisis by taking up the study of vocal anatomy, an endeavour for which she was particularly well prepared as the daughter of the court physician to King Ludwig of Bavaria, sister-in-law of two surgeons, wife of another doctor, and (later) mother of a leading American laryngologist.[10] But her account of personal efforts to reverse the damage to her vocal organs was couched

---

[9] Augustine, *Confessions*, book XI, section 27.

[10] For Seiler's biography, see [unsigned] 1891, 149–62, esp. 151–4; and [unsigned] 1893, 591–2. For a recent evaluation of her pedagogy, see Price 2011. For her son's work, see C. Seiler 1883, whose first chapter treats, appropriately enough, 'The Laryngoscope' (13–26).

in terms that expanded into a broader historical vision. The injury to Seiler's own throat, we are meant to infer from her writings, ontogenetically recapitulated a pattern of degradation of the European voice that had been phylogenetically underway for several generations already. Seiler's 1861 treatise on vocal pedagogy, *Altes und Neues über die Ausbildung des Gesangorganes* (published in English in 1868 as *The Voice in Singing*), nostalgically invoked a golden age of mid-eighteenth-century Italian singing – the era of Porpora and Farinelli – and blamed the comparatively poor state of current practice on a number of historical factors, including the disappearance of the male soprano, the decentralisation and regionalism of pedagogy and theory, and the broader democratisation of musical culture manifest in her era's 'dilettantism without precedent'. Voice teachers from one town to the next hawked idiosyncratic methods without any unified code of knowledge to distinguish quacks from masters. The castrato's historical extinction, moreover, expedited the disunification of vocal practice, for that now lost figure, Seiler suggested, had once united in a single body a quasi-hermaphroditic knowledge of the voices of both sexes.[11]

An insistence on empirical understanding was central to Seiler's project. It was a perceptual intuition of the heard voice, the act of learning through direct imitation, that had distinguished singers of the old Italian school, which she credited with an 'unclouded gift for observation' and a self-awareness and centredness that had been forsaken in the intervening generations.[12]

The old Italian method of instruction, to which vocal music owed its high condition, was purely *empirical*, i.e. the old singing masters taught only according to a sound and just feeling for the beautiful, guided by that faculty of acute observation, which enabled them to distinguish what belongs to nature. The pupils learned by imitation, as children learn their mother tongue, without troubling themselves about rules. But after the true and natural way has once been forsaken, and for so long a period only the false and the unnatural has been heard and taught, it seems almost impossible by empiricism alone to restore the old and proper method of teaching.[13]

Yet this lost, quasi-Goethean 'gift' of intuitive perception – along with the imagined presentness and transparency to the observer it assumed – could only be replaced by something proper to the modern era: in this case, methods and techniques of anatomical and physiological observation, of

---

[11] E. Seiler 1884, 28–9. Related material was serialised as E. Seiler 1865.   [12] E. Seiler 1865, 53.
[13] E. Seiler 1884, 30–1.

Moving through a series of doctors' households, Seiler did not come by her interest in anatomy and physiology out of the blue. Early in her lifelong project, she befriended a medical student who surreptitiously procured a separated throat, which they spent two weeks carefully dissecting together late at night, studying the muscular and cartilaginous structure of the vocal organ under cover of darkness (these practices were considered improper for a woman).[15] Yet by the time she left Dresden, her own larynx in poor condition, Seiler no longer felt compelled to keep her anatomical interests in the dark, and outed herself as an aspiring laryngologist around the time she arrived in Heidelberg in the mid-1850s, where she established contact with several prominent scientists at the university, including the chemist Robert Bunsen, the physicist Gustav Kirchoff and, most pertinent, the physiologist Hermann von Helmholtz (1821–1894), who had just come to Heidelberg himself as part of regional reforms in medical education.[16]

The convergence of Seiler and Helmholtz in Heidelberg perfectly suited their respective agendas at that moment, though in rather different ways. At the time of his move, Helmholtz was turning to the study of vowel sounds from a physical acoustical perspective, and much of this research required the assistance of a trained vocalist who could sing a tone with sufficient steadiness and duration to allow sustained close attention to its qualities. 'While engaged on my book, *Die Lehre von den Tonempfindungen*,' Helmholtz wrote, 'I had the honour of becoming acquainted with Mad. Seiler, and of being assisted by her in my essay upon the formation of the vowel tones and the registers of the female voice. I have thus had an opportunity of knowing the delicacy of her musical ear and her ability to master the more difficult and abstract parts of the theory of music.'[17] Yet these activities were of interest primarily to Helmholtz, and only secondarily to Seiler. Helmholtz was concerned with mapping out a new disciplinary landscape of sensory physiology, one which required unprecedented degrees of control over the production and apprehension of sensory objects normally marginalised or concealed, or even perhaps non-existent for practical

---

[14] On the Goethean 'gift' of natural observation, see Kittler 2002, 155–66.

[15] [unsigned] 1891, 158.

[16] [unsigned] 1893, 592. On science reforms in Heidelberg at this time, see Tuchman 1993, esp. 138–57.

[17] From an 1866 letter quoted in the 'Translator's Preface' to E. Seiler 1884, 7–8. Helmholtz refers to his *Die Lehre von den Tonempfindungen als physiologische Grundlage für die Theorie der Musik* (1863), and 'Ueber die Klangfarbe der Vocale' (1859).

Figure 2.3 'Laryngoscope', Johann Nepomuk Czermak, *Der Kehlkopfspiegel und seine Verwerthung für Physiologie und Medizin* (Leipzig: Wilhelm Engelmann, 1860), p. 16.

purposes, prior to experiment.[18] Though just as attuned as Helmholtz was to sensory marginalia, Seiler took interest less in the texture of new sensations for their own sake, and more in their mode of production. So it is not surprising that the element of their exchange that became magnified in her accounts of their collaboration, in contrast to his, was the practice of the laryngoscopy. This promised to render the mechanics of the voice observable with a previously unimaginable presence and force.

In 1859, the laryngoscope was still relatively new to musical society. It had been four years since the London musical and scientific communities could have read an account by the influential voice teacher Manuel García *fils* (1805–1906), who is often credited with inventing the device itself.[19] Yet in that initial article, García had merely offered a theory about the anatomical mode of production of the various vocal registers, without right away suggesting anything like an intervention in the actual practice of singing itself. In terms of priority in the published record, the latter more ambitious and explicitly pedagogical goal fell first to Seiler, who thus played an important (and almost always overlooked) role in drawing the laryngoscope into a broader network of musical-scientific practice. In Seiler's work, laryngoscopy is identified as a novel mode of observation which could take the place of the Italian 'gift for observation' whose loss she lamented in her singing treatise. But what sort of practice *was* laryngoscopy? Like the ammoniaphone, the laryngoscope was a design of elegant simplicity, consisting of a coin-sized mirror affixed to a long metal rod (Figure 2.3), which was inserted into the throat at an angle that allowed the reflection of the top of the vocal organ to become visible to the eye of a second, observing individual. Of particular interest to singers like García and Seiler were the views of the vocal ligaments (vocal cords), the arytenoid cartilages and the muscles that moved them, and above all the changing shape of the glottis, which refers to the mercurially shifting gap between the vocal ligaments (Figures 2.4 and 2.5).

[18] For discussion of Helmholtz's role in this collaboration, see Steege 2012, 179–93.
[19] García 1854–5, 399–410. Stark 1999, 5, 11 and 16, perpetuates the notion of García the inventor. By contrast, Davies 2014, 133–6, offers a more nuanced interpretation.

Vocal Culture in the Age of Laryngoscopy

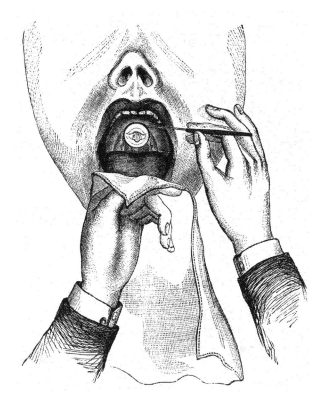

Figure 2.4 Lennox Browne, *The Throat and Its Diseases*, 2nd edn (Philadelphia: Lea Brothers and Co., 1887), p. 47.

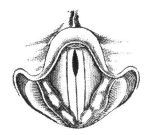 

FIG. 10.—LARYNGOSCOPIC VIEW OF THE FEMALE GLOTTIS IN THE DELIVERY OF A HEAD-NOTE (ORDINARY APPEARANCE).

FIG. 11.—LARYNGOSCOPIC VIEW OF THE MALE GLOTTIS IN FALSETTO SINGING (ORDINARY APPEARANCE).

Figure 2.5 Morell Mackenzie, *Hygiene of the Vocal Organs*, p. 56.

The laryngoscope was morphologically derived from earlier variants dating to the eighteenth century. But not until around 1860 did it become an object of both sustained scientific interest and eventually public fascination.[20] After the publication of Seiler's singing treatise, few manuals on the voice – whether the singing, speaking or ailing voice – failed to include illustrated discussion of how to use the laryngeal mirror and what it might teach.

Given the modesty of this object, it is not immediately clear what about it could have captured the imagination so vividly. One possibility emerges from a retrospective biographical recounting of García's first glimpse of his own vocal organ. In this initial encounter, García is alone, holding a hand-mirror in front of himself, a practice later known as 'autolaryngoscopy':

'During all the years of study and investigation of the problems of the voice-emission,' [García] said, 'one wish was ever uppermost in my mind – "if only I could see the glottis!"'

One day in the September of 1854, when on a visit to Paris, he was standing in the Palais Royal. Suddenly there came to him an idea. 'Why should I not *try* to see it?' How must this be done? Why, obviously by some means of reflection. Then, like a flash, he seemed to see the two mirrors of the laryngoscope in their respective positions as though actually before his eyes. He went straight to Charrière, the surgical instrument maker, asked whether they happened to possess a small mirror, which had been one of the failures of the London Exhibition of 1851. He bought it for six francs.

Returning home, he placed against the uvula this little piece of glass, which he had heated with warm water and carefully dried. Then with a hand-mirror he flashed on to its surface a ray of sunlight. By good fortune he hit upon the proper angle at the very first attempt. There before his eyes appeared the glottis, wide open and so fully exposed that he could see a portion of the trachea. So dumbfounded was he that he sat down aghast for several minutes. On recovering from his amazement he gazed intently for some time at the changes which were presented to his vision while the various tones were being emitted. From what he witnessed it was easy to conclude that his theory, attributing to the glottis alone the power of engendering sound, was confirmed, and thence it followed that the different positions taken by the larynx in the front of the throat had no action whatever in the formation of the sound. At last he tore himself away, and wrote a description of what he had seen.[21]

---

[20] García was perhaps the most influential singing teacher of the nineteenth century, numbering soprano Jenny Lind ('The Swedish Nightingale') and baritone Julius Stockhausen among his students. For a biography by the son of one his students, see Mackinlay 1908. Stark (1999, 3–32) offers a less hagiographic account.

[21] Mackinlay 1908, 203–5.

The simple immediate lesson taken from García's work was just that the position of the larynx – the bobbing up and down of the 'Adam's apple' – did not independently determine pitch and timbre, whereas the changing shape of the glottis now came to play a larger role in explaining these two phenomena. His novel attention to that strangely vacant organ, which is in fact not an autonomous organic tissue at all but an empty space *between* organs, would initially appear to constitute the unique significance of the event. But on a narrative-rhetorical level, the image of García dumbstruck by the very image of the glottis merits some comment. To be 'dumbfounded', as per the biographer's account, is understood here to be a silencing, which, while not absolutely paradoxical in this scene, is at least faintly ironic. The image of the open glottis, the origin of vocal tone, is itself what renders him silent. Following a moment of mute amazement, the shocking image of his own open gullet etched into his memory, García resumes singing with the mirror. The action of 'gazing', typically or at least poetically one of soundless rapture, implicitly sounds here, but the prose account, deferring to mute contemplation, tells us nothing more than that 'various tones [were] emitted', which leaves the object of hearing ambiguous (via an ambivalent 'passive voice', moreover): is García changing the pitch of his voice? the vowel quality? the intensity? In any event, he does not appear to be primarily listening, but rather looking. As the nature of the vocal object changes, García moves from being initially blind to the voice, to being mute, to ending up in a certain sense deaf.

The difficulty of coordinating a simultaneity of singing, hearing and seeing bespeaks the perceptual and somatic disjointedness of laryngoscopy generally. Later commentators reiterated in various ways the uneasy coexistence of perceptual registers, complaining for example that the voice, ideally, is 'necessarily invisible', and that to try thinking of it as something visible either misrecognises its nature or at least distracts singers from some more essential way of perceiving themselves singing.[22] Against the modest frenzy that arose around the new pedagogical device, one detractor insisted:

Never use the laryngoscope. The function of this instrument is to guide the surgeon's hand and probang, and finishes there. Singing is not a question of how a distorted throat looks in an oblique mirror, but how it sounds to a healthy ear. It is not a question of optics, but one of acoustics. Many modern writers have

---

[22] See, for example, Abbott 1924, 932 (along with the preceding and succeeding series of letters to the editor).

56   BENJAMIN STEEGE

deceived themselves and their readers on this point. As Wordsworth says: 'Avaunt, this vile abuse of pictured page! / Must eyes be all in all, the tongue and ear nothing?'[23]

A common alternative to the laryngoscope – one involving not so much direct empirical observation as indirect metaphorical action – was for vocal teachers to appeal to the manipulation of a phantasmal vocal object in an imagined space. Thus, for example: 'to focus the sound; to direct the voice towards the roof of the mouth; against the hard palate; against the upper front teeth; into the head; to the bottom of the chest; to lean the tone against the eyes! to sing all over the face!'[24] But laryngoscopists considered such metaphorical manipulations either too vague to be helpful, or in outright contradiction with themselves. In contrast, the perceived value of the mirror was its demystifying potential to bring imagined and real movements into accord. And yet, as I have been suggesting, the instrument itself hardly paved a clear path to the kind of immediate perception it was held to promise. Even García did not find the laryngoscope especially useful over the duration of a course of training, though he felt that it might serve as an effective propaedeutic, either for the teacher or for the student. In fact, García expressly acknowledged that there was little point in practising song with a mirror in the throat. ('If it is used under the pretence that it can show how one must sing while the throat is opened in phonation, it is clearly an instrument of torture, and deserves to be thrown away without hesitation.'[25]) Rather, its value came in creating the possibility of a self-consciousness unavailable by other means. Once the visual image of the organ was lodged in the memory, knowledge of how to manipulate it effectively would theoretically follow in the same way that one might imagine visualising one's little toe moving before becoming actually capable of wiggling it.

While García, an icon of bel canto pedagogy, remains to this day linked to the singular event of the mythicised origin of laryngoscopy, one might argue (speculatively) that Seiler was substantially responsible for its popularisation.[26] Her treatise, revised and expanded in English after her move to Philadelphia in 1866 and perhaps more widely read in translation than in the original German, set the precedent for subsequent writings that highlighted this new way of perceiving the activity of vocalisation. Where

---

[23] Lunn [1874] 1900, 10.   [24] Browne and Behnke [1883] 1886, 7.

[25] Quoted in Mackenzie [1886] 1891, 87.

[26] Shaw, 'A Book for Orators and Singers', in Tyson 1991, 166, refers to Mackenzie's *Hygiene of the Vocal Organs* (1886) as 'the most interesting English record of laryngoscopic investigation since Mdme. Seiler's', suggesting that she had held the terrain for the intervening quarter century.

Garcia's interest had been initially limited to the various shapes of the glottal opening in the different registers of the male voice, Seiler extended the use of the instrument into a number of other areas, including study of the female voice.[27] In particular, she aimed to synthesise a concern for safe singing habits with Helmholtz's experimental interest in the physiology of vowel qualities. Of personal concern were the precise pitches at which breaks between vocal registers occurred, since singers like herself had increasingly exposed themselves to potential injury when stretching the upper range of one register further than it could safely extend. Laryngoscopy enabled a self-discipline in which a singer might coordinate visual observation of the behaviour of the vocal ligaments at various pitch levels with a correspondingly appropriate mode of vocal production. The ability to visualise strain on the vocal ligaments might help a singer to override muscular habits acquired, but no longer consciously noticed, over years of incorrect and damaging voice study.[28] In fact, laryngoscopic knowledge was explicitly held by Seiler to supplant formal training in song. In a typical historical irony, the way back to the fantasised natural state occupied in the Italian eighteenth century could only be found by stepping through the mirror:

By the kindness of Prof. Helmholtz, I became acquainted with the physical conditions upon which pure musical tones depend, and, after long-continued practice, I succeeded in producing such tones and in making them habitual. Not until I had prepared myself by years of faithful study, and knew the several physical sensations accompanying a perfectly natural musical tone in the different groups, did I begin to observe in myself, with the laryngoscope, the movements in the larynx during the production of tones. In order to draw correct conclusions from such observations, attention must be specially directed to the physical sensations which, in a correct position of the mouth, accompany the formation of a perfect musical tone. For, in using the laryngoscope, the mouth must be opened very wide, and its parts be so drawn aside and so posed that a full view of the glottis shall be afforded. As in this way the resonance and reflexion in the cavity of the mouth become disturbed, it is not possible to distinguish the different groups of tones by their timbre alone. When I succeeded at last in obtaining such command of the parts of the mouth that I could see the whole glottis, I always found the same movements in the

---

[27] E. Seiler 1884, esp. 50–84.

[28] E. Seiler 1884, 69–84. Anyone familiar with the history of vocal pedagogy will be sensitive to the tenuousness of any claims about register breaks, with very little agreement on the facts during the decades before and after Seiler's work. See, for example, Davies 2014, 13–40; and G. Bloch 2007.

formation of the same tones, changing and returning in the same manner. I then sought to make like observation in others, and selected for the purpose persons who never had had any instruction in singing, and whose voices were consequently entirely natural. Professional singers, or such as had received instruction in singing as it is commonly given, I found for the most part to be wholly unfit for the desired observation. For, with a few distinguished exceptions, the voices of such singers are so artificially vitiated that they are no longer in a natural normal condition. The results of the observation of such voices would belong to the class of *facts inexactly observed*, from which every honest inquirer cannot keep too far aloof.[29]

For Seiler, access to self-present song, to the voice 'exactly observed' and 'natural', could only be gained through the defamiliarising practice of seeing it projected onto a surface beyond the bounds of the person.

If the story of García's eureka moment dramatises a rupture in self-knowledge, a sudden coming into contact with oneself as if for the first time, Seiler's rendering of her own experience in contrast emphasises a more resistant and enduring event, requiring a certain *tactus eruditus* almost unrecognisable as the same practice. In contrast to García's instantaneous and improbable enskilling in the art of self-observation, Seiler and later laryngoscopists maintained that it could take months to acquire the technique of singing quasi-naturally with the mirror inserted – a considerable factor which set its musical use apart from its clinical use, wherein a relatively brief glance might be enough to reach a diagnosis.[30] With the introduction of photography of the larynx, or 'photolaryngoscopy', the relative instantaneity of the medical gaze was radicalised. But even in the clinical context, learning to resist the gag reflex (on the part of the singer) and learning to avoid provoking it (on the part of the observer) were demanding enough to motivate the use of a so-called 'Laryngo-Phantom', a life-size dummy singer with a realistic oral cavity, for the physician to practise on before working with living subjects.[31] In short, with laryngoscopy, we are clearly dealing not with a simple and transparent form of knowledge or perception, but with a complex process of training that demanded sustained commitment and some degree of passion on the

---

[29] E. Seiler 1875, 63–5; original emphasis.   [30] See, for example, Mackenzie [1886] 1891, 36–8.

[31] The Laryngo-Phantom 'consists of an imitation of the throat, the larynx, and the mouth, and "is intended to familiarise students with as many of the details connected with the use of the laryngoscope as it is possible to learn before the application of the instrument to the living subject." A number of little paintings representing different laryngoscopic appearances may be slipped into this Phantom, unknown to the student, who has to discover what has been done by the usual process.' Behnke [1880]., 77.

part of its practitioners. If the ammoniaphone promised a short cut to self-transformation, the laryngoscope made the self-transformation all the more plausible by foregrounding the resistances overcome in each minute habitual muscular motion.

One paradox of the laryngoscope noticed in passing earlier bears reiterating here: while it promised wholeness and fluidity to otherwise broken and strained voices, it introduced a disruptive caesura at the heart of the vocal act, marked by the incompatibility of hearing one's voice and seeing it. Or, at any rate, seeing *something*, though the emptiness of the glottal opening, which García and Seiler were now identifying with voice itself, meant that 'seeing' the voice was really a matter of witnessing a negative space established precisely by the absence of the singer's body. J. Q. Davies aptly describes this phenomenon in terms of an infinite regress in which 'the singer's object of study was moving ever back: from external instruments or mouths in the early century, to the back of the throat, to the glottis, and then beyond, the voice eventually disappearing from ordinary view'.[32] Yet to indicate how laryngoscopy might have rendered the voice strange and exterior is in a certain sense historiographically anticlimactic, given the numerous ways in which the same could be claimed of earlier contexts, including, most famously, Wolfgang von Kempelen's spectacular 'speaking machines' of the eighteenth century. The voice's disassociation has not been a singular event.[33] Still, the strangeness of the voice that emerged in laryngoscopic perception was in certain respects *sui generis*. This is perhaps inevitable, given the peculiar fantasy according to which laryngoscopy – less explicitly but just as insistently as the ammoniaphone – was imagined to assume the role once played by an antique Mediterranean song foreign to contemporaneous Heidelberg, London or Philadelphia.

The freighted term 'estrangement' hints at a kind of incipient modernism detectable on the scene of laryngoscopy. I am not the first to propose such a link: Tim Armstrong counts the laryngoscope as one among an expanding battery of roughly contemporaneous technologies of 'intervention' – stethoscope, ophthalmoscope, speculum, high-intensity light,

---

[32] Davies 2014, 128. Holly Watkins and Melina Esse (2015, esp. 165–6) present a slightly contrasting view of laryngoscopy, emphasising the reductive folly of trying to identify anything like 'the' voice, particularly when this (necessarily metaphysical) identity is understood as something dualistically severed from the body that produces it. I certainly acknowledge this folly, though the aim of this chapter is primarily to reflect on the fact that such a belief was historically active at all.

[33] Kane 2014, esp. 180–222, vividly elaborates a related point from a much broader theoretical perspective.

X-rays and so on – which figure in a history of early modernist perception. Invasive and illuminating devices such as these, Armstrong suggests, tend to crop up in a wide range of modernist literary texts that are peculiarly 'characterised by the desire to *intervene* in the body; to render it part of modernity by techniques which may be biological, mechanical, or behavioural'.[34] An aspiration to render something 'part of modernity', to make it contemporary with oneself in a manner that cannot be claimed of everyday sensory experience, would seem to describe a central strand of laryngoscopy in García's and Seiler's practice insofar as they were trying to stabilize something so inherently and notoriously fleeting and inaccessible to immediate knowledge. Making the vocal body 'contemporary', visually at hand at roughly the same moment that it is being actualised in song, however, could never have been an *intended* outcome for anyone who, like Moffat or Seiler, was so explicitly nostalgic for the lost voice of another time and place. It is not possible to conceptualise 'modernity' in this regard as a matter of absolute synchronisation of imaginative and technological resources but rather more as an aspiration constantly and constitutively frustrated.

We may perhaps begin to make sense of this incongruity between an impulse to make 'present' and an apparently countervailing one to look backward to a lost past by recalling how often modernist nostalgias are in fact, ironically, a matter of future orientation.[35] To be sure, it is not self-evident how we might imagine a sense of futurity in the present context, aesthetically conservative as it appears to have been, but I would propose that one possible, if somewhat unexpected, interpretative context for appreciating such a perspective is the broader study of phonetics, a field I have mentioned only in passing and can do no more than to indicate quite loosely here. Phonetics research, overlapping with Helmholtz's and Seiler's collaboration around 1860, was at the time a new discipline explicitly concerned with foreign vocal sounds, and both abutting the traditional philology and anticipating the unapologetically defamiliarising discipline of modern linguistics.[36] That Helmholtz and Seiler found themselves making use of the laryngoscope in conjunction with the intensive study of vowel sounds draws this practice into alliance with the grand project, common to every colonial context, of standardising languages according to

---

[34] Armstrong 1998, 2–6.

[35] For a recent collection of reflections on this theme, see Clewell 2013.

[36] I have addressed the affiliations of music theory, phonetics and early modernism in Steege 2012, 1–6, 178–206 and 229–34. For related explorations, see Brain 1998, 249–84; and Bergeron 2010.

'rational' orthographic and phonological schemes. More interesting than the banal fact of standardisation or rationalisation, though, are the resistant historical circumstances to which these processes responded: namely the vast and rapid expansion of languages and dialects that were coming into contact with one another with increasing intensity in the major metropolitan centres, especially in the later decades of the nineteenth century. Raymond Williams and Michael North have highlighted the significance of the late-Victorian conversion of language from a social custom into a malleable medium within urban immigrant and class-bending cultural environments. In tracing the emergence of linguistic modernism from within the rapidly urbanizing late nineteenth century, Williams has emphasised artists' experience of being

liberated or breaking from their national or provincial cultures ... In this the artists and writers and thinkers of this phase [of modernism] found the only community available to them: a community of the medium; of their own practices. Thus language was perceived quite differently. It was no longer, in the old sense, customary and naturalised, but in many ways arbitrary and conventional.[37]

Though Seiler's and Helmholtz's phonetics research took place near the beginning of this shift and was primarily orientated toward the understanding, appreciation and conservation of a canonical central European musical tradition, it can nonetheless be seen as part of the wider response to a new perception of aesthetic contingency and adaptability, and hence a perceived need to prepare conceptual, technical and cultural resources with which to meet the future emergence of unruly forms of vocal self-presentation.

In short, if the laryngoscope rendered speech and song elemental, particulate and decontextualised, it did so in affiliation with much broader cultural transformations than the seemingly parochial scenes we have been considering here. It is from this perspective that we might interpret the simultaneously affirmative and disruptive self-fashioning of larynogoscopy (as of the controlled inhalation of ammonia) as a kind of proto-modernist practice. Crowding around the margins of the make-shift, middlebrow operatic community that Shaw derided, we glimpse the nascent image of a reworking of the aesthetic persona common to avant-gardes everywhere, despite the constrained moral universe in which these particular behaviours were playing out. Shaw's sketch betokens a wider cultural environment in which, as Williams writes, 'the new relationships

---

[37] R. Williams 1989, 45–6. Also see North 1994, 3–34.

of the metropolis . . . forced certain productive kinds of strangeness and distance: a new consciousness of conventions and thus of changeable, because now open, conventions'.[38] However starry-eyed they may appear in retrospect – or, indeed, to Shaw himself – the transformative cultural force of such scenes was not to be underestimated.

[38] R. Williams 1989, 46.

3 | Operatic Fantasies in Early Nineteenth-Century Psychiatry

CARMEL RAZ

In his celebrated essay on insanity in the *Dictionnaire des sciences médicales* (1816), French psychiatrist Étienne Esquirol marvelled at the earlier custom of allowing asylum inmates to attend theatrical productions at Charenton. Noting that these performances had often led to dangerous relapses or delirium, he reported on his own experience of taking patients to the opera:

> I once accompanied a young convalescent to a Comic Opera. Everywhere, he saw his wife conversing with men. Another, after the space of a quarter of an hour, felt the heat in his head increasing – and said, let us go out, or I shall relapse. A young lady, seeing the actors at the Opera armed with sabres, believed that they were going to assail her.[1]

This passage exemplifies three ways in which attending the opera could exacerbate pre-existing mental conditions. The first patient experienced the performance through the prism of his obsessions, the second had a negative physical response to the venue itself, and the third was unable to distinguish between the onstage action and her own delusions.

Esquirol's account of the dangers of the opera to the mentally ill foreshadows subsequent discourses around the pathological effects of the music of Rossini, Meyerbeer, Wagner and others.[2] As James Kennaway has demonstrated, the idea that music might have a dangerous influence on the nerves became increasingly popular during the early nineteenth century, reflecting not only changing medical theories of the mind–body connection but also the emergence of early romantic conceptions of music as capable of inducing sublime or dangerous physical responses.[3] Echoes of this discourse played out within psychiatry as well, where

---

I would like to thank Annelies Andries, Tom Fogg, Céline Frigau Manning, Elina Hamilton and Nori Jacoby for their helpful comments on this chapter.

[1] 'J'ai conduit un jeune convalescent à l'Opéra-Comique, ajoute Esquirol ; il voyait sa femme causant avec des hommes. Un autre, après un quart d'heure, sentit la chaleur lui gagner la tête. Sortons, me dit-il, ou je vais retomber. Une demoiselle étant à l'Opéra, voyant les acteurs armés de sabres, crut qu'ils allaient se battre.' Esquirol 1816, 228–9. English text adapted from Hunt 1845, 81.

[2] See Walton 2007; Kennaway 2012a; Kennaway in this volume, Chapter 14.

[3] Kennaway 2012a, 48.

experiments with musical and theatrical entertainment in insane asylums became increasingly common as well as subject to debate.[4]

This chapter investigates the role of opera within early nineteenth-century psychiatry. I begin by discussing the concept of opera as therapy, focusing on the Charenton asylum's notorious theatrical productions, which took place between 1805 and 1813 under the direction of the Marquis de Sade. I then survey different approaches to spectacle within the context of early nineteenth-century psychiatry, showing how physicians were divided about the potential benefits and dangers of incorporating theatrical representations into patient treatment. Finally, I present a close reading of two case histories from Peter Joseph Schneider's *System einer medizinischen Musik* (1835), an 'indispensable guide for medical students, directors of lunatic asylums, practical physicians, and unmusical teachers from different disciplines'.[5] The first concerns a young lady mourning the death of her lover, a Spanish tenor; the second recounts the cure of a sailor who could only communicate by singing. Situating the ambivalent depictions of opera that emerge in Schneider's accounts within the history of early nineteenth-century psychiatry, I argue that these cases reflect competing discourses about the alternately therapeutic and pathological power of music and spectacle.

Opera as Therapy

The early nineteenth century saw the gradual rise of a new 'moral treatment' of mental illness across Europe.[6] Characterised by a more humane approach towards patients, 'moral' therapies focused on rehabilitation through distractions such as menial work or entertainment. Mental asylums that had recently chained their patients adopted new methods of therapeutic treatment: patients were now encouraged to enjoy the outdoors, to benefit from regular physical exercise, to read and to attend concerts.[7] In place of bloodletting or purging, diversion became regarded as one of the main techniques of treatment for insanity. Music was widely

---

[4] See Raz 2017.   [5] Schneider 1835, vol. 1.

[6] See Goldstein 1987; Dowbiggin 1991; Scull 2005; Foucault 2013; Knowles and Trowbridge 2015.

[7] Notable here is Jean-Baptiste Pussin and Philippe Pinel's famous freeing of patients from their chains at the Bicêtre and later Salpétrière hospitals. See Weiner 1979. Under Esquirol, the Salpétrière would later feature concerts with some of the most renowned musicians in Paris. See Esquirol 1838, 2: 584–6. These efforts were subsequently expanded by Ulysse Trélat. François Leuret would likewise institute music classes and a patient choir at the Bicêtre. For a review of Trélat and Leuret's innovations see [unsigned] 1847b.

Operatic Fantasies in Early Nineteenth-Century Psychiatry

understood as a positive force, and its usage in the service of therapy and diversion was recommended by both physicians and asylum directors.[8] Theatre and spectacle were likewise regarded as powerful means of affecting the mind, and some early nineteenth-century doctors thought they might usefully be deployed to combat irrational obsessions and delusions.[9]

Philippe Pinel, a pioneer of moral treatment, discussed the advantages of ceremonies and role-playing in his influential *Traité médico-philosophique sur l'aliénation mentale* (1801). He praised the annual mass exorcism at Besançon, in which priests healed the possessed by means of an elaborate ritual accompanied by martial music and the sounds of cannons, and suggested that physicians likewise incorporate theatrical elements into their practice. In a famous example, Pinel described his treatment of a tailor obsessed by delusions of guilt through staging of a mock trial in which visiting physicians played the role of a government deputation. (Unfortunately, the patient had a nervous breakdown after inadvertently learning that both his trial and acquittal had been fabricated.)[10]

In his *Rhapsodien über die Anwendung der psychischen Kurmethode auf Geisteszerrüttungen* (Rhapsodies about the Application of Psychological Treatment to Mental Breakdown; 1803), Johann Christian Reil cited Pinel's example of mass exorcism in recommending the use of music and theatre to both entertain and heal the insane. He argued that every asylum should offer a theatre complete with masks, sets and stage machinery. This would allow the physician to stage scenarios reflecting the patient's own condition; such dramatic enactments would allow patients to engage with, and ultimately resolve, their fears.[11]

---

[8] Roller (1831, 199–203) summarises contemporary approaches to music therapy and provides the reasoning of sixteen major psychiatrists in support of music.

[9] See Goldstein 1987, 87. For more on opera and spectacle in early nineteenth-century Paris see S. Williams 2003; Hibberd 2013; Andries 2018.

[10] 'The principal part was assigned to the eldest and gravest of them, whose appearance and manners were most calculated to command attention and respect. These commissaries, who were dressed in black robes suitable to their pretended office, ranged themselves round a table and caused the melancholic to be brought before them. One of them interrogated him as to his profession, former conduct, the journals which he had been in the habits [sic] of reading, and other particulars respecting his patriotism … In order to make a deep impression on his imagination, the president of the delegates pronounced in a loud voice the following sentence … "It is, therefore, by us declared, that we have found the said Citizen a truly loyal patriot; and, pronouncing his acquittal, we forbid all further proceedings against him."' Pinel 1806, 227.

[11] Reil 1803, 209–10: 'Ich bemerke bloss im Allgemeinen, dass jedes Tollhaus zum Behuf ihrer imposanten Anwendung und zweckmässigen Zusammenstellung ein für diese Zwecke besonders eingerichtetes, durchaus praktikabeles Theater haben könnte, das mit allen nöthigen Apparaten, Masken, Maschinerien und Dekorationen verfehen wäre. Auf demselben müssten

The leap from spectacle to therapeutic theatre was made in the early 1800s by Abbé François de Coulmier, director of the Charenton lunatic asylum, and his head physician, Jean-Baptiste Gastaldy.[12] Beyond the resolution of irrational fears, Coulmier claimed that dramatic performances also had the potential to 'awaken the minds of hapless people completely lost in the cruel illness of dementia'.[13] For nearly a decade, plays, comic operas and ballets were produced on a monthly basis at the institution, which featured a spacious auditorium complete with a stage, orchestra pit, tiered stalls and a director's box. These semi-professional productions, which typically featured patients acting alongside local actors, musicians and dancers, attracted audiences from all over Paris.[14]

Contemporary accounts provide intriguing glimpses of Charenton's theatrical spectacles (I use this term in the nineteenth-century sense of the word to refer to stage performances of all kinds including plays, operas and ballets). The actress Flore Corvée recalled visiting in 1813 in order to see opéra comique star Jeanne-Charlotte Saint-Aubin perform alongside the patients. The programme included Molière's five-act play *Le Dépit amoureux* (1656) followed by Dalayrac's comic opera, *Les Deux petits savoyards* (1789), and new verses by the asylum's most infamous inmate, the Marquis de Sade.[15] Corvée described each of the patients in detail, evaluating their success (or failure) in performing their assigned roles. Some of them he deemed completely capable of fulfilling their duties, and Corvée had particular praise for a beautiful black-haired patient who sang new verses by de Sade.[16] Others were clearly troubled, however, such as the actor who suddenly threw his wig into the prompter's box.[17] Corvée seemed secretly thrilled to have met de Sade himself, whom she compared to a monster in a cage.[18]

Claude de Rochefort, a playwright and vaudeville actor, had a similar reaction when encountering de Sade at the Charenton production of

---

die Hausofficianten hinlänglich eingespielt seyn, damit fie jede Rolle eines Richters, Scharfrichters, Arztes, vom Himmel kommender Kugel, und aus den Gräbern wiederkehrender Todten, nach den jedesmaligen Bedürfnissen des Kranken, bis zum höchsten Grad der Täuschung vorstellen könnten. Ein solches Theater könnte zu Gefängnissen und Löwengruben, zu Richtplätzen und Operationsfälen formirt werden.'

[12] For more on the Charenton theatre see Tucker 2007. In 1964, Peter Weiss wrote a play set in the Charenton in 1808, entitled *The Persecution and Assassination of Jean-Paul Marat as Performed by the Inmates of the Asylum of Charenton under the Direction of the Marquis De Sade*.

[13] Archives Nationales, F15 1946. Letter from Coulmier to Emperor Napoleon, 1811, as quoted in Murat 2014, 99.

[14] Esquirol 1838, as translated in Earle 1841, 141–2.   [15] Corvée 1845, 2:172–8.

[16] Corvée 1845, 2:182.   [17] Corvée 1845, 2:181.   [18] Corvée 1845, 2:175–6.

Marivaux's three-act comedy *Les Fausses confidences* (1737). Having sat next to a charming older gentleman at dinner, Rochefort was stunned to discover that this was in fact the author of the infamous novel *Justine*.[19] The poet Jean de Labouïsse reported on a Charenton performance of de Desmahis's comedy *L'Impertinent*, in which de Sade ably performed the lead role. Labouïsse described him as 'cet infâme scélérat' (this infamous scoundrel) and wondered whether it was right that he was allowed to distract himself from the memory of his crimes.[20]

The Charenton's theatre also generated controversy in the German-speaking world. In a report on Parisian lunatic asylums from 1808, August Schweigger gave his impressions of a Charenton performance of the comedy *Le Sourd, ou l'Auberge pleine* (1793) by Desforges that featured incidental music and a small ballet; this was followed by Grétry's one-act comic opera *Le Tableau parlant* (1770).[21] Schweigger noted that such productions appeared to have therapeutic potential but regarded comedies involving romantic intrigue as too stimulating for invalid actors and spectators.[22] The physician Carl Andrée took a more extreme view, criticising the Charenton theatre for forcing lunatics, who were already alienated from themselves, to inhabit yet another persona in front of a curious public.[23]

There was significant dissent within the Parisian medical community regarding the therapeutic benefit of such performances. Gastaldy's successor as head physician, Antoine-Athanase Royer-Collard, was adamantly opposed to theatrical productions, and Coulmier's intimacy with de Sade, who had honoured him with an allegorical masque praising the therapeutic use of theatre, soon proved to be a liability.[24] In a letter dated 2 August 1808, Royer-Collard complained to Joseph Fouché, Minister of the Police, that Coulmier had a 'theatre erected for the performance of comedies and did not think of the harmful effects of such a tumultuous proceeding upon the mind. De Sade is the director of this theatre.'[25] Royer-Collard's efforts were supported by a critical assessment of the Charenton by Hippolyte de Colins in 1812. Colins was appalled at de Sade's participation in the hospital's dramatic productions, and attacked the Charenton for exploiting its patients as 'objects of curiosity in an amphitheatre before the avid gaze

---

[19] Rochefort-Luçay 1863, 241.   [20] Labouïsse 1827, 154.   [21] Schweigger 1809, 19–23.

[22] Schweigger 1809, 11–12, 26.   [23] Andrée 1810, 220.

[24] In *La Fête de l'amitié*, an allegorical play, de Sade extols Coulmier while advocating for the power of theatre to cure the mad.

[25] Cited and translated in I. Bloch 2010, 170.

of a shallow, inconsequential and sometimes nasty public'.[26] In 1813, the Ministry of the Interior banned all theatrical performances at the Charenton.[27]

The loudest voice in response to the Charenton scandal came from the aforementioned Esquirol, who would succeed Royer-Collard as chief physician of the institution in 1825. In a series of works published between 1816 and 1838, Esquirol strongly condemned the theatrical productions at the asylum, noting that they were useless at best and dangerous at worst.[28] He disagreed with the very premise of enclosing patients 'for three hours in a confined, heated and noisy place, where everything tended to produce headaches'.[29] Crucially, Esquirol consistently advocated for a separation between opera and concert music, stating that the former was dangerous because it exalted the imagination and passions, whereas the latter could be 'a valuable remedial agent, particularly in convalescence'.[30] His separation between music and spectacle was subsequently adopted by Gottlob von Nostitz und Jänkendorf, who cited the Charenton episode in dismissing all theatrical productions as dangerous while reporting on weekly concerts performed by patients at his asylum for the insane at Sonnenstein (1829).[31]

In spite of Esquirol's considerable stature in the field, his distinction was contested by a number of physicians. Only a year after Esquirol's initial excoriation of the Charenton theatricals in the *Dictionnaire des sciences médicales*, François Fodéré (1817) responded that this critique of the Charenton productions had not convinced him that spectacle was categorically dangerous for patients.[32] Fodéré continued to recommend that every insane asylum be outfitted with a hall dedicated to spectacles and concerts, as well as baths, gardens and fountains.[33] A similar opinion was held by Viennese psychiatrist Bruno Görgen (1820), who encouraged his patients to attend both concerts and plays.[34] Belgian psychiatrist Joseph Guislain (1826) also refused to rule out the possibility that theatrical representations could be of some therapeutic use.[35]

---

[26] Hippolyte de Colins, *Notice sur l'Etablissement consacré au traitement de l'aliénation mentale, établi à Charenton près Paris*, excerpted in Pinon 1989, 77.

[27] I. Bloch 2010, 171.

[28] These writings include his article 'Folie' in *Dictionnaire des sciences médicales* (1816), the *Rapport statistique sur la Maison Royale de Charenton* (1818), and his monograph *Maladies mentales et des asiles d'aliénés* (1838). Esquirol reused the same text in all three of these works with minor alterations.

[29] Translation adapted from Hunt 1845, 1:80.   [30] Hunt 1845, 1:81.

[31] Nostitz und Jänkendorf 1829, 1:336–41.   [32] Fodéré 1817, 2:216.   [33] Fodéré 1817, 2:218.

[34] Görgen 1820, 27.   [35] Guislain 1826, 277.

In *Die Irrenanstalt nach allen ihren Beziehungen dargestellt* (A Portrait of the Madhouse and All Its Dealings; 1831), Christian Roller included a four-page review of contemporary opinions on the use of music and theatre, listing its pros and cons alongside the reasoning each physician provided for his view.[36] Roller's final tally comes out even: seven physicians against (including himself), and seven in favour.[37] This shows how, in the early 1830s, spoken and sung theatre had an ambiguous status within the psychiatric community. Some physicians argued that it was explicitly dangerous for the mentally ill while others regarded it as a beneficial distraction. There were distinguished supporters on both sides of the argument, and the issue remained largely unresolved. In what follows, I discuss the reverberations of this debate within contemporary music therapy, focusing on two case histories reported by Schneider. As I will show, the construction of his diagnoses and cures interacts with both approaches in a complex fashion. As such, they shed light on the ways in which discourses around opera and psychiatry around 1835 were imbricated with early romantic fantasies about music, gender, class and mental illness.

Medico-Operatic Case Histories

At nearly 750 pages, Schneider's *System einer medizinischen Musik* (1835) combines medicine with music history, theory and aesthetics. It contains abundant references – in German, Latin, Greek, French and English – to physicians and musicians from antiquity as well as the author's contemporaries. Teetering between the ancient tradition of compiling sources on the effects of music and the emerging field of modern psychiatry characterised by experimental methods, the book ends with the detailed case histories of Lina and Bals, two patients suffering from 'musical afflictions'.[38] Mirroring a long-standing cultural practice of situating music between entertainment and spiritual edification, Schneider aligns arias and recitative with sickness, and religious chorales and work songs with health. In both accounts, he himself cures his

---

[36] Roller 1831, 203–6.

[37] According to Roller, the doctors Reil, Langermann, Heinroth, Guislain, Görgen, Schweigger and Rush are in favour of theatrical spectacle, and the doctors Esquirol, Royer-Collard, Haldat, Nostitz und Jänkendorf, Andrée and Frank are against it.

[38] Schneider lived near Bonn for the duration of his short life, and should not be confused with his namesake and contemporary, the renowned physician Peter Joseph Schneider (1781–1871) from Baden, who also authored numerous medical texts. François-Joseph Fétis conflates them in his *Biographie universelle* (1835–44, 8:126).

patients of their operatic excesses, allowing them to resume their designated place within the social order.

Schneider recounts a research trip in the summer of 1831 to the Netherlands accompanied by one Dr Zober, a friend and colleague. Their first patient is Lina, the nineteen-year-old daughter of wealthy Dutch merchants who had remained in an intractable melancholy for over two years. Upon questioning her parents, Schneider establishes that her condition had been caused by the death of Antonio, her father's Spanish apprentice, whom she had secretly loved. The youth had unexpectedly died after contracting a nervous fever, plunging Lina into a depressive state that Schneider diagnoses as *melancholia attonita*.[39]

Lina and Antonio had met during weekly house concerts put on by the girl's uncle, an accomplished amateur musician. These performances featured works for male choir, as well as the occasional instrumental piece or opera aria. Antonio, Schneider learns, was 'a tenor possessing such qualities as man and musician, in spirit and body alike, as to command the attention of both sexes'.[40] Proficient also on the mandolin, his performances at the house concerts had 'enchanted the daughter of the house through the enticing singing and playing summoned out of his Spanish throat and fingers'.[41]

Lina's parents insist that Antonio had been unaware of her feelings and that a relationship between the two was unthinkable. However, Schneider doubts their account: he discovers that the youth had regularly performed the romance from Daniel Auber's *Fra Diavolo*, 'Pour toujours, disait elle, je suis à toi', and the cavatina from Auber's *La Muette de Portici*, 'Ferme tes yeux, la fatigue t'accable'. In a footnote, he includes the texts of both in German, and muses, 'could these words, passionately and expressively sung by the powerful tenor of our Spaniard, fail to make their intended impact?'[42]

Alongside her depression, Lina exhibited minor physical distress, and her period had been absent for nine months. Schneider decides on two courses of treatment: one physical, to target the body; the other musical, to

---

[39] The term comes from Johann Jacob Müller's *De melancholia attonita raro litteratorum affectu* (1741). According to Müller, this was a specific species of religious melancholy, in which one 'is rendered first depressed, then for a long time mute, immobile, senseless, with limbs almost rigid, emaciated, with very few movements left to him, e.g. with the result that he swallows only immediately after food has been thrust into his mouth and blinks when fingers have been moved before his eyes, and sometimes sleeps'. Müller, as translated in Rubin 2004, 177.

[40] Schneider 1835, 2:255.   [41] Schneider 1835, 2:266.   [42] Schneider 1835, 2:258.

Operatic Fantasies in Early Nineteenth-Century Psychiatry 71

cure the mind. After considering and rejecting a course of emetics – copper sulphate dissolved in cherry laurel water – he decides to prescribe a hydropathic treatment, of the kind much in vogue during the 1830s.[43] The water cure soon vanquishes all of Lina's physical symptoms, with the exception of her absent menses.

Schneider maintains that Lina's soul requires a different approach: a 'purely psychic treatment, to consist of ethereal sounds [*ätherische Klängen*]'.[44] He therefore decides to stage a musical intervention with the aid of the girl's family, accompanied by himself on the aeolodicon, an early type of harmonium. The event takes place in the evening: Lina is seated upon the sofa in her bedroom, illuminated by a weak lamp. Dr Zober is concealed in a corner, observing her, and Schneider joins her uncle, father and a musical friend in an adjacent room. Schneider decides to begin the cure with his own improvised prelude on the aeolodicon, followed by one of the patient's favourite chorales sung in four voices. He hopes the former will brighten the patient's mood and amplify her receptivity, so that the latter can awaken dormant memories. Schneider assigns the melody to the uncle, who possesses a powerful tenor voice, and asks the other singers to sing softly. The cure goes according to plan:

I began to improvise in E♭ minor, one of the keys corresponding to deepest melancholy. Softly, and so, swelling to the strongest fortissimo, and then decreasing to a moderate piano, giving way to pure triads, and thus through the various voicings and turns of the harmony. At the beginning of the third crescendo and then immediately after, Zober observed the patient gasp and shiver in what appeared to be a complete seizure of her full nervous system. Yet she remained dumb and immobile. I preluded to G♭ major and began the chorale, swelling from the lightest breaths and back again, and then the quartet began to sing the first few words. We were not yet at the end, when clearly, supported softly by the choir, the tenor took the melody. Suddenly, the invalid cried loudly, 'O! Antonio! Antonio!' (the name of the Spaniard); and began to cry so deeply that we had to stop our chorale; the young girl had to be carried to bed. Upon illuminating the room we observed the good news that upon crying 'O! Antonio', at once her monthly flow had suddenly begun, as the floor was thoroughly soiled by it.[45]

Schneider muses that '[o]ne should almost believe that the soul had been nourishing itself from this blood, but was now returned to its old domain. Was this due to the ethereal sounds?'[46] In closing, Schneider recommends

---

[43] Schneider goes into considerable detail regarding the construction of a shower in the greenhouse, as well as her dietary and bathing schedules. See also Steward 2002.

[44] Schneider 1835, 2:265.   [45] Schneider 1835, 2:267–8.   [46] Schneider 1835, 2:268.

that the girl travel abroad or visit the home of a country pastor for convalescence, and that her parents find her a groom as soon as she recovers. The case ends with a postscript telling that Lina married one of her father's apprentices shortly after and had a child.

Let us now turn to Schneider's second study. This relates to Bals, a 'coarse and uneducated' sailor, thirty-three years of age, who can only communicate through singing.[47] Known today as psychogenic dysphonia, this condition is characterised by an alteration of the voice due to mental rather than physical causes.[48] The origin of Bals's affliction soon emerges: the sailor had moonlighted as a smuggler. Ambushed by the Ostend border police, he beat one of the officers so badly that the man later died. Bals was subsequently sentenced to a long prison term. Upon his release, he appeared on the cusp of a nervous breakdown, obsessed with 'morbid ideas concerned not only with pride, but also with greed, and especially with an exaggerated fear of the future'.[49] Most peculiar, however, was the following symptom:

Whenever a physician attended the patient, (and there were many of these [visits],) the patient welcomed them all with a strange song: 'A good day sir, my good doctor, you are well, that pleases me, I was always thinking of you, help me.' The patient performed these and comparable speech-songs in the form of a ghastly recitative in a terrible voice; and all the questions that were put to him were also answered in the form of a recitative, singing, or rather howling.[50]

As this passage illustrates, Bals is completely unable to control his vocal production. Schneider notes that a local physician had initially obtained some improvement through regular bloodlettings in conjunction with the counsel of an experienced preacher. However, this success was only temporary, and the sailor had since relapsed. Schneider thus offers to conduct a musical cure.

Schneider begins by preparing the musical performance. He gathers a group of local musicians – two horn players, two clarinets, a bassoonist, a trombonist and a drummer – and four sailors, and decides that they will sing 'Matrosen, die Anker gelichtet', a song composed in 1823 by Christian Pohlenz to a text by Wilhelm Gerhard. Schneider asks the sailors to sing this piece in their 'Dutch dialect', and instructs the musicians to accompany and the drummer to play 'more softly than usual'.[51]

---

[47] Schneider 1835, 2:287.   [48] For further reading see Butcher, Elias and Cavalli 2007.
[49] Schneider 1835, 2:288.   [50] Schneider 1835, 2:289.   [51] Schneider 1835, 2:291.

Operatic Fantasies in Early Nineteenth-Century Psychiatry 73

Next Schneider embarks on the treatment. He visits Bals and inquires after his health. The sailor sings in response: 'Sir, I know not who you are, but I remain who I am! Trillerum da da! etc. If I am damned, then I am damned. But I did not beat him to death.'[52] Schneider then invites the band into the room, and asks them to perform their ditty. The effect of the music upon the patient is striking:

The eyes of our patient sparkled, his entire body jerked, he moved his hands and feet, and joined in the singing with a terrifying energy. When we were at the end, he called *Da Capo!*, and jumped from his bed and joined his sailor fellows. We then sang the second verse, after which his wife distributed brandy, which he drank. After this I requested a waltz to be played, and he grasped his wife, kissed and embraced her (for the first time since his sickness) and danced with her, in such a furious way that the sailors, one after the other, had to replace the poor woman. In the end he was so damp and exhausted, that he fell on his bed and slept.[53]

The merry sounds of Schneider's band seem to galvanise the sailor: his eyes sparkle, his entire body twitches, he moves his limbs and joins in the singing with an energy that Schneider describes as terrifying (*schauderhaft*) – the same adjective he initially used to describe the quality of the sailor's recitative. The power of music and dance restore Bals's vital forces to the point that the next day he is glimpsed chopping firewood in the courtyard. No longer emasculated by the uncanny singing voice, he can now resume his position as provider and head of the household. After six months, Schneider writes, Bals had fully recovered his health and returned to sea.

While both of these cases have successful outcomes, they are plagued by a number of strange inconsistencies. Schneider dates his trip to July 1831, and informs us that Lina had been depressed for two years. Antonio would thus appear to have died in 1829, yet Lina recalls that he frequently sang an aria from *Fra Diavolo*, which only received its premiere in 1830. There are discrepancies in Bals's case history as well. An uneducated sailor is inexplicably fluent enough in musical terminology to cry out '*Da Capo!*' at the end of the performance. Freshly released from jail after a lengthy prison sentence, he is apparently familiar with a recently composed German art song, a piece so popular that street musicians in the Netherlands have added it to their repertoire in Dutch. Moreover, in 1831, Ostend, the town in which Bals's case transpires, was already part of Belgium, rather than the Netherlands.[54]

---

[52] Schneider 1835, 2:291. [53] Schneider 1835, 2:292.
[54] I thank Annelies Andries for bringing this to my attention.

There is a remarkable explanation for these irregularities. It seems that the medical details of both case histories were plagiarised verbatim from *System der höhern Heilkunde für Ärzte, Prediger und Erzieher* (System of Higher Healing for Physicians, Preachers and Educators; 1826), a medical text aimed at both physicians and religious clergy published by the physician and theologian Ernst de Valenti nearly a decade earlier.[55] De Valenti's first case history, the source for Schneider's account of Bals, describes the treatment of a thirty-five-year-old German peasant who had lost his voice following a fatal encounter with a forest ranger who had caught him poaching. Jailed for a lengthy period for beating the ranger to death, the man emerges with an obsessive mania manifesting in the compulsion to communicate by singing in a ghastly recitative. De Valenti treats him with bloodlettings combined with frequent evangelical counsel, some of which he reproduces in his book. The man makes steady progress, and occasional relapses are treated with the herbal sedative belladonna. Four weeks later, he is cured.[56]

De Valenti's second report, the basis of Schneider's account of Lina, concerns a twenty-year-old peasant woman who has been suffering from *melancholia attonita* for over a year. The causes of this sickness are unclear, but her parents inform him that she had previously complained of bone pain and that her menses had stopped. As Schneider would claim later, de Valenti treats her with a course of emetics consisting of a gram of copper sulphate dissolved in cherry laurel water. The first dose brings about immediate improvement, and over the next few months her menses return, her mood improves and her health is restored.[57]

It appears, then, that Schneider grafted de Valenti's case histories onto an elaborately detailed course of musical treatment – the originals feature no music whatsoever. He takes some care to cover his tracks, reversing the order of the case histories, employing a synonym here and there, as well as altering the geographical location, occupation, age and social class of his

---

[55] This finding transpired by chance: while translating the second case study, I stumbled across an unfamiliar hat: Bals wears a 'dirty *Baschkirenmütze* pulled over his ears'. By sheer luck, I come across perhaps the only word that could have led me to Schneider's secret: a variant spelling of the more common *Baskenmütze* specific enough to conjure up de Valenti within the search results, while hardy enough to have withstood Google Books' capricious Fraktur optical character recognition. It should be noted that the diagnostic questions Schneider poses to Lina's parents in the first case history incorporate substantial verbatim text from *Handbuch der Pastoral-Medicin für christliche Seelsorger* (1823) by the physician and chemist Christian Schreger. These questions are presented as Schneider's own. Compare Schneider 1835, 2:251–2 to Schreger 1823, 462–3.

[56] de Valenti 1826, 1:95–103.   [57] de Valenti 1826, 1:104–7.

Operatic Fantasies in Early Nineteenth-Century Psychiatry 75

Table 3.1 A comparison of de Ernst de Valenti's and Peter Schneider's reports of the patient's speech

de Valenti, *System der höhern Heilkunde* 1: 97–98	Schneider, *System einer medizinischen Musik* 2: 288–91	Schneider, *System*, my translation
Willkommen Herr Doktor, ich freue mich Sie wohl zu sehen, ich habe immer an Sie gedacht, machen Sie mich doch wieder gesund.	En guten Tag Herr, mein guter Herr Doktor, Sie sind wohl, das freu't mich, dacht' ich doch immer an Sie, helfen Sie mir.	A good day sir, my good doctor, you are well, that pleases me, I was always thinking of you, help me.
Mein lieber Herr Doktor, ich wollte gern anders reden, ich kann aber nicht, ih muss singen.	Mein liebes Doktor'chen, gerne wollt ich anders reden, ich kann doch nicht anders, ich muss nun einmal singen.	My good doc, gladly would I speak differently, but I cannot, I must first sing.
——	Herr, Sie kenn' ich nicht, wer sie sind, wie Sie sind, so bleib ich doch, wie ich bin! Trillerum da da! u.s. w. Bin ich verdammt, nun dann bin ich verdammt. Ich hab'n aber nicht todt geschlagen!	Sir, I know not who you are, or what you are, thus I too remain what I am. Trillerum da da! etc. If I am damned, then I am damned. But I did not beat him to death!

patients. He even gives them first names, in contrast to de Valenti, who reports on two anonymous German peasants. Table 3.1 is an example of corresponding passages in de Valenti and Schneider's versions. Beyond the consistent rearrangement of the word ordering, there are hardly any differences between de Valenti's transcription of his patient's words and the remarks that Schneider assigns to Bals.

As Table 3.1 shows, de Valenti and Schneider's first two quotations correspond perfectly. But the third response, which has no correlate in the original text, is markedly different in content and tone: the patient appears not to recognise his physician, and addresses him as 'sir' rather than 'doctor'. It also includes a denial of guilt and acceptance of damnation, details reflecting Schneider's own lively imagination. Most striking, however, is the addition of the melodic vocalisation 'trillerum da da!' This embellishment suggests that Schneider misunderstood the symptoms described by de Valenti: he appears to believe the man was singing a musical phrase, rather than speaking in a singsong voice.

Knowing that Schneider invented all of the musical details of these accounts puts the information he provides in a new light. We can regard his reports as an expression of the author's fantasies about the healing power of music; a calculated attempt to install music as a bona fide medical tool capable of restoring the health of lovelorn maidens and rough-hewn sailors alike. The correlations drawn between sickness and health, opera and chorales, and the carnal tenor and ethereal harmonium, are now exposed as the author's dreams about the power of music operating on the mind and body. Finally, we can see the calculated extent to which these cases were designed to argue in favour of music-theatrical treatment.

Throughout Lina's case history, Schneider uses opera to provide implicit commentary upon the situation at hand. The character of Antonio embodies a conception of an operatic tenor as seductive, foreign and dangerous: a 'Spanish throat and fingers'[58] seducing by means of French words and music. Adhering to operatic conventions regarding the habits of Spanish lovers, Antonio accompanies his serenades on a mandolin.[59] The perilous effects of these sounds leave a fatal mark upon Antonio's person: shortly after capturing Lina's heart, he dies of a nervous fever, a fate reflecting the social transgression implicit in the forbidden attachment of a wealthy merchant's daughter and a poor apprentice. Their courtship, scandalously conducted within the family home despite the watchful eyes of the girl's parents and uncle, relies solely upon the sensuous sounds of opera arias. Antonio's sudden death from nervous fever fails to restore social order, and Lina likewise contracts a debilitating nervous malady.

In spite of the moralising undertones of this situation, Schneider's selection of Antonio's repertoire displays a surprising compassion for the lovers' plight. In the aria from *Fra Diavolo*, the impoverished but noble-minded soldier Lorenzo vows his eternal love for the innkeeper's daughter Zerline, who at this point in the opera will be forced to wed the wealthy Francesco. A similar sensitivity appears in the aria from *La Muette*, during which the fisherman Masaniello comforts his sister, the mute Fenella, who has been seduced and abandoned by the son of the Viceroy of Naples. Masaniello promises his exhausted sister that he will watch over her as she sleeps. If during the initial house concerts Lina and Antonio were akin to *Fra Diavolo*'s star-crossed lovers, by the time Schneider enters the picture

---

[58] Schneider 1835, 2:256.

[59] As a comparison, Count Almaviva serenades Rosina with a mandolin in Paisiello's *Il barbiere di Siviglia* (1782), and Don Giovanni serenades Elvira's maid with the same instrument in Mozart's *Don Giovanni* (1787). In Grétry's *L'Amant jaloux* (1778), which is set in Spain, French officer Florival serenades 'Léonore' / Isabelle with a mandolin.

they have transformed into *La Muette de Portici*'s brother and sister. Antonio watches over Lina from the afterlife, while she has adopted the traits ascribed to Fenella: she is mute and half asleep.[60] It therefore evidences medical knowledge by way of a musical narrative.

Schneider's account of the staging of his musical cures likewise evokes an operatic performance. He schedules the musical cure in the evening, giving it the flavour of a theatrical performance. Lina sits on a sofa in a dimly lit room. A minor character – Schneider's friend, the silent Dr Zober – is hidden in a dark corner of the chamber as an observer. There are other roles in this musical drama: Schneider casts Lina's uncle as Antonio, rather than her father, who sings a supporting line within the chorale, probably to avoid the implication of any kind of incestuous substitution. Like offstage musicians, the soloist, chorus and instrumentalist are concealed in an adjacent room. This description provides us with the exact layout of the event, ranging from the lighting to the distribution of characters and musicians.

The musical parameters of this cure, particularly the selection of instrument and key, have explicit affective associations developed earlier in *System einer medizinischen Musik*. Schneider's account of modulating from E♭ minor to G♭ major is charged with symbolic meaning drawn from Christian Schubart's storied key characteristics. In *Ideen zu einer Ästhetik der Tonkunst* (Reflections on an Aesthetics of Music; 1806), Schubart claims that E♭ minor represents 'feelings of anxiety and deep turmoil of the soul; of suppressed despair, of blackest melancholy, of the gloomiest state of mind. Every fear, every quake of the shuddering heart is aired.' By contrast, G♭ major represents 'triumph over difficulty, breathing freely having climbed a hill. Echo of a soul that has struggled valiantly and conquered.'[61] It would seem Schneider's employment of these keys as reference points models the affective transition that he intends to induce in Lina.

The selection of the aeolodicon is likewise laden with association.[62] Invented around 1810 by Gabriel-Joseph Grenié in France and independently in Germany a few years later, this was a new instrument, distantly

---

[60] Schneider depicts Lina as 'partly stupefied and partly sensible, mostly mute, she sat the whole day on the sofa, half of the time dazed [*stauend*] and the other half musing, staring straight ahead'. Schneider 1835, 2:251. For more on the early nineteenth-century medical context of Fenella's mutism see Smart 2004, 32–68.

[61] Schubart translated in Macdonald 2008, 163.

[62] As I have shown elsewhere, Schneider's selection of the aeolodicon also aligns with the contemporary practice of using this instrument to treat predominantly young female patients displaying the (frequently hysterical) symptoms of catalepsy. See Raz 2014. When

based on the harmonium.[63] Because Schneider assumed his readers might be unfamiliar with its sounds, he reprints a description of the instrument from Gustav Schilling's *Universal-Lexicon der Tonkunst* (1834) in full, which includes the following:

The aeolodicon is an instrument whose tone is produced when air or wind is conveyed over freestanding metal pipes ... [It] affords the creation of very regular and well-balanced crescendo and decrescendo effects, according to the rate at which the air in the bellows flows over the tongues. It has six full octaves, and its tone is certainly pleasant in certain respects (in the high octaves it resembles the flute and clarinet, in the middle the horn, and in the low range the contrabassoon) ... the tone itself, a kind of ghostly breath, truly has something ethereal in its nature, and easily moves certain susceptible minds with its gentle sounds.[64]

Schilling compares the aeolodicon's timbre to various woodwind instruments, and comments on the instrument's crescendo and decrescendo effects. He further emphasises that its novel sounds have a special influence on certain sensitive psyches. The idea that particular sonic characteristics – novel timbres combined with dynamic swelling – had a privileged access to the nerves can be traced back to the prototypes of early romantic ethereal sounds: the glass harmonica and the Aeolian harp.[65] The harmonica had long been associated with a dangerous effect on the nerves, a link made notorious by Franz Mesmer's employment of the instrument in his magnetisations.[66]

By contrast, the gently swelling tones of the Aeolian harp, a set of strings stretched over a resonating board and brought into sound by the action of the wind alone, were frequently regarded as the benign resonance of nature or the *Weltgeist*.[67] Through a complex series of relays between physicians, scientists, philosophers and poets, the Aeolian harp became a popular symbol of subjectivity in early romantic aesthetics.[68] The aeolodicon was widely understood to inherit some of the Aeolian harp's ethereal sonic

---

writing this article I was not yet aware of Schneider's plagiarism, and discuss his case study alongside other medical reports.

[63] For more on the emergence of free reeds and harmonium instruments in Germany see Jackson 2006. See also Orde-Hume 1986; Ahrens and Klinke 1996; Gellerman 1996.

[64] Schilling 1834, 1:75, as quoted in Schneider 1835, 2:266.   [65] Dolan 2008, 13.

[66] This connection may have originated in the effects of the lead used in the manufacture of the harmonica's forerunners, musical glasses. See Hadlock 2000, 525; Finger and Gallo 2004, 226.

[67] See Abrams 1971, 51.

[68] As literary scholar Shelley Trower observes, the Aeolian harp provided at once 'a model for a human mind/body conceived as a machine for translating sensory vibrations into consciousness' as well as a metaphor for the artistic process of inspiration by 'transforming the force of the wind into harmonious sounds'. Trower 2012, 13.

qualities, in particular its ability to gradually swell into sound.[69] This sonic similarity was discussed by a number of nineteenth-century musicians, and enthusiastically promoted by harmonium builders, who gave their creations names such as aeolharmonica, aeolophon and aeolomusicon.[70]

Adhering to early romantic tropes of sonic ethereality, Schneider's description of Lina's response to the aeolodicon foregrounds her embodied attunement to its swelling effects. He begins his improvisation by gradually 'swelling to the strongest fortissimo, and then decreasing to a moderate piano', and starts the chorale, 'swelling from the lightest breaths and back again'. Lina entrains herself accordingly: 'at the beginning of the third crescendo and then immediately after [there] began a deep intake of breath and a strong shiver; that is, a complete seizure of the full nervous system'.[71] While opera clearly defines Lina's illness, it also appears to inform her cure. Having lost her heart and mind to the suggestive sounds of love arias, she regains her health to the ethereal tones of religious music performed in an expressly theatrical context.

In the second case history, Schneider likewise employs a number of theatrical parameters to amplify the effect of music upon his patient's mind and body. These include repertoire, instrumentation, staging and dance. Notable here is the choice of the German song, which has four verses, in which a sailor bids his sweetheart farewell as he sets off on his ship, bemoans their parting, and outlines the pleasures and dangers of seafaring life.[72] As in Lina's case, the selection of repertoire stands in a close relationship to Bals's circumstances, though in this case it is motivational rather than biographical. 'Matrosen' is a work song, and the sailor must leave his wife and go to sea in order to recover his mental health. It is aspirational in other aspects as well. Bals is consumed by 'an exaggerated fear of the future'.[73] By cheerfully celebrating the risk inherent in a seafaring career, this song encourages the patient to return to work by placing his morbid fears into perspective.

Schneider informs us that the quality of the performance was excellent, as 'the street musicians of this harbour town take care to perform this sailor's ditty exceptionally well'.[74] Like the refined domestic music that characterised Lina's treatment, these performers come from Bals's own social milieu. Schneider emphasises this by calling them *Musikanten* rather than *Musiker*, and specifying that they are street musicians, or

---

[69] See Raz 2014, 115–44.   [70] Notable here is Gleichmann 1820; see also Dodd 1853.
[71] Schneider 1835, 2:267.   [72] W. Gerhard 1826, 1:143.   [73] Schneider 1835, 2:288.
[74] Schneider 1835, 2:291.

Schnurranten. Finally, he compounds the theatrical elements of the cure by specifying that the music causes the man to violently jerk his body and limbs, almost as if he were performing a St Vitus dance or tarantella. This bodily response to music is swiftly converted into a furious waltz followed by a physical collapse.

Both of Schneider's cures are highly theatrical. In the case of Lina, the musicians themselves are hidden, but the drama is implied through the allocation of vocal parts supported by a specific repertoire and instrumentation. This play-within-a-play induces a dramatic response from the patient, who herself is being observed by a proxy of her physician. Likewise, Bals is at first a spectator, observing his colleagues singing and the musicians playing. Observing this theatrical representation of his former life as a sailor ignites his desire to return to worldly pleasures, and he soon joins in as a participant, leaving his sickbed to dance with his wife and friends.

It is illuminating to compare Schneider's approach to opera with those of his (unattributed) sources. In his *System der höhern Heilkunde* (1826), the very volume from which Schneider lifts his case studies, de Valenti proposes that young men aspiring to good physical health avoid 'painted women and maggoty hothouse fruits, Ovid's *artem amandi* and Homer's accounts of Jupiter's flirtations, as well as bravura arias from well-known operas'.[75] De Valenti's *Medicina clerica* (1831), a practical companion volume to *System der höhern Heilkunde*, offers a similar critique. Writing for a clerical audience, de Valenti describes how a complete village descends into sin after opening an amateur theatre. The pastor is complicit, and his daughter even lends the 'prima donna' her outfit for a comedy.[76] This secular fall culminates in the introduction of operas, a 'monstrosity that the government promptly shut down'.[77]

Schneider appears to have a complex relationship to de Valenti. He writes at length about the importance of religion in conjunction with medicine, and repeatedly declares his intention to produce his own book on the pastoral care of the mentally ill. He also seems to regard *System der höhern Heilkunde* as a model, writing that of the approximately fifteen extant works dealing with pastoral medicine, only de Valenti's had any value.[78] He may even have based his title page affiliation, 'der Philosophie und Musik Doktor' (the doctor of philosophy and music), on de Valenti's

---

[75] de Valenti 1826, 1:150.　[76] de Valenti 1831, 256.　[77] de Valenti 1831, 257.
[78] Schneider 1835, 2:372.

signature of 'der Philosophie und Medizin Doctor' (the doctor of philosophy and medicine).

Given Schneider's respect for de Valenti and the cause of pastoral care, we might regard his decision to plagiarise these case histories as an act of appreciative criticism. Lacking any formal training in medicine himself, he was surely reluctant to simply fabricate medical details. The act of inserting himself into de Valenti's cases represents something of a fantasy of authority. Moreover, in rewriting his text and imagining how music might have played a positive role in the healing process, Schneider undercuts his role model's dismissal of music, and of opera in particular. Yet this revision is only partial: Lina loses her heart to the very same 'bravura arias' that de Valenti deplored, and regains her health through the wholesome sounds of a religious chorale performed within the family domicile.

Conclusion: Between Therapy and Pathology

Schneider's fictional case histories suggest that the author himself held conflicting views about opera. His musical cures adhere to Reil's and Pinel's theories regarding the importance of role-playing, and appear to support theatrical interventions in the treatment of mental illness. Moreover, his depictions revel in operatic clichés such as star-crossed lovers, melancholy, murder, guilt and ethereal sounds as well as the curative potential of staging and role-play. On the other hand, his explicit alignment of opera arias and recitative with sickness, and religious music and work songs with health suggest that he believed – or thought that his readers believed – that opera had a deleterious effect on health. Schneider's theatrical interventions are therefore especially designed to enact the transformation of opera into other genres: in Lina's case, Antonio's arias are supplanted by a four-part chorale, while Bals's ghastly recitative is replaced with a familiar sea shanty. The author's conflicted attitude is further evident in his decision to plagiarise and subvert de Valenti, a religious physician who was pointedly opposed to opera in all forms.

This ambiguous conception of opera is mirrored in *System einer medizinischen Musik*. Schneider time and again states that music is a healing medium; but while he treats church, chamber and concert music at length, opera is almost entirely excluded from discussion. Schneider devotes only six pages to 'theatrical music', in which he repeatedly states that opera is harmless. He maintains that while operas do not serve a morally edifying purpose, they cannot corrupt children or the 'pure of heart'. Moreover, he argues that they are no worse than plays for adults and adolescents.[79] In support of this claim, he cites Markus Herz's 1797 case history of a female amnesiac who had forgotten attending a performance of *Die Zauberflöte*.[80] Once recovered, Herz notes, she held the unusual distinction of having enjoyed the opera for the first time on two separate occasions.

It is no coincidence that Schneider's anecdote regarding opera was nearly four decades old by 1835, as it was actually plagiarised from the Viennese physician Peter Lichtenthal's influential book on music therapy, *Der musikalische Arzt* (The Musical Doctor; 1807).[81] Schneider's treatment of opera borrows heavily from Lichtenthal's corresponding chapter, lifting many passages verbatim and paraphrasing others without attribution. However, as in his other plagiarisms, there is a crucial difference: Lichtenthal has no concerns about potential dangers inherent in opera, and enthuses about *Die Zauberflöte*, which he claims to have seen ninety-three times. He further praises the genre of opera for affording a truly magical variety of characters, emotions, scenes and impressions.[82] Having excised Lichtenthal's operatic effusions, Schneider's attempt at defending opera from its detractors appears to be fully his own.

It seems the plagiarism in *System einer medizinischen Musik* was never discovered, and the book garnered positive attention from the musical community. The *Allgemeine musikalische Zeitung* (1835) commended the author for his diligence in compiling abundant source material,[83] and the *Allgemeiner musikalischer Anzeiger* (1836) praised it as a 'significant summation of original and varied insights, historical discoveries and testimonies, and factual compilation'.[84] In his annotated bibliography *Systematisch-chronologische Darstellung der musikalischen Literatur* (1839), Carl Ferdinand Becker commented on Schneider's erudition and evident love for his subject matter.[85] An entry in the *Musikalisches Conversationslexikon* of 1840 celebrated the author's multifaceted scholarship and set high expectations for his future.[86] This was a poignant note, given that Schneider had died three years earlier at the age of twenty-seven, poisoned by his assistant, who committed suicide shortly after.[87]

The ethics of inventing medical case histories notwithstanding, Schneider's reports make significant innovations in theorising the affective treatment of the causes behind mental illness. First of all, unlike the exoneration of Pinel's patient in a mock trial, Lina and Bals are not

---

[79] Schneider 1835, 1:236–7.   [80] See Herz 1798.   [81] Lichtenthal 1807, 69.
[82] Lichtenthal 1807, 66–7   [83] [unsigned] 1835, 779.   [84] [unsigned] 1836, 65.
[85] Becker 1839, 8.   [86] [unsigned] 1840, 407.   [87] Henseler 1959, 119.

Operatic Fantasies in Early Nineteenth-Century Psychiatry 83

dosed with a fraudulent reality manufactured to suit their pathology; music is used to suggest rather than replace. De Valenti's cures result through chemical means: the melancholy girl is simply treated with a powerful emetic. By contrast, Schneider replaces de Valenti's methods with staged performances of music, which targets his patients' minds and bodies through sonorous vibrations.

In featuring music rather than words, Schneider's case histories exemplify how sound can permit direct access to the unconscious by reconfiguring the musical and musically inspired symptoms of mental illness into symbolic communication to be treated on its own terms – that is, by music. This idea of 'symptom as symbol' prefigures ideas about hysteria that would be developed by psychoanalysts over fifty years later. This step is original to Schneider, and is nowhere to be found in de Valenti, Schreger or his other sources. The tension manifested between Schneider's own operatic imagination and medical ideas about the genre's potential dangers reveals a transitional moment in which opera was simultaneously correlated with sickness and health in the early romantic imagination.

4 | Opera and Hypnosis
Victor Maurel's Experiments with Verdi's Otello

CÉLINE FRIGAU MANNING

One day in his private home on the avenue Bugeaud, in Paris's sixteenth arrondissement, the famous baritone Victor Maurel hosted a meeting which combined music with hypnotism of a young woman. This is how Maurel recounts the experience:

A very beautiful young girl was involved in M. le colonel Derochas's experiments as his subject. – M. Jules Bois, whose intellectual curiosity is always aroused, was at that time interested in everything related to hypnotism, and agreed one day to bring me Lina. – He put her to sleep and one of his friends sat at the piano, for Lina was especially sensitive to musical suggestions. A minuet was played first. Lina's robust frame did not fit well with the somewhat mawkish graces of this kind. – But, after several instants of hesitation and fumbling, as the musical intentions were repeated, the rhythm of the dance finally took hold of her and inspired within her its laws. We then saw her sketch out delicate little steps, bending over in exquisite bows; a fan that was held out to her was handled with delightful affectation. – Then, with no transition, the *Marseillaise* suddenly resounded on the piano; Lina leapt, waving her fan, which was transmuted into a sort of imaginary banner. – Her chest was pounding, her wild and exalted eyes had become disproportionately enlarged, all her beautiful tensed body, raised up by a fanatical enthusiasm, seemed the living emblem of the great days of old. Finally, forcing myself to make no gesture, I sung to her Cassio's *Dream* from Verdi's *Otello*, putting into it the best of my art, and I had the surprise, which deeply moved me, to see her use, among other excellent gestures, some of those I had used myself in this famous piece.[1]

---

[1] 'Il s'agissait d'une fort belle jeune fille qui servait alors de sujet aux expériences de M. le colonel Derochas. – M. Jules Bois, dont la curiosité intellectuelle toujours en éveil s'intéressait à ce moment aux choses de l'hypnotisme, voulut bien, un jour, m'amener Lina. – Il l'endormit et quelqu'un de nos amis présents se mit au piano, car Lina était spécialement sensible aux suggestions musicales. On joua d'abord un menuet. La plastique robuste de Lina s'accordait mal avec les grâces un peu mièvres de ce genre. – Mais, après quelques instants d'hésitation, de tâtonnements, au fur et à mesure que se répétaient les desseins musicaux, le rythme de la danse s'empara d'elle enfin et lui inspira ses lois. Nous la vîmes alors esquisser des pas menus et délicats, se courber en des révérences exquises; un éventail qu'on lui tendit fut manié avec une délicieuse afféterie. – Puis, sans transition, la *Marseillaise* retentit tout à coup au piano; Lina bondit, brandissant son éventail, transmué en je ne sais quel drapeau imaginaire. – Son torse haletait, ses yeux exaltés et farouches s'étaient démesurément agrandis, tout son beau corps tendu, soulevé par un fanatique enthousiasme, semblait l'emblème vivant des grands jours d'autrefois. Enfin, m'astreignant à ne faire aucun geste, je lui chantai, en y mettant le meilleur de

In this account, which was part of one of Maurel's lectures published in 1904, the figure of the singer does not appear, as in other medical enquiries of the time, as a patient or object of study. Maurel sings, but he is not the centre of attention, which is focused instead on the hypnotised woman. Nor is he a mere spectator, as he actively participates in the experiment that he himself stages and later recounts. Such hypnotic experiments featuring music and musicians were frequent occurrences at the time; they were staple events in the social life of salons, as well as in occultist and scientific circles, and accompanied the emergence of a modern discipline: psychology.[2] Less frequent are descriptions originating from singers themselves. What matters here, however, is not merely Maurel's experience of hypnosis, nor his recollection of the anecdote, but rather the wide range of questions and hypotheses, both scientific and artistic, to which the episode gives rise.

In my analysis of Maurel's text, I will argue that musical hypnosis was not just a fashionable pretext for bourgeois scientific performances and sensational public exhibitions. Nor was it merely an alternative therapy for unexplainable or otherwise untreatable diseases. Scholars such as the anthropologist Clara Gallini and the historian Jacqueline Carroy have shown that hypnosis throughout the long nineteenth century was a powerful culture in itself, which was widely engaged with across the working, middle and upper classes.[3] It did not concern only medical contexts, but had its own actors, functions, practices and sites.

Through Maurel's lecture, I would like to explore the prominent role played by music in hypnosis at the time and to investigate how Maurel went further than usual, thereby placing opera squarely in the spotlight. Among a number of important questions raised by this episode of musical hypnosis – ranging from the authenticity or stimulation of Lina's state to the questions of ecstasy and the relationship between the male observer and the female hypnotised subject – I would like to investigate some crucial aspects of Maurel's approach. To do so, I will first reconstitute the pedagogical and research context in which Maurel recounts this hypnotic event. I will then show how Maurel's experiment was simultaneously

---

mon art, le *Rêve* de Cassio, tiré de l'*Otello*, de Verdi, et j'eus la surprise, qui ne fut pas sans m'émouvoir vivement, de lui voir employer, parmi d'autres excellents, quelques-uns des gestes que j'employais moi-même dans ce morceau fameux.' V. Maurel 1904, 4–5.

[2] Psychology at this time was seeking to become part of the medical sciences and the clinic, thus extricating itself as a discipline from its discursive and institutional ties to philosophy.

[3] 'Au siècle dernier, l'hypnose a été également une culture.' Carroy 1991, 19. See also Didi-Huberman 1982; Gallini, 1983; Gauld 1992; and the works of the philosopher Isabelle Stengers, especially Stengers 2002.

representative and unique, especially in the choice of 'Era la notte' from Giuseppe Verdi's *Otello*. I propose elements of a reading of the opera through the lens of hypnosis before finally attempting to shed light on Maurel's psychological theory and method of acting, founded on the imagination and inspired by hypnosis.

Opera and Hypnosis at the École des Hautes Études Sociales

Victor Maurel not only experimented with hypnosis, he also made use of it in his reflections on his art, which he then explored in his pedagogy. He also found a prestigious and appropriate context for his teaching: the École des Hautes Études Sociales, where he presented his findings on acting and hypnosis in 1904, at 16 rue de la Sorbonne 'in the learned quarter of the Sorbonne and the Collège de France'.[4]

How could a singer find himself in such a position? The École, founded in 1900, followed in the wake of the École Pratique des Hautes Études (EPHE), created in 1868 in the context of higher educational reforms. Academics and practitioners were brought together at the EPHE in order to develop new ways of teaching and conducting research. The goal was to create active citizens, in the spirit of the comparative pedagogy of the *Universités populaires*.[5] When the École des Hautes Études Sociales (EHES) opened an Art School in 1903, Maurel was invited to join the faculty, and was appointed 'Chair of Vocal and Scenic Aesthetics'. This chair aimed at 'facilitating the open presentation of questions relating to the technique of singing and acting and the overall aesthetics of the art of the modern lyric interpreter'.[6] Maurel's courses were featured not in the musical curriculum, but in that devoted to theatre. Academics, critics and even politicians taught in the curriculum's first two sections, namely 'History of Theatre' and 'Theatre Abroad', while the third section, 'New Ideas and Forms', was entrusted to six pedagogues, including two artists: André Antoine, Director of the *Théâtre libre*, and Firmin Gémier, a figure emblematic of the *théâtre populaire*. As for Maurel, he was in sole charge of

---

[4] 'dans le docte quartier de la Sorbonne et du Collège de France'. Bois 1903.

[5] The objective of the École Pratique des Hautes Études (EPHE), later undertaken by the École des Hautes Études Sociales, was to create a 'young Sorbonne'; see Prochasson 1985.

[6] 'destinée à faciliter l'exposition libre des questions relatives à la technique du chant et de la scène et à l'esthétique générale de l'art de l'interprète lyrique moderne'. In *Le Ménestrel* (17 May 1903) and *Gil Blas* (18 May 1903).

the fourth section, presented in detail by *Le Guide musical* as a 'course on musical, vocal and scenic aesthetics: vocal training: doctrines and their advocates; attempts made to introduce scientific notions into the study of the art of singing; what a science of singing should be: its method and means'.[7] Maurel conducted his teaching in front of a large audience of students, society ladies and various figures of the musical, artistic and academic worlds.[8] The question of hypnosis was already omnipresent in both scientific and artistic debates (some journalists suspected Sarah Bernhardt, for instance, of acting under a state of self-hypnosis);[9] but thanks to Maurel, hypnosis was placed centre stage from the very beginning of his series of lectures, which took place every Friday afternoon during the early months of 1904. The inaugural lecture, published the same year in a small volume, only underlined the multiple interests of one of the nineteenth century's most famous singers.

Creator of the roles of Iago and Falstaff, Maurel was convinced that the singer must be an actor, and a true collaborator with the composer.[10] A 'polymorphic artist', in the words of Jules Bois, Maurel worked with painting, theatre and cinema, and wrote in depth about specific roles and his art in general.[11] He was always seeking to discover more and to perfect his art: studying philosophy, with *Thus Spoke Zarathustra* as his bedside reading, learning about sciences, laryngoscopy or psychology, visiting hospitals or close friends such as the mathematician Manœuvrier, as well as practising gymnastics and boxing.[12] What is less well known, however, is Maurel's commitment to the potentially fruitful relationship between opera and the sciences, one which he defends in *Le Chant rénové par la*

---

[7] 'Cours d'esthétique musicale, vocale et scénique: L'enseignement vocal: les doctrines, les hommes; tentatives faites pour introduire des notions scientifiques dans l'étude de l'art du chant; ce que doit être une science du chant: la méthode et les moyens.' *Le Guide musical* 49 (1903), 561; the same article reproduces details of the entire course, along with the names of the teachers.

[8] See, for instance, the description in *Gil Blas* (30 January 1904). The presence of a variety of society figures is indicated, including 'Mmes Ambroise Thomas, Camille Erlanger, Bergounhioux de Wailly, comtesse de Ghinsel, Mlles Jane Morel et Villain, M. et Mme Lombard, le prince Bibesco, MM. Gustave Bret, René Doire, André Pirro, le docteur et Mme Letulle, M. et Mme Brunswick et d'autres'.

[9] See, for instance, [unsigned] 1892.

[10] V. Maurel 1897, v. On Maurel as an acting singer, see Henson 2015, 19–47.

[11] Bois 1903; see V. Maurel 1897, 1–148; and B. Maurel [1923?].

[12] On reading Nietzsche, see Bois 1903. Published in German between 1883 and 1885, Nietzsche's text was fully translated into French for the first time by Henri Albert (Paris: Le Mercure de France, 1898). On Maurel's exposure to scientific and mathematical discourses, see *Gil Blas* (3 January 1904), which published a portrait of the mathematician Manœuvrier in which Victor Maurel is presented as one of his best friends.

science (Singing Renewed by Science). This brief pamphlet, published in 1892, argues that 'concerning vocal technique, there are two paths, and two paths only, which a pedagogy truly worthy of the name may take: empiricism and science'.[13] Art and science are not incompatible, Maurel contends, but rather complementary. Science begins with positive facts in order to elaborate a general law: an idea which is a truth. In contrast, 'the starting point of art is an Idea ... which has to be ... part of the truth, or, more simply, a truth'.[14] Art thus gives rise to positive facts and effects, while science begins with positive facts in order to observe causes, to compare them and relate them to others. Moreover, 'all the arts in which the artistic effect is achieved only through an expenditure of the organism itself are closely related to physiological science'.[15]

In his course at the EHES, Maurel developed his scientific vision of the actor-singer's art more fully. While physiology was considered in *Le Chant rénové par la science* as the basis for all vocal training, as well as for dancing or gymnastics, the singer now integrated new elements, inspired by contemporary research, especially psychology. At the time, some of psychology's first partisans were scholars fascinated by music: for instance, Lionel Dauriac, Professor of Musical Aesthetics at the Sorbonne, also conducted hypnotic experiments with Lina de Ferkel. It is within such a context that Maurel's inaugural lecture, in its published form, focused entirely on hypnosis.

Musical Hypnosis

The extensive history of music's relationship to hypnosis remains unwritten.[16] Such an account could begin with Mesmer's use of the glass harmonica in his therapeutics and follow subsequent developments throughout the nineteenth century. Music was valued as an accompaniment to trance states, as a way to produce new suggestions or as a form of hypnosis itself. It was part of the sadistic experiments that Lafontaine

---

[13] 'Pour la technique du chant, il est deux voies, et il n'est que deux voies que puisse prendre un enseignement vraiment digne de ce nom: l'empirisme et la science.' V. Maurel 1892, 12.

[14] 'L'art a pour point de départ une Idée, ... qui forcément doit être ... une des facettes de la vérité, ou, plus simplement, une vérité.' Maurel 1892, 25.

[15] 'tous les arts où l'effet artistique se réalise uniquement dans une dépense de notre organisme lui-même sont en un rapport étroit avec la science physiologique'. Maurel 1892, 28.

[16] For some elements of this nascent history, see Kennaway 2012b. I am currently working on a monograph exploring aspects of this history during the nineteenth century.

Opera and Hypnosis 89

conducted both in public and private spaces, and was frequently the main attraction of large-scale hypnotic performances, such as the ones staged by Donato.[17] In *fin-de-siècle* Paris, music was still qualified by Doctor Foveau de Courmelles as 'one of the best ways to reach a state of ecstasy'.[18]

What had changed by the last decades of the nineteenth century, though, was that music was no longer used in a vague or generic way. Until that time, doctors and practitioners of hypnosis had only mentioned 'joyful', 'sad' or 'martial' pieces, polkas, minuets or religious hymns, whose titles and composers were almost never specified.[19] These musical pieces were generally played only on the piano, in order to provoke effects which were analysed in terms of automatism: hypnotised bodies were described as automata, 'forced' to move or to dance according to certain kinds of music. What Maurel described, however, corresponded to a new, more sophisticated approach to music, typical of the *fin de siècle*.

Maurel's experiment took place thanks to Jules Bois, a fascinating omnifarious figure who wrote many historical, spiritual and journalistic essays, as well as literary texts ranging from novels and poetry to theatre. Bois also wrote a tragedy, *Hippolyte couronné*, in which Maurel played the role of Thésée in Orange on 30 July 1904, and at the Odéon on 22 March the following year.[20] Like many other occultists, Bois had attended hypnotic sessions organised by Albert de Rochas, the administrator of the École polytechnique and prolific author of books devoted to hypnosis or past lives – including *Les Sentiments, la musique et le*

---

[17] Born in France, Charles Lafontaine, who failed as an actor, became wealthy as a travelling magnetiser. He created a kind of stage demonstration that he toured across Europe between 1840 and 1852, using trained subjects as well as volunteers from the audience. He created a public sensation by inserting needles into his subjects, thus playing on sadism, transgression and fear (see Lafontaine 1852, 1866). Donato was the pseudonym of Alfred Édouard D'Hont, a former Belgian navy official, who in the 1870s and 1880s conducted successful tours all across Europe. Donato had recourse to complex techniques, ranging from several kinds of sleep induction to authoritarian suggestion, which eventually gave rise to Donatism. He used his gaze rather than his hands, applying his methods publicly, and quite violently, not only on selected and trained individuals, but on groups of mostly young spectators from the audience. Doctors such as Jean-Martin Charcot, Cesare Lombroso and Charles Richet attended Donato's highly controversial performances (see Gallini 1983, 211–56). In both Lafontaine's and Donato's performances, music was involved.

[18] 'La musique est l'un des meilleurs moyens d'extase.' Courmelles 1890, 104.

[19] See, for instance, Pitres 1884, 23.

[20] Jules Bois (1868–1943), one of Joris-Karl Huysmans's only close friends, would later become a traditionalist Catholic. He was also the partner for many years of the soprano Emma Calvé, who was one of Maurel's pupils. See Dubois 2006.

90 CÉLINE FRIGAU MANNING

Figure 4.1 Cover illustration for Albert de Rochas, *Les Sentiments, la musique et le geste* (Grenoble: Librairie Dauphine, 1900) (collection Frigau Manning).

geste, published in 1900.[21] This book is magnificently illustrated, and features on the cover a portrait by Alfons Mucha of Lina de Ferkel allegorising *La Marseillaise* (see Figure 4.1), with many other photos of her inside, including some by Nadar.

---

[21] de Rochas 1900.

Lina was a professional model who worked for painters such as Mucha and Georges Rochegrosse. In fact, it was thanks to Mucha that she began to work with de Rochas.[22] She was subsequently one of the two most famous hypnotic prima donnas of the time, along with the subject hypnotised by Émile Magnin, Magdeleine G.[23] Magdeleine G., a pseudonym for Madeleine Guipet, came from a family of professional dancers. According to Magnin, she never received any specific training in dance, but attended the Conservatoire de musique, where she took piano and singing classes with good results. Magnin claimed that timidity and laziness prevented her from embarking on a professional artistic career. She married, had two children, and first consulted Magnin in the hopes that he could heal her chronic headaches. Both women abundantly fuelled contemporary debates on the status of their performances. Were such displays imitations of art, or even fake art, intentionally created by simulators bored by the routine domestic life that was the lot of women at the time? Or were they, for contemporary spectators, in fact true artistic visions, inspired under influence by 'unconscious artists'?[24] This very question played a crucial part in their growing publicity and success. As far as Lina is concerned, for instance, Bois helped to create her celebrity by organising public events at La Bodinière in Monte Carlo in 1898. It is important to realise, meanwhile, that these exhibitions cannot merely be understood as society events that instrumentalised the female body for the pleasure of male audiences. Bois was a determined feminist, and his hypnosis sessions were included in an extensive programme which boasted occultist presentations from 'the thought-reader' Mr Ninoff, presentations promoting feminism – with subjects ranging from George Sand to 'the failure of marriage' – and *tableaux vivants* entitled 'The Greatest Feminine Figures of History'.[25]

In spite of such contexts, Bois's engagement in contemporary feminist discourses does not, of course, preclude the potential objectification of the

---

[22] See Arnauld 2009.
[23] Magnin [1906]. Magnin's book was illustrated with Fred Boissonnas's photographs: see Eidenbenz 2011. The expression 'prima donna' was used at the time, typically in an ironic way, to qualify the women who were magnetised in public performances or shows throughout the nineteenth century (see, for example, Alexandre Erdan's (1860, 1:39) description of a session featuring the magnetiser Dupotet). Some of these women, however, achieved prominent reputations, such as Prudence Bernard, married to the magnetiser Auguste Lassaigne, or, among Charcot's subjects at the Salpêtrière, Geneviève de Loudun, Augustine G. and Blanche (Marie) Wittman. In *fin-de-siècle* Paris, Lina de Ferkel and Magdeleine G. were, as far as I know, the only women whose status as artists was least considered and discussed.
[24] See Gallini 1983, 115–37; and Carroy 1991, 65–96.   [25] See [unsigned] 1898.

hypnotised female subject. In a situation combining spectacle, revelation, authority and control, the sexualisation of the observed female body is never far away, even (or especially) among artists and spectators who aspire to a state of primarily aesthetic apprehension. Crucially, hypnosis thus lends its weight to an apparent sexualisation of the female artistic body, yet not in the way we might expect. Though the hypnotised female subject is nominally under male control, the autonomy and self-determination of her gestures invests her with an agency that implicitly opposes unwanted male power. The erotic context is complicated further by the possibility that it was precisely this increased agency that male spectators found sexually appealing: the fantasy not of the helpless female somnambulist, but of the animated heroine, instilled with knowledge of what she desires and determined to attain it.

Though it would be reductive to see this spectacular, gestural revelation as a simple instrumentalisation – with the hypnotic experience as an 'excuse' for sexual excitation – the two aspects are far from mutually exclusive, and indeed participate in a complex interplay of spectacle, desire and belief. Is such a performance part of a sexual, and not merely social, emancipation? Against this optimistic vision, however, we are confronted in Maurel's text with the clear progression of Lina's corporeality when in a hypnotic state, from her 'robust frame', evoking the actual presence of the flesh, to the increasingly more subtle manners of a codified bourgeois woman. Beginning with childish or crude 'hesitation and fumbling', she progresses under hypnosis to 'delicate little steps' and 'exquisite bows', as though the hypnotic experience were paramount to her discovery, or at least heightening, of her own bourgeois feminine identity – and there is of course a specific kind of excitement provided by the transformation of a common woman into the projected image of an upper-class lady. Given Lina's provisional access to a superior social and sexual status, the passage's eventual climax appropriately participates in a peculiarly orgasmic rhetoric, as though Lina were reproducing an ecstatic state of sexual intensity filtered through a distinctly male gaze: 'Her chest was pounding, her wild and exalted eyes had become disproportionately enlarged, all her beautiful tensed body, raised up by a fanatical enthusiasm.'

Lina's association with classical models, primarily via her dress, is similarly sexually ambiguous. Does it increase her sexualisation for the reason that it connects her with an Attic and divine sensuality, or rather decrease it because of the soberness of the classical ideal? When Bois brought Lina de Ferkel to Maurel, the event remained private, despite being recorded by a journalist and by de Rochas.

Such a context reinforced the intimacy on which Lina and Magdeleine played; garbed in free-flowing clothes recalling antique togas or Isadora Duncan's tunics, they appeared to express, in poses of self-abandonment, the secrets of their unconscious.[26] Both performed their musical suggestions with a minimalist *mise en scène*: generally only a piano, occasionally accompanied by other instruments or voices, a rug to create the 'stage',[27] and sometimes some accessories, like the fan evoked by Maurel (see Figure 4.2). The musicians, all relevant figures of their time, were announced by name either in the media or in the programmes that Magnin includes in an appendix, and comprised such singers as Emma Calvé and Jane Hatto, and composers like Léopold Ketten and Joseph Bizet. The precise nature of the music played mattered greatly: both de Rochas and Magnin give extensive details about the pieces chosen from the works of Richard Wagner, Frédéric Chopin or Charles Gounod. They do not simply aim at drawing general correspondences between the music and the sequence of gestures. What matters is to carefully close-read musical sections and gestural syntax. Generic oppositions such as sad, joyful, martial, etc., are refined into subcategories, with precise examples of pieces, gestures and images for each. Automatism is still at work here: for de Rochas, melody is expressed by the upper part of the body, rhythm by the lower part, and there is a link between certain notes – low or high, sharp or flat – and certain gestures. But automatism is made more complex by parameters such as heredity, culture, education and national origins. What now takes place in the theorisations of musical hypnosis is a holistic reflection on specific individuals (gifted with individual names), whose specific histories, personalities and psychological features are investigated.

But what can we say in all this concerning opera? What does it stand for in these programmes and reflections? First, opera seems perfectly adapted to the hypnotic musical session, which relies on the union of gesture and music. Of course, these are not united within the same body (the actor-singer's), for in the hypnotic theatre, gesture is enacted by the

---

[26] Coined in German (as *Unbewusste*) by Friedrich Schelling in his *System of Transcendental Idealism* (1800) and later introduced into English by Samuel Taylor Coleridge in his *Biographia Literaria* (1817), the term 'unconscious' was frequently used as an adjective as well as an adverb ('unconsciously') before imposing itself as a noun. Both forms commonly appear in writings related to magnetism and hypnosis throughout the nineteenth century. On the history of the concept, covering the early history of psychology and psychoanalysis and including Franz Anton Mesmer, Sigmund Freud, Carl Jung, Alfred Adler and Pierre Janet, see Ellenberger 1970.

[27] See, for instance, Carbonnelle 1903.

Figure 4.2 *Un Vieux menuet dansé par Lina*, in Rochas, *Les Sentiments*, 169 (collection Frigau Manning).

body of the hypnotic subject, while music comes from the singer's body, which restrains itself from making any kind of gesture. Opera, furthermore, provides well-known music for the audiences of the hypnosis sessions. Lina, however, is in a different situation: she is familiar with the famous operatic pieces played during these sessions, but not with the operatic spectacle itself. Last but not least, opera is considered 'objective music' which has a more precise force of suggestion and, according to de

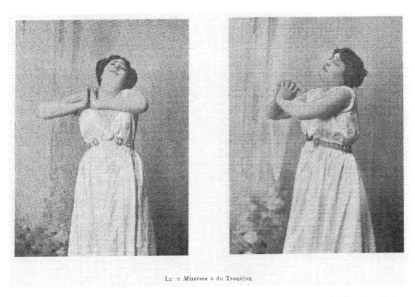

Figure 4.3 Le 'Miserere' du Trouvère, in Rochas, *Les Sentiments*, 177 (collection Frigau Manning).

Rochas, gives better results when combined with hypnosis than 'subjective music'. De Rochas takes and refines this distinction from Sully-Prudhomme's reflection on 'subjective' and 'objective' expression of a musical piece, according to an emotional barometer that allows the listener to associate particular music more or less precisely with a particular emotion.[28] With Verdi's music, considered to be more 'objective' by de Rochas, the great aesthetic battles of the time seem re-enacted in the hypnotic session, for the rivalry between the two 'unconscious artists', Lina and Magdeleine, plays on the storied Verdi/Wagner opposition: Lina being more Verdian (see Figure 4.3), while the more avant-garde Magdeleine becomes a Wagnerian.[29] It is in this context that Maurel went beyond the musical themes usually played on the piano. 'Victor Maurel ... who is not only a singer of great talent, but also an erudite psychologist, hummed some Italian songs.' This, at least, was what a journalist reported; but while Lina was being hypnotised, Maurel, as we have seen, in fact chose a very specific Verdi piece: 'Era la notte' from *Otello*.[30]

---

[28] Sully-Prudhomme, quoted in de Rochas 1900, 139.   [29] de Rochas 1900, 97.
[30] 'Victor Maurel ... n'est pas seulement un chanteur de grand talent, mais aussi un psychologue conscient de son métier, fredonna quelques chansons italiennes.' Quoted in de Rochas 1900, 186.

Hypnotic Verdi: Reading *Otello* through the Prism of Hypnosis

Considering his relationship with the role of Iago, Maurel's choice is perhaps unsurprising. Verdi had been thinking of the baritone since the opera's genesis, and indeed Maurel created the role in 1887 at La Scala in Milan.[31] But given the opera's plot and the musical rhetoric of suggestion rooted in Iago's role, 'Era la notte' also seems to musically parallel the situation of hypnosis, as Iago simultaneously lulls Otello's reasoning faculty to sleep and awakens his suspicions. Indeed, the whole opera might be fruitfully considered through the prism of a kind of obsession akin to hypnosis. Though the notion has not yet been treated to an in-depth analysis, some Shakespeare scholars have linked hypnosis to *Othello* in passing – not as a basis for a reading of the work, but as a descriptive analogy, with Iago being presented as a 'hypnotic villain' and Othello acting 'as if hypnotised'.[32] Concerning Verdi's opera, Daniel Albright even suggested that 'Othello is an ideal hypnotic subject, infinitely susceptible, carried away by Iago's suggestions.'[33] And indeed, many elements of Arrigo Boito and Verdi's *Otello* can be fruitfully read in light of the nineteenth-century culture of hypnosis and psychology.

Why such recourse to the hypnotic hypothesis? Jealousy, even supreme jealousy, may indeed be insufficient to understand how Otello – presented for the entire first act as the noble 'Duce' of the explosive 'Esultate', triumphant over Venice's enemy and the storms of the sea – could become the victim of Iago's Machiavellian insinuations. And inversely, describing Iago as cruel, even radically cruel, may be insufficient to explain his attitude. 'Your demon drives you, and I am that demon. And I am driven by mine, in which I believe, a merciless god'[34] (Act II scene 1). Iago's circular credo must be understood literally: he is a 'demon' able to influence any victim he latches onto, from Cassio and Roderigo to Otello, whose spirit and heart he manages to infect,

---

[31] Conati and Medici 2015, 95.   [32] See, for instance, Burke 2007, 244.

[33] Albright 2014, 111. Moving instead from medicine to performance studies, the link between Othello and hypnosis has also been mentioned, albeit in a cursory way, in medical and psychology texts, such as by David B. Cheek: 'The mechanisms by which hypnosis can do harm are not different from the tools which Lady Macbeth used on her husband, which Cassius used on the honorable Brutus, which Iago used on Othello. We can do more harm with ignorance of hypnosis than we can by intelligently using the forces of suggestion' (Cheek 1958, 177; quoted in Kroger 2008, 104).

[34] 'Ti spinge il tuo dimone, / e il tuo dimon son io. / E me trascina il mio, nel quale io credo / inesorato Iddio.'

Opera and Hypnosis 97

contaminate and control. He presents himself as being similarly under influence, yet in a spiralling hierarchy of control wherein he is gifted with greater power. For a nineteenth-century audience versed in constantly circulating stories of magnetism and hypnosis, Otello's drama may not immediately have seemed that of a brave, noble general who happens to have one tragic flaw – jealousy – which leads him to be duped by Iago and to murder his beloved wife. In Boito and Verdi's *Otello*, Iago does not appear as the instrument of a tragedy that would have occurred in any case. This implies another vision of *Otello*'s drama: as the fruit of destiny and bad luck more than the effect of tragedy.

Otello is thus in many ways the unfortunate story of a noble man who happens to meet an 'evil spirit', as defined, for instance, by the anonymous 1911 *Traité sur l'obsession* (A Treatise on Obsession) with its subtitle *L'obsession a pour base la suggestion* (Suggestion as the Basis for Obsession).[35] Indeed, the notion of obsession had recently been medicalised. In Dechambre's medical dictionary, obsession – drawn from the 'occult sciences' – was defined as 'the state of a person tortured by a demon, while possession refers to the enduring presence of the demon within the body. Dreams and set delirious ideas, voices which hallucinating people hear, can take on the character of obsession.'[36] Otello, like many other nineteenth-century figures who inhabit fantastical tales, embodies one of the era's most terrifying nightmares: that of a man who, in spite of his lofty spiritual qualities, and perhaps because of his 'nervous temperament', is fundamentally unable to escape the negative influence of a magnetiser who succeeds in abolishing any interior resistance in his victim.[37] Such a magnetiser accomplishes this not only by what he says (or sings), but by the way he says it, with his powerful gazes, manners, intonations and modes of speech. Like hypnosis, Verdi's musical language may induce a specific type of vocal interpretation, somewhere between speaking and chanting, with work on rhythms, breathing and intonation.

---

[35] 'Esprit malveillant'. [unsigned] 1911b, 3. On obsession, see Davis 2008, esp. 31–104.

[36] 'Dans les sciences occultes, l'obsession est l'état d'une personne tourmentée par un démon, tandis que la possession indique le séjour permanent du démon dans le corps. Les rêves et les idées délirantes fixes, les voix qu'entendent les hallucinés peuvent prendre le caractère d'obsession.' Dechambre 1875, 14:71.

[37] For two canonical examples of such figures, see Hoffmann 1982, 85–126; and Poe 1998, 239–48. Not all nineteenth-century scientists agreed with Charcot that hypnotism was a pathological effect of hysteria. According to many, however, nervous individuals – especially women – were more likely to respond to hypnotism and suggestion. See, for instance, Richer and Tourette 1875, 15:73.

Hypnosis had in fact long been considered as a form of psychic power and abolishment of free will: a way to take control of another person for better or for worse – to heal the subject or, on the contrary, order him to commit crimes.[38] In writings of the time related to hypnosis, two fantasies dominate: first, the unconscious woman raped or abused in her sleep either by a cruel, premeditating criminal, or else by a weak man influenced by her unintentional charms; a woman who in both cases is completely amnesiac and unable to remember anything that occurred. And second, the honest, resourceful man who, when manipulated by a criminal hypnotiser, becomes a criminal himself, ready to commit the most hideous of crimes under influence.

Otello is arguably an operatic incarnation of the latter. The murder is Iago's own suggestion: 'It's much better to suffocate her in her bed where she has sinned.'[39] Throughout the entire opera, Otello corporeally shows both the psychological and physiological effects of Iago's influence – such as his headache after his violent refusal to intervene in Cassio's favour at Desdemona's request (Act II scene 4), his fainting after the malediction scene at the end of Act III, and – ultimately – his suicide.[40] But the question is not only a medical one, for the juridical issues concerning hypnosis were also widely explored at the time: 'Has a crime been committed? Immediately, hypnotism is invoked, and the suggestion appears, dominating everything. It is claimed that free will is an empty word and the hypnotised subject is called an automaton.'[41] To the question: is a man guilty when he commits a crime under another's direct influence, or more explicitly in a state of hypnosis? – the answer is repeatedly: yes.[42] But the question hides a deeper interrogation connected with free will. Specifically, is the hypnotised subject acting without any participation of his or her will? Can or could he or she resist the

---

[38] Though there is not enough space here to fully explore the complex historical shifts in the history of hypnosis, the question of resistance is one of the fundamental differences in the nineteenth-century approach to hypnosis when compared to the modern one. Though the question of loss of control is still present in the popular imagination, twentieth-century approaches more frequently argue that hypnosis is rooted in an interpersonal relationship, and that the question of resistance is not of central importance.

[39] 'Val meglio soffocarla, / Là, nel suo letto, là, dove ha peccato' (Act III scene 7).

[40] At the time, suicide itself was in the process of being medicalised, considered as a chronic disease or a fit of insanity; see Frigau Manning 2016.

[41] 'Un crime est-il commis? Aussitôt, l'hypnotisme est invoqué, et la suggestion apparaît, dominant tout. Il est affirmé que le libre arbitre est un vain mot et le sujet hypnotisé, un automate.' Courmelles 1890, iii.

[42] See, for instance, Tourette 1887.

hypnotist's influence? At the same time, criminal anthropologists such as Wilhelm Wundt or Cesare Lombroso dreamt about the utility of hypnosis for the moral reform of society: in a utopian future, criminals would be hypnotised by prison officers in order to transform them into good, trustful subjects, and to reintegrate them into society once the hypnotic redemption was complete.

Victor Maurel explores the penal dimension of hypnotism in his lecture, and this can also help to explain why Verdi chose not to call his opera *Iago* as he had initially planned. The final title, *Otello*, was of course a way for Verdi to claim that he was adapting Shakespeare's tragedy, while also openly competing with Rossini's *Otello*. 'I prefer them to say "He chose to wrestle with the giant and was crushed,"' Verdi told Boito in January 1886, 'rather than "He wanted to hide behind the title of Iago."'[43] But this change was above all a way to place Otello in the spotlight: 'they continue to say and to write to me "*Iago, Iago*". He is (this is true) the Demon who moves everything; but Otello is the one who acts: *He loves, is jealous, kills*, and *kills himself*. And for my part it would seem hypocrisy not to call it *Otello*.'[44] Verdi and Boito thus chose to focus the action on the murderer under influence, who is also a victim; this underlines the complexity and paradoxical issues of a crime caused not only by love or jealousy, but committed under the influence of an evil creature. 'Otello is like a man moving in a nightmare, and under the fatal, mounting domination of this nightmare he thinks, acts, moves, suffers and commits his dreadful crime', Boito wrote to Verdi in October 1880.[45] The question of Otello's loss of free will under influence remains open, as it would in the contemporary debates on hypnosis.

Victor Maurel's choice of a number from this opera for his hypnotic session thus seems highly appropriate, and gives a special aura to his experiment. But as the journalistic account states:

Lina does not know Italian and, moreover, is one of the rare Parisians who have never listened to M. Victor Maurel. The latter felt tears come to his eyes when he saw this mere hypnotic subject, on the basis of the barely articulated vibrations of his voice, interpret the different pieces by way of gestures and

---

[43] Conati and Medici 2015, 96. The 'giant' was very likely Shakespeare himself and not Rossini, as suggested by the editors of the correspondence.

[44] Conati and Medici 2015, 96. There may be a distant reference here to the authority of Goethe's *Faust*, whose famous revision of Genesis was: 'In the beginning was the deed' ('Am Amfang war die Tat'). My thanks to David Trippett and Benjamin Walton for this suggestion.

[45] Conati and Medici 2015, 7.

expressions identical to those which he himself had been able to find only after many years of work.[46]

While insisting on Maurel's emotion when confronted with Lina's spontaneous gestures, the journalist does not delve into what is perhaps one of the most intriguing aspects of this experiment: how does the singer explain the fact that Lina is able to perform the same gestures? And to what extent does the use of a specific operatic piece allow him to go further in his own theoretical and practical method as an actor-singer?

A Psychological Method of Acting

Victor Maurel's approach to acting appears to be based fundamentally on psychological categories associated with hypnosis, such as identification and *objectivation*. Indeed, for the baritone, objectivation is the basis of his art. The concept is recurrent in theories of hypnosis. Charles Richet, for instance, defines objectivation as any situation in which the subject conceives of a character type, performs and 'objectivises' it: 'It is no longer like hallucinating people who contemplate, as spectators, images which unfold before their eyes; it is like an actor who, overcome by madness, imagines that the drama he acts out is reality, not a fiction, and that he has been transformed in his body and soul into the character he has been entrusted to play.'[47] Thus, when Mrs A. is told to be a peasant woman, then starts to act like one; and then is told to be an actress, a general, etc., and begins speaking and acting for each suggestion according to the 'type': 'It is not a simple dream,' as de Rochas states, quoting Richet, 'it is a *lived dream*.'[48] Mrs A. is not just imitating the emblematic poses of an actress or a general: she is truly living them. Objectivation is thus for Maurel the possibility, in an altered state of consciousness, of exteriorising passions, with major effects on the audience, through expressions and gestures which are not merely signs of the states of the

[46] 'Lina ne sait pas l'italien et, de plus, est une des rares Parisiennes n'ayant jamais entendu M. Victor Maurel. Celui-ci sentit les larmes lui venir aux yeux en voyant ce simple sujet hypnotique, aux vibrations à peine articulées de sa voix, interpréter ces différents morceaux par des gestes et des expressions identiques à ceux qu'il n'avait pu trouver qu'après bien des années de travail.' de Rochas 1900, 186.

[47] 'Ce n'est plus seulement à la façon de l'halluciné qui assiste en spectateur à des images se déroulant devant lui; c'est comme un acteur qui, pris de folie, s'imaginerait que le drame qu'il joue est une réalité, non une fiction, et qu'il a été transformé de corps et d'âme dans le personnage qu'il est chargé de jouer.' Charles Richet, quoted in de Rochas 1900, 79.

[48] de Rochas 1900, 79.

soul, but *are* these states themselves. To him, 'the intensity of objectiva-tion is always linked to the intensity and appropriateness of the prior mental identification'.[49]

In this sense, Maurel firmly denies Denis Diderot's famous theory. Acting is not about elaborating exterior images of characters, but rather about creating and working with internal images. Giving the most pro-minent place to imagination in his psychological theory, Maurel seems to follow contemporary research conducted by psychologists such as Lionel Dauriac or Théodule Ribot. In the case of voluntary weeping, for exam-ple, Dauriac argues that 'it is not by the action of their will that these people cry, but thanks to representative images: they imagine the state they want to produce'.[50] As for Ribot, he devotes a whole 'Essay on the Creative Imagination' to the question, stating that 'imagination, in the intellectual order, is the equivalent of will in the realm of movements'.[51] He goes on to identify the imagination's various factors, intellectual, emotional and unconscious: 'All forms of the creative imagination imply elements of feeling,' he argues, and in the case of aesthetic creation, 'affective states become material for the creative activity'.[52] Ribot's the-ories had at the same period a remarkable influence on Constantin Stanislavsky, whose famous 'system of acting' relies on his reading of the distinction between intellectual and emotional memory, the latter involving a change in bodily state.[53] Indeed, the parallel with Maurel's reflection is striking:

What you see of great artists on stage is in no way the most difficult aspect of their art. The difficult and strenuous part is what you cannot see at all, it is the inner state which lies beneath all this mimicry, all these accents, all these vocal inflections, and gives them that appearance of life which makes such an impression on you; it is this

---

[49] V. Maurel 1904, 2.

[50] 'ce n'est pas par l'action de leur simple volonté que ces personnes pleurent, mais par l'intermédiaire d'images représentatives: elles se représentent l'état qu'elles désirent produire'. Lionel Dauriac, paraphrased in Cabanès 1926, 156.

[51] Ribot 1906, 9. Ribot was the first person to complete a PhD in psychology based on a scientific method, the first to be in charge of a course on experimental psychology at the Sorbonne, and the first psychologist to be awarded a chair of 'Experimental and Comparative Psychology' at the Collège de France. See Nicolas 2005, 6.

[52] Ribot 1906, 32–3.

[53] As reported by W. Rose (2008, 56), Stanislavsky underlined in red the following text from Ribot's conclusion to *The Psychology of the Emotions* (1911, 163): 'The recollection of a feeling, it will be said, has this special property, that it is associated with organic and physiological states which make of it a real emotion. I reply that it *must* be so, for an emotion which does not vibrate through the whole body is nothing but a purely intellectual state.'

state that artists must laboriously organise, to create in themselves, and in which they can only maintain themselves on stage by a continuous effort of innervation and voluntary imagination.[54]

Maurel encourages the actor to work with his or her imagination not in order to create images which are externally imitated or presented to the audience, but to internalise them, or to find them in their inner self – images which thus become active, and are accompanied by all the requisite expressions and gestures.

Autosuggestion plays a central role here, for the question Maurel asks is: 'Do we have the means to create in ourselves a state of even transitory hypnosis?'[55] Drawing from theories such as those of the Swedish psychiatrist Fredrik Johan Björnström, he presents hypnosis as being 'caused ... by central excitation in the brain, by psychical action on the imagination, or by *suggestion* – as it is called in modern language'.[56] In a renewed approach to acting, autosuggestion allows the actor-singer to draw on his or her profound interiority not only to recall memories of lived moments, but also to let rise within spontaneous, detailed creations of the imagination, bringing a range of gestures up to the bodily surface. Such gestures, with no intervention from the faculty of reason, are more than simple signs of an affect which captures the soul: they are truly *part* of this affect, allowing the singer to use interiority as a space for creating artificial but true emotional states – true because they are free from any historical determination.

Where, though, do these gestures actually come from? What happens, according to Maurel, when Lina is able to locate gestures that she cannot possibly have observed on the operatic stage? How does he explain that the subject is able to find the same gestures herself – or more precisely, why does he want to believe this, and want us to believe this in turn? Maurel provides no definitive answers, presenting only the events of this strange situation. The mystery remains absolute. We can only sketch out hypotheses, evoking some of the theories then in vogue. Those concerning telepathy, for instance, may have been used to explain why Lina, without

---

[54] 'Ce que vous voyez d'un grand artiste sur la scène, cela n'est point le difficile de son art. Le difficile, l'ardu, c'est ce que vous ne voyez point, c'est l'état intérieur qui sous-tend toute cette mimique, tous ces accents, toutes ces inflexions vocales et leur donne cette apparence de vie qui vous étonne; c'est cet état que l'artiste a dû péniblement organiser, créer en lui et au niveau duquel il ne se maintient à présent sur la scène que par un effort continu d'innervation et d'imagination volontaires.' V. Maurel 1904, 9.

[55] 'Avons-nous ... les moyens de créer en nous un état d'hypnose même passager?' Victor Maurel 1904, 11.

[56] Björnström 1889, 18.

knowing any Italian, seemed to read in the singer's mind the appropriate gestures – and indeed the hypnotised subject as a thought-reader is a common trope. Other hypotheses might have connected Lina's performance with her potential access to a collective memory: her gestures emerging from an individual unconscious which, thanks to hypnosis, would be able to communicate with a collective one, deeply rooted in the self, thereby creating a truth of expression liberated from social conventions and historical bounds. Other explanations may have been inspired by a sort of Schopenhauerian aesthetics, and predicated on faith in the musical power of reminiscences.

As is well known, Arthur Schopenhauer's theories influenced a range of contemporary philosophers and readers, including two of Maurel's most influential figures of reference, Wagner and Friedrich Nietzsche. For Schopenhauer, every human existence, and indeed existence itself, is subject to the continuous, unavoidable repetition which defines the principle of Will. Only art allows men to free themselves from repetition, at least for a brief moment, through creation or contemplation. These moments are characterised by phenomena that resonate with the process of hypnosis: a detachment from space and time, absorption and projection in the act of contemplation. 'If life is iteration,' as Cécile Wolff puts it, 'art is reminiscence (obscure reminiscence of what was, before anything, the origins of repetitions).'[57] Imagination, as inspired by the receptive state created by hypnosis, allows the self-hypnotised actor to find gestures conceived as primary reminiscences.

Maurel does not then merely consider hypnosis as a way to train artists or to perfect his own art, as was the case in de Rochas's or Magnin's approach wherein Lina and Magdeleine were presented as 'ideal models', sources of inspiration or proof that a gesture, applied to this or that emotion, was the right one.[58] Rather, Maurel seeks to transmit a range of techniques he locates in hypnosis in order to train the imagination, to define and refine its skills in autosuggestion. To demonstrate how powerful the imagination can be in constructing new moral or immoral images of the self, he uses a provocative example, exploring the juridical dimension to make an unusual point. He chooses the Hugoesque figure of a man who has committed homicide in order to save his family. Ten years have passed, the perpetrator of the crime has not been found and the man has lived an utterly honest life – that is, until he begins to fall under suspicion. Being guilty, the man is unable to imitate the convincing accents of indignation

---

[57] See Wolff 2009, 155.   [58] See, for instance, de Rochas 1900, 47–8.

that would be characteristic of an innocent man, and the 'innocent man' is truly a role that he must approach gradually, internalising it before he is able to embody it. 'This man, in this moment, is in an intermediary region between life and art,' Maurel says; he has to 'provoke within his inner self an artificial state' which cannot merely be simulated, 'to go directly to the greatest art, the one which, in one word, in one gesture . . . would overcome all resistance and implant conviction'.[59] He needs to develop a 'process of incubation' founded on an act of autosuggestion and language: searching for the similarities between the guilty man he is, and the innocent man he wants not to appear as, but to become. 'What he needs above all is an inner fire of sincerity where, at the proper time, he would draw on the impulse which will charge his voice, his gestures, his entire being, with truth.'[60] The work of the actor – as occurs in hypnosis – involves a transformation. Once the new image of the self is born, once the autosuggestion is enacted, all the rest – gestures, intonations, states of being – will naturally perfect and complete the character.

Conclusions

Maurel's experiment with hypnosis seems to have been a singular event, never repeated. But it came to occupy a significant place in his theory of acting. Beyond the social event, the episode reveals a vital aspect of the singer's professional life. On the one hand, his teaching, extending into the context of higher education, was not confined to private classes with singers such as Emma Calvé, or the school he founded in Paris in 1906 and later took to New York. On the other hand, and in contrast to what Verdi's letters may lead us to believe, his position as chair at the EHES proves that Maurel's research towards a 'singing renewed by science' was not an eccentric part of his activities; rather, there emerges the figure of a researcher active across a wide epistemological spectrum, and within a dynamic research community of artistic and scientific knowledge.[61]

---

[59] 'Cet homme, en l'instant, est dans une région intermédiaire à la vie et à l'art . . . susciter en lui un état artificiel . . . aller tout droit au grand art, à celui qui dès le premier mot, dès le premier geste, impressionne, empoigne, terrasse les résistances et implante la conviction.' V. Maurel 1904, 12–13.

[60] 'processus d'incubation'; 'ce qu'il lui faut à tout prix, c'est un foyer intérieur de sincérité où, le moment venu, il puisera l'impulsion qui animera de vérité sa voix, ses gestes, tout son être'. V. Maurel 1904, 13.

[61] See Henson 2007.

Engrossed in the changing relationships between body, the psyche and the moral self, Maurel contributed to the *fin-de-siècle* search for various forms of non-rational knowledge. This is the reason why, at the crossroads of the history of medicine, psychology and opera, we find in Maurel's text a valuable way to rethink the relationships between the epistemologies of science and music at the dawn of the twentieth century. Maurel's acting theories were not 'inspired by' a comparison with hypnosis: they were deeply interwoven with the concepts, ideas and images of hypnosis itself. Hypnosis constitutes here a proactive artistic method: it is both an experiment and an experience, in the dual senses of the French *'expérience'* – an experiment, for it is a test that Maurel carries out in the intimacy of his salon transformed into an imaginary laboratory. It is also, however, a veritable lived experience, as it allows Maurel to acquire dreamt knowledge through a body in action: the body of the other, and, in this case, the body of the unconscious artist – Lina's body.

PART II

Ears

5 | Hearing in the Music of Hector Berlioz

JULIA KURSELL

Introduction: Imagination and the Position of the Subject

For a long time, Hector Berlioz was thought to hold a singular, even an isolated position in music history. Among the first to offer a new perspective was Pierre Boulez, who suggested that Berlioz's position in music history could be explained by 'the fact that a large part of his *œuvre* has remained in the realm of the imaginary'.[1] With this remark, Boulez alluded to the *Grand traité d'instrumentation et d'orchestration modernes* (1844/55), and more specifically to the chapter on the orchestra that closes the treatise. Speculations on the sound of an orchestra that would unite 'all the forces that are present in Paris and create an ensemble of 816 musicians' were, for Boulez, typical of Berlioz: 'mixing realism and imagination without opposing one to the other, producing the double aspect of an undeniable inventive "madness" – a fairly unreal dream minutely accounted for'.[2]

This chapter takes Boulez's diagnosis as a point of departure for the argument that the imaginary and the real mingle not *despite* both referring to the actual features of – in this case – an orchestra, but *because* they do so. As I will argue, 'inventive "madness"' indicates the way in which the real and the imaginary become indistinguishable in Berlioz's work. For this, I will analyse the role of hearing in his work on the one hand, and embed the analysis within a historical account of hearing, on the other. The guiding assumption is that the sense of hearing poses a peculiar challenge to the Romantic concept of the subject. Idealist philosophy had left the subject with the task of reconquering space from the subject's own position within it. Sensory physiology reacted to this by developing a new concept of experimentation that was exploratory rather than hypothesis-driven.

The first part of this chapter surveys this development with an emphasis on research into hearing. Building on this survey, I then reconstruct

---

[1] Boulez 1986, 175.   [2] Boulez 1986, 177; 1985, 229.

perceptual positions emerging from Berlioz's music that draw on changes in intensity as the basic data from which a subject can understand its own position. As will be shown using the example of the *Symphonie fantastique* (1830), this can result in indistinguishability between the subject's perception and imagination. In the later opera *Les Troyens* (1856/63), Berlioz stages ghosts as figures that blur this distinction. Changes in intensity will again provide the main cue for making the ghosts' unstable nature plausible on stage. Both the example of the *Symphonie fantastique* and the apparition of Hector's ghost in the second act of *Les Troyens* strongly relate to the Romantic topic of the 'fantastic'. By contrast, the focus in my analysis will be to look at how Berlioz instantiated the perceptual aspect of the characteristic ambiguity between natural and supernatural explanations within the 'fantastic'. If previous analyses emphasised the pathological, my focus is on how realistic aspects create the condition for hearing.

One can assume that Berlioz was familiar with the contemporary discourse about experimental science through his studies in medicine that he pursued up to the degree of a baccalaureate in *sciences physiques*.[3] If this provides a basis for looking at how certain musical moments construct certain perceptual positions, it does not yet explain the specific situation on the opera stage. To investigate this, a final example will be discussed in which four shadows from the underworld urge Aeneas (Énée), the hero of *Les Troyens*, to leave his beloved Dido in Carthage and reach the shores of Italy. The conflict between present and absent spaces (both literal and spectral) in this scene will be used as the central argument for relating orchestration as the focus in Berlioz's theoretical work to his exploration of auditory perception. If the opera is a space for experimentation – my principal hypothesis – it is one that can include complex negotiations between acoustic situations.

Background: Sensory Physiology, 1800–1830

The listener of the early nineteenth century who notes or even analyses the quality of a sound seems something of an exception. Berlioz was such a listener: in his *Memoirs*, he described his experiences at the Paris Opéra:

Not all places were equally good for hearing, I had tried them all and knew the defects and advantages of each. Thus in one you were on top of the horns, in

---

[3] On Berlioz's biography see Bloom 1998.

another you could hardly hear them. On the right the trombones were too prominent, on the left you got an unpleasant effect from the sound bouncing off the stall boxes. At the front you were too near the orchestra, and the voices were drowned; on the other hand, at the back you were too far from the stage to make out the words or the expressions on the actors' faces. The orchestration of this work should be heard from here, the choruses in that work from there. In one act, where the scene was a sacred grove, the stage area was enormous; the sound tended to disperse and lose itself about the theatre; in that case you had to go nearer. Another took place in the interior of a palace, and the design was what is called a box set, an apparently unimportant change which doubled the power of the voices: so it became necessary to move a little farther back to allow voices and orchestra to find a better balance.[4]

If this quote suggests a hearing subject that is aware of specific acoustic properties of the sound in the opera, this is not how the emergence of the nineteenth-century listener has been generally described. At first glance, the new Romantic listener seems characterised instead by the way in which he or she got rid of all allegedly objective references. As James Johnson has pointed out, listeners became convinced 'that their musical experience was unique', discovering along the way the diversity of subjective feelings in their own listening, and, rather than referring to shared emotions, declared with Adolphe Guéroult that music 'speaks to the soul without appearing to the senses'.[5]

Yet this is only one aspect of a new concept of the subject that emerged around 1800. No less important was the quest for the conditions in which subjectivity becomes possible.[6] The shift towards an inherent self-relation has been identified as the defining trait of this modern concept of subjectivity. As Jonathan Crary has argued, a quest for understanding perception during the nineteenth century began with Johann Wolfgang von Goethe's *Farbenlehre* (1810) and can be pursued in contemporary physiology.[7] Goethe proposed that to understand perception one should try to perceive perception itself.[8] Following Goethe's turn towards subjective experience, physiologist Jan Evangelista Purkyně scrutinised what he called 'subjective phenomena'.[9] He

---

[4] Berlioz 1969, 91–2.

[5] Johnson 1995, 274; Guéroult, 'L'Eglise et l'opéra', quoted in Johnson 1995, 274.

[6] Dieter Henrich (1993) has formulated this problem for Early German Romanticism and the emergence of idealistic philosophy.

[7] Crary 1990. On Romantic science more generally cf. Cunningham and Jardine 1990; Poggi and Bossi 1993.

[8] Crary 1990, 17. On Goethe's *Farbenlehre* see also Schäfer 2011.

[9] On Goethe and Purkyně cf. Vogl 2007.

established that perceptual phenomena that did not exist outside human perception – such as after-images – nevertheless occurred lawfully and could be considered as appropriate objects for scientific investigation.

This new physiological approach to subjectivity distanced itself from the study of perception that sought to understand how an outer world entered the human mind. Broadly speaking, whereas German physiologists opposed this view in researching 'subjective phenomena', French physiologists most explicitly called for a radical change from a qualitative and descriptive operational mode to a quantitative use of experimentally generated data. Within the history of French physiology, François Magendie has long been considered a key proponent of this change.[10] Whereas eighteenth-century physiology based its understanding of the organism on anatomy and tried to explain the functions of the organs from this perspective, Magendie first looked at functions and then went towards the organs involved. He reproached previous physiologists for using a notion of experimentation that was only able to confirm preconceived classifications: 'One seeks that which must be, and not that which is.'[11]

Instead, he pleaded for a mode of experimentation that would discover new phenomena: physiology had to adopt an exploratory mode of experimentation.[12] Magendie explained this new approach in his textbook, *Précis élémentaire de physiologie* (1816–17), in which he also summarised the state of knowledge in physiology, including his own experimental studies. Although he was modest in his assumptions about the book's appeal – which he claimed was written simply to introduce students of medicine to human physiology – the methodological tenets articulated there have been seen in French history and philosophy of science as a decisive step towards the modern life sciences.[13]

Magendie's new concept of experimentation freed physiology from anatomy, as it no longer assumed that the only secure knowledge of living organisms could be won by post-mortem anatomy. Instead he claimed to base his research solely on the 'observation of healthy and ill men and experiments on living animals'.[14] Sensory perception was a case in point. Too little was known about the ear in particular to permit a conclusive understanding. Anatomical studies of the ear had provided important findings, including the first description of the membranous labyrinth; but

---

[10] This historiography goes back to Magendie's disciple Claude Bernard; see Albury 1977.
[11] Magendie 1816–17, 1:6. [12] See Steinle 2001, 2016.
[13] Cf. Rothschuh 1968; Albury 1974.; Canguilhem 2002, 226–74. [14] Magendie 1816–17, 1:v.

its author, Antonio Scarpa, could only warn physiologists not to speculate about the functions of the nerves that he had found to end in a muddy substance in the labyrinth.[15] For the moment, anatomy had reached its limits.[16]

Nevertheless, Magendie insisted that experience permitted certain observations. He was the first, for instance, to prove experimentally that both ears are used for discerning the direction from which a sound reaches us. After having someone produce a sound in a dark place, he noted he was unable to identify that sound's direction with one ear plugged. Using both ears, this became possible again.[17] Magendie ascribed his finding to the possibility of comparing the intensity received by both ears. Intensity, however, was a problematic concept in itself: it was the cue for understanding auditory space, but it was also a source of constant error. To some extent, the distance of a sound could be judged based on that sound's intensity because a sound that is nearer would sound stronger, and a distant sound softer. In order to judge this, however, the nature of the sound had to be familiar. A soft sound could just as well come from a source nearby and a loud sound from a distant source. Magendie concluded: 'We are easily deceived about the point where a sound originates.' Hearing was therefore subjected to frequent 'acoustic errors'.[18]

The ambiguity Magendi noted for auditory intensity was one of the main characteristics of intensity more generally. For the physiologist and comparative anatomist Johannes Müller, intensity was an integral part of his new concept of perception.[19] Müller published two treatises on vision in 1826, where he laid out his theory of the relation between perception and nerve physiology.[20] In the first, *Zur vergleichenden Physiologie des Gesichtssinnes des Menschen und der Thiere*, he presented a comparative physiology of the sense of vision in humans and animals. Building on Goethe and Purkyně's studies of subjective phenomena, the second treatise, *Ueber die phantastischen Gesichtserscheinungen*, presented Müller's theory of 'specific sense energies'. According to this theory, every nerve was imbued with a specific capacity to produce sensations or to stimulate action. This capacity was independent of any concrete stimulus. A stimulated nerve would thus always produce the reaction for which this

---

[15] See Magendie 1816–17, 1:141. Magendie refers to Scarpa 1789.

[16] On microscopy before and after the development of microtomes see Schickore 2007.

[17] Magendie 1816–17, 1:107.   [18] Magendie 1816–17, 1:151.

[19] On Müller see Hagner and Wahrig-Schmidt 1992; Otis 2007; Meulders 2010, 43–54.

[20] J. Müller 1826a, 1826b.

particular nerve was appropriate, rather than reflecting the properties of the stimulus. A nerve leading to a muscle would always make this muscle contract; the optic nerve would always produce sensations of light; and the auditory nerve sensations of tone – regardless of how it was stimulated: mechanically, through chemicals or electricity, or any other means.

Given that a nerve could be excited by any stimulus, intensity – that is to say, the degree of 'energy' conveyed – remained the only aspect of sensation that related to the stimulus and thus potentially the outer world. A nerve could specify sensory perception in two respects: it could bring its own specific energy to the awareness of the subject, and it could convey the degree of its stimulation. As Müller noted, changes in sensory energies played a critical role in helping the subject to construct a relation to the outer world. He later specified: 'The mind not only perceives the sensations and interprets them according to ideas previously obtained, but it has a direct influence upon them, imparting to them intensity.'[21]

Based on his theory of sense energies, Müller tried to develop a purely physiological concept of the mind. Imagination, he assumed, eventually had to be explained as a product of nervous activity. Müller did not spare himself from self-experimentation to explore those nervous activities that appeared to the perceiving subject as the mind. He drove himself to hallucinate through artificially induced insomnia, hoping that this would make him better understand the laws that regulate 'phantastic visions'. He published the results in his treatise on hallucination and suffered a nervous breakdown shortly thereafter.[22]

Hearing in the *Symphonie fantastique*

Johnson's cultural history of listening and Crary's analysis of the history of perception both centrally address the role of the subject. Similarly, musicologists in the 1990s revisited the role of the listening subject – with the aim of re-establishing hermeneutics in response to the predominance of structuralism that had held sway in the post-war humanities, often with an underlying intention of getting rid of a problematic past.[23] For the new musicology, the diversity of listeners' interpretations also offered the possibility of readdressing the hegemony of absolute music. Part of this

---

[21] J. Müller 1843, 717.   [22] See Otis 2007, 44–5.

[23] Critical approaches to this pervade current musicology up to N. Cook 2002.

enterprise was to change the status of allegedly extra-musical aspects and to emphasise their value for understanding music.

Although this critique was directed against an essentialist concept of music in the first instance, it was also brought to bear on musical performance. Listening and hearing were separated once again, reducing sensory perception to a negligible precondition. Updating early nineteenth-century claims that music speaks more to the soul than to the ear, various musicologists now assumed that if a concept of music exists, it is to be looked for in the individual subjects. Similarly, the way in which nineteenth-century listeners conveyed the individuality of their feelings spoke to the hermeneutics of the late twentieth century. Support for the new mode of interpretation came from literary studies, and more specifically, narratology. Consequently, the study of nineteenth-century symphonic music has, in the context of new musicology, tended towards understanding music in narrative terms.[24]

In the case of Berlioz's *Symphonie fantastique* this situation is reversed. While programme music seems a case in point for studying a composition's 'verbal tale', it did not have the appeal of idiosyncrasy. Ever since Berlioz himself distributed the programme notes to the first performance, the story of an opium-induced vision of unfulfilled love and gruesome death amid the scenery of Paris in the 1820s has established the task for the listeners' imaginations.[25] As Francesca Brittan has argued, narration, and more specifically the genre of the fantastic, is the key to this composition, providing an unexpected bridge to contemporary attempts to objectify knowledge of the individual.[26] Fantastic narration, as it has been defined since Tzvetan Todorov's *The Fantastic: A Structural Approach to a Literary Genre* (1975), departs from a characteristic ambiguity between natural and supernatural explanations of related occurrences.[27] This enabled a reference to discourses of 'objectivity' in a new way, mediated through medicine and psychiatry. The *Symphonie fantastique* fits seamlessly into this context. This piece demonstrates that this new approach, in taking the narrative seriously, would neither drop subjectivity nor overstate objectivity.

One of the most prominent instances of the fantastic in the *Symphonie fantastique* is the beheading of the hero in the fourth movement.[28] As French epistemologist George Canguilhem has pointed out, the guillotine

---

[24] Classic texts on narration in music include Nattiez 1990; McClary 1997; Hepokoski 2002.

[25] See, for instance, Kregor 2015, 70–9; for another perspective, including a reference to Berlioz's own statements on this matter see Langford 2000, 54.

[26] Brittan 2006, 2007.   [27] See, for instance, Langford 2000.   [28] See Ritchey 2010.

obsessed physiologists in the aftermath of the French Revolution. The question of whether or not head and body would continue to sense after the beheading turned nerve physiology into a pressing topic.[29] Scottish anatomist Charles Bell first advanced the hypothesis that two different kinds of nerves lead from the body towards the brain and from there back into the body. Magendie provided the first empirical evidence, but the dogs he used in his *in vivo* experiments were in too desperate a state to allow for further differentiation.[30] Müller repeated the experiments and, using frogs instead of dogs, was able to corroborate Bell's hypothesis.

Taking this fascination with beheading as a point of departure, the following comments on the *Symphonie fantastique* suggest that the history of physiology offers a reference not only for understanding nineteenth-century art, as demonstrated by Crary, but also musical composition. Reconsidered in this way, the oft-analysed fourth movement of the symphony can be described as a play with aural perceptions in the context of the situation depicted by the programme. More specifically, the music provides cues for an implicit position of a hearing subject. This is not to say that this position is homogeneous, nor that there is only one such position. Rather, it is necessary to differentiate between at least two types of position: that of a subject who listens to Berlioz's composition, and that of a perceptual position – or several of them – from which the acoustic events in the music are presented. Borrowing a term from theatre studies, these two positions could be called the intra-diegetic and extra-diegetic levels in the overall acoustic presentation.[31]

Yet the construction of these positions cannot be achieved by imposing the programme upon the sonic events. This would reduce the role of hearing to the intra-diegetic position of a hearing subject within the narration that is detached from the concert-listener's position to be then attributed to the narrated events *ex post facto*. This, however, is insufficient for describing Berlioz's music. Rather, the intra-diegetic position is and must be constantly corroborated through acoustic features in the music. To this end, the music also reflects accidental features of the sounds that reach the implicit position of hearing. Sounds can, for instance, arrive earlier or later at that position, they are clear or muffled, louder or softer. In other words, the concert-listener must be aware of cues that point to the effects of

---

[29] Cf. Canguilhem 1993; Schmidgen 2006.

[30] Magendie 1822; see also Otis n.d., 4. For Magendie's research on nerve sensitivity see Canguilhem 1955; 2002, 295–304.

[31] See Pfister 1988.

Example 5.1 Hector Berlioz, *Symphonie fantastique*, arr. F. Liszt, IV: March to the Scaffold, bb. 17–25

hearing for construing the intra-diegetic level. In this way, the hero emerges within the narration as a position of intra-diegetic perception along with the music.

This double play of listening to hearing begins from the very first bars of the 'march to the scaffold' that convey the sound of an approaching marching band. Already here, a fixed position is implied, from which the band's arrival is observed. Yet, at this moment in the music, this could be anyone's position except the concert-listeners'. The position that the concert listeners must construe is clearly fictitious, even if it is not yet clear to them whose position it will be. They see the instrumentalists remaining in their places, while the sounds get louder, and they are invited to accept an additional position within the narrative, from which the increase in loudness makes acoustic sense as a nearing marching band. The approach of these sounds is set to music with considerable acoustic realism. Soft drums are heard first; the motif that next appears in the French horns enters pianissimo, as if as yet too far to be properly discerned. The increasing proximity of the sound is further depicted by foregrounding low instruments, whose sonic energy disperses less quickly and therefore reaches further than high-pitched notes. Higher registers gradually join in, making the orchestration ever more detailed and thus appearing as a sound mass that approaches ever nearer.[32]

That said, the music does not fully map onto the acoustic image of a marching band that becomes louder and louder, either. Abrupt switches to

---

[32] For an analysis of spatial effects in the orchestral timbre of the *Symphonie fantastique* see Tan 1997; and on Berlioz's orchestration treatise see F. Kolb 2016.

Example 5.2 Hector Berlioz, *Symphonie fantastique*, arr. F. Liszt, IV: March to the Scaffold, bb. 62–71

high-pitched fortissimo notes which are followed by a release of tension in all musical parameters, as if becoming exhausted (see Example 5.1), present a different perspective to that of an approaching sound mass. Whereas the acoustic image of the marching band refers to a growth in tension for external reasons, the repeated alternation between soaring effort and exhaustion suggests a layer of intensity that is not acoustic in the same sense, but instead is inward bound. The role of this superimposed dynamic layer remains ambiguous, however, as long as the overall increase in loudness persists and as long as each of the release-phrases lands on a last accented note, thereby creating the association with a heavy, slow gait. When a triumphant new motive (see Example 5.2) shifts the accent of the phrase to the first beat in the measure, this gives the concert audience to understand that the marching group has arrived at its destination: the spot where the execution takes place.

The next step the music depicts is catastrophic. The position of intra-diegetic hearing within the musical texture and the concert listener's position collapse into one. The main theme is now so close to the implicit perceptual standpoint that it cannot be attributed to one single instrumental line any longer. All instruments seem now to be at the same distance from this position, encircling the spot where it is located. As Example 5.3 shows, after a fanfare in the brass (bb. 78–81), the notes of the main soaring theme jump from one instrumental group to the next so swiftly that they hardly form motivically coherent sections of their own (bb. 82–85).[33] They seem reduced to a stutter – or, in the terms of the implicit perception – a disorientation: the intra-diegetic position of perception now emerges as that of the subject-to-be-executed. The concert listener, too, cannot distance him- or herself from that position, and must share the sense of disorientation. Nothing but the distorted position of that hearing subject is given in the music. After this collapsing of the two perspectives, the rhythmic structure of the march breaks down, descending in a tumbling hemiola. What follows depicts the execution, after which only silence is left for an implicit hearing subject or, as we learn retrospectively, hallucination.

All these observations corroborate a reading of the *Symphonie fantastique* as relating to the narratological category of the fantastic, in that they demonstrate once more the ambiguity between what can be explained as realistic and what appeals to other modes of explanation, including the appeal to supernatural forces. This also applies to the various acoustic positions in the music. The positioning of the audible events oscillates between a precise rendition of possible acoustic relationships and musical features that reach beyond such realism, creating at the same time a tension between the local specificity of such a position and the encompassing and extra-diegetic position of the concert listener. If this multiplicity of perceptual modes is to include the implicit perceptual position of the hero, who now appears to be the executioner's victim, this is not achieved through a mere representation of a narrative, but instead employs the double play of listening which constantly refers to instances of imagination *and* of hearing. Hearing – as opposed to listening – does not imply knowledge about what will be heard. It is a mode of gaining knowledge rather than of communication. The musical process of juxtaposing acoustic positions and creating tensions between the perception of outer and inner worlds provokes such a concept.

---

[33] Tresch 2011.

Example 5.3 Hector Berlioz, *Symphonie fantastique*, arr. F. Liszt, IV: March to the Scaffold, bb. 78–86

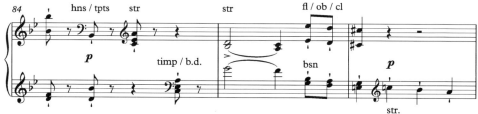

Hector Speaks

In his collection of essays *À travers chants*, Berlioz listed among the basic 'elements of music' the 'degree of intensity' and the 'point of departure' of sounds. Both refer to qualities of sound that are considered irrelevant for a notion of musical composition whose essence is rooted in the symbolic operations of counterpoint. Berlioz, by contrast, referred to audible effects as constitutive for his compositional practice. He explained: 'By placing the listener closer or farther away from the performers and, on certain occasions, placing instruments at a distance from each other, one can bring about changes in the musical effect that have not yet been adequately studied.'[34] In the *Symphonie fantastique*, he not only used this as a device for orchestration – think, for instance, of the dialogue between an oboe and

---

[34] Berlioz 1998, 5; on this collection see K. Kolb 2009.

English horn across the space of the concert hall – but he addressed the listener's imagination in a play of distance and intensity, as the analysis above has sought to demonstrate.

When it comes to operatic music, the compositional treatment of intensity in space shifts to a different level. Points of perception can now be embodied in the actors on stage, and the semantics of audible cues can be delivered together with the sounds. This, in turn, affects the role of imagination. Arguably, Berlioz could lean on his vast knowledge of opera for developing the acoustic image of the march in his *Symphonie fantastique*. The contrast between the real and the imaginary that created the peculiar musical fantastic, however, is enhanced in the symphony by the fact that no visible narrative explains to the listener which sounds have to be understood as being intra-diegetic. When comparing this to Giacomo Meyerbeer's excessive use of offstage sound, for instance in *Les Huguenots*, the difference becomes apparent. As Mary Ann Smart has shown, Meyerbeer uses an encoding of meaning to integrate offstage sounds into the operatic narrative, in addition to employing them for acoustic effect.[35] The offstage choral singing in *Les Huguenots* that alternates a Protestant chorale with a belligerent chorus of the intruders who are about to massacre them cannot be seen on stage, but it is understood through the semantics attributed to each of the alternating fragments. The acoustic effect is subordinated to the narrative. Berlioz, in contrast, needs acoustic realism to pair it with the uncanny also on the operatic stage. Reimporting the effects that originated from opera into his own operatic music, he still employs such juxtapositions of modes of hearing.

A compelling case in point is the presence of ghosts, who appear in several of Berlioz's vocal compositions. Most prominently, they give voice to fate in *Les Troyens*. The plot, constructed around Aeneas' destiny to found the Roman Empire, employs supernatural authorities to communicate to Aeneas what he should do instead of dying for Troy or staying with Dido in Africa. At first sight, the ghosts seem yet another token of the fantastic. Yet on stage, the nature of the ambiguity between natural and supernatural explanations shifts. Ghosts on stage undermine the secure demarcation between the tangible and the figment of imagination.

Hector's ghostly appearance in the second act of *Les Troyens* can be seen as a model for how this ambiguity is embodied on the stage. The same problems identified by Stephen Greenblatt for staging a ghost in the

---

[35] Smart 2004, 102–31, esp. 105f.

theatrical space (where does the ghost come from? how can it be present without being there?) also occur in opera, yet with other means of resolution.[36] The stage directions for the apparition of Troy's dead hero are simple. He enters the stage and walks slowly towards the sleeping Aeneas, who awakens because of the battle noises of the falling city. Hector then conveys his message and walks away again, disappearing into darkness. That he is not just another human actor but a shadow from the underworld is indicated in several ways. The music shows a calculation of sound intensities that stages the ghost as heard, combining the two aspects of hearing and intensity in a liminal moment between the living and the dead. If his moment of visual appearance requires nothing more than an 'obscure corner' from which he solemnly advances, his exit is set both visually and musically as a gradual fade-out, thereby challenging the limits of auditory perception.[37] In fact, the acoustic exit already begins with the first words he addresses to Aeneas. The recitation gradually descends in chromatic steps through the octave b♭ to B♭. The score indicates that Hector's voice should become more and more feeble as he recites ('*La voix d'Hector doit s'affaiblir graduellement jusqu'à la fin*').

The descending line of the ghost's utterance takes up a figure that Berlioz had already explored in the song 'Spectre de la rose' from the song cycle *Nuits d'été* (1840/41). Here it is set to a line in which the ghost explains where he comes from. The descending, non-legato chromatic line ends on the words 'De profundis', i.e. the incipit of Psalm 130, which stands here for a part of the Christian funeral rite. Berlioz embeds this connotation within an opposition of musical registers. Having reached the lowest point, a melodic upsurge gives way to the ghost declaring that he comes from Paradise.

This spatial contrast is transformed on Hector's first appearance. The ghost seems to be in a state of speaking only after an initial blow in the orchestra has prepared the appropriate energy level for him to enter the acoustic world. From there, his voice glides down on the declining energy of that blow to end in silence. Berlioz stages the utterance of the ghost according to a surprisingly precise idea of sound energy, as it could be described in modern terms: a peak of energy must precede any sound that enters the audible realm. Yet this acoustic envelope at the same time

---

[36] Greenblatt 2001.

[37] Here and in the following I use the New Berlioz Edition (Berlioz 1967–2005), indicated as NBE; quote cited in Hector Berlioz, *Les Troyens*, 3 vols. (NBE 2a–c), ed. Hugh Macdonald, vol. 2a (1969), 211, 215.

reveals that the ghost's existence is not granted. Hector's materialisation depends on an effort that cannot be stabilised.

Hector's entry is embedded in music and scenic action that bear witness as much to his being there as to his liminal state. From the very beginning of the act, the acoustic scenery had been split in two layers. The stage directions – 'distant battle noises' – describe an acoustic layer that is not per se musical and whose source is invisible.[38] Although there is no indication of how the battle noises are put into effect, this in fact gives them a status that for Boulez would be imaginary: it is clear from the indications that they are meant to be independent of the music. In addition, the score specifies that four instruments – two trumpets and two cornets à piston – are located behind the scenes. The military fanfares they interpolate do not coincide with the indication of the battle noise in the score; however, nor do they picture the events described in the stage directions. Rather, the offstage instruments subsume the outside noise into the main musical stratum whose status is not intra-diegetic. The players join the orchestra before the curtain is drawn.

The first activity on stage is a pantomime: Ascanius enters and sees his father, Aeneas, soundly asleep. Ascanius 'harkens' to the outside noises, but as the noises become weaker, he exits without having dared to wake his father. His action confirms the two acoustic layers: the music articulates Ascanius' movements, whereas the battle noise is now marked as belonging to the diegetic world, which – although offstage – can be perceived on stage. That Ascanius could hear the noise, whereas it did not rouse Aeneas, has become a meaningful detail of the acoustic scenery.

Hector enters only after this confirmation of the battle noise's diegetic role. With his entry, the music drastically changes in character. Four horns tuned to chromatic steps from d to f set the tone for a slowly creeping melody in the first horn. Berlioz purposefully asks for stopped notes in the horns, although he prescribes both cylinder and natural horns.[39] The uncanny, hesitating atmosphere is further enhanced through pizzicato and tremolo notes in the strings and a heartbeat-like rhythm in the

---

[38] Berlioz, *Les Troyens* (NBE 2a), 1:203. I thank David Trippett for pointing me to Berlioz's mention in the 1844 edition of the treatise that the bass drum, struck softly, gives the sound of distant cannon fire. I agree with him that some instantiation of the stage directions in line with such suggestions is implied here, without, however, changing the status of these stage directions as being a linguistic description whose function cannot fully be replaced by concrete indications.

[39] See Macdonald's (2002, 160–3) commentary on the horn section in the *Grand traité*.

timpani. To these sounds, the shadow walks towards the sleeping human, giving a deep sigh as he stops next to Aeneas.

As long as Aeneas remains asleep, the relation of the music that accompanies the apparition to the diegetic world remains ambiguous. Aeneas obviously neither sees nor hears the ghost. For the moment, only the spectator can observe the spectre. The new orchestral colouring does not integrate any of the sounds connected to the battle outside Aeneas' room. With a fortissimo blow in the orchestra, a sudden clash of the world of humans and ghosts turns Hector into a perceptible phenomenon for Aeneas. Aeneas is said to awaken from an offstage rumbling of some building collapsing outside that is 'heavier than those before', and he immediately becomes aware of Hector.[40] After these two blows the two worlds begin to interact, and the stage indications referring to outside noise cease. The music now forms a realm wherein the shadow and the human can encounter one another.

Aeneas addresses the apparition, asking Hector what has brought him back to the human world. His utterances demonstrate vivid agitation, as expressed in the agile rhythm and variety of his articulation. Nevertheless, they resemble Hector's utterance to some extent, as they compress its features into the extension of less than a single bar. A stepwise downward movement prevails, but it is enlivened through melodic upward peaks and a heavy oscillation between dynamic extremes in the orchestra. Aeneas' prosody is fully in possession of such expressive features: he imposes his own articulation upon what is indicated in the score as 'recitation'. By contrast, the ghost is bound to a non-expressive articulation that reduces all musical parameters to a minimum. He recites on one note, making only small melodic steps, finishing one phrase with a minor second downward or beginning a phrase a minor second below the previous one. The rhythm is reduced to a syllabic declamation of the text. No agogic freedom is foreseen. The score indicates the ghost's articulation to be 'measured', resembling in this respect the diction of the Commendatore in Mozart's *Don Giovanni*. Most significantly, the dynamics indicate a loss in tension. Hector's last words are barely audible. Human and ghost follow the same prosody, but differ in their ability to enliven it.

The appearance of the ghost onstage creates a peculiar relation to the perceiving subject. The situation it creates does not engage the spectator in a play of subject positions, but of acoustic layers.[41] The human actors

---

[40] None of the available audio-visual recordings follows these instructions.

[41] Bockholdt (1979) carries out analyses of such strata.

implement their points of perception and thereby confirm the intra-diegetic presence of sounds. The liminal state of the ghost interferes with the intra-diegetic sounds in complex ways. The music that accompanies the ghost oscillates between an extra-diegetic function and an utterance that is audible for Aeneas. While the utterance of the ghost appears less expressive than Aeneas' lively human speech, it is also more musical in that it emphasises the skeleton of musical and acoustic parameters that allow the shadow to enter the perceptible realm. The materialisation of the ghost thus involves music in a way that transforms the relation between the imaginary and the real into an ambiguity between the extra- and intra-diegetic roles of sound and music onstage. The presence of the ghost is translated into the presence of sound. The ghost needs to be heard before one can listen to it.

Contrasts of Space and Colour

The second part of *Les Troyens* centres on a conflict between spaces. Aeneas' fate ordains that he will reach Italy, but his love of Dido ties him to Carthage. Troy and Italy, that is to say the absent spaces, exert pressure on the hero, who wishes to stay in the here and now. His fate intervenes through the utterances of supernatural voices. Named and unnamed voices haunt him, calling from offstage. Aeneas' resistance to leaving Carthage eventually provokes Hector's second appearance, this time accompanied by his father, Priam, his sister Cassandra and her groom Chorebus, all of whom died in Troy. This apparition marks a turning point in the plot. After all the authorities from Troy are summoned onto the scene, their calls finally reach Aeneas.

The ghosts literally leave him no escape. A choir of bass voices opens the scene, incanting his name on the note D that remains present as the ghosts' reciting tone throughout the scene. The veiled ghost of Priam then appears on the left side of the stage and pronounces a first call on the same pedal D. He urges Aeneas not to postpone the departure, joined by the as-yet-invisible Chorebus, Hector and Cassandra. After these interpellations, a crown of pale flames lights up on Priam's head. He identifies himself to Aeneas and conveys his message: 'I am Priam, you have to live and part.' Aghast, Aeneas recoils from the spectre, only to encounter Chorebus on the other side of the stage. The ghost appears and identifies himself in the same way and continues the message: 'you have to part and conquer'. Again, Aeneas recedes, but this time the ghosts of Hector and Cassandra hinder his way. Aeneas immediately recognises them and they finish the message, always remaining on the pedal tone *d*: 'you have to conquer and found!' Aeneas bows to his fate and awakens his men to leave for Italy.

The crowns that make the ghosts visible epitomise the embedding of the opera into a framework of energy transfer. The flames use the same technology as do manometric flames that came into use at this time for scientific instruments. The Paris-based instrument maker Rudolph Koenig, with whom Berlioz was acquainted through the eminent violin builder Jean-Baptiste Vuillaume, used such flames in his *analyseur du timbre d'un son*, a device that showed the strength of the harmonic components in a musical tone with the help of such a flame. A sung vowel, for instance, would be rendered as a series of smaller and larger flames in a turning mirror next to the flame. The drawings arising from such analyses circulated widely, appearing as rows of flames of different height, although the image actually was made of a chronological decomposition of different states in one single flame.[42]

Although we can exclude the idea that Berlioz connected the appearance of the spectres to a notion of the spectrum – the transfer of this term to acoustics only happened in the twentieth century – the detail is nevertheless characteristic for the concept of timbre at stake in this scene. In Koenig's *analyseur* the vowels had to be sung on the same pitch, for the pitches of the analysing devices could not be changed, yet the flames showed the vowel sounds to be composed differently.[43] Similarly, the entrance of each ghost is accompanied by a chord on the pedal tone *d*, on which they also recite their message. As their utterances become more and more pressing, the harmonic tension in the chords rises. The ghosts appear as instantiations of the voice of fate that is articulated more and more urgently, yet without changing its core message: Aeneas must part.

No less significant in this scene is the orchestration. Along with the flames, four solo violins play piercing flageolet-chords, indicated in the score as *sons harmoniques*, whose high pitches stand out against the predominantly low register of the orchestral sound. More importantly, flageolet-tones come close to a single frequency and their sound contains

---

[42] On Koenig, see Pantalony 2009.

[43] Koenig later builds resonators whose size can be changed, thereby making them able to react to different frequency components in incoming sounds. He calls the corresponding complex of resonators 'analyseur du timbre des sons'. On the history of the resonator see Pantalony 2009, Kursell 2018.

little noise. This makes them particularly hard to localise for human hearing. The acoustic marker for the ghost's visibility withdraws spatial cues from the sound.

Orchestration is the main device in this scene. It opposes a non-localisable, insisting tone to the haecceity and fluidity associated with human actors. The ways in which Berlioz achieves this can be seen as substantiating the concept of timbre he coined in his *Grand traité*. In the introduction he explains that the aim of orchestration is to produce 'impressions *sui generis* (whether or not motivated by expressive intention) and independent of the three other musical powers [*sc.* melody, harmony, rhythm]'.[44] With this remark he declares timbre to be a factor independent of the overall musical texture that has its own specific relation to expression. Acting as a truly independent force, timbre's expressive value is described by a gradient of its own that ranges from paucity to prevalence over the other musical powers.

The second part of *Les Troyens* translates this into the central topic of spatial conflict. The intervention of 'fate' is characterised by a zero-degree of spatial orientation. Sounds in the second ghost scene create a tension without melodic change and localisable movement. The force that encircles Aeneas has no spatial identity and can appear everywhere. The depth of the pedal tone *d* reaches beyond the regular orchestral range, as the double basses tune their lowest string a second down to the contra-octave *d* during this passage. The flageolet notes, as well as the other instrumental colours, such as the bass clarinet and the four horns, which this time all transpose at the same pitch to support the pedal tone, are chosen to create 'ghostly music', as Berlioz describes it in the *Grand traité*. The voices of the ghosts recite their texts on their lower range. The middle range, in which human hearing distinguishes acoustic parameters particularly well, is left empty.

Within this setting, the pedal note acts as a motif that is reminiscent of Aeneas' fate. As shown, this pedal's function is not purely harmonic. Rather, one might refer to it as a *note-son*, a term coined by Jean Barraqué to connote a recurring pitch that becomes notable within a sonic environment.[45] For this, the *note-son* oscillates between functioning as a pitch and a timbre. Similarly, the pedal on *d* is motivated in two ways. Even though it is at times disconnected from the overall harmonic

---

[44] Hector Berlioz, *Grand traité d'instrumentation et d'orchestration modernes*, ed. Peter Bloom (NBE 24), 5.

[45] Barraqué (1962) calls this a *note-son*, as opposed to the *note-ton* that refers to the note as a symbolic element.

progression, it must continue because it allows the ghosts to articulate their messages. In addition, it gains a characteristic colour through the fact that the low *d* marks the low end of the voices' articulatory range where they seem to neither speak nor sing. What is more, the *note-son*'s persistence adds to the rising harmonic tension. Remaining constant against the background of chromatically shifting diminished seventh-chords and an oscillation between harmonically unstable chords with low functional tension and a high degree of dissonance, the pedal becomes all the more insistent. Only after turning the *d* into a dominant does the last utterance resolve to G major on the word 'found'. Its semantic function is now exhausted. With the resolution to the tonic, the call is no longer necessary. Motion returns on stage as Aeneas takes action again.

Berlioz earned enthused reactions from his contemporaries for his use of pedals in *Les Troyens*. Joseph d'Ortigue, who attended the dress rehearsal of the 1863 premiere of the opera's second part, wrote to Berlioz: 'What an [achievement in] instrumentation as that of the Septet with its pedal c in the treble, and these pedals in the low registers with the *piano* [sounds of the] bass drum!'[46] It is characteristic that d'Ortigue mentions both the pedal as device and the instrumentation in one breath, and that he refers to pedals in the bass and the treble. Julian Rushton has pointed to the central role of both types of pedals for the composer, noting that Berlioz prefers pedal tones with a freely floating character that reinforce harmonic ambiguity rather than stabilising harmony.[47]

A comparison of the ghost scene with the Septet reveals that the pedal tones relate to opposite expressive values in both scenes, although each scene in its own way creates a sense of immobility. In the Septet, all the main actors – Trojans and Carthaginians – join in a hymn to the sea that praises the beauty of the moment. The gently rocking movement of the waves epitomises their desire for the situation to endure. Their simultaneously moving voices every now and then create dissonances with the pedal tone, when the harmony oscillates between F major and its submediant D♭ major. The resulting dissonances, however, seem absorbed by the feeling of rest suggested by the movement to and fro. The human voices that gather in the middle range create a dense sound as opposed to the 'hollow' sound that will later characterise the ghost scene. In this praise of Venus and her element, the sea, the question of whether the pedal tone can be said to represent fate remains ambiguous. Just as the pedal note *d* confirms its function of embodying fate when it disappears, resolving to *g*, so the strikes of the bass drum that are

[46] Berlioz 1995, 6:504. [47] See Rushton 1983, 111.

interpolated within the vocal harmony only reveal a threatening character when they reappear at the end of the act. Now they introduce the uncanny use of a hidden tamtam on stage. Hitting Aeneas' weapons, Mercury produces a tamtam sound – that seems to come from far away, before he calls: 'Italie'.

Calling the pedal a *note-son* emphasises a colouristic use of pitch. Additional evidence for this view may be found in Berlioz's reaction to an invention of nineteenth-century instrument making: pneumatic instruments with freely vibrating metal tongues that could produce stable tones for an unlimited time that allowed for nuancing in intensity. In the second edition of his *Grand traité*, Berlioz included a chapter about new inventions, where he mentioned an instrument called '*mélodium avec prolongement*'.[48] This instrument added a 'prolongation' register to a regular harmonium or piano. In the regular pianoforte, raising dampers by using the sustaining pedal brought the inconvenience that all notes would resonate. Lifting a single damper had previously required keeping the key pressed down, and the same was true for the harmonium, where the key had to be pressed to keep a tone constant. This prolongation register instead freed the fingers from this task and opened up new possibilities of combining long and short notes. The exploration of pedal notes in a musical setting therefore profited from this new invention, as Berlioz demonstrates, showing in particular examples of treble notes to be held by the prolongation mechanism. In this way, these keyboard instruments would finally enable composers to probe orchestral effects, as Berlioz declared enthusiastically. His scepticism towards the piano, whose sounds did not ostensibly allow distinguishing layers of sounds, seemed remedied.

The mechanism used for the prolongation functioned using knee levers, both in its piano and harmonium versions. Berlioz hastened to add that, as for the regular harmonium – or, as the instrument produced by his favourite brand Edouard Alexandre is called, the *orgue mélodium* – the prolonged notes could be modified in their intensity. The *orgue mélodium*, he emphasised, was 'expressive': it possessed crescendo and decrescendo, applicable to any note while resounding. As opposed to regular organ pipes, in which changes in dynamics would destabilise pitch, instruments with freely vibrating tongs like the *orgue mélodium* allow for dynamic nuancing that leaves pitch unaffected.[49] With these instruments' constant

---

[48] Berlioz, *Grand traité* (NBE 24), 472–4 (L'orgue mélodium d'Alexandre) and 475–7 (Pianos et mélodiums d'Alexandre à son prolongé).

[49] On the history of these instruments see Restle 2002.

but nuanced tones, the pedals in Berlioz's musical setting share important features. They are fully flexible in their expression, yet their length can be adjusted to the needs of the dramatic situation, rather than being restricted by human breath. This very feature allows pedal tones in *Les Troyens* to embody fate and its inhumane message that forces Aeneas to renounce his love and his comfort in the here and now.

Whenever Berlioz commented on new technological developments in keyboard aerophones, he emphasised the possibility of nuancing the tone. He notes this for the newly developed swelling stop in Aristide Cavaillé-Coll's organs; for the metal tongs in the *orgue mélodium*; and he also noted in the *Grand traité* that the melodium was often portable, therefore introducing an additional spatial index to its use: 'a greater or smaller volume of sound can be obtained depending on the way the feet propel the bellows mechanism and on the location of the instrument'.[50] All these features resurface in the first part of *Les Troyens*, where he uses the concept of a fade to stage the ghost of Hector. In the second part, by contrast, the possibility of indexing space through intensity is inverted. Here, the voice of fate has no spatial index and therefore cannot undergo nuances in its intensity. Tension is created through harmony and omnipresence of the sound.

Perhaps most importantly, Berlioz is interested in expression as it is embodied in such technical innovation because these instruments externalise the main index of spatial perception. In the *Symphonie fantastique*, intensity could be described as an index of the outside world for the sensing subject. With 'expressive' instruments, by contrast, intensity is now a matter of regulation and control. Listener, composer and musician participate in the same flux of expression. 'Expression' in these instruments, in turn, is synonymous with dynamics. In short, expression is the result of externalising the nuancing of intensity.

Against this background, Berlioz's notion of timbre as 'impression *sui generis*' obtains a new meaning. As the two scenes analysed above demonstrate, timbre takes the lead: first, in the subtraction of time – when the beauty of the moment is celebrated against the will of fate – then, in the subtraction of space when Aeneas is finally forced to submit to his fate. In both situations, the human actors are no longer just witnesses to an acoustic presence. Instead, they act against or in accordance with the voice of fate that is unnoticeably present or dominant in the musical sound. Accordingly, the pedal is either masked, through integrating it

---

[50] Macdonald 2002, 311.

into the overall harmonic immobility, or it is bent towards a resolution, through accepting it as the harmonic function of the dominant. The co-presence of humans and supernatural elements now reaches beyond a dichotomy of the dead and the living. Timbre here contributes to creating yet another function for the imaginary. While the implosion of the dichotomy between the dead and the living sets the warriors of Troy in action and makes them face an as-yet unknown future in Rome, it leaves the Carthaginians without any option to act. They can only watch the boats that have left their shores. Yet, instead of acting, they are seized by a state of 'clairvoyance', as one could say using a notion developed by Gilles Deleuze for a type of (cinematic) image that emerges from cutting perception of its prolongation into action.[51] Bound to remain in their space, the Carthaginians see the future that will turn the conflict into one between their state and that of Rome.

Conclusion: Spatial Imagination and Experiment

Imagination as a mode of producing the new is what intrigued Boulez about the work of Berlioz; however, that which is new escapes prescription. Writing a treatise about instrumentation, Berlioz admitted that good instrumentation requires inventiveness, even genius, but these could not be taught. Some of the conditions for the emergence of new and convincing orchestration were nevertheless accessible to description and to control. To become a visionary for musical sounds meant first of all to use one's hearing. It required an awareness of the flows of sound that take place in a performance. Here the listeners' role was not much different from that of the musician and, especially, the conductor, as the use of hearing is not restricted to either of these roles but must be part of all of them. Its function and tasks are imposed by the musical sound as soon as this sound begins. The exploration of musical sounds is shared by all parties.

If – as suggested by Magendie – experimentation had to become a means to explore what is not yet known, this also holds to some extent for the musical exploration Berlioz envisages in his composition. Space as an object of exploratory experimentation was shown to be problematic. For the Romantic subject, space was not a given. The need to explore, experience and construct space comes to the fore when Berlioz mixes his precise

---

[51] Deleuze 1997, 18–24.

empirical observation of hearing with his visionary grasp of sound. When the real and the imaginary become indistinguishable, as happens in the musical description of hearing subjects as well as in the liminal figure of the ghost, the exploration of the auditory space becomes particularly productive. Orientation in space can be achieved through a distinction of acoustic cues that create points of perception, and the opposition of absence and presence in space can be stages with the help of timbral features. Both are recurring issues of Berlioz's music, as I have tried to show in this chapter. Within his peculiar mode of exploration, the listener could join the composer in exploring these questions. They could experience how intensities guide or mislead us about the distances of sounds, they could witness the acoustic emergence of a figure that has no bodily existence, and they could follow acoustic properties of a sound with enhanced individuality and spatial identity in opposition to a sound that lacks these characteristics. In each case, the listener would not be left with their individual interpretation of the musical processes they heard, but would have to compare their actual experience with the conditions of sensory perception more generally. If this does not translate into science, it nevertheless approaches an empirical mode: exploration through experimentation.

Today Berlioz's explorations of auditory space seem accessible to scientific scrutiny. Spatial hearing is understood to be composed of a multifactorial input from intensities, difference in phase and intensity between both ears, and timbral filtering through the shape of our ears. During Berlioz's lifetime, however, experimental research on auditory spatial perception barely got further than Magendie's first findings. Too little was known about what constitutes sound and how sound was perceived. A decussation of the auditory nerves – that is, a connection that links the two ears before they reach the brain – was only discovered long after Berlioz had died. In 1875, Lord Rayleigh would still summarise the state of research on auditory space perception in a pessimistic tone:

I am obliged to leave the question in rather an unsatisfactory state, for my calculations are very far from explaining the facts; in fact, they rather go to take away the force from what had hitherto been supposed to be the explanation. At one time I was almost inclined to suppose that we did not distinguish through our ears at all, but in some other mysterious way.[52]

---

[52] Rayleigh 1875, 79.

A clearly comprehensible concept of auditory space was unavailable, and an experiential realm, such as the one Berlioz accessed in the Paris Opéra, did not translate into workable scientific concepts. Both for him and for his listeners, then, Berlioz's explorations of auditory space had to remain within the realm of 'inventive "madness"'.

6 | From Distant Sounds to Aeolian Ears
Ernst Kapp's Auditory Prosthesis

DAVID TRIPPETT

Introduction

A well-known depiction of collective listening on the operatic stage occurs in Act I of Wagner's *Lohengrin* (1850): the Herald asks the assembled Brabantians whether there is a champion among them to defend Elsa against the accusation by her former suitor, Friedrich, that she murdered her younger brother Gottfried, the Duke of Brabant. These are uncomfortable moments for Elsa. There is an eerie silence after the first question ('he is surely a long way off and could not hear'), and there appears – for a time at least – to be no reply to the second question either (Example 6.1). Wagner's stage directions describe these as a 'long silence' and a 'long, awkward silence' respectively,[1] implying that the growing tension of the second silence – with added tritone in the bass tuba – is akin to that moment after an awkward exchange in public, where the tumbleweed rolls, the wind blows. A doubtful four-part chorus enters *piano* after both points of asking, confirming retrospectively that it was principally the collective that had been listening.

Quite how the Herald's question, via a four-strong trumpet call, reaches Lohengrin nearly 400 miles away has intrigued media theorists for some time – with suggestions ranging from the use of radio waves to the telephone and an extended organic nervous system.[2] For present purposes, I am more concerned with the theories of listening that such a moment suggests, and how the emergent concept of aurality, defined for our purposes as the phenomenal and discursive field of sounding culture, establishes common ground and even a certain reciprocity with contemporary discourses of signalling within the physical and biological sciences.

---

[1] 'Langes Stillschweigen' / 'Wiederum langes, gespanntes Stillschweigen', *Lohengrin*, Act I scene 2. See Wagner 1911–14, 2:72.

[2] On radio waves, see Kittler 1987, 206. On the telephone, see Rehding 2006, 266. On the extended organic nervous system, see Trippett 2013, 377–9.

Example 6.1 Richard Wagner, *Lohengrin*, Act I scene 2, bb. 551–575

Petitions to 'listen' in a libretto are happily ignored by characters within opera plots. Dramaturgically, this stokes narrative tension. Witness the Rhinemaidens' forlorn entreaty against taking the gold ('Höre, was wir dich heissen!') or Wotan's threat against Loge to keep his word ('Jetzt hör', Störrischer! Halte Stich!'). When warnings *are* taken seriously, they tend merely to fulfil established plot lines, e.g. the Queen's caution for Anna to abandon her son in Marschner's *Hans Heiling* ('Hör' auf mein Wort, Betörtes Menschenkind, Ich bin gekommen dich zu warnen'). Anna had already rediscovered her love for Konrad before the Queen warded her away from Heilig; her words become a redundant prop that brings about what was already in train. The imperative to *listen!* is rarely diagnostic, in other words, and remains on the surface of an operatic narrative.

With diegetic objects to listen *to*, moments of listening in opera can also convey a character's sensory orientation, placing them in spatialised, tactile communication with their environment: Tamino hears a flute ('Was hör ich? Wo bin ich? Welch' unbekannter Ort!'); Siegfried hears a bird ('Du holdes Vöglein! Dich hört' ich noch nie: bist du im Wald hier daheim?'); Gurnemanz hears Christian bells as Kundry receives her baptism ('Mittag: – Die Stund ist da'); Pelléas asks Mélisande if she hears the closing of the castle doors ('Écoute! Écoute!'). Such statements direct the audience's attention to sonic objects as much as the character's. By drawing attention to the non-diegetic scene as something artificial they arguably give rise to a certain self-consciousness, making listeners self-aware of being listening subjects within a performance. In each case, sensory immersion on stage conveys a character's proprioception, serving as a point of orientation wherein characters cannot control their reaction; the conventions of stage realism dictate that they must ask after sound or noise rising above the non-diegetic threshold, ever that *frisson nouveau* for an audience.

As inserted layers of media, diegetic sounds provide tactile moments of distraction, then, moments that for Walter Benjamin 'should be conceived as a physiological phenomenon'.[3] He reads sensory attention and distraction as part of the currency of epiphany, a kind of corporeal catharsis inherent within our relation to any media where distraction is accompanied by cognitive realisation. Beyond an idealist metaphysics that understands 'listening as thinking', in other words, modern concepts of listening relate to sense organs and must harbour an irreducibly physical element, what Helmholtz – perhaps the most widely read acoustician and physiologist of the nineteenth century – called 'the corporeal ear' (*das körperliche Ohr*) in contradistinction to 'the mental ear' (*das*

---

[3] Benjamin 2008, 56.

geistige Ohr).[4] Yet *how* a character on stage listens, and the physiological status – if any – of their ears, is less easy to grasp.[5] It relates in the first instance to contemporary discourses of audition, itself a reflexive historical category, but one that draws together in a continuous movement the separate discursive layers of operatic narrative and empirical science. By positing a structural link between activities of the stage and in the stalls, this approach offers up a liminal space wherein each can be read in terms of the other: historical operatic narrative vis-à-vis contemporary scientific understanding; acts of performance vis-à-vis acts of witnessing.

Even if we accept this approach, to listen is, at first blush, to be attentive, passive and, by implication, silent.[6] Yet the fabric of nineteenth-century opera, as a continuous audio-visual experience, is bound to active powers of expression, movement and persuasion – qualities basic to the semiotic exchange within which opera's narrative structures can function: from non-diegetic topoi to *Leitmotive*, or – adopting contemporary language – what E. T. A. Hoffman called the combination of opera's 'individualized language' of word, action, and music 'with the universal language of music'.[7] In the context of music's expressive powers, traceable to the hypertrope of Orpheus, to depict the sound of *listening* in opera would be to depict music's negative or opposite – the silent condition of one's openness to receiving auditory expression. It is music's vacuum. Such logic holds that it is counterintuitive to portray auditory attention because sound itself is both its object and its principal means of expression.[8] The channels are in conflict.

---

[4] On listening as thinking see Bonds 2006, 29–43; Helmholtz 1863, 456. For an extensive discussion of Helmholtz's dualism and his positioning between discursive fields, see Steege 2012, 58–79.

[5] In an enquiry into the semiotic levels of Wagner's *Leitmotive*, Edward Cone asked what level of awareness characters have of the 'denotative significance – nay the very existence – of the motifs they employ'. His concept of 'motivic emergence', where symbolic sounds emerge into the world of actual sounds while retaining their symbolic character (e.g. Siegfried's horn call), is based on a deductive reading of individual characters' psychology – awareness, memory, comprehension – across the history of such motives. See Cone 2010, 80–105.

[6] This obtains principally in relation to listening in the historical age of the musical work, an 'ideology' of aesthetics and etiquette mapped out by Lydia Goehr (2007). But see also Johnson's source-rich account of the shifting listening practices at the Paris Opéra, and the competing hierarchies of attentiveness and individual judgment vis-à-vis the influence of received opinion: 'audiences now paid at least as much attention to the performance as to the notable in the boxes' (Johnson 1995, 69).

[7] Hoffmann 1989, 152.

[8] Illustrating the extent to which listening *within* music is a deceptively simple idea, Jean-Luc Nancy (2008), after considering a composer's tempo marking of *ascoltando* (listening) – music

Yet listening has always been a two-way street. It involves actively making sense of what is heard as well as receiving any intrinsic properties of the sound produced. This is perhaps most pronounced in verbal speech, though structural linguists from Saussure to Jakobson have long maintained that all communication rests on a principle of common coding.[9] In his *Sensualist Philosophy* of 1876, the American theologian Robert Dabney underscored this principle in response to the question: 'Do [physical] sensations cause volitions?' His negative answer was justified by a simple illustration:

Let us suppose that the sturdy Briton knows only his mother-tongue; and then shout the insult in French. No flush burns in his face; no muscle is moved to strike. But now let a bystander translate the insult into English, reciting it in the softest tone, and the forcible manifestations of anger are at once made. Why this? Evidently because sound was not even the occasion, much less the cause, of resentment, at all: but *an idea*, a thought, of which the sound was the symbol.[10]

Beyond the frame of language and representation, Edward T. Cone made much the same point for our comprehension of musical sounds when he identified 'a complicated interchange between hearing the music and knowing the music', which amounts to passively receiving the sound and mentally retracing the composition, which would then recursively feed back into one's experience of future hearings.[11]

Both examples touch on what we could call *listener*-response theory, and while the methods of such criticism emanate from the Constance School of *Rezeptionsästhetik* and reader-response theorists of the 1970s and 1980s, such methods find a number of nineteenth-century precedents. A decade before Charles Wheatstone's playful 'experiments in audition' reported how cranium resonance appears to augment sound, the German political economist Adam Mueller argued in his 1816 essay on 'The Art of Listening' that 'to be receptive, to *receive* with understanding and dignity is everywhere just as great an art as to act, or to *give* with intelligence, with taste, and with power'.[12] In essence, his thesis was that the arts of oratory and listening were interdependent for those on stage. But he also effectively presented a typology of listening – fully a century and a half before Theodor W. Adorno's sociological types – in which he distinguished the phenomenon of collective attention from individual perception.[13] While,

---

to be played as though listening – concluded that the implied listening subject could only be the music itself, that the 'musical work' is listening to itself.

[9] See Jakobson 1971; 1987, 451.   [10] Dabney 1876, 150–1.   [11] Cone 2010, 59.
[12] Wheatstone 2011a; A. Müller 1996, 131.   [13] Adorno 1989, 2.

in theatres, the best actors listen through social codes of response – laughter, coughing, silence – 'a large assembly may be overwhelmed by the power of speech in such a way that it forgets the conventional response, that it listens as with a single ear and every breath is concerned only with how to fit in the speech's occasional pauses'.[14] This breathless silence would seem to be written into the score in the response Wagner assigns his Brabantian crowd in *Lohengrin*. Its focus on attention to the absence of audible sound (from the grail knight) seemingly foregrounds the need – in Wheatstone's words – for 'an instrument which, from its rendering audible the weakest sounds, may with propriety be named a Microphone'.[15] In such a reading, Elsa's technological problem is as much one of listening as it is of signal transmission, in other words.

Auditory Science and the Lute of 3,000 Strings

Since Ernst Chladni's experiments with sound figures on glass in 1787, the physiology of the ear has been a corollary to the study of acoustics. It was of course Helmholtz who was chiefly responsible for disseminating the view, advanced in a public lecture at Bonn University during the winter of 1857, that there is a physical basis to our perception of harmonic consonance in music. As is well known, he articulated a purely physiological theory for how complex waves were analysed into their constituent periodic forms, after Joseph Fourier's *Théorie analytique de la chaleur* (1822). This explained the impression of consonance and dissonance by a theory of ratios or coincidence between periodic frequencies, that is, by the coincidence or separation of harmonics. Non-coincident harmonics cause beats and unevenness through the mixture of different tones that occur, and these are manifest through physical sensations within the Organ of Corti. By comparison with the work of later researchers, notably Carl Stumpf's theory of fusion (*Verschmelzung*), it becomes clear, however, that this was not a theory of consonance, but a theory of dissonance, in which consonance is defined negatively by the absence of physiologically determinable dissonant features.[16]

---

[14] A. Müller 1996, 135.   [15] Wheatstone 2011a, 32.

[16] Stumpf's concept of fusion is first advanced in the second volume of *Tonpsychologie* (1883–90); the two tones of perfect consonances are perceived as a single entity, where their degree of consonance is determined by the integer ratios of their frequencies. For the relationship between Helmholtz and Stumpf, see Motte-Haber 2012, 3–16.

On this material basis, John Tyndall, the English physicist remembered principally for his work on heat and infrared radiation, gave a series of public lectures at London's Royal Institution in 1867 entitled 'Sound' in which he described the laws that determine the physical behaviour of vibrational frequencies under different conditions, their propagation through air, water and solid matter, as well as the physiological structure of the ear and its means of transmitting sound to the auditory nerve. (It may be no coincidence that earlier that year, Giuseppe Verdi's latest opera *Don Carlos* would open by establishing an auditory perspective within space and time; the eponymous bass first becomes rooted, dramaturgically, by listening to the dying strains of an offstage horn-call: '[*he stops and listens*] . . . the sound . . . dies away among the deep shadows . . . [*he listens*] All is silent!') Tyndall had read Helmholtz's *Die Lehre von den Tonempfindungen* (1863) with its diagnosis of the automatic mechanism of sympathetic resonance, and praised the 'thoroughness and excellence of the work' in his preface.[17] By co-opting the physiology of the ear within a system of physical laws, his approach tacitly rejected the contemporary doctrine of psychophysics, representing instead a mechanical epistemology of sound perception in which the ear becomes a physical instrument, representative of a view traceable to the French monists from Julien Offray de la Mettrie to the positivism of August Comte: that the human body is a self-regulating machine that obeys the same Newtonian laws as must any matter.

Here is Tyndall's summary of the transmission of force that results in the perception of sound:

when the tympanic membrane receives a shock, that shock is transmitted through the series of bones [hammer, anvil, and stirrup], and is concentrated on the membrane against which the base of the stirrup bone is planted. That membrane transfers the shock to the water of the labyrinth, which, in its turn, transfers it to the nerves.[18]

Based on the principle of blind causality, this is little more than a summary of existing knowledge. But it is the stark absence of mental activity that gives us pause, for the interior perception of music is intimately, and not straightforwardly, linked to its material status as vibrational stimuli – it's easy to get lost in this inward space, in other words, and the inner ear has, for centuries, been likened to a 'labyrinth' for reasons poetic as well as

---

[17] Tyndall 1867, viii.   [18] Tyndall 1867, 324.

mimetic.[19] ('The Labyrinth' is of course the anatomical term for this region of the inner ear.)

Yet following the work of Ernst Heinrich Weber on tactile sense perception during the 1830s, the question of how sound sensations were transmitted to the brain attracted a number of mechanistic theories from Anglo-German scientists that rejected the basis of sensory perception in the psyche alone.[20] And there is flinty common ground here between the so-called scientific materialists (Ludwig Büchner, Jacob Moleschott, Karl Vogt) and the more respected academic psychologists centred at the Berlin Academy of Sciences (Helmholtz, Emil du Bois-Reymond, Ernst von Brücke and Carl Ludwig – the so-called 'physiological reductionists'). The latter unveiled a new programme for physiology in 1847 that denounced *Naturphilosophie*, vitalism and speculative metaphysics just as vehemently as did materialists, even if materialists constituted 'intellects of a lower order' due to their insufficiently critical attitudes towards empirical methods.[21] Such distinctions detracted little from the fact that an array of scientists involved in anatomy had been working on the assumption of a mechanical body conceivable as an assemblage. This material model of the body had the character of orthodoxy, rather than radicalism, within non-theological circles, lending credibility to Hoffmann's playful deceit of Olympia as a passable, lovable human in *Der Sandmann* (1816) or Carlo Collodi's animate puppet *Pinocchio* (1883).[22]

But materialism is perhaps a misleading term to the extent that its mid-century proponents were still driven by *ideas* in their pursuit of an understanding of the world. And as Frederick Gregory argued long ago, they were all scholarly children of Ludwig Feuerbach, for whom: 'Truth, reality, and sensation are identical.'[23] A striking case – coeval with Helmholtz's research into the physiology of the ear at Bonn University between 1855 and 1858 – is Heinrich Czolbe, perhaps the most fanatical academic physician of the century to pursue a worldview exclusively through principles of sensation. Czolbe's Sensationalism (*Sensualismus*) constituted a monist stance – advanced in his *Neue Darstellung des Sensualismus* (1855) – that sought to consolidate into a single worldview what he felt had been advanced only in discontinuous fragments by figures such as Feuerbach, Vogt and Moleschott. 'Clear concepts' are only accessible via direct sensations, he maintained, where what is supersensible amounts to an 'unclear concept':

---

[19] Politzer 1907/13, 1:27.   [20] Weber 1834.   [21] Merz 1903–14, 3:560.   [22] See Pizzi 2012.
[23] Feuerbach 1986, 51.

If we want to clarify by deduction what is unknown, this can only occur through mediation with what is known, not through what is again unknown. If someone wishes to make a fluid clear, and at the same time casts something unclear into it, one would naturally call him foolish. Yet a similar absurdity appears to govern our common logic.[24]

It is on the basis of such logic that Czolbe articulated a worldview based exclusively on immediate sensation. He argued that this, or sensory qualities, are the effect of stimuli propagated mechanically in precisely the form in which they are created and received, i.e. unchanged; hence the quality of sound (or colour, or heat) is somehow inherent in the very form of its propagation along nerves.[25] It was, in effect, a theory of psychic automatism – the 'making-material' of thought and expression – half a century before André Breton's surrealist manifesto.[26]

In his subsequent monograph, *Die Grenzen und der Ursprung der menschlichen Erkenntniss im Gegensatze zu Kant und Hegel* (1865), Czolbe ignored the complaint that there was a great discrepancy between the tiny area of stimulation within the optical and auditory nerves compared to the powerful impression received by our eyes and ears, declaring simply that the discrepancy 'seems to me explicable through the mechanical propagation of disturbance or outward projection'.[27] He also maintained that the world in its physical condition is eternal, and disregarded the counter-proofs of science as 'mere illusion, which on further investigation would disappear'.[28] These arguments failed to persuade a majority of respondents, and Friedrich Lange, the leading mid-century historian of materialism, impugned the theories of unchanging matter and individual character of sense propagation as two 'incurable weaknesses' of Czolbe's philosophy.[29]

---

[24] 'Wenn wir Unbekanntes durch Schlüsse erklären wollen, kann dies doch nur durch Vermittelung des Bekannten, nicht aber wiederum durch Unbekanntes geschen. Will jemand eine Flüssigkeit klar machen und wirft dabei Unklares hinein, wird man ihn doch thöricht nennen. Eine ähnliche Absurdität aber scheint in der gewöhnlichen Logik zu herrschen.' Czolbe 1855, 2.

[25] Czolbe 1855, 13–14.

[26] Czolbe's philosophy should be distinguished from the more recent concept in social psychology of conscious automatism, a deterministic philosophy that holds humans are conscious but respond as automata according to prior conditioning; free will, in this context, is seen as illusory. See particularly Kane 2011.

[27] 'Die gewaltige Größe des Sehfeldes beim Sehen und auch des Tonraumes bem Anhören von Musik im Verhältnis zu den ungemein kleinen gereizten Stellen im Verlaufe des She- und Hörnerven scheint mir durch obige mechanische Ausbreitung der Störung, oder Projection nach Aussen erklärlich.' Czolbe 1865, 205.

[28] Friedrich A. Lange's ([1865] 1880, 2:291) characterisation .   [29] Lange [1865] 1880, 2:291.

Could directed attention also become explicable through physiology? With a similar reluctance to embrace concepts of a supersensible mind in dialogue with the sensory world, the philosopher-psychologist Georg Elias Müller offered a more metaphysical theory of perception in his *Zur Theorie der sinnlichen Aufmerksamkeit* (1873). Relying on neurophysiological speculation, Müller argued that 'the capacity to affect the soul, which *certain physical processes in the brain* possess, will be increased or decreased or entirely suspended under the influence of the activity of sensory attention'.[30] In other words, attention directed to sounds – whether internally or externally directed thinking: the Brabantians listening out for Elsa's champion – enacts physical changes in the listening body, rendering auditory perception, at root, still a material form of perception in Müller's schema.

There is, of course, a rich array of possible contributors to the Anglo-German discourse on theories of audition; returning to Tyndall's mechanical epistemology, it is perhaps with such debates in mind that he admits the process of sound transmission is 'not direct' within the inner ear but in passing through the membranous labyrinth, where the numerous hair-like appendages are set in motion according to their individual periodic frequencies, he refers to the central agent of signal processing, the Organ of Corti, as a kind of mechanical technology, namely:

a wonderful organ, which is to all appearance a musical instrument, with its chords so stretched as to accept vibrations of different periods, and transmit them to the nerve filaments which traverse the organ. Within the ears of men, and without their knowledge or contrivance, *this lute of 3,000 strings* has existed for ages, accepting the music of the outer world and rendering it fit for reception by the brain. Each musical tremor which falls upon this organ selects from its tensioned fibres the one appropriate to its own pitch, and throws that fibre into unisonant vibration.[31]

While a more common metaphor was the overstrung piano (traceable to 1737, and notably employed in Helmholtz's *Tonempfindungen*),[32] Tyndall's 'lute of 3,000 strings', poetically responsive to the slightest external stimulation by each string's predetermined frequency response,

---

[30] 'Die Wirkungsfähigkeit auf die Seele, welche gewisse physische Vorgänge im Centralorgane besitzen, [wird] durch die Thätigkeit der sinnlichen Aufmerksamkeit beeinflusst, vermehrt oder vermindert oder ganz aufgehoben.' G. Müller 1873, 1–2. Emphasis added.

[31] Tyndall 1867, 325. My emphasis.

[32] The metaphor of the piano's set of tensile strings, progressively ordered by resonating frequency, and hence capable of analysing the mass of acoustic vibrations projected onto a piano – per a Fourier analysis – would be adopted by Helmholtz, Herbert Spencer and James Sully among others.

belongs to a broader archetype of instruments that draw on naturally occurring sound. The oldest model is more familiar under a different name, that most natural and most automatic of instruments: the Aeolian harp. Other scientists made the same connection more directly. The German acoustician Franz Josef Pisco asked rhetorically: 'Can we not conceive of the hairs of Corti as a harp in the ear that is excited to sympathetic vibration through resonance?'[33] The Leipzig-based physiologist Johann N. Czermak mooted the same analogy in a series of popular lectures from 1869: 'while the rods of Corti, corresponding to the narrowing of the lamina spiralis from bottom to top, gradually decrease in length, they thereby form a kind of regular, graded stringing that we recognise in the *harp* and in the piano. The cochlea is in fact a type of miniature piano with nerves that we have in our ears.'[34] And even from the other side of the Atlantic, in a quite separate discursive field, a Pittsburgh-based medical doctor, William Henry Winslow, declared simply in a treatise on diseases of the ear from 1882, that 'the organ of Corti *is* the Aeolian harp, which responds to every vibration of the tympanic membrane, and furnishes the music of the universe'.[35]

Aeolian Ears

With this substantialist claim, the impulse towards automatic audition voiced by Pisco, Czermak, Winslow et al. broaches the expansive literary trope of the Aeolian harp as the romantic analogue of mind – that figurative mediator between outer motion and inner emotion. In this pairing, both pieces of apparatus – ear and Aeolian harp – are at once deterministic and inscrutable. The harp's response to vibrating air is automatic, irresistible, just like the microscopic hairs lining the cochlea duct; yet the harp brings forth sounds whose emotional effect within the mind are as physically untraceable as the source of the harp's stimulation.

---

[33] 'Und kann man die *Corti*'schen Fasern nicht auch als Harfe im Ohr auffassen, welche durch die Resonanz zu Mitschwingungen angeregt wird?' Pisco, *Die Akustik der Neuzeit* (n.d.). Cited in Kapp 1877, 92.

[34] 'Indem die *Corti*'schen Stäbchen, entsprechend der Verschmälerung der Spiralplatte von unten nach oben, allmälig an Länge abnehmen, so bilden sie eine Art regelmässig abgestufter Besaitung, wir [sic] wir eine solche an der *Harfe* und am Clavier kennen. Ein solches Miniaturclavier mit Nerven ist in der That die *Schnecke*, die wir im Ohre haben.' In Czermak 1869, 51.

[35] Winslow 1882, 73.

The same tension arguably pervades the many poetic evocations of wind harps within European poetry of the early nineteenth century. Samuel Taylor Coleridge lucidly connected nature to the creative imagination through the emblem of a harp that itself is physically part of nature:

And what if all of animated nature
Be but organic Harps diversely fram'd,
That tremble into thought, as o'er them sweeps
Plastic and vast, one intellectual breeze,
At once the Soul of each, and God of all?   (*'The Eolian Harp'*, 1795–96)

And the concealed origins of the breeze, the metaphor par excellence for divine stimulation, finds voice in Novalis's claim for artworks that are ontic, sensorially complete in themselves, independent of any viewers' perception: 'The phenomena must be there, like the notes on an Aeolian harp, all at once, without origin – without revealing their instrument.'[36]

This is not the place to retrace the rich metaphor of the harp in all its poetic resonance.[37] Suffice it to say that in its earliest instantiation in Western literature, the wind harp was a scientific instrument coupled to automation; Athanasius Kircher referred to it a 'self-operating harmonic device' (*machinam harmonicam automatam*) in his *Musurgia Universalis* (1650).[38] Hence the poetic valency of the device, typified in Percy Bysshe Shelley's call to 'make me thy lyre, even as the forest is' or William Wordsworth's *Prelude*, which speaks of 'Aeolian visitations', can be considered chronologically secondary to the scientific principle of an automatic sounding instrument.

By the 1870s, the poetic associations of this fabled instrument were consonant, if also contrastive, with the modern scientific discourse of the wind-harp. Its principle of air-powered sound was not structurally distinct to Cagniard de la Tour's siren, which emitted tiny puffs of air through a perforated rotating disc to create the desired pitch. And in an earlier lecture, Tyndall explains the wind harp as a purely physical apparatus, as a mechanical process, devoid of poetic association:

---

[36] Novalis 1967, 446.

[37] See Brown 1970, 3: 73–90; and Hankins and Silvermann 1995. For a specific study of breeze as a signifier for mental creativity, see M. H. Abrams (1957, 113), for whom it comes as no surprise that the poetry of Coleridge, Wordsworth, Shelley and Byron should be 'so thoroughly ventilated'.

[38] Kircher [1650] 1970, 2:352.

The sounds of the Eolian harp are produced by the division of suitably stretched strings into a greater or less number of harmonic parts by a current of air passing over them. The instrument is usually placed in a window between the sash and frame, so as to leave no way open to the entrance of the air except over the strings.[39]

As if to underscore the de-poeticised conception, he even passes on practical advice about how to build one. Drawing on Wheatstone's writings, he recommends readers find an ill-fitting door, and place a violin string at the bottom of it. 'When the door is shut, the current of air entering beneath sets the string in vibration', he explains, 'and when a fire is in the room, the vibrations are so intense that a great variety of sounds are simultaneously produced.'[40] Practical exemplification here sits alongside poetic association without implying any synthesis.

Perhaps the apex of profane adaptions of the Aoelian harp or 'voice of nature' is the so-called weather harp. Already eighty years old by the time of Tyndall's lectures, this apparatus is indicative of the scientific identity that persisted alongside the poetic conception of automatic harps among Romantic poets in the early decades of the nineteenth century. It had been invented by Giulio Cesare Gattoni in Como back in 1785, and replicated by Wilhelm Hass in Basel two years later. This saw the device adapted to barometric purposes where changes in weather were announced through sound. Haas trained fifteen iron wires – each 320 feet in length, of varying thickness, and positioned two inches apart – from atop his garden house to the bottom of the garden. As Georg Lichtenberg, put it in 1797: 'with every change in the weather, the strings resonate, sometimes we think we hear the sound of a tea kettle before the water come to the boil, sometime a harmonica, here a distant chiming of bells, there an organ. Often the sound is so loud that it disturbs the garden-room concert.'[41] Such comic utilitarianism contrasts with the Greek heritage of Aeolus, ruler of the winds, and his instrument's iconographic precursor, the lyre, which, as Friedrich Kittler once argued, is not to be regarded as a simple tool or instrument for illustrating harmonic ratios but a gateway between what exists and what is perceptible. It is 'a magical thing that connects mathematics to the domain of the senses' because it translates the sensual and the symbolic directly into one another.[42] Likewise, the jangling weather harp, automatically

---

[39] Tyndall 1867, 123. [40] Tyndall 1867, 123.

[41] 'Bey jeder Veränderung des Wetters tönen diese Saiten, bald glaubt man den Ton eines Theekessels zu hören, ehe das Wasser in demselben zum Sieden kommt, bald eine Harmonika, bald ein fernes Geläute, bald eine Orgel. Oft wird das Getöne so stark, daß das Concert im Garten-Saale gestört wird.' Lichtenberg 1789, 130.

[42] Kittler 2006, 56.

responsive to nature's inconstant breezes, was more profound as a gateway between nature and expression than as acoustic sound.

However unlikely the ear-as-automatic-harp may appear alongside emerging theories of psychology, what Helmholtz called 'the mental ear of the imagination', the cultural work accomplished by the analogy presents an unfamiliar model of the listening subject.[43] Listening – in this view – approached the automatism of a mechanical reflex; its pretext was the morphological kinship between the centre of the inner ear and the fabled scientific instrument, but the correspondence exceeds morphology alone, as we shall see.

Organprojektion as Prosthesis

The conceptual basis for reading human organs in terms of technologies – whether mythic or scientific – in the late nineteenth century was established by Ernst Kapp, often credited as the first modern philosopher of technology, after Robert Willis's rhetoric about human mechanics. Kapp was a philologist and historian, who, after being exiled from Germany in 1849, spent sixteen years in Texas before returning to his homeland. Twelve years later he published what would become his most influential work, *Grundlinien einer Philosophie der Technik* (*Principles of a Philosophy of Technology*), a philosophical study of the effects on human society of the use of technology.[44] In this text Kapp first coined the phrase 'philosophy of technology', and for this reason is commonly cited as the originator of this field of inquiry.[45]

In his second chapter, Kapp argued that tools and technologies are projections of human organs: the eye is the model for the camera obscura, the teeth provide a formative image of the saw, the forearm with clenched fist does the same for the stone hammer, the crooked finger becomes a hook, etc. Such relationships, as Kapp puts it, constitute 'a projection of organs [*Organprojektion*] or the mechanical after-image of an organic form'.[46] The book drew broadly on Aristotelian principles of *techné*,[47] and more specifically on Democritus' view of technology as the imitation of nature, in which human house-building and the craft of weaving were

---

[43] '*das geistige Ohr des Vorstellungsvermögens*', Helmholtz [1857] 1884, 1:103. [44] Kapp 1877.

[45] Accounts that cite Kapp as the originator of the field of Philosophy of Technology include: Rapp 1981, 4; Ferré 1988, 10; Fischer 1996, 309; Zoglauer 2002, 9; de Vries 2005, 68; Ropohl 2009, 13.

[46] 'eine Organprojektion oder die mechanische Nachformung einer organischen Form.' Kapp 1877, 71.

[47] The ability to make (something) that depends on correct awareness of, or reasoning about, the thing to be made.

first invented by imitating swallows building their nests, and spiders weaving their webs.

Before going further, there are two aspects of Kapp's projection of organs that need to be separated: on the one hand, he is concerned with technological genesis, where the technical means are seen as unconscious after-images (*Nachbilder*) of human organs. On the other hand, he thematises the cultural dimension of technology, wherein this technical means is posited as a medium through which we recognise ourselves.

The latter is illustrated most clearly in Kapp's view that the locomotive is not distinct from the animal system in principle. Like animals, it 'needs feeding' in order to power the system of locomotion through heat produced by the chemical oxidation process. Helmholtz had made much the same point in the context of thermodynamics (and is cited as *auctoritas* by Kapp),[48] and as early as 1848, du Bois-Reymond's study of animal electricity had emphatically laid the ground for a new organic physics with his conclusion that:

It can no longer remain doubtful what is to be made of the question of whether the difference we recognize as the sole possible one between the processes of dead and inanimate nature in fact actually does exist. *No such difference exists....* The separation between so-called organic and inorganic nature is an entirely arbitrary one.[49]

But for our purposes, it is Kapp's theory of technological genesis that pertains to the fragile notion of automatic listening under discussion. The most widely accepted instance of organ projection, one that Kapp cites simply as 'obvious', is that between the nervous system and the networks of telegraphic communication being established throughout Europe and North America during the middle of the century. This parallel – asserted by such respected academic physiologists as du Bois-Reymond, Helmholtz and Werner Siemens – serves to authenticate his conception of organ projection: 'nerves *are* cable installations of the animal body,

---

[48] Helmholtz's view, at least in the context of thermodynamics, was on the brink of a non-humanist subject in 1854: 'the animal body ... does not differ from the steam engine as regards the manner in which it obtains heat and force, but ... in the manner in which the force gained is to be made use of.' Helmholtz, 'On the Interaction of the Natural Forces' [1854], in Cahan 1995, 37.

[49] 'Es kann daher nicht länger zweifelhaft bleiben, was zu halten sei von der Frage, ob der von uns als einzig möglich erkannte Unterschied zwischen den Vorgängen der todten und unbelebten Natur such wirklich bestehe. *Ein solcher Unterschied findet nicht statt....* Die Scheidung zwischen der sogenannten organischen und der anorganischen Natur ist eine ganz willkürliche.' du Bois-Reymond 1848, xliii.

From Distant Sounds to Aeolian Ears   149

telegraph cables *are* human nerves. And, we might add, so must they be, for the characteristic feature of organ projection is the unconscious occurrence.'[50]

Auditory media historians studying Kapp's discussion of the ear will encounter a cache of sources that, after Helmholtz, liken the Organ of Corti to both the harp and the piano. While Kapp felt it unnecessary to deliberate between these, to decide upon a single technology or after-image (*Nachbild*) to which the ear gave rise, he cites the accumulation of sources itself as proof of concept:

We have hereby persuaded ourselves afresh that a mechanism pieced together by human hands [wind harp] can be construed as being in the most striking accordance with an organic entity without the slightest knowledge of that organ's functions.... What had been an earlier unconscious model to humankind, is revealed in its precedence by means of the later after-image.[51]

At this juncture, I want to draw together the separate discursive fields of materialist and psychological (cf. romantic) theories of listening here by asking what cultural work Kapp's analogy performs. What is at stake, in other words, when historical ears become a formative model for the Aeolian harp – in Kapp's specific sense of projections of bodily organs? The list must exceed the space available, but might include: a critical methodology that involves thinking *both in and of* mediality; modes of hearing we attribute to historical audiences; aspects of a work ideology figured through such works' historical recipients; a materialist challenge, perhaps an affront, to the nascent foundations of experimental psychology in Germany under figures like Wilhelm Wundt and Carl Stumpf; and a tool for rereading the music of the period, particularly moments of listening within a narrative or (opera) plot. To take our earlier example from Wagner: in the context of opera, we might ask, with due hermeneutic licence, why three successive instruments play the 'long, awkward silence' after Elsa's second call for a champion – three expectant dominants, three

---

[50] 'Die Nerven *sind* Kabeleinrichtungen des tierischen Körpers, die Telegraphkabel *sind* Nerven der Menschheit! Und fügen wir hinzu, sie müssen es sein, weil das charakteristische Merkmal der Organ projection das unbewußte Vorsichgehen ist.' Kapp 1877, 141. For a detailed, discursive study of the parallelism between nerves and networked telegraphic cables in nineteenth-century Germany, see Otis 2001.

[51] 'Wir haben uns hierdurch aufs neue überzeugt, dass ein von Menschenhand aus Stücken zusammengesetzter Mechanismus in auffallendster Uebereinstimmung mit einem organischen Gebilde ohne die geringsten Kenntnisse von dessen Functionen construirt werden konnte.... [W]as als das Frühere dem Menschen ein unbewusstes Vorbild gewesen war, mittels der späteren Nachbildung in seiner Priorität zur Erscheinung kommt.' Kapp 1877, 93.

different vibrations of the same string, three gusts of thwarted expectation? The music thematises musical silence, whose sonic void also points to an absence of conscious activity in the listener. Might we, at an interpretative push, think of this as a thematic depiction of auditory automatism – the sound of attentive expectation unfulfilled?

When Winslow remarked that 'the organ of Corti *is* the Aeolian harp', his bald metaphor was literary rather than media-technological, yet it imbricates, carrying overlapping associations. While the Kappean reading of listeners' ears as unconscious acoustic technologies is unappealing to a liberal model of the human subject, the soft bed of Romantic poetry that cushions our understanding of the Aeolian or wind harp during the nineteenth century has had wider treatment within a musical context.

To take a second opera as an example, Franz Schreker's *Der ferne Klang* (1903) is far more discursively concerned with the idea of listening than is Wagner's *Lohengrin*. Fritz, the protagonist, is in need of a hearing aid. He cannot hear the 'distant sound' – figured as a metaphor for divine artistic inspiration – and is driven from his young love, Grete, in search of this. In the opera, we recall, the sought-after sound is associated in the first instance with the Aeolian harp. As Example 6.2 shows, Fritz's first explanation of 'the puzzling other-worldly sound' (*der rätselhaft weltferne Klang*) couldn't be clearer:

Do you know, Grete, how when the wind wafts over the harp with a ghostly hand– afar, afar. And I seek the master who stirs the harp. And I seek the harp that brings forth the sound. And when I possess the sound I shall be rich and free – an artist by the grace of God.[52]

The harp, in this reading of the work, becomes not the voice of nature, but a mode of listening to nature, which is to say a mode of being receptive to nature, to what Wordsworth called 'mild creative breez[es]'. Such a literal reading of Fritz's ears brings together Schreker's neo-romantic imagery with the scientific discourse of his age. It seems he did not know of Kapp's writing, nor did he make statements to the effect of the prevalent analogies between the harp and the ear, but these were voiced by scientists whose discourse forms a sedimented layer in the cultural reception of the opera.

And at the end of the work, it is hard to read Fritz's words as other than a confession over auditory technology, that is, his harp-like apparatus has

---

[52] 'weisst du, Gretel, wie wenn der Wind mit Geisterhand ueber Harfen streicht. Weit, weit. Und die Meister such' ich, der die Harfe ruehrt; und die Harfe such' ich, die den Klang gebiert; und halt ich den Klang, bin ich reich und frei ein Kuenstler von Gottes Gnaden!' *Der ferne Klang*, Act I scene 1.

Example 6.2 Franz Schreker, *Der ferne Klang*, Act I scene 1

been retuned, establishing a media link-up between his ear and the environment; he has learned to hear anew via a technology that consolidates his erstwhile loneliness:

Do you hear the sound? How blessed – transfigured – no May wind and no summer storm. Just a shudder of air – a sensual trembling billows through the treetops and a thousand strings shiver with the divine breath of spring! Do you hear the sound? It no longer escapes me, I grasp it just as tightly as shall I never leave you. Birds are singing, bells are ringing – gloriously they burst forth with the mightiest splendour. That is not spring – earlier summer delivers a festive arrival. Harps resound to me as powerfully and sonorously as the sounds of the spheres.[53]

Comparable confessions are scattered throughout nineteenth-century European literature (e.g. Gustave Flaubert's *Novembre*), and Schreker, who famously wrote his own libretto, assigns the harp arpeggios a range of chromatic sevenths during this final passage.[54] Such diegesis predictably drew the ire of commentators like Walter Niemann who regarded the literal depictions of nature's breezes as 'a spiritual fallacy' (*seelischer Fehlschluß*), i.e. augmentations of the artificiality of the instrument. 'If we elevate these elements themselves to the impetus for creation,' he continued, 'we rob music of its highest value and of that which sets it apart from nature: its soul, its inner experience.'[55] Niemann's scepticism at musical mimesis, at the profane afflatus of implicitly representing nature's breezes as man-made, only underscores the modernity of Schreker's work in seeming to place the science of 'psychic automatism' at the centre of the inner ear.

The opera has, of course, inspired a number of different readings that hear in Schreker's music the staging of its own epoch: from the critique of marginalised female voices and anticipation of Hollywood underscoring, to the creation of psychological perspectivism and the Freudian id through sound.[56] In this tradition, Ulrike Kienzle sought to deepen the semiotic role

---

[53] 'Hörst du den Ton? / Wie selig verklärt / kein Maienwind und kein Sommersturm / ein Beben der Luft nur ein lustvolles Zittern geht durch die Wipfel und tausend Saiten erschauern unter des Frühlings göttlichem Hauch! / Hörst du den Ton?! Der schwindet mir nimmer, den halt' ich so fest, wie ich dich nicht mehr lasse. Es singen Vögel, es läuten Glokken glutvoll erbraust es in hehrster Pracht. Das ist nicht Frühling / ein früher Sommer hält festlichen Einzug / die Harfe erklingt mir, als klängen die Sphären machtvoll und rauschend.' *Der ferne Klang*, Act III scene 14.

[54] 'I tried to discover, in the rumour of forests and waves, words that other men could not hear, and I pricked up my ears to listen to the revelation of their harmony.' Flaubert 2005, 15.

[55] 'Erheben wir diese aber selbst zur bewegenden Ursache des Schaffens, so rauben wir der Musik das Höchste, was sie von der Natur auszeichnet: die Seele, das innere Erleben.' Niemann 1913, 216.

[56] See particularly Peter Franklin's (1991, 2013) interpretative readings.

of the Aeolian harp by figuring it as an emblem that explains Schreker's irregular phrase structures and unpredictable harmonic progressions through the perceived irregularity of the billowing wind.[57] Perhaps this analogy-based connecting process is what Roland Barthes had in mind when he defined the picture or image as 'the organisation of the various readings that can be made of it: a picture is never anything but its own plural description.'[58] We might conclude that the emblem of the harp itself must remain multivalent, pivoting between the impetus for analytical interpretation, narrative rereading, and scientific instrument.

***

In the end, the fragile notion of automatic listening under scrutiny is consistently undermined by the discourses of psychophysics and empirical psychology from the 1860s onward. Helmholtz himself was irretrievably caught between these two discursive fields.[59] 'You might almost think Nature has intentionally fallen into the keenest contradictions here, by resolutely wishing to destroy any dream of a pre-existing harmony between the outer and the inner world', the scientist observed in 1868.[60] To recall my earlier claim, a theory of the ear as wind harp is based on mechanical principles of causality voided of cognitive agency. It forms a subspecies of what William James called the 'conscious automaton-theory', which maintains that in everything outward we are purely automatic mechanisms.[61] Feeling is a mere collateral product of our nervous processes, unable to react upon them any more than a shadow reacts on the steps of the traveller whom it accompanies. James, for one, passionately refuted such materialism. Common sense, he asserts, shows that even a live frog with an intact brain will not respond in predictable ways to stimuli: 'the signal may be given, but ideas, emotions or caprices will be aroused instead of the fatal motor reply'.[62] An ear's thinking mind is no different.

That a theory of auditory automatism could arise in the context of nineteenth-century materialism speaks to the attitude of scientists hearing musical sounds, and the authority of the contemporary model of listener as pure recipient of musical works. While opera's connection to theories of automatic listening must remain tentative, such theories serve to enmesh a

---

[57] Kienzle 1998, 79.   [58] Barthes 1988, 150.

[59] See Steege's concept of the 'third ear' within Helmholtz's acoustic epistemology (2012, 43ff.).

[60] 'Fast könnte man glauben, die Natur habe sich hier absichtlich in den kühnsten Widersprüchen gefallen, sie habe mit Entscheidenheit jeden Traum von einer prästabilirten Harmonie der äusseren und inneren Welt zerstören wollen.' Helmholtz [1868] 1884, 1: 294.

[61] W. James [1890] 2007, 133ff.   [62] W. James 1879, 4.

hermeneutics of opera within contemporary discourses of aurality. And here, the capacity for operatic narrative to brush against that which is anathema to its means of expression – i.e. directed listening, whether as an event (*Lohengrin*) or a theme (*Der ferne Klang*) – speaks to the flexibility of the medium during the nineteenth century and its ongoing dance with technological inflection.

7 | Wagner, Hearing Loss and the Urban Soundscape of Late Nineteenth-Century Germany

JAMES DEAVILLE

On 4 July 1878, the inhabitants of New York City quietly celebrated the festive day, with 'no public exhibitions of fire-works, and no fire-crackers', based on the municipal decision 'to exclude noise and bombast on holiday occasions ... because the interminable din of city life operates as a silent and impalpable force' in citizens' lives.[1]

A decade later, the Victorian periodical *All the Year Round* – edited by the son of Charles Dickens – issued the following in a diatribe against noise in London:

The dweller in London ... has to put up with many annoyances ... There is none more aggravating, none more harmful than noise. Few realise what noise really means and implies – a disturbance not merely of the ears, but of the brain and nerves, is involved by the continual rattle and roar with which we are surrounded; and physicians tell us that nervous ailments are frequently produced – more frequently rendered doubly severe – by the continued tension thus called into existence.[2]

Within twenty years, the noise of metropolises had become so intolerable that the philosopher and noise-abatement crusader Theodor Lessing was compelled to publish his classic text *Noise: A Polemic against the Noises of our Lives*, in which he viscerally evokes the soundscape of the modern city, in this case, Berlin:

Hammers thud, machines rumble, the wagons of butchers and the carts of bakers roll past the house before daybreak. Countless bells wail uninterruptedly. Thousands of doors open and close. Thousands of hungry people ... haggle and

---

[1] [unsigned] 1878a, 5. The muted celebration took place in a time of auditory crisis for the city, since a group of 138 physicians had just petitioned the court to alleviate the noise created by the trains of the Metropolitan Elevated Railway Company, which 'disturbs and interrupts all mental processes ... [and] is capable of doing, and undoubtedly will do, great and permanent injury to those who may be compelled to live within reach of its force'. [unsigned] 1878b, 8. See also Thompson 2004, 145, for a brief discussion of Edison's attempts to measure the railway's noise levels.

[2] [unsigned] 1889, 474.

scream, they scream and argue beside our very ears and fill the streets of the city with their business and their trade . . . The streetcar screeches. A train rolls over the iron bridge. Straight through my aching head, straight through our finest thoughts.[3]

It was this noisy, modern urban environment, this acoustic excess that invited contemporary commentators on Wagner to apply their experiences of the metropolitan soundscape to his music, inspired by a burgeoning medical discipline dedicated to studying the ear and its diseases and injuries. In this chapter, I will examine the emergence of the science of otology and its response to the urban sonic environment of the late nineteenth century, and then explore the literature about music and Wagner for evidence of this new 'otic' vocabulary. Along the way, we shall observe how the new-found interest in the act of listening ties in with burgeoning discourses of materiality in the late nineteenth century.

At the outset, it is important to separate the threads that bind together our investigation of Wagner, hearing loss and the urban environment: (1) sober assessments by medical experts inform the fear of Wagner's impact upon hearing; (2) prevalent criticism of the loudness of his music was grounded on the prevailing uncertainty over the thresholds for tolerating auditory volume; (3) as a result of that unease, any kind of change – whether social, industrial or musically stylistic – became the lightning rod for anxieties, which found voice in music criticism that latter-day musicologists have all too easily been able to dismiss as hyperbole.

Well before Lessing's description of urban noise pollution, municipal authorities had recognised the disruptive capabilities of urban noise. Already in 1595 the city of London came under an ordinance limiting domestic and industrial sound between the hours of 9 p.m. and 4 a.m.[4] Regulations of this sort multiplied as the Industrial Revolution of the nineteenth century brought industry and traffic into the city – for example, in 1842 the city council of New Orleans passed a law that restricted the blowing of horns by carriage drivers.[5] The seeming universality of the remediation of urban noise nuisances through municipal ordinances is indicative of a broader move within industrialised cities to regulate their auditory environment.[6] Before mid-century the ordinances pertained to human agents in unlawful noise production, in the form of 'any noise,

---

[3] Lessing, cited in Fritzsche 1998, 172–3.

[4] Goldsmith 2012, 45. Noise ordinances that regulate the human production of nocturnal sounds have persisted to the present. Most pre-industrial societies imposed curfews after sunset, however, which would have enforced the noise ordinances.

[5] Young 2011.   [6] Smilor 1979.

Wagner, Hearing Loss and Urban Soundscape   157

disturbance or improper diversion in the streets'.[7] As the century progressed, however, corporations and municipalities served more frequently as the objects of legal complaints regarding noise, reflecting the increasing levels of urban noise pollution.[8] Jacques Attali culturally positions the rise of noise ordinances in the modern urban soundscape: 'In the codes that structure noise and its mutations we glimpse a new theoretical practice and reading: establishing relations between the history of people and the dynamics of the economy on the one hand, and the history of the ordering of noise in codes on the other; predicting the evolution of one by the forms of the other; combining economics and aesthetics.'[9]

Concurrent with the criminalisation of disturbing the peace through noise was the growing recognition that it was unhealthy: popular and scholarly writers of the late nineteenth century increasingly identified noise as one of the sources of personal harm in the metropolis. For example, in the essay 'Über den Lärm' from 1879, Emmy von Dincklage proclaimed that 'no age since the creation of the world has made so much and so egregious noise as ours'.[10] In the same year the noted English psychologist James Sully produced a major study 'Civilisation and Noise', in which he observed: 'persons at all sensitive to noises are exposed to an amount of suffering which may appreciably colour their conscious existence'.[11] A few years earlier, Army Corps of Engineers road specialist Quincy Adams Gillmore could assert the following: 'The writings of eminent medical practitioners are full of testimony to the pernicious influence of street noise and din upon the health of the population, particularly upon invalids and persons with sensitive

---

[7] *The Revised Laws and Ordinances of the City of Troy* (Troy, NY: Tuttle, Belcher & Butler, 1838), 118.

[8] The landmark British legal case *Sturges* v. *Bridgman* from 1879 decided against the noisemaker defendant, a confectioner's shop, opening the way for other lawsuits against commercial disturbers of the peace. See also Karin Bijsterveld's (2008, 69–71) discussion of hearing loss among boiler boys in the context of late nineteenth-century Amsterdam. A legal encyclopedia from late in the century establishes that 'inconvenience and annoyance occasioned by noise and confusion of passing trains has also been allowed an injury for which compensation has been claimed'. 'Noise and Vibration', The *American and English Encyclopedia of Law*, ed. John Houston Merrill, 31 vols. (Northport, NY: Edward Thompson Company, 1888), 6:547.

[9] Attali 1985, 5.

[10] 'Kein Zeitalter seit Erschaffung der Welt hat soviel und so ungeheuerlichen Lärm gemacht wie das unsrige.' Dincklage 1879, 413.

[11] Sully 1879, 233. Sully studied with Herrmann von Helmholtz in Berlin and authored several studies on the psychology of music, and the interest in apperception that an earlier article – 'Physiological Psychology in Germany' from 1876 – had displayed in the first issue of a quasi-populist journal (*Mind*) has caused Benjamin Steege (2012, 118) to remark on the 'urgency' with which the topic of auditory attention was being taken up by the mid-1870s.

nerves.'[12] Furthermore, under the title 'Noise Nuisance', the *Cincinnati Lancet and Clinic* of 1883 complained that 'to the sick and convalescent, and to "nervous people" – a class rapidly increasing in number with the progress of our civilization – street noise is an intolerable nuisance which, in some cases, may result in positive injury, and is a penalty paid for living in the city'.[13] And to the extent that insomnia is counted among modern diseases by such an eminent medical authority of the late nineteenth century as British physician Benjamin Ward Richardson, its causes – including the noise of modern life – came under fire:[14]

The development of insomnia is a fatal drawback to the many gains which modern life has brought us ... While insomnia has many causes, it is always kept alive by noise, and in cities like London and Paris noise is always going on day and night.[15]

Such proscriptions against injurious urban noise cut across municipal and national boundaries in the late nineteenth century, in so far as the same clamorous technologies were introduced to cities across Europe and North America: streetcars, factory whistles, steam engines and other factory machinery.[16] As a result, the evidence from a variety of urban soundscapes and medical practices – where the hazards of technologically produced noise, as well as the otological responses to their effects, achieved their own discourses – elides regional and national differences.

These attributions of injury to sounds, whether physiological or psychological, may have originated in response to what seemed to be the increasingly loud and complex soundscape of the modern metropolis, yet they also arose within the context of an increasing concern over otic health after mid-century.[17] Jonathan Sterne has argued that an augmented interest in issues of listening and hearing predates the introduction of recording technologies in the late nineteenth century, remarking that 'the new science of otology or ear medicine constructed diseases of the ear as a

---

[12] Gillmore 1876, 205.   [13] [unsigned] 1883b, 264.

[14] Richardson 1882, 241. For an extended discussion of the relationship between insomnia and modernity, see Scrivner 2014.

[15] [unsigned] 1897, 12–13.

[16] Fritzsche 2015. See also physician Walter B. Platt's 1888 article 'Injurious Influences of City Life', which identifies 'the incessant noise of a large city' (485) as injurious to residents of various European and American cities (487).

[17] It is telling that around mid-century, popular literature about the preservation (and loss) of hearing begins to appear in print in Europe and North America, such as Clark's (1856) practical guide *Sight and Hearing: How Preserved, and How Lost*, Fowler's public lecture from 1865, 'The Eye and Ear, and How to Preserve Them', and the unsigned 1854 essay 'Das menschliche Ohr'.

problem separate from the eye'.[18] Indeed, the discipline had advanced so far in the second half of the nineteenth century that in 1884 the noted Scottish otologist Thomas Barr could remark with pleasure on 'the increased interest in diseases of the ear taken both by the public and the profession, and especially as the result of fuller and more correct knowledge of the serious consequences which may attend them'.[19]

Already in 1822, occupational hearing loss is a topic for the French physician Philippe Patissier, whose *Traité des maladies des artisans* prominently mentions noise as hazardous for craftsmen: 'The noise that these craftsmen make with their hammers disturbs the neighbours of their studios as well as they themselves.'[20] Still, the medical literature before 1850 tends to reference natural sources of auditory damage, like Jacob Breder Heidenreich's 1850 summary of Kramer's advice for ears: 'You should be careful of factories that produce noise, song birds, loud speech, etc.'[21] It stands to reason that the earliest otologists of the century would invoke the sound world around them in describing hazards for human hearing, which generally did not yet encompass noises from boiler shops, trains and streetcars: thus, writing in 1827, the venerable French specialist Jean Antoine Saissy references harmful environmental 'violent noises' like those of thunder, (church) bells and artillery, but not industrial machinery.[22]

If, as Sterne argues, the ear and its diseases had received scholarly attention primarily in the context of the other sensory organs (especially the eye) earlier in the nineteenth century, during the second half of the century study of the ear, its function and dysfunction preoccupied a variety of medical specialists.[23] It was German-speaking Europe that led

---

[18] Sterne 2003, 51. Otology is the medical study of ear physiology and pathology, while audiology is a health-care discipline that assesses hearing loss and treats it through therapy.

[19] Barr 1884, 358–9.

[20] 'Le bruit que ces artisans font avec leurs marteaux incommode les habitans voisins de leur atelier, et les affecte eux-mêmes.' Patissier 1822, 81.

[21] 'Man habe Acht gegen Fabriken, die Lärm veranlassen, Singvögel, lautes Sorechen u. s. w.' Heidenreich 1850, 152.

[22] Saissy 1827, 178.

[23] Sterne nevertheless overstates the case for otology emerging from study of the sensorium, omitting reference to the various medical specialists in Great Britain, France and the United States who were devoting themselves exclusively to pathologies of the ear in the early nineteenth century. Among these texts are Saunders 1806, Itard 1821, Buchanan 1828 and Pappenheim 1840. See Esmail 2013, 41. For a history of otology, see especially Pappas 1996. The comments of American scientist Benjamin Silliman are indicative of the attitude that the eye and ear belonged together: 'the eye and the ear, each in pairs, corresponding to the double brain, are placed close to that intellectual organ, and communicate directly with it; they are the most elevated and dignified of the senses'. Silliman 1840, 80.

160 JAMES DEAVILLE

the way in the newly established medical science of otology, with landmark studies about the ear's health and pathology by Wilhelm Kramer (1801–1876), Anton von Tröltsch (1829–1890) and above all Adam Politzer (1835–1920).[24] Politzer established the first ear clinic in 1863 at the University of Vienna and subsequently founded with Tröltsch and Hermann Schwartze (1837–1910) the first international journal of otology as the *Archiv für Ohrenheilkunde* in 1864.[25] Hermann von Helmholtz's classic text *Die Lehre von den Tonempfindungen* of 1863 falls squarely within this initial period of heightened European interest in the physiology of the ear,[26] but only Helmholtz (1821–1894) significantly forges a link with the psychology of hearing and – more importantly – listening. Helmholtz had already drawn that distinction in the noted lecture from 1857, wherein the audiologist distinguishes 'between the material ear of the body and the spiritual ear of the mind'.[27] Later in the century, Politzer proceeded to publish (in 1878) the first volume of his comprehensive textbook of otology *Lehrbuch der Ohrenheilkunde*, whose second volume appeared in 1882. At the same time, pioneering research on the ear and its maladies was being carried out in France, England and the United States,[28] by figures like Prosper Ménière (1799–1862), Joseph Toynbee (1815–1866) and Daniel Bennett St John Roosa (1838–1908).[29]

The texts authored by these otologists and their colleagues feature both general introductions to the field and specialised studies of hearing problems. (Table 7.1 presents a selection of key nineteenth-century texts on the ear and its diseases and injuries.) As aids to students and members of the medical profession, the manuals, handbooks and treatises from the second half of the century treat not only diseases of the ear but what Laurence Turnbull, writing in the *Medical and Surgical Reporter* of 1865, called 'acoustic injury'.[30] In the general volumes on otology the specialist reader would find diverse chapters on conditions of the ear, systematically leading the reader from basic physiology through common and then

---

[24] Primary publications of these otologists are as follows: Kramer 1867, Tröltsch 1862, and Politzer 1878/82 and 1907/13.

[25] On Politzer's accomplishments as an otologist, see Mudry 2000.   [26] Helmholtz 1863.

[27] Helmholtz 1883, 88. Helmholtz's research and lectures in Bonn in the mid-1850s already demonstrated this interest in the physiology of the ear: his appointment there was as a professor of physiology and anatomy. See Steege 2012, xi, 40.

[28] It is important to recognise that these scientists working on auditory damage were physiologists, not acousticians, i.e. they were investigating pathologies of the body, which are quite separate from the nature and effects of sound that are the topics of research in acoustics.

[29] Their primary texts: Toynbee 1860, Ménière 1861, Roosa 1873.   [30] Turnbull 1865, 88.

Table 7.1 Key nineteenth-century texts on the ear and its diseases and injuries

1806	John Cunningham Saunders, *The Anatomy of the Human Ear*
1821	Jean Marc Gaspard Itard, *Traité des maladies d'oreille et de l'audition*
1827	Jean Antoine Saissy, *Essai sur les maladies de l'oreille interne*
1828	Thomas Buchanan, *Physiological Illustrations of the Organ of Hearing*
1840	Samuel Pappenheim, *Die specielle Gewebelehre des Gehörorganes*
1859	Julius Erhard, *Rationelle Otiatrik nach klinischen Beobachtungen*
1860	Joseph Toynbee, *The Diseases of the Ear: Their Nature, Diagnosis, and Treatment*
1861	Prosper Ménière, 'Mémoire sur des lésions de l'oreille interne'
1861	Wilhelm Kramer, *Die Ohrenheilkunde der Gegenwart*
1862	Anton von Tröltsch, *Die Krankheiten des Ohres, ihre Erkenntniss und Behandlung: Ein Lehrbuch der Ohrenheilkunde*
1867	Wilhelm Kramer, *Handbuch der Ohrenheilkunde*
1870	Josef Gruber, *Lehrbuch der Ohrenheilkunde*
1873	Daniel Bennett St John Roosa, *A Practical Treatise on the Diseases of the Ear*
1877	Charles H. Burnett, *The Ear: Its Anatomy, Physiology, and Diseases*
1878, 1882	Adam Politzer, *Lehrbuch der Ohrenheilkunde*, 2 vols.
1884	Thomas Barr, *Manual of Diseases of the Ear*
1884	Ludwig Löwe, *Lehrbuch der Ohrenheilkunde*
1907, 1913	Adam Politzer, *Geschichte der Ohrenheilkunde*, 2 vols.
1908	Georg Boenninghaus, *Lehrbuch der Ohrenheilkunde für Studierende und Aerzte*

specialised disorders.[31] Typically the organisation of the pathological sections works its way inward, from the readily observable conditions of the external ear to the subjective assessment of maladies involving the inner ear, called the 'nervous apparatus' by Toynbee.[32] These authors may devote a brief section of their texts to damage from sonic sources, usually situating sound injuries both in the eardrum and in the organ of Corti, the former due to concussive pressure, the latter to a wide range of traumatic sounds. However, their opinions differed on the actual neuro-mechanisms affected by the injury, even as other disorders of the inner ear such as Ménière's disease – identified by Prosper Ménière in 1861 – had to await an empirical diagnosis until well into the twentieth century.[33]

The studies devoted exclusively to auditory pathologies still valorise conditions caused by disease, but also consider non-physiological sources. These

---

[31] For example, Charles H. Burnett's standard textbook (1877).   [32] Toynbee 1860, 348.
[33] Gangadhara Somayaji 2015.

include environmental sources, among which harmful noise represents only one of several factors. Adverse weather conditions and atmospheric dust appear with regularity as environmental hazards to hearing, as well as injuries arising from occupational noises.[34] Although not stated as such, the fear of the times over the deleterious effects of industrial, commercial and transportation noise in the modern city finds support in these publications that establish the medical foundations for auditory injury through sound.

Even contemporary fiction – that arbiter of cultural temperament – carried the discourse surrounding injurious sounds, and perhaps nowhere more clearly than in a short children's tale by Timothy Shay Arthur, in *The Children's Hour* of 1872. Beating on an old tin pan with two bits of iron, ten-year-old Hartley greatly disturbs his mother, who attributes her strong response to nerves.[35] After explaining what nerves are, she establishes, "'If you had struck me on the head with your fist, you hardly could have hurt me worse ... My nerves are very sensitive" ... "But how can a noise touch your nerves?" asked the boy. "It touches the nerves of hearing, and through these jars all the rest".'[36] Such a medicalised narrative reflects the anxieties behind embodied responses to hearing noise, which characterises equally contemporary reaction to Wagner's music, as we shall observe.

Thus otologist John Roosa's 1883 article 'The Effects of Noise upon Diseased and Healthy Ears' discusses in detail the long-term damaging impacts of environmental sounds, invoking some of the most common urban noises of the era: railway carriages, clattering wagons and, especially, boiler shops.[37] Already in 1859 Julius Erhard's general text on otology had cited the environmental factor of noise in work in hammer mills and with pieces of artillery as being harmful to hearing, and over two decades later, Politzer would identify the occupations of locksmith, blacksmith, miller and cooper as typifying those that led to hearing loss among their practitioners.[38]

---

[34] Burnett, for example, names mill hands, carpenters, boilermakers and female domestics as examples of workers who are susceptible to hearing loss through environmental factors. Burnett 1877, 403.

[35] One possible reading of the story is that Arthur is depicting the human response to the mechanical noise of the industrialised city.

[36] Arthur 1872, 11. The modern term for this phenomenon of heightened sensitivity to sound is 'hyperacusis'. Another story that refers to hyperacusis is the novel *The Woman in White* by Wilkie Collins (London: Sampson Low, 1860).

[37] Roosa 1883. In his *A Practical Treatise on the Diseases of the Ear*, Roosa sets up a binary between 'musical' and 'unpleasant' sounds, as heard in ongoing repetition: 'the continual recurrence of a kind of sound, that has no musical, but on the contrary, an unpleasant character, must at last cause a hyperæmia of the ultimate nerve-fibres of the cochlea' (1885, 667).

[38] Erhard 1859, 126–8; Politzer 1883, 190. One year after the English-language edition of Politzer and publication of Roosa's article, Thomas Barr indicated the professions of boilermakers,

However, Roosa conducted specific, extended testing in boiler shops: 'Boiler-makers, and those who become deaf from an exposure to the continuous shock of loud sounds, suffer a lesion of the acoustic nerve.'[39] One of his boilermaker interviewees remarked that 'Those heavy hammers jar every nerve in the body.'[40] The evidence compelled Roosa to conclude that 'the hearing-power of persons working in such a din as that of a boiler-shop invariably becomes impaired'.[41] This important article appeared in the influential *Archives of Otology* and was translated and reprinted in 1884 in the *Zeitschrift für Ohrenheilkunde*, where it was cited by other specialists throughout the decade.[42] Roosa himself would incorporate its findings into later editions of his 1873 text *A Practical Treatise on the Diseases of the Ear*.[43]

The physiological approach to audition advocated by such medical authorities works from the assumption that the body represents a quasi-mechanical apparatus, leaving little space for cognition and the life of the mind.[44] Their discourses of damaged listening acuity are grounded in materialist attitudes toward medical conditions and diagnoses, which explains why the otological literature they produced pathologises physio-logical phenomena – damage to the eardrum from concussive sounds, for example – rather than cognitive impairment.[45] As a result, the late nine-teenth century became an era of rapid growth in the understanding of ear structures and their functions and dysfunctions.

The materialist paradigm also explains how musical sounds and envir-onmental noises could be rationalised within a single taxonomy of auditory stimuli, which would lead to the argument that certain instruments and manners of performance could be injurious to the ear. For example, Wilhelm Kramer's *Die Ohrenheilkunde der Gegenwart* of 1861 provides a more detailed taxonomy of damaging noise sources that includes sounds produced by musical instruments:

---

riveters and railway engine drivers as exemplifying types of work that could be hazardous to hearing. Barr 1884, 54.

[39] Roosa 1883, 108.

[40] Roosa 1883, 111. Roosa's introductory comment locates the source of the nerve-jarring effect in the ear: 'Boiler-makers speak in graphic language of the effects of the fin upon their ears.'

[41] Roosa 1883, 118. The injury was so common among workers in such factories that it became known as 'boilermaker's disease' or 'boilermaker's ear'.

[42] See, for example, R. 1883; Montgomery 1884, 52; and Baber 1888, 298.

[43] The book appeared in seven revised editions through 1892.

[44] Historians of science date this attitude towards the human body back to the Cartesian separation of body and mind, which conceived of it 'using physical, chemical and materialist vocabulary'. Hirjak et al. 2013.

[45] For a discussion of medical materialism, see H. Cook 1997.

If at all possible one should go out of the way to avoid noise in mills, factories with clanging machinery, workshops of metal workers, copper smiths and boiler-makers, hammer mills, target practice of the artillery and infantry, the use of firearms in hunting, *the proximity of wind instruments and violins of heavily staffed orchestras*, screeching parrots and canaries . . .[46]

Politzer also writes about 'the action [upon the ear] of loud noises . . . while driving in loudly rattling carriages or in a railway train, in noisy factories and workshops, while listening to music loudly instrumented, etc.'[47] Under the sub-category 'Subjective Ear Sensations' of the category 'Subjective Symptoms', Politzer considers the condition *Hyperæsthesia acoustica* ('excessive sensitiveness to noises'), in which 'all sorts of music and loud speaking give rise to an unpleasant and often worrying sensation'.[48] And in the revised 1896 edition of his manual, Barr observes how 'even in persons who may be very deaf, loud sounds, such as speech through a conversation tube, or a railway whistle, or loud music such as that of a large organ, are sometimes very disagreeable or even painful'.[49] These physiological medical references to heavily orchestrated or merely loud music and its potentially harmful or painful impact upon the hearing of the individual – however realistic they may be – share a precedent that pre-dates the work of Politzer, Helmholtz and their otologist contemporaries: already in the 1853 *Ästhetik des Hässlichen*, Karl Rosenkranz complained about the 'tickling of deadened nerves . . . [through] colossal instrumentation'.[50] What unites this family of references is the recognition that musical sound can function as an imminent threat to the well-being of an individual, in the manner of the noises produced by the urban soundscape of the street and workplace. Once again we encounter anxieties over music, and sound in general, whose levels of sound intensity could exceed the thresholds for health and human tolerance.

When these medical specialists cite potential injury or pain from music by virtue of its heavy orchestration or 'loud instrumentation', they are marking the characteristics of volume and timbre that have become confused and conflated in contemporary parlance about sources of otological harm. In the introduction to his 1953 *Lexicon of Musical Invective*, entitled

---

[46] My italics. 'Dem Lärm in Mühlen, Fabriken mit klappernden Maschinen, in Werkstätten der Schlosser, der Grob-, Kupier- und Kesselschmiede, in Hammerwerken, bei Schiessübungen der Artillerie und Infanterie, beim Gebrauch der Schiessgewehre auf der Jagd, in der Nähe namentlich mit Blaseinstrumenten und Geigen starkbesetzter Orchester, schreiender Papageien und Kanarienvögel … geht man möglichst aus dem Wege.' Kramer 1861, 34.
[47] Politzer 1883, 203.   [48] Politzer 1883, 341.   [49] Barr 1896, 38.
[50] ' … sinnlich verweichlichende Melodien, koloffale Inftrumentirung'. Rosenkranz 1853, 52.

Wagner, Hearing Loss and Urban Soundscape 165

'Non-Acceptance of the Unfamiliar', Nicholas Slonimsky addresses this problem when he famously quips, 'New music always sounds loud to old ears. Beethoven seemed to make more noise than Mozart; Liszt was noisier than Beethoven; Strauss, noisier than Liszt.'[51] While Slonimsky's equating of loudness with noisiness may be problematic today because the two attributions index different modes of perception (in essence, physiological and cognitive), writers in the nineteenth century regularly blended these sources of aural discomfort.[52] This should be familiar territory to anyone who has worked with the reviews quoted in Slonimsky or with Wilhelm Tappert's 1877 publication *Ein Wagner-Lexikon: Wörterbuch der Unhöflichkeit*, the inspiration for Slonimsky.[53]

Academics have tended to read the anti-Wagnerian criticisms collected by Tappert as metaphorical hyperbole, whereby commentators registered disapprobation by situating the unfavourable experience of the music in its auditory reception.[54] In light of the clinical and popular responses to the harmful audible environment of the metropolis, however, is it possible that Wagner's music evoked embodied materialist representations of that discourse? David Trippett suggests as much when he notes that in such literature 'the body's response to melody is no longer a literary metaphor'.[55] Such visually rich tropes of exaggeration as 'ear splitting' and – in German – 'ear-torturing' (*ohrenmarternd*) denote more than just colourful feuilletonist polemics: they arose in the context of medical discussions over auditory well-being within the injurious/painful urban soundscape of the time.[56] Hence it was natural that such comparisons

---

[51] Slonimsky 1953, 18.   [52] See Hugill 2012, 52–3.

[53] The full title reads *Ein Wagner-Lexikon. Wörterbuch der Unhöflichkeit enthaltend grobe, höhnende, gehässige und verläumderische Ausdrücke welche gegen den Meister Richard Wagner seine Werke und seine Anhänger von den Feinden und Spöttern gebraucht worden sind: zur Gemüths-Ergötzung in müssigen Stunden* ('A Wagner Lexicon. Dictionary of Rudeness, Containing Coarse, Mocking, Scathing, and Defamatory Expressions Which Have Been Used by Enemies and Mockers of and against Master Richard Wagner, His Works, and His Followers, for Entertainment in Idle Moments').

[54] See for example Dreyfus 2010, 35.   [55] Trippett 2013, 9.

[56] 'Ear-splitting' is used in [unsigned] 1883a, 604. André Gill's 1869 caricature of Wagner 'splitting' his auditor's ear with a Nibelungen spike and hammer visualises the metaphor in one of the century's most notorious satirical representations of Wagner. One critic's comments about Wagner approach Gill's caricature more closely in referencing the 'ruptured eardrums' (*gesprengte Trommelfelle*) of Wagner's audience members (Tappert 1877, 5). The German *ohrenmarternd* is attributed to a letter by writer Eduard M. Oettinger to Alexandre Dumas from 1860, cited in Tappert 1873, 672. Oettinger follows this auditory neologism with another medicalising compound descriptor, *nervennörgelnd*, which translates as 'irritating for the nervous system'. Combined, the two terms suggest that the brutal sounds impacted the listener's emotional (nervous) state.

would be drawn when listeners were confronted by music that performed acoustic excess, over and above that which had been experienced in the concert hall to that point. The music critics were accessing contemporary tropes of sonic harm rendered all too familiar through the sheer volume of contemporary urban noise.

It is no coincidence that such language first appears in musical literature after 1860, even as otological terms like *Hörverlust* ('loss of hearing'), *Gehör-Schaden* ('hearing injury') and *Gehör störend* ('damaged hearing') were establishing themselves in German- and English-language medical discourse.[57] The more specialised and graphic designations for auditory injury in the German language, such as *ohrenzerreissend* ('ear rupturing'), arose even later in the century, and that specifically in relation to Wagner's music dramas, in particular, *Tristan und Isolde*.[58]

Tappert recognised the importance of such language in referencing the audible effects of Wagner; his widely circulated lexicon deserves closer consideration not only as an aggregator for *bons mots* about Wagner from the daily and musical press of the time, but also as a study of the neologisms and derisive vocabulary that the new music provoked. The Wagner lexicographer includes four ear-related entries in the book's primary alphabet: *Ohrenschindend* ('ear flaying') and *Ohrenzerreissend* ('ear rupturing'), and *Ohrenschmerz* ('ear ache') and its synonym *Ohrenzwang*.[59] The adjectives designate injurious actions upon the ear, while the nouns describe a condition of the ear, all of which could have occurred in the otological literature of the time.[60] Elsewhere in the lexicon he quotes (i) the term *ohrenzerfleischend* ('ear mangling') in reference to Wagner's operas, (ii) the audience member for *Die Walküre* who needs a goodly amount of 'cotton in his ears' to avoid long-term damage, and (iii) the 'new' introduction to *Tannhäuser* as 'murderous noise' (*Mordlärm*).[61]

---

[57] Vocabulary of this kind can be found throughout such standard texts as Gruber 1870 and Löwe 1884.

[58] Tappert (1877, 27) attributes *ohrenzerreissend* to the *Berliner Montagszeitung* of 1874 with regard to an announced performance of *Tristan* in Munich. The very first reference to Wagner and hearing loss seems to occur in the notorious oppositional journal *Niederrheinische Musik-Zeitung*, in a review by 'C.D.' of the Viennese premiere of *Lohengrin* from 1858. The critic cites a colleague as saying, 'The twenty-four keys do not provide a good basis for hearing' ('Die vierundzwanzig Tonarten geben keine Basis für das Gehör ab') (C.D. 1858, 299).

[59] C.D. 1858, 290.

[60] For example, in an 1878 article about the abuse of locomotive steam whistles, the author uses the descriptor 'ohrenzerreissen' for their shrillness to the ears of listeners ([unsigned] 1878c, 155).

[61] '... The critic from the *Sporn* [Hieronymus Truhn] discovered a sea of ear-mangling music of torment [in *Siegfried*]' '... Ein Meer von ohrenzerfleischbender Quallenmusik entdeckte der

Wagner, Hearing Loss and Urban Soundscape

If Tappert primarily draws upon commentators' neologisms that were applied to listening to Wagner, other authors invoke the sources for those experiences of his music. This is where his material becomes more directly aligned with the urban soundscape. References to Wagner's use of percussion and brass are not uncommon in the sources, which obliquely connect with the injurious noise of the city, such as this Weimar report from *Signale* of 1865: 'Earlier [!] the Musicians of the Future made a din in our ears until the full complement of cymbals, tam-tam, triangle, and other such beautiful instruments burst through.'[62] Another allusion to industry and hearing loss is encountered in the study by German psychiatrist Theodor Puschmann (1844–1899), *Richard Wagner: Eine psychiatrische Studie*, where the author suggests the need for aural fortitude to survive Wagner: 'Your auditory nerves must be as thick as ship's cables if you want to come away unharmed from the noise [of a Wagner opera].'[63]

The humorist Daniel Spitzer more overtly positions the composer's work within the noisy milieu of the city in a 'Wiener Spaziergang' from May 1866, entitled 'Die Prater-Ausstellung': 'Where shall I go now? Shall I really plunge into the turmoil of the steam machinery, which creaks, roars, whistles and screeches as if it were performing an overture by Wagner?'[64] The notorious Wagner opponent, who would publish the letters between the composer and a Viennese 'Putzmacherin' in 1877, satirically attempts to re-auditise Wagner's music through the vocabulary of modern auditory trauma: language that accesses lived sound from the reader's somatic experience of such audible effects within the urban environment of the time.[65]

It is possible to argue that as a feuilletonist, Spitzer would have used such metaphorical constructions naturally as a part of the humorist's toolkit. However, a small body of specialised late nineteenth-century literature that

---

Kritiker des "Sporn"' (Tappert 1877, 30); 'A garnish of ear plugs for *Valkyrie* visitors' 'Eine Garnitur Gehör-Wattons für, Walkyren'-Besucher' – Tappert found this passage in the *Berliner Montagszeitung* of 4 May 1874 and cited it (Tappert 1877, 5); quotation by Ludwig Speidel in the *Wiener Fremdenblatt* of 1872, cited in Tappert 1877, 25. The reference must have been to the Bacchanale in Act I from the Paris version, which was used in Vienna for the 1872 production.

[62] 'Früher rasaunten uns die Zukunftsmusiker die Ohren bis zum Zerspringen voll mit Becken, Tamtam, Triangel und dergleichen schönen Instrumenten.' Cited in Tappert 1877, 30.

[63] 'So dass ... die Gehörnerven so dick wie die Schiffstaue dazu gehören, um aus deratigem Lärm [einer Wagner'schen Oper] unversehrt und heil hervorzugehen.' Puschmann 1872, 30.

[64] 'Doch wohin jetzt? Soll ich mich wirklich in das Gewühle der Dampfmaschinen dort stürzen, die knarren, dröhnen, pfeifen und kreischen, als wenn sie eine Ouvertüre von Richard Wagner aufführten?' Spitzer 1877, 35–6.

[65] Spitzer 1906.

reports on Wagner from the perspective of medical science exists, and makes precisely the same connection. The authors are otologists, who would have had some familiarity with Wagner's music – or at least with the major Wagner tropes in circulation at the time; as medical specialists, however, their assessments of the physiological effects of the composer's works acquire special validity for the present investigation.

In the sixth edition of his textbook from 1885, otologist Roosa – whose 1884 assessment of harmful noises we encountered above – clearly brings the injurious effects of Wagner into the urban soundscape of his time: 'If Galen had lived in the nineteenth century, and in New York with its uneven pavements, boiler shops, locomotive whistles, elevated railways, and Wagner music, he might have added largely to his category of sounds unpleasant to the ear.'[66] Leopold Damrosch's first Metropolitan Opera season (1884–5) featured *Tannhäuser*, *Lohengrin* and *Die Walküre* in 44 of its 101 performances, which obviously left its impact upon New Yorker Roosa, who would surely have attended at least one performance.[67] As one of New York's more prominent personalities, the otologist could hardly have escaped what Horowitz describes as the city's 'hunger for Wagner', whatever his own misgivings. Roosa's mild adjective – 'unpleasant' – describes the sensation of the assorted urban sounds he itemises, but when equated with such noises as those of boiler shops and locomotive whistles, the harmful material impact of Wagner's music on the ear becomes unmistakable.

At almost the same time, physician and ear specialist Dr Carl von Reichert published a study entitled 'Versuch einer Richard Wagner-Studie' in a medical journal from 1884, subsequently releasing it as an offprint.[68] In it the author speculates about the effects of Wagner's music upon the listening layperson, such as in the following passage: 'It is fully in the nature of the layman that to the extent his relatively inflexible eardrum and his insufficiently developed hearing will continuously and most intensively be shattered by powerful new masses of tones; [he] will tend to interpret this musical noise [of Wagner] as never before heard.'[69] Through the last clause Reichert hoped to explain the negative responses to Wagner, but he was also advancing an argument for the physiological basis for

---

[66] Roosa 1885, 17.   [67] Horowitz 1994, 76–8.   [68] Reichert 1884a, 1884b.

[69] 'Es liegt ja so ganz in der Natur des Laien, dass er in demselben Maasse, als sein schwer bewegliches Trommelfell und sein mangelhaft entwickeltes Gehör fortwährend und in der intensivsten Weise erschüttert, von neuen gewaltigen Tonmassen … gereizt wurde, im selben Maasse dann natürlich auch geneigt ist, diesen musikalischen Lärm als noch nie dagewesen zu interpretiren.' Reichert 1884a, 24.

Moreover, Reichert alludes to the noise of modern life when he connects Wagner's followers with 'crass materialism, the golden-calf cult and the general tendency towards degeneration and machinizing, which is the mark of today'.[71]

The third doctor under consideration does not directly bring Wagner into the noisy cityscape, yet his admonitions on opera and otic health are nevertheless revealing. In his textbook on auditory pathology, Ludwig Löwe refers to the harmfulness of operatic music for one's ears without specifically naming any composer, while two passages from 1884 point to Wagner. Firstly, a fairly straightforward warning: 'The ear patient should not be permitted to attend noisy operatic performances.'[72] The second section of text explains the reason for the cautionary note: '[the other senses] are so occupied at a noisy and sumptuous operatic performance that they are not in a position [to substitute for the ear]'.[73] Löwe is suggesting that the listener would experience sensory overload at an opera like Wagner's, an observation that provides a degree of medical verification for the more fanciful descriptions of the music's material impact given by critics. Löwe's concern with overstimulation serves as further evidence for the contemporary unease over the seemingly unbridled cultural transformation wrought by Wagner's music.

Finally, the infamous Wagner caricature by André Gill from 1869 (see Figure 7.1) warrants consideration in this context, for it visualises the otic assault, the physiological impact of Wagner's music.[74]

Here Wagner is depicted as driving a note-spike into an ear with a Nibelungen hammer, drawing blood from the eardrum. Various authors feature this illustration either on the covers or as illustrative material for their Wagner books, and indeed, Gill's work invites multiple readings and

---

[70] The notion of aural over-stimulation through the experience of Wagner's music is certainly not novel, but the implicit reversal of Slonimsky's terms for new music sounding loud to 'loud' (dense) music sounding new does introduce a cognitive response that takes the critical reactions recorded by Tappert one step further.

[71] ' ... [in Folge des] crassen Materialismus, des goldenen Kalb-Cultus und des allgemeinen Verflachungs- und Vermaschinirungs-Strebens, welches die Signatur der heutigen Tage ist'. Reichert 1884a, 42.

[72] 'Dagegen soll man Ohrenleidende zu rauschenden Opernaufführungen nicht zulassen.' Löwe 1884, 300.

[73] ' ... werden sie bei einer lärmenden und prunkvollen Opernaufführung so in Anspruch genommen, dass sie hierzu nicht im Stande sind ... ' Löwe 1884, 301.

[74] After the *Ring des Nibelungen* premiere, Gill also drew the caricature 'Le Tétralogue Wagner' for *L'Éclipse* of 3 September 1876, in which Gill uses the same facial features for Wagner while showing the composer beating a large cooking pan.

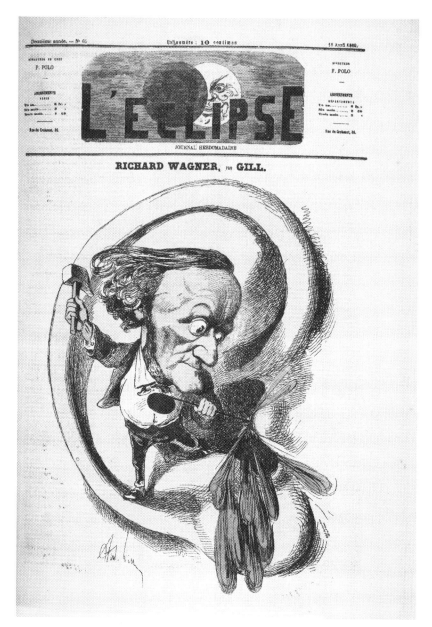

Figure 7.1 André Gill, 'Richard Wagner', *L'Éclipse*, 18 April 1869 (collection Trippett).

interpretations. Most obviously, the chisel of the Nibelungen is the work tool of the gold-mining dwarves, who were exploited by 'industrialist' Alberich: this exegesis of Wagner's *Ring* equates Wagner's music with the physical aural harm from the late nineteenth-century industrial soundscape. Trippett suggests that Gill's caricature 'captures something of the literalism of this material mode of communication', referring to what he terms 'galvanic' or automatic 'listening', which foregrounds the physiological, sensory economy of the musical experience, something that cannot be resisted by thought and that is grounded in contemporary beliefs in the sensorium's irreducibly material condition.[75]

To sum up this investigation: Wagner's music entered cultural discourse at a time when the medical science of otology was emerging in tandem with issues of ear physiology and hearing pathophysiology. Of particular concern to such medical specialists were the reasons for hearing loss, one cause of which was the noisy urban soundscape of an industrialised modern world. The fears associated with sonic injury would lead to noise abatement societies, literature about the physically and psychically injurious nature of noise and improved ear plugs, but in the late nineteenth century, anxieties over aural thresholds mapped onto the 'loudest' music of the day, that of Wagner. Ear specialists and music critics found common cause in decrying the composer's newly created sound world, mutually shrinking back from what they believed was the limit of material and perceptual endurance for hearing. Of course, in attacking the apparently deafening qualities of Wagner's music, they were not merely warning about dynamic levels, but were conflating a host of musical qualities such as textural density, harmonic complexity and orchestral brilliance, the combined experience of which could well have sounded too 'loud' to contemporary ears, much like the overwhelming noise complex of the modern metropolis.

Wagner's music dramas arrived in a European urban soundscape that rumbled, rattled and roared its way into the ears of citizens, 'straight through their finest thoughts', as Lessing opined. In the same year as Lessing's jeremiad against noise (1908), Breslau audiologist Georg Boenninghaus proclaimed in his *Textbook of Otology for Students and Physicians*: 'We modern musical human beings no longer sense any discomfort [*Unbehagen*] over [Wagner's] music; our ear is accustomed to it, and consonance and dissonance are hence not a problem for Helmholtz's theory, but that of psychology.'[76] This citation well illustrates the difference a few decades make, from the materialist sensory response to Wagner documented in this chapter to the cognitive, mind-based

---

[75] Trippett 2013, 367.

[76] 'Wir modernen musikalischen Menschen aber empfinden bei dieser Musik [von Wagner] kein Unbehagen mehr, unser Ohr ist daran gewöhnt, und Konsonanz und Dissonanz ist daher nicht Problem der Helmholtzschen Theorie, sondern der Psychologie.' Boenninghaus 1908, 62.

perspective that still prevails today. It also reinforces the historical engagement of medical science with Wagner and his music, a topic that remains under-researched in the literature. And Boenninghaus's remark may well inspire us to ask, where does the threshold of discomfort stand today, and what does that say about listening acuity in our own audible environment?

PART III

Technologies

8 | Science, Technology and Love in Late Eighteenth-Century Opera

DEIRDRE LOUGHRIDGE

It is a tale told by countless operas: young love, thwarted by an old man's financially motivated marriage plans, triumphs in the end thanks to a deception that tricks the old man into blessing the young lovers' union. Always a doddering fool, the old man is often also an enthusiast for knowledge. Such is the case, for instance, in Carlo Goldoni's comic opera libretto *Il mondo della luna* (1750), in which Buonafede's interest in the moon opens him to an elaborate hoax that has him believe he and his daughters have left Earth for the lunar world; and also in the Singspiel *Die Luftbälle, oder der Liebhaber à la Montgolfier* (1788), wherein the apothecary Wurm trades Sophie, the ward he intended to marry himself, for a technological innovation that will make him a pioneering aeronaut.[1]

In both of these operas, the outlines of well-worn comic stereotypes are easily visible.[2] And the very visibility of these stereotypes helps bring to view another, more broadly significant phenomenon: the reworking of operatic conventions to channel changing ideas and feelings about 'science'. For while many eighteenth-century operas lampoon devotees of bookish scholasticism, in these two cases the pursuit of knowledge appears in more modern-scientific guise: centred on observation and exploration of the natural world, its advance linked to technology and the augmentation of human powers. And whereas the pedant obsessed with antique learning was a reliable target for ridicule, science and technology represented a domain of growing importance and fashionability during the eighteenth century – a kind of activity and topic of conversation in which opera-goers were now likely to participate.[3] As a result, the figure of the fool becomes complicated: in *Il mondo della luna*, Buonafede explores the lunar world as an attentive – though deluded – observer, while in *Die Luftbälle*, aeronautic pursuits are not those of the foolish old man alone: the opera's hero Karl, Sophie's true love, has himself made and flown a hot air balloon. In both

---

[1] Fegejo 1750; Bretzner 1786, adapted as a Singspiel in 1788.

[2] On the foolish philosopher or pseudo-scholar type in opera, see Farkas 1967; Hunter 1999; and Goehring 2004, esp. 53–121.

[3] For further discussion of the popularisation of science through literature and performance in connection with opera and musical life, see Loughridge 2016.

operas, furthermore, scientific inquiry occasions special music. Indeed, replacing bookish scholasticism with observation and adventure altered the operatic potential of knowledge-pursuit; and putting music to such plots at once underlined the pleasure in scientific inquiry, and encouraged sympathy for epistemophilia.

Roy Porter has described the eighteenth century as a period of 'consolidation' for scientific knowledge: the revolutionary discoveries and methods of the likes of Galileo and Newton having already been established, the period mainly saw scientific approaches to the natural world disseminated and institutionalised across Europe.[4] The 'consolidation' image, however, carries the risk of leaving out sources of resistance and acts of reinterpretation. *Il mondo della luna* and *Die Luftbälle*, I argue, show the dynamic nature of the 'consolidation' process: more than examples of opera capitalising on contemporary scientific fascinations, these operas reflect and contributed to an ongoing adjustment of earlier attitudes towards the pursuit of knowledge; in this, they belong to the history of science as much as to the history of opera. Yet such operatic cooperation in advancing scientific interests was short-lived; as we shall see, Mozart's *Die Zauberflöte* evidences a newfound preference for separating operatic magic from scientific achievements.

Opera's Anti-Science Heritage

From *commedia dell'arte*, opera inherited a robust tradition of satirising the pursuit of knowledge, at the centre of which stood the stock character of the Dottore. This 'scholar-windbag', as Peter Jordan aptly describes him, was 'an incarnated lampoon of learning, tending towards long sententious and often nonsensical speeches' intended by the speaker to display his erudition but having the opposite effect of exposing his foolishness and ignorance.[5] In the case of *Il mondo della luna* the line of descent from the Dottore to Buonafede is clear, for Goldoni adapted the story for the opera from an earlier *commedia dell'arte* piece. First performed in 1684, Nolant de Fatouville's *Arlequin, Empereur dans la lune* – like Goldoni's opera – tells the tale of a man curious about the moon, whose curiosity is exploited by others to further their own marriage interests.[6] The earlier scenario begins at a telescope, as the Dottore and Pierrot debate the existence of a world on the moon. The Dottore maintains that such a world exists,

[4] Porter 2003.   [5] Jordan 2015, 66.   [6] See Brago 1984, 310.

reasoning with typically comic logic: 'if there is twilight in the moon, there must be generation and decay; and if there is decay and generation, animals and vegetables must be born; and if animals and vegetables are born, ergo the moon is a habitable world like ours'.[7] Thus even as he stands at a telescope, the Dottore privileges logic and philosophical doctrine over empirical observation. Indeed, it was a mixture of empiricism with doctrinaire logic – reasoning by analogy that if the moon has mountains like Earth it must also be inhabited like Earth – that gave birth to widespread speculation about a world on the moon in the mid-seventeenth century, and found popular expression in Bernard le Bovier de Fontenelle's natural-philosophical work of 1686, *Entretiens sur la pluralité des mondes* (*Conversations on the Plurality of Worlds*), a text widely translated and republished throughout the eighteenth century.[8]

When Arlequin discovers that the Dottore intends to give his servant Colombine to an apothecary in marriage, he uses the Dottore's belief in a lunar world to secure Colombine as his own wife. Disguised as a foreigner, Arlequin presents himself to the Dottore as 'Ambassador Extraordinaire, sent by the Emperor of the moon'. Arlequin proceeds to convince the Dottore through fantastic descriptions of lunar life, as well as a faked conversation with the lunar emperor through a speaking trumpet. The Dottore listens to these voices of authority and ultimately believes what they tell him, frequently contributing his own insight – consistent with his logical deduction of a world on the moon – that 'it is just as it is here'. (In an example of circular exchange between theatre and philosophy, Gottfried Wilhelm Leibniz cited this theme from Fatouville's play – unironically – to explain his postulated 'Principle of Uniformity': 'everywhere and all the time, everything is the same as here'.)[9]

The pretentious erudition, the reliance on logic and doctrine, the resulting failure to distinguish reality from fantasy – these traits displayed by the Dottore in *Arlequin, Empereur dans la lune* remained favourite targets for satire in comic opera. The stock character of the Dottore often reappeared as a philosopher, an 'eccentric [purveyor] of arcane lore', as Edmund Goehring has described, 'who, in defiance of common sense, sought to impose a rigid system of thought upon experience'.[10] An archetypal

---

[7] 'S'il y a des Crepuscules dans la Lune, bisogna ch'a vi sia una Generation, & una Corrution; e s'al ghé una corrution, & una generation, bisogna ch'a ve nasca dei Animali, e dei Vegetabili; e s'al ghe nasce dei animali, e dei vegetabili, ergo la Luna é un Mondo abitabile com'al nostro.' Fatouville 1721, 180–1.

[8] On the history of the idea of a world on the moon, see Crowe 1986, esp. 9–21 and 59–73.

[9] Letter to Sophie Charlotte, 8 May 1704, cited in Lodge 2004, 200. [10] Goehring 2004, 54.

example comes from Giovanni Bertati's *I filosofi immaginari*. Composed by Giovanni Paisiello initially for the court of Catherine II in St Petersburg in 1779, the opera had several dozen performances in German adaptation between 1781 and 1803 in cities including Vienna and Dresden, under the titles *Die engebildeten Philosophen* and *Die engebildeten Astrologen*.[11] The plot is preserved across the opera's various versions: the father Petronio is a Dottore-type character, whose primary concerns are 'scholarship and science'.[12] One of his two daughters follows in his footsteps: Cassandra is interested in philosophy and rejects the idea of marriage. Clarice, on the other hand, regards philosophy as useless and is concerned primarily with marrying her lover, Giuliano. Philosophy, in this story, is scholastic and logical, disengaged not only from the social world but also from empirical observation. As Cassandra declares, she is 'already accustomed to treating sense perception with scorn'.[13] Her métier, like her father's, is to seek knowledge in the pages of books by such authorities as Plato and Descartes. Musically, their epistemophilia is depicted through march-style arias that capture their pomposity, or patter arias that heighten the ridiculousness of their pseudo-erudite speech.[14]

Concurrent with such depictions of the philosopher in the latter half of the eighteenth century, meanwhile, were portrayals of a new species of knowledge-seeker. In *Il mondo della luna*, Goldoni transmuted the scholar-windbag Dottore into someone curious to gain knowledge through sensory observation. At the start of the opera, Buonafede does not already believe there must be a world in the moon. Instead he visits the astronomer Ecclitico in order to inquire what the moon is. Ecclitico has just built a giant telescope, and tells Buonafede he has discovered that on the moon is another inhabited world. This notion had largely fallen out of favour by the mid-eighteenth century, as mounting empirical evidence failed to support it.[15] Buonafede is thus surprised by Ecclitico's claim, and remarks that only his grandmother (a figure of the past) had ever spoken of such things. But when he looks through Ecclitico's telescope and sees people interacting not

[11] See the entry for Paisiello's *I filosofi immaginari* in *Die Oper in Italien und Deutschland zwischen 1770 und 1830*, www.oper-um-1800.uni-mainz.de/einzeldarstellung_werk.php?id_werke=317&herkunft=; and Hadamowsky 1966, 1:34.

[12] 'scienza, e dottrina'; 'Gelehrsamkeit und Wissenschaft'. Bertati 1784, 19; 1783, 24.

[13] 'E a trattar con disprezzo / I sensi e la material io già mi avvezzo'; 'bin schon gewohnt, die sinnliche Empfindung mit Verachtung zu unterdrücken'. Bertati 1784, 7; 1783, 6.

[14] See Hunter 1999, 110–24; and Goehring 2004, 78–82.

[15] See Crowe 1986, 59–73; as Crowe observes, refraining from speculation about lunar inhabitants was crucial for astronomers to establish a professional reputation by the latter half of the eighteenth century.

at all like they do on Earth, he immediately accepts the visual evidence. Unbeknownst to Buonafede, his faith is misplaced: Ecclitico is a fraudulent astronomer and his telescope a fake. What Buonafede sees through the instrument is not a world in the moon, but an illuminated machine with moving figures, hanging just beyond the end of the optical tube.[16]

The scene of telescopic observation initiates the moon-world hoax, undertaken for the same reason as in *Arlequin, Empereur dans la lune.* But in this case, the hoax involves Buonafede's extensive empirical investigation of the lunar world. At the end of Act I, Buonafede drinks a sleeping potion believing it will transport him to the moon. At the start of Act II he wakes up on what he takes to be the world in the moon – in fact Ecclitico's garden, decorated with 'extravagances' (*stravaganze*) to give it an appropriately exotic appearance. Guided by Ecclitico, Buonafede observes the lunar environment – and Goldoni's libretto calls for particular nature sounds. 'Listen to the harmonies from those saplings shaken by quick breezes,' Ecclitico instructs Buonafede; the subsequent stage direction reads, 'a short concert begins with violins and oboes in the orchestra, echoed by hunting horns and bassoons from behind the scenery'. Other musical stage-directives include 'nightingales are heard singing', and 'off-stage echoes answer from all sides'. Unlike the view through the telescope, which only Buonafede can see, these sounds give Buonafede and opera spectators alike the opportunity to observe lunar nature – and the composer the opportunity to render that nature either patently ridiculous or seductively otherworldly (and hence to characterise Buonafede as a total fool or a more sympathetic dupe).

Throughout his telescopic and first-hand encounters, Buonafede finds lunar behaviour to be very different and preferable to that on Earth (a change from the Dottore's doctrine 'it is just as it is here'). To the harmonious tree rustling, Buonafede responds with typical enthusiasm: 'Bravo! Bravissimo! In this world the trees can play much better than our musicians.' In the tradition of the Dottore, Buonafede's efforts to acquire and display knowledge reveal his comical ignorance and gullibility. But whether one laughs at or sympathises with Buonafede depends much on the music, and how familiar or exotic, patently ridiculous or beautifully otherworldly, it makes Ecclitico's tricks seem.

First set by Baldassare Galuppi for performance in 1750, *Il mondo della luna* subsequently received numerous new settings (and numerous textual

---

[16] For further discussion of the relationship between Goldoni's telescope scene, Haydn's setting and popular scientific culture, see Loughridge 2016, 25–45.

revisions) into the 1790s.[17] Galuppi's version, composed for the carnival season in Venice, presents no major musical surprises, investing Ecclitico's lunar garden with little sense of otherworldliness, and preserving Buonafede in the familiar role of the foolish old man. Later composers, by contrast, seized upon, and even expanded, the opportunity to portray an exotic lunar soundscape. When Haydn and Paisiello composed versions of *Il mondo della luna*, in 1777 and 1783 respectively, each departed from Goldoni's instructions in ways that encourage opera spectators to share Buonafede's delight and wonder at 'lunar' phenomena.

Haydn's Act II starts with a Sinfonia that previews some of the nature sounds that Buonafede will encounter after he wakes (Example 8.1). The Sinfonia begins with material from the tree branch symphony (bb. 1–8). The phrase segues into an idea (bb. 8–11) that will recur as singing birds in Buonafede's aria 'Che mondo amabile', where he lists the delightful things he has seen and heard on the moon ('the trees play music, the birds sing, the nymphs dance, the echo replies'). Through differences in orchestration between the Sinfonia and these later instances, Haydn first introduces opera spectators to a strangely beautiful 'lunar' environment, then presents Buonafede with more ordinary, even ridiculous 'lunar' sounds at odds with his enthusiasm. In the Sinfonia, for instance, the melody from the tree symphony is scored for violins with a solo violin added an octave above, imparting a lustrous sheen. The tree symphony Buonafede applauds, by contrast, features a melody on bassoon, an instrument often spotlighted for comedic effect (Example 8.2).

In Buonafede's aria 'Che mondo amabile', the birdcalls are scored for flutes, oboes, bassoons, and horns, accompanied by Buonafede's whistling (Example 8.3). In the Sinfonia, they are scored for the special effect of strings playing flageolet – that is, playing harmonics by lightly stopping the string at natural nodes, thereby yielding a different, airier tone. Flageolet harmonics were so called because they were thought to sound like the flageolet, a wooden predecessor of the tin whistle.[18] By setting birdsong for *strings* playing flageolet in the Sinfonia, Haydn thereby called for an imitation of an imitation. The result is appropriately distanced from the original: the naturally unequal strengths of the violin's harmonics turn the descending thirds on the page into ascending fourths in performance, transforming the most stereotypical birdcall into something hardly

---

[17] See Polzonetti 2011, 29–32.

[18] Jean-Joseph Cassanéa de Mondonville introduced violin harmonics in *Les Sons harmoniques: Sonates à violon seul avec la basse continue*, Op. 4 (Paris, *c.*1738), explaining how to produce them in an introduction and featuring them in the sonatas.

Example 8.1 Haydn, *Il mondo della luna*, Act II, Sinfonia, bb. 1–10. (*Joseph Haydn Werke*, series 25, volume 7/2, ed. Günther Thomas (Munich: Henle, 1979).) Used by permission

suggestive of birdcall at all. It seems altogether fitting to respond to these lunar birdcalls as Buonafede would – to find them delightful and different, perhaps even better, than any birdsongs heard on Earth. Haydn thus grants opera spectators two sources of pleasure: first in experiencing a fantastic lunar world for themselves, and subsequently in knowing better than Buonafede as he falls for the illusion.

In Paisiello's setting, an instrument unmentioned by Goldoni defines the sound of the lunar world: the still-uncommon clarinet.[19] The instrument is

---

[19] Paisiello produced *Il mondo della luna* in a number of versions; here, I refer to the *festa teatrale* version performed in St Petersburg, 1783, which served as the basis for the version performed in Vienna in 1786.

Example 8.2 Haydn, *Il mondo della luna*, Act II, 'tree symphony', bb. 1–14

reserved for numbers that conjure the lunar soundscape, and combines with horns and bassoons to form wind ensembles of a kind that carried magical associations in eighteenth-century opera.[20] Disregarding Goldoni's specifications for the tree symphony, Paisiello scored the number for a wind quartet of clarinet, bassoon and two horns. Paisiello also

[20] See Buch 2008.

Example 8.3 Haydn, *Il mondo della luna*, Act II, 'Che mondo amabile', bb. 44–49

added an instrumental number to depict the 'healthy' lunar air that Ecclitico points out to Buonafede (Example 8.4). Scored for two wind quintets, each composed of two clarinets, bassoon and two horns, the 'healthy air' number features a back-stage wind ensemble echoing the one in the pit (the spatialised sound, here as elsewhere, contributing to the sense of being in another world). Paisiello thus supplied lunar music at which opera spectators could marvel along with Buonafede, and through which they might gain sympathy for his enthusiasm.

Haydn composed *Il mondo della luna* for a wedding celebration at Esterháza, and Paisiello his as a *festa theatrale* for the court of Catherine II in St Petersburg. Adding musical to visual splendour may thus have been uppermost on these composers' minds as they marshalled their instrumental resources to heighten the music-theatrical spectacle of *Il mondo*

Example 8.4 Paisiello, *Il mondo della luna*, Act II, 'air', bb. 1–21. Österreichische Nationalbibliothek Musiksammlung, Mus.Hs.17806/2

della luna. But Haydn's and Paisiello's choices also had ramifications for the characterisation of Buonafede and his scientific curiosity, and reflect a new scientific consciousness in opera – one cognisant of the spectacular potential of sensory observation and its technological enhancements. These composers discovered this potential in a mid-eighteenth-century libretto still strongly marked by opera's anti-science heritage. But librettists working in the 1780s and 1790s found new source materials in the scientific developments of their day. In fact, the same year that Paisiello composed *Il mondo della luna* to sonify the lofty perspective of the moon, scientific consciousness received further impetus from a new technological innovation: the hot air balloon.

Approaching the Gods

'Thanks to the Montgolfiers, whom genius inspires ... the feeble mortal can approach the gods', a poet observed on the occasion of a balloon launch at Lyon in January 1784.[21] The Montgolfier brothers had launched the first hot air balloon before a crowd of 60,000 spectators at Versailles in June 1783, and sent up the first manned balloon – flown by Pilâtre de Rozier – a few months later. News of the hot air balloon quickly spread throughout Europe, as did ventures in flight.

Johann Wolfgang von Goethe described hot air balloons as experiments from a time 'when the scientific world was busily occupied with determining the different kinds of air'.[22] He might equally have noted the wider world's preoccupation with the spectacle of hot air balloon launches: a spectacle that could turn operatic. For instance, at the ascent of the 'Marie Antoinette' that took place at Versailles on 23 June 1784 to entertain visiting royalty from Sweden, musicians played the overture from Pierre-Alexandre Monsigny's comic opera *Le Déserteur* (1769). More common are references to unidentified military music or cannon fire; but celebratory sounds regularly complemented the awe-inspiring sight of a balloon ascending into the heavens.[23]

As the celebratory atmosphere at balloon launches suggests, aeronauts were cultural heroes. They became a focus of national sentiment, arousing

---

[21] Quoted in Darnton 1968, 20.
[22] 'als die naturforschende Welt sich eifrig beschäftigte die verschiedenen Luftarten zu erkennen'. Goethe 2014, 53.
[23] See the numerous contemporary reports translated in Jobé 1971.

pride in the achievements of one's countrymen, a competitive desire to surpass other nations, and prompting races to become the 'first' at various localities. The winner of many of these races was J.-F. Blanchard, a French mechanic who became an aeronaut by financing his flights through ticket subscriptions. With this entrepreneurial approach, Blanchard travelled throughout Europe introducing people to the phenomenon of human flight. He cultivated the spectacular side of ballooning, fashioning himself a brave explorer more than a natural philosopher. Sometimes, however, he was joined by a scientific companion: the physician John Jeffries accompanied Blanchard on certain flights, and recorded such metrics as temperature and barometric pressure.[24] On 3 October 1785, Blanchard ascended in a balloon at Frankfurt am Main to become the first to fly in Germany. Though he advertised himself as a 'French aeronaut', he also appealed to national feelings, as in a promotional poem that espoused the greatness of air balloon flight and proclaimed 'they were *Germans* / Who recognised all this'.[25]

To become the first German to fly remained a prized title – one that the Baron Lütgendorf sought to claim on 24 May 1786. Much promotional material was published ahead of the launch. One pamphlet (reproduced in Figure 8.1) celebrates Lütgendorf as the first German aeronaut, with verses such as, 'Hark sons of Germany! A German will dare / To be carried by an air balloon through the air: / Baron von Lütgendorf will become Germany's Blanchard / And invites you to admire the show and regard.' The poem concludes by calling upon those who share scientific interests as well as sensibility to attend the launch, and linking their attendance to civic pride: 'O come, ye who honour your arts / Ye who nurture your knowledge and good feelings / Come, ennoble our city, and ennoble the balloon! / And think – a German flies, and fame is his only reward!'[26]

The competitive and potentially nationalistic nature of ballooning, as well as the question of reward, runs through Christoph Friedrich Bretzner's Singspiel *Die Luftbälle, oder Der Liebhaber à la Montgolfier*. As the story

---

[24] See Gillespie 1984. On the spectacular-cum-scientific culture of hot air balloons, see also Keen 2006, Holmes 2008 and Brant 2011.

[25] 'Das waren *Deutsche* zwar, / Die alles dies erkannten'. Quoted in Westheim 1908, 310.

[26] 'Auf, Söhne Deutschlands, hört! Ein Deutscher wird es wagen, / Durch einen Luftballon sich durch die Luft zu tragen: / Baron von Lütgendorf wird Deutschlands Blanchard seyn, / Und ladet euch zur Schau und zur Bewund'rung ein.'; 'O, kommet doch herbey, ihr, die ihr Künste ehret, / Ihr, die ihr Wissenschaft und Schöngefühle nähret, / Kommt, adelt unsre Stadt, und adelt den Ballon! / Und denkt – Ein Deutscher fliegt, und Ruhm nur ist sein Lohn!' [unsigned] 1786, [1, 3].

Science, Technology and Love   187

Die
Luftbälle
oder
der **Liebhaber**
à la Montgolfier
eine Posse in zween Akten
von
Brezner.

Aufgeführt auf dem kurfürstlichen National-
Theater in München, 1786.

Figure 8.1 Christoph Friedrich Bretzner, *Die Luftbälle, oder der Liebhaber à la Montgolfier* (Leipzig: Friedrich Gotthold Jacobaer, 1786), title page. Bayerische Staatsbibliothek München, P.o.germ. 175, urn:nbn:de:bvb:12-bsb10106328-3.

starts, Sophie laments the absence of her true love Karl, and her impending marriage to her guardian, the apothecary Wurm. Karl's sister Lottchen, however, produces a letter for Sophie from Karl, in which he announces he is on his way to her in a hot air balloon. As Sophie worries over Karl's safety, Wurm enters, talking about the 'amazing thing' ('unglaubliche Dinge') that soon everyone will be able to read about in the newspapers. In guessing what 'amazing thing' Wurm has in mind, Lottchen proposes both traditional alchemical pursuits as well as a more modern, institutional achievement: perhaps Wurm has invented a universal medicine, become a member of the Academy of Sciences in Paris, or discovered the philosopher's stone and can now make gold. But it is none of these 'trifles'. Rather, with the help of Magistrate Senf, Wurm has readied and is about to fly a hot air balloon.

Wurm's casting as an apothecary resonated with contemporary life as well as satirical tradition. Goethe recorded the efforts of local Weimar apothecary Wilhelm Sebastian Buchholz to keep up with the latest scientific experiments by launching a hot air balloon in 1784, at first unsuccessfully, but ultimately getting off the ground.[27] Wurm is interested less in keeping up with current science, however, than in becoming famous as the first great German aeronaut. Modelling himself on 'the brave Blanchard', Wurm intends for Senf and himself to become famous as the first Germans to fly. Senf, meanwhile, believes they will make a trip to the moon, and has grand plans for their pioneering space exploration. His projected studies range from the natural-scientific to the cosmological and anthropological, with topics including the spots on the moon, the 'existence and being of more worlds', and the character of those worlds' peoples and societies.

What starts as a mutually beneficial collaboration between Wurm and Senf turns acrimonious when – in the course of pompously describing the celebrity they will enjoy after their flight – Wurm inadvertently insults Senf with the remark that he will no longer be a 'miserable, simple Magistrate' ('elenden simplen Magister'). Lottchen interrupts the ensuing spat by letting slip the secret that her brother Karl has made an air balloon. Wurm and Senf each rush to make themselves indispensable to the younger aeronaut. Senf asserts that a young man like Karl needs a savant (*Gelehrten*) like him. He envisions himself conducting experiments while Karl steers: he will be the Dr Jeffries to Karl's Blanchard. Wurm, on the

---

[27] Goethe 2014, 53–4.

other hand, maintains that Karl, being a young man, needs him as a sponsor.

Once Karl arrives – waving 'the flag of love' – Lottchen hatches a plan to exploit Wurm's aeronautic dreams in order to unite Karl and Sophie. It is a simple deception: Karl tells Wurm and Senf that he has invented a steering mechanism and is going to the moon since, having no hope of marrying Sophie, there is nothing for him on Earth. At this, Wurm offers to let Karl marry Sophie if he will tell Wurm how to steer the balloon and let him take credit for the invention. At the ensuing launch, however, Wurm and Senf go up and quickly fall back to earth, while Karl and Sophie fly away in Karl's balloon, to live happily ever after.

Because Karl is a successful aeronaut, Wurm and Senf embody less lampoons of learning than of incompetence; what comes in for satire is not the pursuit of knowledge so much as the selfish motivations for such pursuit, and the character of the pursuer. Wurm spells out the values he stands for early on, telling Sophie and Lottchen: 'head, head, head, head must one have! Sciences, talent, erudition, spirit of invention!'[28] Karl exposes the incompleteness of these values. He is, as Lottchen says, a genius, whose ballooning will probably earn him a title, pension and fame. But his intellectual pursuits and economic success flow from his bravery and love. As Lottchen describes Karl, he has a 'brave, adventurous head' (*kühner unternehmender Kopf*). And Karl calls his hot air balloon not a ticket to fame and fortune but his rescuer, saying he has it to thank for the happiness of his life – his reunion with Sophie. If there is a secure moral reading of all this, the story arguably draws distinctions between laughable and admirable forms of scientific venture, finding it possible for intellectual genius to be united with a warm heart and brave soul.

Bretzner established himself as a popular librettist in 1779, with the publication of four operettas. Today, the Leipzig-based writer is chiefly remembered as the librettist whose *Belmont und Constanze, oder Die Entführung aus dem Serail* (written for the composer Johann André and published in 1781) was 'freely adapted' by Gottlieb Stephanie to become Mozart's *Entführung aus dem Serail* (1782).[29] But *Die Luftbälle* he wrote not as an operetta but rather as a spoken play – a two-act farce (*Posse*). The play was performed in Hamburg and Breslau in the summer of 1785,

---

[28] 'Kopf, Kopf, Kopf muß man haben! Wissenschaften, Talente, Gelehrsamkeit, Erfindugsgeist!' Bretzner 1786, 13.

[29] The title page of the 1783 *Entführung aus dem Serail* libretto reads 'nach Bretznern frey bearbeitet'.

according to Bretzner's preface to the first edition, which was printed in Leipzig the following year.[30] While this edition sees a 'choir of musicians with trumpets and drums' participate in the climactic balloon launch, there are no numbers for the main characters to sing, and no composer is credited.

That *Die Luftbälle* would be adapted as a Singspiel is not surprising, given Bretzner's popularity as a librettist, the common plot elements, and the musico-spectacular appeal of the hot air balloon. In 1788, song texts 'from the Singspiel' *Die Luftbälle* were printed in Hamburg, under the names of Bretzner as author and Ferdinand Fränzl as composer.[31] For Fränzl, *Die Luftbälle* was his first stage work. After he wrote the music in Strasburg, where he studied composition with Franz Xaver Richter and Ignaz Pleyel, the Singspiel premiered at the Mannheim Nationaltheater on 15 April 1787 (where Fränzl's father – also a composer and violinist – was musical director). It continued to be performed there until 1795, and also had a Munich premiere in 1788, though the music seems never to have been published.[32] Unlike the free adaptation of Bretzner's *Belmont und Constanze*, the adaptation of *Die Luftbälle* to the musical stage stayed true to Bretzner's plot, the song texts being inserted between or replacing the spoken text. The narrative fidelity of the adaptation brings into focus the effects of 'opera' on the telling – of song texts and music on the tone and messages of the stage production.

As one might expect, Fränzl musically heightened the spectacle of the hot air balloon. The launch scene involves celebratory music likely akin to that provided by the choir of musicians Bretzner had scripted, and by musicians at actual balloon launches. But in addition, the scene features dramatic action music. The balloons ascend to the accompaniment of a seventeen-measure pedal point on D major, with gradually increasing activity and dynamic level in the orchestra (Example 8.5). It is music of a sort used to represent sunrises, as well as marvellous entrances like that of the Queen of the Night in Mozart's *Die Zauberflöte*. The conventionality of the musical gesture serves to liken the hot air balloon launch to such

---

[30] A playbill gives 23 May 1785 as the date of first performance in Hamburg, according to the catalogue of the Staats- und Universitätsbibliothek Hamburg. This date precedes de Rozier's balloon accident, which is referenced in the added song texts.

[31] Whether these song texts were penned by Bretzner or were the work of another, uncredited author is unclear. Friedrich Walter proposed Friedrich Schiller as author, citing a letter of 17 May 1786 in which Schiller mentions meeting Ferdinand Fränzl, and having completed some operetta texts; see F. Walter 1909.

[32] See F. Walter 1899, 399; Bolongaro-Crevenna 1963, 249.

Science, Technology and Love 191

Example 8.5 Ferdinand Fränzl, *Die Luftbälle, oder Der Liebhaber à la Montgolfier* (1785), Act II finale; instrumental ritornello while the balloons ascend. Staats- und Universitätsbibliothek Hamburg Carl von Ossietzky, ND VII 130: 1

natural and fantastic phenomena, and to invest the aeronautic technology with a similar sense of awesome power.

Other changes come with the endings to each act, which were redesigned to suit the conventions of operatic finales. The first act of the play ends with

Wurm and Senf making amends and exiting arm-in-arm with a renewed commitment to their venture. By contrast, the Singspiel Act I finale proceeds from an added plot element: news of a hot air balloon accident. Lottchen reads the story of a fallen aeronaut from a newspaper, and shocks Wurm and Senf with the revelation that the victim was none other than Pilâtre de Rozier, the first man to ascend in a hot air balloon. The accident in question took place on 15 June 1785, when de Rozier attempted to fly across the English Channel with a new balloon design combining 'inflammable gas' (hydrogen) and hot air. When the balloon caught fire, Pilâtre and his flight companion plummeted to their deaths, becoming the first aeronautic casualties – to widespread lamentation.[33] The finale thus amplifies the idea of mortal risk whose focal point in the play is Sophie's concern for Karl's safety. And the news report leads to an added moral that Sophie, Lottchen, Wurm and Senf sing together to end the first act: 'the higher the flight, the further the fall' ('Je höher der Flug, je tiefer der Fall'). Fränzl's setting dwells on the line: sung in unison and in imitation, it homes in on the danger inherent in scientific advance. But as the end of the first act, it is a sentiment that stands to be superseded.

And so, at the end of the opera, it is. Bretzner's play ends with Senf, undeterred by his flight's failure, comically advertising pre-subscriptions to his account of his air trip. The opera instead ends with the chorus: 'Viva, viva, to live / and Montgolfier besides! / Music resounds / All cry / They live high!'[34] The affirmative sentiment is especially striking compared with the conclusion of Goldoni's *Il mondo della luna*, where all sing together, 'in the end he will repent / who would believe in the moon' ('All fin si pentirà / chi lunatica sarà'). Where seeking to go beyond natural boundaries had been opera's recipe for comic downfall, it was – in the wake of ballooning – something opera could celebrate.

Fairy-Tale Endings

If astronomy and aeronautics supplied novel opportunities for musico-spectacular display in comic operas that portrayed bourgeois life, however, in the marvellous domains of mythology and fairy-tales they raised a new question: what were the creators of opera to do when their intentionally

---

[33] On the reception of de Rozier's death, see Hallion 2003, 60.

[34] 'Vivant, vivant sollen leben, / und Montgolfier darneben! / Musik erschalle, / Auf ruft alle, / Sie leben hoch!' Bretzner and Fränzl 1788, 20.

fantastic devices became the stuff of everyday reality? Such a question became pressing in the milieu of Mozart's *Die Zauberflöte*. In the summer of 1791, Blanchard was building up to perform the first air balloon launch in Vienna. Two operas inspired by J. A. Liebeskind's story 'Lulu, oder die Zauberflöte', from the third volume of Christoph Martin Wieland's fairy-tale collection *Dschinnistan* (1786–9), were conceived for the city at this time: *Die Zauberflöte* as well as *Kaspar der Faggotist, oder Die Zauberzither*. Like their source material, both operas feature air transport – but deal differently with the fact that such travel was no longer solely the stuff of myth and fairy tale. Their approaches thus suggest another shift in attitudes towards the operatic potential of science and technology.

In the tale 'Lulu, oder die Zauberflöte', the fairy Perifirime recruits Prince Lulu to recover her magic tinder-box from an evil magician. Like numerous fairy-tales and myths, 'Lulu' features a cloud chariot. After Perifirime gives Lulu a magic flute and ring to help him in his task, a castle door opens by itself and the 'chariot, designed like a cloud' ('Wagen, wie eine Wolke gestaltet'), floats out and lands before them. They get in, and the chariot rises and flies 'as smoothly and quickly as a swallow through the forest'.[35]

The cloud chariot was staple stage machinery for operas based on fairy-tales or mythology. But when librettist Joachim Perinet wrote *Kaspar der Faggotist, oder Die Zauberzither* for composer Wenzel Müller and the Theater an der Leopoldstadt, he turned the cloud chariot into a 'hot air balloon' ('Luftballon' or 'Luftmaschine'). As in 'Lulu' (but for some name changes), the fairy Perifirime charges the Prince Armidoro with retrieving a golden tinder-box that the Sorcerer Bosphoro has stolen from her. After bestowing upon Armidoro a magic zither and magic ring, Perifirime and her genies present the prince and his comic sidekick Kaspar with a hot air balloon. The balloon appears at a wave of Perifirime's hand, as she tells Armidoro and Kaspar: 'this hot air balloon will take you comfortably to the spot'.[36] The moment is exploited for comic effect: Kaspar circles the basket sceptically and expresses trepidation at getting inside, but Armidoro commands him to be brave, and they fly off to Bosphoro's palace.

While *Die Zauberflöte* also features a prince (Tamino) and comic sidekick (Papageno) sent on a rescue mission equipped with magical gifts, the

---

[35] 'Der Wagen erhob sich, und flog so sanft und schnell wie eine Schwalbe über den Walde hin.' Wieland 1789, 3:298.

[36] 'Dieser Luftballon wird euch bequem an Ort und Stelle bringen.' Perinet 1792, 15.

flying machine is not among the tools put at their disposal. Instead, they are told that, 'three boys, young, handsome, / noble and wise / will hover around you on your journey; / They will be your guides; / follow only their advice.'[37] At critical moments in the unfolding drama, these three boys appear in a flying machine (*Flugwerk*). Numerous commentators claim that at the premiere of *Die Zauberflöte*, this flying machine was made to look like a hot air balloon. And in a number of modern productions – including at the Hamburger Staatsoper (1971), Opéra National de Paris (2001), Houston Grand Opera (2003) and in Ingmar Bergman's 1975 film version – the three boys descend in the 'period' apparatus; Figure 8.2 shows a further example from 2013.

Yet, the claim that a hot air balloon graced the stage at the premiere of *Die Zauberflöte* circulates without evidence, and seems to be a spurious invention of later critics who connected the *Flugwerk* with Blanchard's contemporaneous ascent. David J. Buch has observed that interpretations of Mozart's *Die Zauberflöte* have largely proceeded without considering the generic context of fairy-tale opera – a context that, when recovered, shows many supposedly Masonic elements of the opera to be conventional fairy-tale elements.[38] The putatively 'aeronautic' *Flugwerk* was similarly a fairy-tale opera convention. Already in the 1770s, one finds comic theatre pieces touting *Flugwerken* in their generic descriptions, and the devices routinely joined other fantastic elements on the stage.[39]

Not for lack of knowledge would the creators of *Die Zauberflöte* have preserved the traditional flying machine rather than update it to a hot air balloon. Five years earlier, Immanuel Schikaneder had authored a Singspiel for the occasion of Baron Lütgendorf's planned Augsburg launch. Set to music by Benedikt Schak (the first Tamino), *Der Luftballon* centres on the multi-suitored Sophie and an aeronaut who fly together and thereafter declare the true love – founded not in financial interest but in 'harmony of soul' – that they feel for one another. A less idealised vision of balloon flight

---

[37] 'Drei Knäbchen, jung, schön, / hold und weise, / Umschweben euch auf eurer Reise; / Sie warden eure Führer sein; folgt ihrem Rate ganz allein.' All translations from *Die Zauberflöte* are after Frey 1997.

[38] Buch 2004.

[39] A 1773 play mocked standing conventions by imagining a piece with the excessive title, 'Leander und Hero, oder der Ueberwinder des Konigs Zamar durch Zauberey, oder die treue Liebe, oder nichts umsonst; eine Heldenkumedie [sic] mit Flugwerken, Maschinen, Verwandlungen, Teufeln und Gespenstern' (Leander and Hero, or the conqueror of King Zamar through magic, or the true love, or not for nothing; a heroic comedy with flying machines, machines, transformations, devils and ghosts); Moll 1773, 12.

Science, Technology and Love 195

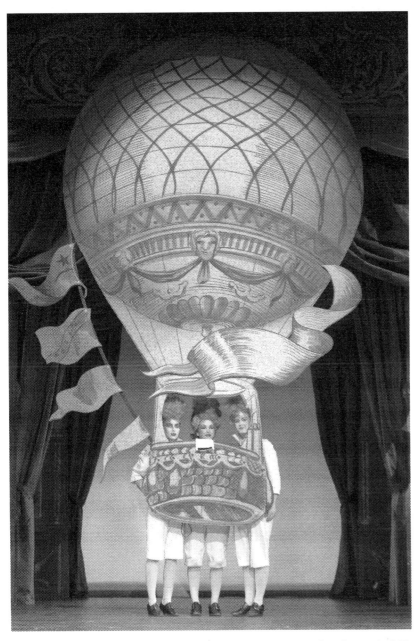

Figure 8.2 'Drei Knaben', press photo from the 2013 Theater und Orchester GmbH production of *Die Zauberflöte*, Neubrandenberg/Neustrelitz. Photo credit: Joerg Metzner.

comes from Mozart himself. On 6 July 1791 – the day Blanchard made his successful ascent in Vienna, after having failed on 9 March and 29 April – Mozart wrote to his wife: 'even as I write these lines Blanchard will either ascend into the air or fool the Viennese for a 3rd time. This whole episode with Blanchard is most unwelcome to me, today of all days – it's preventing me from completing my business.'[40]

The simple prop of a flag – specified for the aeronauts in both Schikaneder and Bretzner's texts, and ubiquitous in period images – would have been sufficient to turn the *Flugwerk* into a hot air balloon. But no flags are mentioned; instead, the three boys are described as carrying silver palm branches, their *Flugwerk* bedecked with roses. In light of *Kaspar, der Faggotist* – the main rival for Schikaneder and Mozart's production – the *Flugwerk* in *Die Zauberflöte* appears a deliberate decision not to engage with the balloon craze. The different approaches to operatic flight in an aeronautic age may have much to do with timing: *Kaspar* premiered on 8 June 1791, when Blanchard had yet to successfully ascend in Vienna, and balloon flight still had the status of a fantastic dream. *Zauberflöte* premiered on 30 September 1791, nearly three months after Blanchard's flight, when balloon flight was a fading memory – the stuff of a new normality.

Today, the obsolescence of hot air balloons grants them much the same status they enjoyed in their pre-normalcy days: they readily read as a fantastic image from a world that is not ours. In this respect, the hot air balloon now makes a fitting 'flying machine' for the three boys. But it is also worth considering the difference a hot air balloon makes for a period reading of the opera. At the start of the Act II finale, 'the three boys descend' ('die drey Knaben fahren herunter') to an instrumental introduction magically scored for clarinets, bassoons and horns, sotto voce (Example 8.6). Then they sing:

Bald soll der Aberglaube schwinden,	Soon shall superstition disappear,
Bald siegt der weise Mann.	Soon the wise man wins.
O, holde Ruhe, steig hernieder,	O gracious peace, descend here,
Kehr in der Menschen Herzen wieder,	Return to the hearts of people,
Dann ist die Erd' ein Himmelreich,	Then is the Earth a heavenly kingdom,
Und sterbliche sind Göttern gleich,	And mortals like gods.

To unite these words with a hot air balloon is to put technology forward as the means to make 'mortals like gods'. To unite them with a cloud chariot is to figure mortals becoming 'like gods' as the attainment of peace rather than

---

[40] Letter of 6 July 1791; quoted in Abert 2007, 1210.

Example 8.6 Mozart, *Die Zauberflöte*, Act II finale, 'Bald prangt, den Morgen zu verkünden'; instrumental ritornello while 'the three boys descend'

power – the difference between Mozart's gentle wind ensemble, and Fränzl's pedal-point crescendo.

***

In the decades before the Montgolfier brothers unleashed their balloons, flight seemed like childish fantasy – especially so on the operatic stage, where flying chariots were a staple of the marvellous that critics seeking a more naturalistic theatre targeted for censure. In retrospect, however, one can see these flying gods and goddesses not as mere 'puerile representations', as Charles Burney described them in 1773, but as stimuli to technological innovation. As Sigmund Freud suggested amidst the swirling changes of the early twentieth century, 'these things that, by his science and technology, man has brought about on this earth ... do not only sound like a fairy tale, they are an actual fulfilment of every – or of almost every – fairy-tale wish'.[41] To put it another way, fairy tales and myths have been incubators for science and technology, helping to set research agendas by archiving dream images of superhuman powers.

Through its stagings of fairy tales and myths, opera has been a site of cross-fertilisation between technological innovations and dream images, and also a site for social commentary on the practice of scientific inquiry. The 1770s–80s mark a remarkable phase in this operatic history, when hard-edged rejection softened to make room for the pleasures of observation, and the possibility that the pursuits of knowledge and of love need not stand in conflict. The *Flugwerk* of *Die Zauberflöte* stands for the end of this phase, when to re-enchant the operatic stage, developments in science and technology were relegated to the wings, to discourses of reception, to performance training and to subtexts – where they can be found in abundance throughout the nineteenth century.

[41] Freud 1989, 737.

9 | Technological Phantoms of the Opéra

BENJAMIN WALTON

Commenting on the emerging 'material turn' in opera studies, Jonathan Sterne recently cautioned about the need to define what we mean by a term as 'seductive yet baggy' as materiality.[1] Yet even if we sidestep the confusion of the competing Marxist, media theoretical, neuroscientific, ontological and ecological materialities that Sterne invokes, to start instead with a more naïve quest for opera's historical material traces – its objects and its things – where might the limits of such a search lie?[2] And must the realm of the material for the opera scholar necessarily function, as Sterne suggests, as a way 'to get at the immaterial, the ephemeral, the mortal'?[3] What, in short, might a material history of opera look like?

Such questions crowd in when writing about the Palais Garnier – principal home of the Paris Opéra from 1875 to 1989 – and when feeling at once impressed and oppressed by its material excess, by its overdetermination as a symbol of grand operatic culture, and by its continued existence as a repository for certain kinds of operatic fantasy, indulged as much by the scholars in its library as by the tourists posing on its grand staircase. Perhaps better, then, to approach the question more obliquely: what might a material history of opera seem most likely to leave out? From recent evidence, it would pass over those material traces that seem least enchanted, or least historically innovative, which often amounts to much the same thing, in pursuit of the sort of 'estranging old-time images, eccentric instruments, outré theories [and] fabulous body parts', listed by Carolyn Abbate as beloved of historians of music and science.[4]

---

[1] Sterne 2016, 160.

[2] On the distinction between objects and things, derived from Heidegger, see Brown 2001. In Brown's terms, objects become things 'when they stop working for us: when the drill breaks, when the car stalls, when the windows get filthy, when their flow within the circuits of production and distribution, consumption and exhibition, has been arrested, however momentarily' (4).

[3] Sterne 2016, 160.

[4] Abbate 2017, 793; see also the objects listed as focal points of a clutch of materially conscious opera books reviewed by Laura Tunbridge (and also quoted by Sterne): 'one large larynx; two dried testicles; a musical score; a shellac disc; symbols all for the continuing search for something beyond opera's materiality': (2016, 299).

Abbate suggests that there is nothing intrinsically wrong with luxuriating in the pleasures of such quirky *objets trouvés*.[5] Sterne, though, is not so sure, arguing that the disproportionate attention given to these kinds of artefacts at the expense of others less seductively bewildering – the design of a stage or the architecture of an opera house, for instance – indicates an estrangement of opera from its technological apparatus, with the result that operatic technologies receive attention only when objects of wonder. And quirky objects can quickly lose their shine. Take, for instance, the chronology that opens Karen Henson's recent edited collection of essays on *Technology and the Diva* – the book for which Sterne's reflections on operatic materiality serve as an afterword. Its authors offer up a trove of heliographs, phonautographs, microphones, wax cylinders, telegraphs, radio broadcasts and moving images. Yet in terms of production history, at least, the resultant catalogue of innovation maps a largely familiar landscape: the invention of limelight in 1803; phantasmagoric grand opéra via the innovative use of gaslight in the 'Ballet des nonnes' in Giacomo Meyerbeer's *Robert le diable* in 1831, the electrical sunrise of *Le Prophète* in 1849; a shift away from Paris in the second half of the century with the use of new technology for *Parsifal* at Bayreuth in 1882; the innovations in scenery and staging proposed in Adolphe Appia's *La Musique et la mise en scène* of 1899.[6] Such a progression chimes with other recent work, such as John Tresch's *The Romantic Machine*, which considers the ways that technology and romanticism, arts and sciences, became thrillingly entwined in Paris in the first half of the nineteenth century, only to unravel faced with 'the mechanistic materialism and rigid disciplinary divisions that took command after midcentury in the Second Empire'.[7]

Not that the broad contours of such a narrative necessarily ring false: the failed attempts during the 1860s to develop a revolutionary new system for the stage machinery of the Garnier Opéra, a system that forms the subject of this chapter, foundered in part through the incompatible disciplinary claims to expertise of machinists, engineers, creative personnel and Garnier himself as architect. Meanwhile, if I were to rephrase and refine the question that ended my first paragraph once more, this time to ask what a mechanistically materialist history of opera might look like, the Palais Garnier would seem an obvious place to turn for answers: it was, after all, an edifice explicitly intended to sculpt and gild the cultural prestige and aesthetic riches of opera into monumental form. The failure to innovate at

---

[5] On the seductions of the quirk, see Mathew and Smart 2015.
[6] Clancy, Gutkin and Vágnerová 2016.   [7] Tresch 2012, 19.

the Opéra, moreover, stands in contrast to more successful innovation elsewhere in Europe soon afterwards, as part of a broader story of changing operatic geographies towards the end of the nineteenth century.

As Tresch suggests, though, any elision of technological and aesthetic progress runs into problems in the second half of the century. In terms of the Palais Garnier, for instance, Evan Baker's recent history of operatic production argues that the fires that burnt down the Opéra's previous home, the Salle Le Peletier, in 1873, and the Opéra Comique in 1887, 'presented unique opportunities to initiate new production styles to accompany the newly replaced theaters'. Baker continues, 'the managements proved timid, contenting themselves with reproductions of the earlier stagings'.[8] But the implied equation here of management timidity with continuity of production style is undercut by contemporary discussions of the machinery on which innovative productions depended. An article that appeared in 1884 in the engineering journal *Le Génie civil*, for instance, listed the 'three principal conditions of theatrical machinery' as follows:

1. To create an illusion for the eyes of the spectator in the hall, through mechanical means as simple and rapid as possible;
2. To offer enough resilience to avoid at all costs any sort of accidental breaking or bending that, seen from the hall, would spoil the progress of the performance and would unfortunately bring down the spectators from the elevated spheres of artistic convention to a petty and sometimes ridiculous reality;
3. To build only scenery that can be taken down quickly and broken down into small pieces, easy to put to one side from one act to the next and to take out of the theatre, when one work is replaced by another.[9]

No Appian calls for revolution here; but instead, innovation figured as a commitment to a spectacular realism that would improve the audience's suspension of disbelief through improvements in construction, speed and

---

[8] Baker 2013, 251.

[9] '1. Produire l'illusion aux yeux du spectateur placé dans la salle, avec des moyens mécaniques aussi simples et aussi rapides que possible; 2. Offrir une résistance suffisante pour ne donner lieu, sous aucun prétexte, à un accident quelconque de rupture ou de flexion qui, vu de la salle, nuirait à la marche de la représentation et ramènerait fâcheusement le spectateur des sphères élevées de la convention artistique, à une réalité mesquine et parfois ridicule; 3. Ne se composer que de parties rapidement démontables et décomposables elles-mêmes en pièces de faible échantillon, faciles à mettre de côté d'un acte à l'autre et à emporter hors du théâtre, lorsqu'un ouvrage cède la place à un autre.' Nansouty 1884, 222.

efficiency.[10] And this implied a fourth condition, widely discussed elsewhere at the time: the replacement of men by machines. The search for new machinery at the Garnier Opéra was as much shaped by ongoing debates about mechanisation and labour costs across the rapidly expanding Second Empire industrial sector as by any vision of a new approach to operatic production. For some, the 'vast factory' of the new Opéra – as one critic described it at its inauguration in January 1875[11] – could benefit from the sorts of rationalisation introduced in other branches of manufacturing in pursuit of maximally smooth workflows; for others, cultural production could not be equated with other forms of industrial production, while the accumulated expertise of machinists could not be bettered simply by the introduction of new machines.

In what follows, then, my exploration of the saga of the Opéra machinery is shaped by several interconnected ideas, some perhaps more familiar to historians of science than of opera. These include Sterne's definition of technologies as 'repeatable social, cultural and physical processes crystallized into mechanisms', and David Edgerton's advocacy of a use-based technological history (rather than a history fixated on novelty), but they also encompass an attention to technological failure alongside success, and to the potential of a dominant discourse – here the discourse of inexorable progress – to shape solutions to technical questions.[12] And behind all such issues lies the attempt to reconnect the realm of the technological with the social and the aesthetic in the study of operatic history. Put bluntly: no spectacular operatic productions without machines, and no machines without people to operate them.

My focus, however, falls here not on the massed ranks of the Opéra's machinists, but on the small group tasked with determining which machinery to install; and above all on the young Charles Garnier himself. Garnier first took on the task of designing a new staging system single-handedly, before participating actively in the Commission (and Sub-Commissions) to seek a workable solution when his initial ideas were rejected. And it was Garnier, too, who committed the most complete account of the whole episode to print: first in *Le Théâtre*, published in

---

[10] Appia ruefully stressed the same thing in the second preface of 1918 to his *La Musique et la mise en scène*, when he wrote that 'the public like the specialists were entirely preoccupied with innovating through an increasing luxuriousness of decorations, or else by an ever-more-perfect realism: and the mise en scène understood in this way condemned the dramaturge to walk on the spot' ('le public comme les spécialistes étaient uniquement préoccupés d'innover par un luxe croissant de décorations, ou bien par un réalisme toujours plus parfait: et la mise en scène ainsi comprise condamnait le dramaturge à piétiner su place'). Quoted in Bablet 1983, 1: 9.

[11] 'cette vaste usine'. Duval 1876, 43.   [12] Sterne 2014, 121; Edgerton 2006.

1871, and then ten years later in *Le Nouvel Opéra*. He was responsible, as a result, for laying down an apparently authoritative history of the ultimate failure to install a new system, owing to lack of time and money, and of shaping his role at the centre of things in a way that left enough room for later writers to cast him as a technological visionary, frustrated by pettifogging bureaucracy.

Garnier's close involvement over many years with the question of the machinery, while he simultaneously masterminded the rest of the building's construction, is quite extraordinary; and his desire to include his own version of the deliberations over the machinery as part of his wider description of the project is entirely understandable. But his narrative is partial in ways that only become clear by returning to the quantities of original plans and reports written at each stage of the deliberations. Not that it would be possible to do justice to all the mechanical and interpersonal intricacies these documents reveal within the confines of a single chapter. Indeed, such a cache would arguably require a full-scale immersion in some kind of 'scientifiction' – Bruno Latour's description for his fusion of 'the novel, the bureaucratic dossier, and sociological commentary' developed in *Aramis, or the Love of Technology*.[13] Numerous striking parallels could be drawn, in fact, between the ill-fated mission to transform the Opéra machinery and Latour's virtuosic account of the thwarted attempts a century later to introduce a personal rapid transit system to Paris. And in homage to his insistence on the essentially fictional nature of any technological project, as well as in light of Garnier's own later retellings of his quest for the ideal operatic machinery, I divide up what follows into five acts: a kind of dramatic sketch, rendered in disenchanted prose, devoid of any novel special effects, and with Garnier as flawed hero.

Act I

The official government decree of 29 September 1860 confirming the construction of a new Opéra – to replace the decrepit forty-year-old theatre on the Rue Le Peletier – was notably terse, referring only to the 'public utility' of the project. But there were plenty of people around willing to spell out the stakes at much higher pitch. César Daly, influential editor of the *Revue générale de l'architecture et des travaux publics*, suggested 'national utility', at the least, given the clear national interest in a project

---

[13] Latour 1993.

designed to confirm Paris as the artistic capital of Europe.[14] And in the months before the decree, Théodore Delamarre, editor of *La Patrie*, had proposed that 'the new opera house, to answer to the splendour of the capital, must be, in its external proportions, in the grandiose character of its interior layout, a theatre without rival in Europe'.[15] The members of a commission set up by the Prefect of the Seine to review possible locations concurred, proclaiming that the building must be of 'a previously unknown magnificence'.[16] And so it came to pass: as the concluding lines of a celebratory hymn written for the eventual inauguration on 3 January 1875 would put it: 'France, mother of the arts, fulfil your destiny: / That they should come, your children, to take their place in the festivities! / That before this palace they raise their heads high; / That their brows might be imprinted with a noble pride … ! / Here is *Progress*; here is *Conquest*; here is *Grandeur* and *Immortality*!'[17]

For all the bombast, this final string of abstract nouns manages to capture something of the near-impossibility underlying the enterprise, stuck between the future imperatives of progress and conquest, and the more ancient claims of grandeur and immortality. How could the Opéra serve both as a showroom for the existing luxury of French and European operatic grandeur, and at the same time look ahead, leading the artform on towards the twentieth century? It is a question that has been posed many times since, perhaps with an eye on the building's ornate classicism, or on the status of the new Opéra as a museum (or mausoleum); a role epitomised by the fact that the night of the inauguration saw a parade of operatic excerpts from the 1820s and 1830s rather than any new composition.[18] But it was in the realm of stage machinery that some of the

[14] Daly 1861, col. 82.

[15] 'La nouvelle salle de l'Opéra, pour répondre à la splendeur de la capitale, doit être, par ses proportions à l'extérieur, par le caractère grandiose de ses dispositions intérieures, un théâtre sans rival en Europe'. Delamarre 1860.

[16] 'une magnificence jusqu'à présent inconnue'. Paris, Archives Nationales (hereafter F-Pan), AJ[13] 531/III, Charles Chaix d'Est-Ange et al., 'Projet d'une nouvelle salle d'Opéra: Avis de la Commission d'Enquête', 33.

[17] 'France, mère des arts, accomplis ton destin: / Qu'ils viennent, tes enfants, prendre part au festin! / Que devant ce palais ils lèvent haut la tête; / Que leurs fronts soient empreints d'une noble fierté … ! / C'est ici le *Progrès*, c'est ici la *Conquète*, / C'est ici la *Grandeur* et *l'Immortalité*!' Buffenoir 1874, stanza 14.

[18] In architectural terms, the Palais Garnier would become a symbol of backward-looking decadence for many twentieth-century modernists, with Corbusier declaring it a 'decor for a funeral' ('un décor d'enterrement'); but such critiques have a much longer history, dating back to the years of the Opéra's construction, and rising in volume in the years after the inauguration. Later defenders of the building's style include Penelope Woolf (1988, 214–35), who argues that it was a successful symbol of Second Empire social progress, and Christopher Curtis Mead (1991), who proposes the building as a demonstration of the 'Renaissance' of French Classicism. At the inauguration O. Le Trioux, writing in the *Chronique musicale*, declared it to have inaugurated nothing, and that it had celebrated 'neither the past, nor the

greatest hopes had initially been invested for the creation of something genuinely new; and not before time. As Daly wrote in 1861:

Who would believe it? In an era when the mechanical rules and governs, in a society founded on industry and commerce, both of which depend on the genius of the mechanical; at the heart of the nation most addicted to pleasure, of the town that wants and deserves to have the first Opéra in the world; on the banks of the Seine, no less, where we have learnt to say as often as on the banks of the Thames: *Time is money* ... who would believe it? The mechanism of scenery has made no progress for two hundred years! In this context, the present Opéra in Paris perfectly resembles the *salle des machines*, as the old theatre in the Tuileries was called. I don't think I am mistaken in saying that the Opéra of the rue Lepelletier [sic] had installed on its stage all the material from the theatre on the rue Richelieu, demolished [in 1820] following the assassination of the duc de Berry.[19]

The decree announcing the initial competition to decide the architect of the new Opéra, published on 30 December 1860, nevertheless passed over the question of machinery completely, specifying only that the stage should be big enough to hold 400 people, of a depth of 32 metres, and a width of at least 14 metres; and that there should be a store nearby to hold materials from the current repertoire.[20] But the vastly more detailed programme released in April 1861 – once the 171 entries for the initial competition had been whittled down to just five – clearly spelt out the problems of the current system: all the scenery had to be brought out of storage by hand, leading to progressive deterioration of materials, and involving lengthy entr'actes while sets were dismantled and others rebuilt. At the same time, many effects had to be foregone altogether because of the time taken to change the décors.[21]

present, nor the future' (1875, 78). For a later (and more positive) account of the inauguration, see Patureau 1991, 9–24. Finally, on the stagnation of the repertory more generally, see Charle 2007, esp. 245–50; Huebner 2003, 303–5; and, especially, K. Ellis 2015.

[19] 'Le croirait-on? à l'époque où la mécanique trône et gouverne, dans une société fondée sur l'industrie et le commerce, dépendant tous deux du génie de la mécanique; au sein de la nation la plus adonnée au plaisir, de la ville qui veut et doit avoir le premier Opéra du monde; sur les bords de la Seine enfin, où l'on a appris à dire aussi bien que sur les bords de la Tamise: *Time is money* (le temps c'est de l'argent), le croirait-on? Le mécanisme des décors n'a pas fait un progrès depuis deux cents ans! Sous ce rapport, l'Opéra actuel de Paris ressemble parfaitement à la *salle des machines*, common on appelait l'ancien théâtre construit aux Tuileries. Je crois même ne pas me tromper en disant que l'Opéra de la rue Lepelletier a vu installer sur sa scène tout le matériel du théâtre de la rue Richelieu, démoli à la suite de l'assassinat du duc de Berry.' Daly 1861, col. 96.

[20] The decree, signed the Minister of State, Count Walewski, appeared in *Le Moniteur universel*, and was reprinted in full in Daly 1861, cols. 82–4.

[21] The full programme ('Programme pour l'étude du projet d'une nouvelle salle d'Opéra, au point de vue de l'administration et de l'exploitation du théâtre') was dated 18 April 1861, and consisted of 107 numbered sections: see Daly 1861, cols. 108–33. A draft copy, complete with

The programme offered a solution with a blithe optimism that in hindsight can only seem poignant: 'Nothing ... would be easier, by means of various mechanical procedures simpler than most of those used daily in the most basic industrial workshops, than to operate the most complicated changes of décor in a handful of minutes.'[22] There followed a detailed outline of the new system, which boiled down to two main ideas, with a possible third for a future date. First, the large flats (the *châssis*) that made up the basic set along with the painted backdrop would slide into place by means of rails attached above the stage, before being turned into position by hand ('since we do not wish to deprive ourselves of the resources of intelligent manual labour, but only to restrict it to operations of detail').[23] For this to work, the spaces in the wings would ideally be at least half the width of the stage itself, thereby removing the need for storage beneath the stage. Second, the large free-standing constructions known as *praticables*, built to simulate mountains or other such structures, could mostly be replaced by 'a simple raising of the ground, if the floor of the theatre were formed of mobile parts lifted by a rack and pinion system'.[24] This, the programme suggested, would also allow the replacement of the current stage floor, crisscrossed as it was with grooves for sliding in scenery from the sides or from below, with something more solid.[25] Taken together, the benefits of these measures seemed clear:

economy of material; economy of personnel, twenty people being able then to do a job that today occupies a hundred. What possible progress might not ensue for the art of décor, if simple and prompt manoeuvres allowed the realisation of effects in a few minutes that one wouldn't dare undertake today or that one could only manage through brute strength and expense and with interminable entr'actes![26]

---

emendations can also be found in F-Pan AJ[13] 451/III. Both Daly 1861 and Mead 1991, 44–98, carry detailed accounts of the competition itself.

[22] 'Rien ne serait plus facile, ... au moyen de quelques procédés mécaniques plus simples que la plupart de ceux employés journellement dans les moindres ateliers industriels, que d'opérer en quelques minutes les changements de décors les plus compliqués.' 'Programme', section 47; in Daly 1861, col. 116.

[23] 'car nous n'entendons pas nous priver de la ressource du travail manuel intelligent, mais le réduire aux opérations de détail'; 'Programme', section 48; in Daly 1861, col. 116.

[24] 'par un simple soulèvement du sol, si le plancher du théâtre était formé de parties mobiles soulevées par des épontilles à crémaillère'; 'Programme', section 53; in Daly 1861, col. 117.

[25] The best summary in English of the staging system at this time can be found in the translation of J.-P. Moynet ([1873] 1976). See also Ault 1983.

[26] 'économie de matériel; économie de personnel, vingt hommes pouvant alors suffire à un travail qui en occupe cent aujourd'hui. Et que de progrès possibles n'entreprendrait pas l'art du décorateur, si des manœuvres simples et promptes permettaient de réaliser en quelques minutes des effets qu'on n'ose entreprendre ou qu'on n'obtient aujourd'hui qu'à force de bras et

Finally, looking ahead, the programme offered one more idea for the future: some kind of hydraulic system that might enable effects impossible to produce at the present time. The dimensions of the plumber's workshop, the programme stated, should be calculated bearing this possibility in mind.

At such an early stage, questions of space understandably loomed large. An anonymous note from 1860 had observed that 'lack of space ... has for two centuries been an obstacle for any progress in theatrical machinery'.[27] And when in early 1863 – a year and a half after the second competition ended – the victorious Charles Garnier turned his attention to the question of machinery: in an extended report for the Minister of State, he agreed to create enough space for storage in the wings, and also called for sufficient height, to avoid folding backdrops or curtains stored in the flies. Having spent most of 1862 having the groundwater pumped out at the site, and overseeing the construction of reinforced foundations, Garnier went against the grain in arguing *for* a deep under-stage area; vital, he insisted, for 'the progress of theatrical machinery'.[28]

As to the two key elements of the programme specifications, at this stage Garnier ruled out replacing the *praticables* with a movable floor, preferring to find ways of making them lighter and more mobile. He went along, though, with the idea of moving scenery in on rails from above the stage, and proposed closing off the flies from the stage with an iron ceiling, to protect any scenery stored there from fire, and to allow the machinists more space to manoeuvre backcloths and lighting safely. More intriguingly, he also laid out a scheme to operate scene changes with a motor, whether operated by hand, steam, gas or electricity (with a preference for the latter two). Each piece of scenery could then be linked to a sort of keyboard, he suggested: at the touch of a key a machinist could make scenery appear or disappear, thus providing quick and effortless transformations.[29]

Here, then, in 1863, we have Garnier as visionary: master of his brief; eyes fixed steadfastly on the future. And although he opened his 1863 report with an account of the many theatres he had visited across Europe

---

de dépenses et avec d'interminables entr'actes!' 'Programme', section 55; in Daly 1861, cols. 117–18.

[27] F-Pan, AJ[13] 453/III: 'Note sur les dimensions que doit avoir la scène de l'Opéra' (1860).

[28] '[les] progrès de la machination théâtrale'; AJ[13] 453/III, Garnier, 'Etude sur les Théâtres: Rapport adressé à Son Excellence Monsieur le Comte Walewsky, Ministre d'État', (n.d.), 34. The original copy of the report was dated 25 February 1863.

[29] Garnier, 'Etude sur les Théâtres', 38.

– from his time in Italy as Prix de Rome laureate around 1850 to a recent trip to northern Italy and Germany with Victor Louvet, his second in command – in terms of machinery they had taught him nothing. 'The stages of foreign and French theatres, more or less vast and more or less well appointed,' he wrote, 'provide no interesting information, and the systems of machinery installed there offer no new element that could resolve such an important question': the question, that is, of how to equip the grandest opera house ever built. 'Only serious study of the needs of the stage,' he went on, 'the adoption of benefits as identified, the rejection of defective practices and the judicious use of new discoveries can lead to a successful result.'[30]

So the way forward seemed clear. Hidden away in this same report, however, were two details that foreshadowed troubles to come. First, a detail of character: over a decade later, after the completion of the Opéra, Garnier would write that 'the architect who constructs a theatre is always placed between two alternatives: if he does something new, he offends all habits and is called a revolutionary; if he proceeds as before, he betrays all hopes and is called a reactionary'.[31] The solution, Garnier suggested, was therefore for the architect to do as he pleased; but in questions of machinery, at least, Garnier himself tended to oscillate between the two extremes. No sooner had he written off existing theatrical machinery in his 1863 report, and called for substantial modifications, than he turned back on himself:

We should fear too radical a reform, however, too great an upheaval, which would tend, not only to change the machinery but also, for a doubtful purpose, lead to the complete alteration of the plants, lighting, and all the services connected to the stage. While the current system has many disadvantages that need remedy, it also has some advantages, which are all the better to maintain, as they have been tried and tested in practice and confirmed by experience.[32]

---

[30] 'En résumé les scènes des théâtres français et étrangers, plus ou moins vastes et plus ou moins bien disposées, ne donnent aucun enseignement intéressant, et les systèmes des machines qui y sont installées, n'apportent aucun élément nouveau qui puisse servir à résoudre une question aussi importante. C'est donc seulement l'étude sérieuse des besoins de la scène, l'adoption des avantages constatés, le rejet des usages défectueux et l'emploi judicieux des découvertes nouvelles qui doit amener à un résultat satisfaisant.' Garnier, 'Etude sur les Théâtres', 39.

[31] 'l'architecte qui construit un théâtre est toujours placé entre deux alternatives: s'il fait du nouveau, il froisse toues les manies et on l'appelle révolutionnaire; s'il fait de l'ancien, il trahit toutes les espérances, et on l'appelle réactionnaire'; Garnier 1878–81, 1:199–200.

[32] 'Cependant il faut craindre une réforme trop radicale, un bouleversement trop complet, qui tendrait, non-seulement à changer la machination, mais, qui entrainerait également, et cela pour un résultat douteux, la modification entière des plantations, de l'éclairage, et de tous les services dépendants de la scène. Si le système actuel a bien des inconvénients auxquels il est

One could read this as Garnier's attempt to draw a line between technology and aesthetics: change the machines, by all means, but only in order to perfect the recreation of existing staging. But one could also see it evincing a more general caution that could easily lead to the blurring of that same line, with Garnier torn between a desire for innovation and an instinctive appreciation for what had worked well in the past.

The second detail was of a more direct kind: a terse footnote, added some time after the 1863 report's completion, and inserted just at the point where Garnier sketched his vision of the machinist moving scenery at the touch of a button. It read: 'since the period when this report was written, this system has been examined and studied by a special commission and has been rejected as offering too many disadvantages'.[33] A new solution had to be found.

Act II

Later in 1863, Garnier took the opportunity to update the new Minister of Fine Arts, Jean-Baptiste Vaillant, on the theatrical machinery, pointing out that if a hydraulic system were considered, as mooted in the 1861 programme, it would have to be integral to the construction of the building, since it would be well-nigh impossible to add later on.[34] A decision was needed fast, in other words, so as not to hold up construction work, and so Emile Perrin, director of the Opéra, could work out the implications for future operatic productions. The most satisfactory solution, Garnier suggested, would be to set up a commission to study the question. Quite why he thought this is unclear. Perhaps he welcomed the thought of external expertise, not least to assess other proposals for the new machinery that had begun to emerge; perhaps he wanted to devote more time to all the other aspects of the Opéra construction; perhaps he really believed that a

---

nécessaire de remédier, il a aussi quelques avantages, qu'il est d'autant meilleur de conserver, qu'ils ont été éprouvé par la pratique, et consacrés par l'expérience.' Garnier, 'Etude sur les Théâtres', 35. Just before this passage Garnier describes Italian and German machinery as 'in its infancy', and French machinery as better but still beset by problems.

[33] 'Depuis l'époque à laquelle ce rapport a été écrit, ce système a été examiné et étudié par une Commission spéciale et a été repoussé comme offrant de très-grande inconvénients. [Voir les rapports faits à ce sujet par la commission des machines théâtrales.]' Garnier, 'Etude sur les théâtres', 38.

[34] F-Pan AJ[13] 453/III: 'A Son Excellence Monsieur Le Maréchal de France, Ministre de la Maison de l'Empereur et des beaux-arts'. The document includes a date of February 1863 added in blue crayon, but must have been later that year, since Jean-Baptiste Vaillant only took up the post of Minister of Fine Arts in June 1863.

commission would help in reaching a quick consensus. Whatever his reasons, time was certainly pressing: in October 1863 Garnier submitted yet another report to Vaillant saying that work was going slower than hoped, and that to finish in time for the 1867 Exposition (as then intended) he would need more money – Garnier's constant plea throughout the construction process – and 'immediate knowledge of the system to use for the stage machinery'.[35]

The machinery of government, though, moved even more slowly than the scene changes at the Opéra; it was only towards the end of July 1864, nine months later, that Vaillant announced the foundation of a commission whose brief went well beyond the narrow question of hydraulics, to assess all the advantages and disadvantages of the present system, and to bring to the future installation the improvements 'that experience, art and science might judge necessary'.[36] Its twelve members included Garnier and his deputy Louvet; Perrin, as director of the Opéra; and Félix Martin as former general secretary. Five others were practitioners: three of the Opéra's most esteemed scene painters – François Nolau, Édouard Desplechin and Charles-Antoine Cambon, all in their sixties – alongside the Opéra's head machinist for over a decade, Jean-Joseph Sacré, and Monsieur Brabant, the head machinist of the Porte Saint-Martin (and later of the new Opéra). And the final three were expert outsiders: Henri Tresca, engineer and assistant director of the Conservatoire des Arts et Métiers; Etienne de Cardaillac, long-time head of the civilian buildings section of the Department of Public Works (and a member of the 1861 jury); and finally, as president, Victor Regnault, physician, chemist, photographic pioneer and director of the Sèvres porcelain factory.

With the Commission in place, Garnier quickly submitted a summary of his proposed system, prefaced by passages from the 1861 programme. Already, though, his ideas had been toned down: manpower was now declared the best option for moving the scenery, and the master keyboard had disappeared. He also included a caveat that his plans were intended 'merely as a basis for discussion', and claimed that his purpose in formulating a system at all had simply been to 'indicate the important points to

---

[35] 'la connaissance immédiate du système à employer pour la machination de la scène'; F-Pan AJ[13] 453/III: 'Nouvel Opéra. Avancement des travaux. Rapport à Son Excellence Monsieur le Maréchal de France, Ministre de la maison de l'Empereur et des Beaux Arts', Paris, 24 October 1863.

[36] 'que l'expérience, l'art et la science jugeraient nécessaires'. The decree was dated 24 July 1864, and was reprinted in the *Revue de l'architecture et des travaux publics* 22 (1864), col. 300, where Daly welcomed the formation of the Commission while questioning why it had not been set up before the initiation of the competition to design the Opéra.

examine'.[37] The Commission, of which Garnier was almost certainly the youngest member, was now in control.

Three sets of responses to Garnier's plan survive. The first, undated, was from the Sub-Commission (consisting of Perrin, the machinist Sacré, two of the scene painters, Cambon and Despléchin, and Garnier himself) set up to assess all proposals received. It was moderate in tone, but declared the movement of the scenery by rails above the stage as problematic and undesirable.[38] The second report, dated 25 October 1864, and signed by all three of the Commission's artists, was less temperate, describing the proposal as combining the problems of the current stage with those of systems abandoned fifty years earlier, and ridiculing the idea of the iron ceiling and of manoeuvring the scenery from above. Contrary to popular opinion, stage machinery had indeed progressed over recent decades, they argued; Garnier's project would send them backwards. The only area on which they agreed with Garnier was that a mobile floor was unnecessary; and they also advocated a semi-circular panorama to replace the current backcloth.[39] The third report, also undated, was from Brabant, machinist of the Porte Saint-Martin; he supported the scene painters in declaring Garnier's system 'completely ... impossible, and a step backwards', although he supported the desire for simplicity and economy of personnel.[40]

Two months later, in December 1864, Garnier collated the Sub-Commission's response to the four other systems for the new Opéra machinery it had received.[41] All followed the programme in outlining some kind of mobile floor; one (by Monsieur Barthélemy of Nancy) also proposed a framework for the under-stage machinery made of iron rather than wood; the other three all echoed the scene painters in imagining some sort of panoramic backdrop, two (by the engineers Raignard and Foucault) complete with a central cupola, while the third (Signor Rouchi, from Milan) threw in hydraulic counterweights and new methods to imitate

---

[37] 'il ne faut y chercher qu'une base de discussion ... mon but ayant été seulement d'indiquer tous les points importants à examiner'. F-Pan AJ[13] 453/III: Garnier, 'Rapport adressé à Messieurs les membres de la commission de décoration et de machination théatrales [sic]' (August 1864), 1.

[38] F-Pan AJ[13] 453/III: 'Projet de Rapport de la Sous-Commission chargée d'examiner, au point de vue de la construction et de la manœuvre, le projet indiqué dans la note de Monsieur Garnier' (n.d.).

[39] F-Pan AJ[13] 453/III: Cambon, Deplechin [sic], Nolau, 'Nouvelle salle de l'Opéra. Etudes des procédés de décors et de machination. Rapport de la sous-commission de Peinture Scénique' (25 October 1864).

[40] F-Pan AJ[13] 453/III: 'Rapport de M. Brabant, chef machiniste' (n.d.).

[41] F-Pan AJ[13] 453/III: Garnier, 'Rapport à Messieurs les Membres de la Commission des machines théatrales' (December 1864).

wind, thunder and rain.[42] After much discussion, all were rejected; in a final summary to the Commission in February 1865, Garnier confirmed that the existing system from the Salle Le Peletier was the only one feasible, subject to necessary modifications.[43]

Having gone so rapidly from pioneer of novelty to defender of the status quo, at times Garnier, in summarising the conclusions of the Sub-Committee, sounds at this point almost brainwashed. 'Through the elimination of all others', he wrote, 'the present system is the only one acceptable, and the only one that at this point . . . can offer all possible resources to the scene painters and to the machinists, enable all effects, and lend itself to all compositions.'[44] Any accusations of falling back on routine were misplaced, he continued, for 'routine is nothing other than experience, and the *status quo* is only a continuation of good practice. Those who . . . not only seek improvements but multiple modifications, but that radically overturn the means currently in use, set themselves up for great disappointment.'[45] As to his own system, unveiled in his initial report of 1863 with such confidence, he now turned against it as 'not my own, but intended to engage with the given programme', and praised the Commission for rejecting it along with the rest.[46] Anything that impeded the art of the decorators, he concluded, 'cannot be accepted; the decoration is the goal, the machinery the means, and one must never sacrifice the first to the second'.[47]

And that might, perhaps, have been the end of the story; the old guard of Opéra stagehands had won Garnier over, and all that remained was to capitalise on the additional space that the new Opéra stage had to offer, and

[42] Raignard would go on to install a new hydraulic machinery system at the Théâtre du Vaudeville when it moved to the Boulevard de Capucines in 1866, which was sufficiently problematic never to be used. See Gosset 1886, 80; and G. Moynet 1893, 45–6.

[43] F-Pan AJ[13] 453/III: Garnier (rapporteur), Perrin, Cambon, Sacré, Despléchins [sic], 'Commission de décoration et de machination théâtrales. Minute du rapport adressé à la Commission par la Sous-Commission. Paris. Février 1865.'

[44] 'Le système actuel . . . par le fait de l'élimination de tous les autres, devient le seul acceptable, est aussi jusqu'à présent le seul, qui . . . peut offrir toutes les ressources possibles aux décorateurs et aux machinistes, permettre tous les effets, et se prêter à toutes les compositions.' 'Rapport adressé à la Commission', 1–2.

[45] 'la routine n'est autre que l'expérience, et que le *statu quo* n'est que la continuité du bien. Ceux donc, qui . . . cherchent non pas seulement des améliorations, mais bien des modifications, qui renverseraient radicalement les moyens mis en usage, se préparent de grandes déceptions.' 'Rapport adressé à la Commission', 2.

[46] 'non comme mien, mais comme me paraissant rentre dans un programme donné'; 'Rapport adressé à la Commission', 2.

[47] 'il ne pourrait être accepté; la décoration est le but, la machination est le moyen, et l'on ne doit jamais sacrifier le premier au second'; 'Rapport adressé à la Commission', 2.

to address any other matters outstanding. Garnier identified just two: first, whether a motor could be brought in to power the counterweight system, thereby economising on machinists. Second, the matter of that movable floor, despite Garnier's continued reservations. But these were mere wrinkles, Garnier suggested, that could best be handled by the appointment of an expert foreman.

With the basic system in place, Garnier returned to his principal task: overseeing during 1865 the completion of the Opéra's exterior shell and the construction of the interior iron superstructure to hold the suspended ceiling, ramps and landings of the auditorium. But in early 1866 he reminded the Minister of Fine Arts that the other details were still to be worked out, and the following month Garnier proposed Sacré, the Opéra's head machinist, as the perfect foreman.[48] He also suggested that the Commission could now be wound down. It might be reconvened briefly, he wrote, to finalise the choice of motor, and the exact mechanism for the stage floor, but just for three or four meetings; beyond that its use 'seems doubtful to me, for in any commission there is always one person who talks and rambles the whole time, and prevents serious people from expressing their opinions'.[49] 'I quite realise', he added, 'that in seeking the dissolution of the Commission, I am taking responsibility for the system, or at least responsibility for its execution, but this doesn't seem to me more weighty that what I already bear for the whole building, and I would find as compensation for this increase in work the enormous advantage of being able to line it up with progress in the construction of the new Opéra.'[50]

Act III

Not only was the Commission not wound down, but in its hands the question of the movable floor transformed rapidly from a detail into a

---

[48] Pan AJ[13] 453/III: Garnier, 'Nouvel Opéra. Rapport à S. E. Monsieur le Maréchal de France, Ministre de la Maison de l'Empereur et des Beaux-Arts. Travaux pendant l'année 1865. Paris, le 19 Janvier 1866', 44; 'Rapport à S.E. Monsieur le Maréchal de France, Ministre de la Maison de l'Empereur et des Beaux Arts. Soumissions diverses: Menuiserie, etc.' (24 February 1866), 10.

[49] 'me paraît douteux, car dans toute commission, il y a presque toujours une personne qui parle et divague tout le temps, et empêche les gens sérieux de dire leur avis'. 'Rapport' (24 February 1866), 10.

[50] 'Je sais bien qu'en demandant la dissolution de la Commission, j'assume sur moi la responsabilité du système, ou du moins la responsabilité de son exécution, mais elle ne me parait pas plus lourde que celle que j'ai maintenant pour l'édifice, et je trouverais comme compensation dans ce surcroît de travail le grand avantage de pouvoir le diriger suivant le degré d'avancement de la construction du Nouvel Opéra.' 'Rapport' (24 February 1866), 10.

full-blown technological challenge, and a last-gasp opportunity to prove the Opéra's commitment to the dictates of progress. And at this point a new protagonist enters the drama. In mid-1866, a civil engineer named Auguste Quéruel, who had previously specialised in the construction of steamships, learnt from the Opéra's manager of building works, Monsieur Sabathier, that plans for new machinery had effectively ground to a halt, and that various engineers – including two of the principal construction firms in Paris, Edoux and Farcot – had been officially invited to help, but had declined.[51] Sabathier therefore passed on to Quéruel the seven official reports so far produced by the Commission, and Quéruel seized the opportunity. By November he had developed a new system, and submitted it to Garnier.[52] Like Barthélemy, Quéruel proposed an iron framework below the stage, and, like Raignard, Foucault and Rouchi, a panoramic back curtain; he also came up with new methods of lighting the stage, and a sprinkler system to put out fires. More importantly, and in a marked departure from all previous systems, he proposed an extensive hydraulic system below stage, with no fewer than seventy-two presses able to open and close the transverse divisions of the stage (the 'trappes' and 'trappillons'), in order to bring up freestanding scenery (known as 'fermes'), and to move the understage trolleys carrying the flats from either side.

Garnier queried the use of iron, while recognising that it brought advantages in terms of stability; Quéruel followed up in March 1867 with a detailed elaboration of the advantages of hydraulics over pulleys for the entire mechanism of the mobile floor.[53] A week later, on 29 March, the Opéra's head machinist, Sacré, presented his new proposal to the reconstituted Sub-Commission (now with engineer Henri Tresca as president), who suggested various objections;[54] in August 1867 a third new proposal

---

[51] A later report revealed that since 1854 Quéruel had been involved with the construction of steamboats using surface condensers and distilled water, before turning to the investigation of theatrical machinery (Quéruel 1869, 737). Quéruel's claim that both Farcot and Edoux had turned down an invitation from the Minister of Fine Arts to involve themselves in designing and installing the machinery came as a response to a question after a talk he gave in 1874; see Quéruel 1874b, 100.

[52] The dates of Quéruel's initial reports are taken from the summary given in a later submission: Pan AJ[13] 453/III: 'Projet de Machinerie pour le Nouvel Opéra, par A. Queruel, Ingénieur Civil à Paris. Septième mémoire' (28 October 1868).

[53] This was Quéruel's third report, dated 20 March 1867; see Quéruel, 'Septième mémoire', 4.

[54] This date is extrapolated from the later revision from Sacré (and his son, who was second-in-command of machinery at the Opéra at the time): Sacré père et fils, 'Mémoire explicatif et rectifié des Plans et d'un Nouveau système de Construction en fer et de Machination de plancher du Nouveau Théâtre Impérial de l'Opéra, adressé à Messieurs les Membres de la Commission de l'Opéra' (29 November 1867), article 20.

arrived, this time from Brabant, the machinist of the Porte-Saint-Martin (like Sacré, a member of the Commission from the start).[55]

Suddenly, the search for a new system – now centred on the question of the mobile floor – was at full steam again, but with the solution further away than ever. What Garnier had framed in 1865 as the sorting out of a few details had transformed into a new competition to design the stage floor mechanism, complicating the Commission's earlier commitment to the existing system and leaving Garnier still unable to estimate the final cost of the machinery. Back in action, the Sub-Commission duly took a trip to the Porte-Saint-Martin to inspect Brabant's model, also studying the hydraulic apparatus installed at the Lyon railway station. Meanwhile, trying once again to draw things to a conclusion, and with time slipping by, in November 1867 Garnier threw his weight behind a revised version of Sacré's plan, adding a lengthy covering note to stress that the system had been approved by all members of the new Sub-Commission bar one, and that Sacré stood ready to address any objections. Garnier then raised several such objections himself – to do with the rigidity of the frame, the sort of mechanism proposed to move the mobile floor, and how to deal with any malfunctions – in an attempt to pre-empt further discussion, and to guide (or force) the Commission's hand.[56]

Unsurprisingly, given his long experience with the machinery at the Salle Le Peletier, Sacré's proposal was not especially revolutionary, beyond the introduction of the mobile floor and the use of iron for the frame below the stage. Other changes were largely pragmatic and small-scale: the size of the trolleys, for example, would be slightly reduced to make them easier to use and to avoid injury; the height of the basement's first level would be raised so that extras holding lances or horses could gather there without bending double.[57] But despite Garnier's support of Sacré, Quéruel kept up his own campaign, in October 1867 submitting a further new plan to the Commission with the number of hydraulic presses now reduced to twenty-seven, and including examples of how the system would suit key works in the repertoire; in March 1868, he came back to them with a new plan, now without Sabathier, but still with the hydraulics in place.[58]

[55] Brabant's project is described in detail in F-Pan AJ[13] 453/III, Henri Tresca, 'Travaux du nouvel opera. Rapport sur la Construction du plancher de la Scène' (August 1869).

[56] F-Pan AJ[13] 453/III, 'Système. Sacré père et fils.' Letter from Garnier to members of the Commission, prefacing Sacré's own 'Mémoire explicatif'.

[57] Sacré, 'Mémoire explicatif', art. 26.

[58] The October 1867 plan is described in Quéruel, 'Septième mémoire'; for the fifth, see F-Pan AJ[13] 453/III, 'Mémoire adressé à Messieurs les Membres de la Commission des machines théâtrales pour le Nouvel Opéra par A. Quéruel, Ingénieur Civil' (15 March 1868).

Then, in mid-1868, came a breakthrough: a sudden meeting of minds between Garnier and Tresca that 'produced, so to speak, an explosion'. 'After numerous meetings, long discussions and serious studies on the various projects presented', Garnier wrote to the Sub-Commission, 'two members of your Commission had, at a single moment, the same intuition of an astounding system for nearly all the data presented so far, that appeared to be able to resolve completely the problem proposed.'[59] Not that their plans were yet perfect, Garnier added; but questions of detail could be debated later if the Sub-Commission could accept the outlines of their new plan.

Such an implausible 'eureka moment', leading to the sudden crystallisation of a perfect solution, can perhaps best be read as one last attempt by Garnier to jump-start the Commission into a decision: it offered them a compromise between the systems of Sacré and Quéruel, but with no acknowledgment to either, and with a new twist in the form of an iron grid placed under the stage to raise or lower it (in whole or in part) by means of four hydraulic presses at each corner (with pulleys as a back-up).[60] After much discussion, and some modifications (including a fifth hydraulic press in the centre of the grid) the Sub-Commission was convinced, and commended the plan to the Commission unanimously, but for a single vote of dissent from Sacré, whose own system – and, by implication, whose expertise – was now sidelined. In the Sub-Commission's final report Tresca pulled rank, dismissing Sacré's arguments against their system as 'instinctive rather than technical'.[61] The laws of progress trumped the cavils of the ageing practitioner.

[59] 'et fit pour ainsi dire explosion'; 'après de nombreuses réunions, de longues discussions et des études sérieuses sur divers projets présentés, il se produisit ce phénomène que deux membres de votre commission eurent à un moment donné la même intuition d'un système renversant à peu près toutes les données présentées jusqu'à ce jour, et paraissant devoir résoudre complètement le problème proposé'. F-Pan AJ[13] 453/III: Garnier, 'Note adressée à Messieurs les Membres de la sous-commission de machination scénique', 1.

[60] The initial proposal included the possibility of a second grid to act as a counterweight to the first, but this was not supported by the Sub-Commission.

[61] 'des observations plutôt instinctives que techniques'. F-Pan AJ[13] 453/III: Tresca, 'Travaux du nouvel Opéra. Rapport sur la Construction du plancher de la Scène' (1 August 1869), 35. Tresca also outlines Brabant's queries about the system, which he developed in a 'Note adressée à Monsieur Tresca, président de la Sous-Commission des études de machination du Nouvel Opéra'.

Act IV

Sacré, however, was not to be silenced easily. In a letter to Regnault, president of the Commission, in August 1868 he tore apart Garnier and Tresca's design, declaring the iron framework a monstrosity and launching a strong attack on using hydraulics in place of pulleys, not least in terms of the safety of the backstage crew.[62] Moreover, he rejected the implication that progress in staging should be measured according to the criteria of industrial efficiency:

The Theatre is not a factory, and it can never be assimilated to this type of industry. Theory is all very well, it often produces excellent ideas; but the practitioner, the man of practice may not be as backwards as a certain report [i.e. the 1861 programme] addressed to us suggested, [claiming] that for a hundred years and more, the Theatre had remained stationary, and that no progress had been made. In that case, the scene painters and the machinists would be entirely irrelevant.[63]

After a stormy meeting of the Commission in December, at which his intervention was discussed, Sacré wrote again, complaining that Perrin was strongly in favour of the Garnier/Tresca plan only because he saw the chance for 'grand effects', without understanding the mechanics of how to achieve them. Progress drives contemporary life, Sacré wrote, 'but if what we might have accepted as a benefit turns out only to be a mistake, then it would be better to give it up'.[64] And in these terms, the mobility of the stage floor was altogether unnecessary, he argued, since the spectator would not care how effects were achieved. 'Let us perfect what we know, whatever people might say', he pleaded, one last time, adding that 'the smooth running of a theatre is very simple to understand and to establish'.[65]

Quéruel was not to be silenced either. In October 1868 he submitted his own thoughts on Tresca and Garnier's system, describing it ironically as a 'curious mechanical wonder', and suggesting that the attempt to do

---

[62] F-Pan AJ[13] 453/III: Sacré, 'A Monsieur Regnault, président de la Commission de machination et décoration théâtrale' (11 August 1868).

[63] 'Le Théâtre n'est pas une usine, et l'on ne pourra jamais l'assimiler à ce genre d'industrie. La Théorie est une grande chose, il en sort très souvent d'excellentes idées; mais le praticien, l'homme exercé, qui ne serait pas aussi arrière que dit un certain rapport qui nous a été adressé, que depuis cent ans et plus, le Théâtre était resté stationnaire, qu'aucun progrès n'avait été fait. Alors les décorateurs et les machinistes seraient de bien grandes nullités.' Sacré, 'A Monsieur Regnault', 9.

[64] 'Mais si ce que nous aurions accepté comme un bienfait, ne devenait qu'une déception, il vaudrait mieux y renoncer.' F-Pan AJ[13] 453/III: Sacré, letter to Regnault (20 December 1868), 3.

[65] 'Perfectionnons ce que nous connaissons, malgré tout ce que l'on peut dire. . . . Le bon fonctionnement d'un théâtre est très simple à comprendre et à établir.' Sacré, letter to Regnault, 3.

everything with such a small number of hydraulic presses was as foolhardy as creating 'an omnibus with 500 seats'.[66] A few days later, he renewed his bid to persuade the Commission of the superiority of his own plan, inviting them to see a model built at 1/20 scale. He also pointed out that he was the only interested party without a defender on the Commission, and the only one who had had no opportunity to see the other projects. Not that he was complaining, he added; just that he hoped for a serious competition, since 'everyone would gain by it'.[67]

Unfortunately for him, when the Commission visited his model they did so unannounced, and Quéruel lacked the extra help needed to work the machine properly.[68] But he invited them back in January 1869, and laid out the benefits of his system one last time. 'No doubt you are amazed by my perseverance in studying this project', he suggested, 'and you might ask yourself how, after lack of success with the Sub-Commission, I still allow myself to keep developing my project for you in the hope of a better outcome. Allow me, I pray, to tell you the reason. I have dug so deep into the question that I can't see how anyone could imagine anything better and more complete than my proposals.'[69] This time, he bolstered his claims with multiple endorsements. One of the Farcot brothers – whose firm had earlier turned down the invitation to develop their own system – was quoted as saying 'for me, the problem is resolved'; Quéruel collected similar puffs from two railway engineers, and from Ferdinand Mathieu, head engineer of the firm of Schneider and Co., who had been responsible for reconstructing the Gare d'Austerlitz a few years before. He ended his pitch at full throttle: 'so you see, among engineers there is but one opinion: the structure is stable and elegant. The mechanism is simple and powerful, the floor rigid and secure; multiple and precise in its movements; at last the problem of the complete mobility of the floor is fully resolved.'[70]

---

[66] 'un tour de force mécanique curieux'; 'un omnibus à 500 places'. F-Pan AJ[13] 453/III: 'Projet de Machinerie pour le Nouvel Opéra par A. Queruel. Sixième Mémoire' (22 October 1868), 6.

[67] 'tout le monde y gagner'. Quéruel, 'Septième Mémoire', 6.

[68] The unsuccessful visit is mentioned in F-Pan AJ[13] 453/III: 'Projet de Machinerie pour le Nouvel Opéra par A. Queruel, Ingénieur Civil, à Paris. Huitième Mémoire' (20 January 1869), 4.

[69] 'Sans aucun doute, Messieurs, vous avez dû vous étonner de la persévérance que je mets dans l'étude de ce projet, et vous avez pu vous demander comment, après un insuccès dans la sous-Commission, je me permets encore de développer devant vous mon projet et d'en espérer un meilleur sort. Permettez-moi je vous prie de vous en dire la raison. J'ai tellement creusé la question, je crois la posséder si bien, que je ne vois pas ce que l'on pourrait imaginer de meilleur et de plus complet que mes propositions.' Quéruel, 'Huitième Mémoire', 4.

[70] 'Pour moi, le problème est résolu'; 'Ainsi, Messieurs, vous le voyez, parmi les ingénieurs il n'y a qu'un avis: la charpente est stable et élégante. Le mécanisme est simple et puissant, le plancher

Later in 1869 Quéruel presented his system to the Société d'encouragement pour l'industrie nationale; in March 1870, he installed – at his own cost – a limited version at the Théâtre de la Gaîté, with hydraulics used to lift the curtain, after Sacré refused him the use of the Opéra stage. Then on 13 July he sent his presentation to Perrin, bemoaning what he called the 'fake competition for machinery at the new Opéra'.[71] But if he hoped for one last chance, time was not on his side. Less than a week later, the Franco-Prussian War broke out, and all construction of the Opéra came to a complete halt.

Act V

In the period of enforced rest brought about by the war and then the Commune, Garnier worked on his book *Le Théâtre*: ostensibly a general reflection on theatre as physical space, but in practice all about the unfinished Opéra. He mixed new observations with material filleted from his reports over the previous decade, with chapters on such subjects as lighting, acoustics, heating, interior design and, of course, theatrical machinery. This last opened with some familiar themes: the lack of progress in machine design; the vast numbers of machinists required and time taken for basic manoeuvres; the difficulties of transporting scenery; and the challenges to the successful creation of illusion. Characteristically, however, he also paid tribute to past achievements, and to the flexibility of the system handed down over generations. Then he turned to the work of the Commission, narrating the rejection of the plans by Barthélemy, Raynard, Ronchi and Foucault before rerunning verbatim his 1865 defence of routine as a continuation of good practice. Then came the mission to design the movable stage, and the proposals of Sabatier and Quéruel, Sacré and Brabant, and of course the eureka moment with Tresca.

---

en place rigide et sûr; dans ses évolutions, multiple et précis; enfin le problème de la mobilité universelle du plancher est pleinement résolu.' Quéruel, 'Huitième Mémoire', 4.

[71] 'le faux concours de la machinerie du nouvel Opéra'. The charge was made by Quéruel in the cover letter he sent to Perrin along with his description of the Gaîté project: F-Pan AJ[13] 453/III, letter dated 13 July 1870, followed by 'Mémoire adressé à M. Magne, Architecte Président de la Commission chargée par M. le Préfet de la Seine, d'examiner un *moteur hydraulique* appliqué à la manœuvre des rideaux du théâtre de la Gaîté, par A. Queruel, Ingénieur Civil.' An undated letter from Quéruel to Perrin held in the same folder states that Garnier will be visiting the Gaîté the following day after attending a meeting of the Commission, indicating that Garnier did pay attention to the experiment; a much later account claimed that it had been abandoned due to excessive humidity and water leakage from the hydraulic motor, along with other problems in operation: Vaulabelle and Hémardinquer 1908, 37.

Garnier's entire narrative in his chapter on machinery is so worthily (so tediously) compendious that it would be hard to imagine that anything has been left out. Yet not only does he omit any mention of his original system, thereby remaining silent about its rejection; he also passes over all subsequent tensions and disagreements, delays and frustrations, adopting the serene tone of a magnanimous chronicler. Each inventor is both praised and critiqued; Quéruel's multiple plans are all declared of interest; Sacré's bitter dissent against Tresca and Garnier's system and even his identity as sole dissenter go unmentioned. Such a fraught period, with the Opéra unfinished and his own position as architect uncertain, was no moment to settle scores. Instead he sought to smooth both the ructions of the past and indicate the way forward. 'One might hope that the new Opéra will inaugurate [the Garnier/Tresca] system,' he concluded, 'but it will perhaps come down to a question of money. The projections in the budget, having used as a point of departure the existing machinery, are manifestly insufficient for the new machinery.'[72] Either way, his work – and that of the Commission itself – was presented as complete and of value, regardless of future events:

whatever the outcome ... [these deliberations] will have served to elucidate important points; if the project is not carried out at the new Opéra, it will perhaps be tried in another theatre; if, on the contrary, as I greatly hope, the attempt will be made at the Opéra, the constructors of scenery will soon be able to study with their own eyes a new and distinctive method, which will open up a path previously unknown.[73]

Coming after so many pages in which all hint of drama has been so studiously excised, this conclusion amounted to a cliffhanger of sorts – if one whose resolution for the later reader remains the best-known part of the whole story. But to hear Garnier's own reaction to the ultimate failure to install a new system at the Opéra, we need to jump ahead – past the Siege of Paris and the Commune, and also past Perrin's replacement as Opéra director by Olivier Halanzier in 1871, past the fire at the Le Peletier in late

---

[72] 'on pourrait espérer que le nouvel Opéra inaugurera ce système, mais il faudra peut-être compter avec la question d'argent. Les prévisions du devis ayant eu pour point de départ la machinerie actuelle sont manifestement insuffisantes pour la machinerie nouvelle'; Garnier 1871, 305.

[73] 'Dans tous les cas ... ils auront servi à élucider bien des points importants; si le projet n'est pas exécuté au nouvel Opéra, il pourra peut-être être essayé dans un autre théâtre; si au contraire, comme je le désire vivement, l'essai se fait à l'Opéra, les constructeurs scéniques pourront bientôt étudier *de visu* un moyen nouveau et typique, qui leur ouvrirait une voie inconnue jusqu'alors'; Garnier 1871, 305–6.

October 1873 and the rushed completion of the new house, without a mobile stage floor, for its inauguration in early 1875 – all the way to Garnier's next publication, *Le Nouvel Opéra*.[74] This was on a monumental scale, consisting of two volumes of text in quarto, together with two of steel engravings and chromolithographs, and four that contained 115 albumen silver print photographs, all of elephant folio size; the whole enterprise described by Martin Bressani and Peter Sealy as 'obviously in metonymic relation to the lavishness of the real building', and as 'probably the longest summation for the defense ever pronounced by an architect over a single piece of his work'.[75] Yet the chapter on theatrical machinery that opens the second text volume, published in 1881, consists simply of a direct copy of the earlier chapter in *Le Théâtre*, prefaced by a light-hearted defence of self-plagiarism ('Since God recopies, I don't see why I ... can't imitate his example'),[76] and followed by a resigned summary that leads directly from the earlier conclusion:

Ah well, this new and distinctive method will barely be studied; money for one thing, time for another, have prevented me from putting into action the project I have just spoken of and, as with most commissions, the theatrical commission did little good.[77]

On the upside, Garnier continued, the below-stage area was now prepared so that if a future director ever wanted to install the mobile stage floor they could do so without great expense, since all that was missing was the beams of the grid and the hydraulic motors. For now, though, it was 300,000 francs gone to waste on an unrealised system.

And then, at last, the pent-up frustration of many years breaks through:

Why then this commission, which worked for so long and that seemed duty bound to renew all the scenic machinery? Why all these complaints of the decorators, who pretended that they would no longer be able to produce anything unless the floor could rise and fall at their demand?[78]

---

[74] Garnier 1878–81, with six atlas folios of plates and photographs (1876–1880).

[75] Bressani and Sealy 2011, 199–200.

[76] 'Puisque le bon Dieu se recopie ainsi, je ne vois pas pourquoi moi ... je n'imiterais pas son exemple'; Garnier 1878–81, 2:2.

[77] 'Eh bien, l'on n'étudiera guère ce moyen nouveau et typique; l'argent d'un côté, le temps de l'autre, ne m'ont pas permis de mettre à exécution le projet dont je viens de parler et, comme la plupart des commissions, la commission théâtrale n'a pas servi à grand'chose'. Garnier 1878–81, 2:48.

[78] 'Pourquoi alors cette commission, qui a travaillé si longtemps et qui semblait devoir renouveler toute la machinerie scénique? Pourquoi enfin toutes ces plaintes des décorateurs, qui

As in earlier writings, this was followed by a retreat into the values of convention: 'Alas! This is what it is like with many things. One often calls tradition routine, when it means wisdom, and novelty progress when it signifies irrelevance.'[79] Whether the unfinished machinery at the Opéra would be such an irrelevance was not yet clear, he added, since it had never been tried; but 'I greatly fear that this commission had for its goal and its desiderata nothing but some floating sticks thrown into the water by so-called innovators, and that the absolute utility of a mobile floor in a theatre amounts only to a seductive mirage that disappears when approached.'[80] He concludes with the hope that one day he might complete a part of the plan at the Opéra, to avoid future money being spent on a project that might not work.

It is an extraordinary moment in the expensive pages of a book designed to commemorate and disseminate a full account of the successful completion of the grandest opera house in the world. So extraordinary, in fact, that later writers tended to see only the Garnier of *Le Théâtre*, proud of his work, rather than the Garnier of *Le Nouvel Opéra*, so wary of the imperatives of progress. Alphonse Gosset, for instance, in his *Traité de la Construction des Théâtres* of 1886, cited the Opéra project as a provocation to engineers to innovate, for machinists to awake, and for public opinion to demand the sort of progress visible elsewhere in new buildings.[81] Similarly, Germain Bapst, in a book on theatre production published in 1893, celebrated the foresight of Garnier's 'ingenious' unrealised project for the movable stage floor; while Edwin Sachs, in his monumental 1896 survey of modern opera houses and theatres, described the failure to innovate at the Opéra 'a great opportunity lost', but added that 'Charles Garnier, I know, still mourns this lost opportunity'.[82] In his preface to Georges Bourdon's study of English theatres, published in 1903, Sachs went further, noting that in the years since the opening of the Opéra, 'astonishing' innovations in theatrical machinery had appeared in other parts of Europe, but that these had been enabled by the 'strong impetus' created

---

prétendaient ne pouvoir plus rien composer si le plancher n'avait à leur demande un fux et un reflux alternatifs?' Garnier 1878–81, 2:50.

[79] 'Hélas! C'est qu'il en est ainsi de bien des choses. On appelle souvent la tradition routine, tandis qu'elle veut dire sagesse, et la nouveauté progrès, tandis qu'elle signifie inconséquence.' Garnier 1878–81, 2:50.

[80] 'j'ai grand'peur que cette commission n'ait pris pour but de ses *desiderata* que quelques bâtons flottants jetés dans l'eau par de soi-disant novateurs, et qui l'utilité absolue d'un plancher mobile dans un théâtre ne constitue qu'un séduisant mirage se dissipant lorsqu'on s'en approche'. Garnier 1878–81, 2:50–1.

[81] Gosset 1886, 83.   [82] Bapst 1893, 605–6; Sachs 1896–8, 3:24.

by Garnier's researches during the 1860s at the Opéra; not only did the world's architects and theatre directors remain in his debt, so did all stage engineers.[83] Bourdon elaborated the point, claiming that 'if it had been up to Charles Garnier alone, [the Opéra] would surely have become the sumptuous palace of modern machinery'.[84] Georges Vitoux, in *Le Théâtre de l'Avenir* (also published in 1903), agreed, casting Garnier with Tresca as heralds of the future.[85] This image has persisted: George C. Izenour's authoritative *Theater Technology*, for instance, celebrates Garnier for 'expanding existing French theater technology to the utmost', before listing a variety of 'spatial and technical superlatives' in the design of the Opéra's machinery.[86]

So Garnier got his apotheosis in spite of all his doubts. But other endings to the story are possible. At the Opéra's inauguration, for instance, critics were for the most part too bedazzled by (or disgruntled with) all the finery of the building to pay attention to the machinery; when they did mention it, they welcomed it as just one more element comprising the building's statistical sublimity, wheeling out figures such as the total mass of the counterweights (122,000 kilogrammes of iron and lead), or the total length of cable (223,100 metres of hemp, and 12,700 metres of iron).[87] Many later writers have remained similarly bedazzled, with much of the secondary literature on the Opéra exploring every aspect of the building but the machinery.[88] Not that the subject disappeared altogether in the years following the inauguration, of course, nor the same old astonishment at how little theatrical machinery had changed in recent centuries, and how many machinists the Opéra employed; but it would be another forty years before the machinery of the Opéra was overhauled again, and all the wood and hemp finally replaced with metal.[89]

As to Quéruel, last heard of in July 1870, he continued to spread the word about his new system, and to grumble to anyone who would listen

---

[83] Sachs, in Bourdon 1903, vii.

[84] 'S'il n'avait tenu qu'à Charles Garnier, elle fût devenue à coup sûr le palais somptueux de la machinerie moderne'; Bourdon 1903, 257–8.

[85] Vitoux [1903], 166.   [86] Izenour 1996, 22.

[87] See, for example, the statistical section that concludes Nuitter 1875, 239–52. Garnier himself includes a chapter rejecting the need to account for the Opéra statistically in his own *Nouvel Opéra* (1878–81, 2: 237–9).

[88] Alongside all the coffee table books on the Opéra (and serious works like Mead's study), it is telling that when the text of Garnier's *Le Nouvel Opéra* was reprinted in 2001 (available for purchase from the Opéra's bookshop), the second volume was left out, thereby silently omitting the chapter on the machinery (as well as chapters on expenses, heating, lighting, construction, works of art and so on).

[89] See F-Pan AJ[13] 1190.

about Garnier's behaviour. He published a stinging review of *Le Théâtre* in the *Gazette des architectes* in late 1871, in which he mocked Garnier and Tresca's supposedly explosive discovery of the perfect system that turned out to borrow so heavily from his own design; and compared his own reliance on multiple hydraulic motors (criticised by Garnier) with the thousands upon thousands of pulleys, ropes and counterweights in the systems of Sacré and Brabant.[90] In April 1872 he received a bronze medal for his experiments at the Théâtre de la Gaîté from the Society for the Encouragement of National Industry, and later that year presented his work to the Society of Civil Engineers. And he returned to the latter Society again one evening in early 1874, explicitly to discuss the machinery at the new Opéra.[91] He gave an exhaustive account of all the various systems proposed, including his own, grandly concluding that 'public interest cannot remain indifferent to the success of this attempt for reform, proposed on the grandest stage in existence'.[92] Members of the Society seem to have disagreed; for all Quéruel's detail and passion, he received just two questions from the floor before the company moved on to a lecture on developments in the manufacture of phosphorised steel rails at the foundries of Terrenoire; a topic that generated considerably more interest.

Unable to build much support outside the Opéra, Quéruel turned to the pursuit of internal recompense, writing to Garnier on 26 December 1874, after a tour of the completed building, to profess shock at finding a system of machinery so reliant on his plans in a variety of ways, even without hydraulics.[93] Garnier denied the charge and suggested he write for a second opinion to Tresca or to the Minister of Public Works.[94] And so he did, in the form of a pamphlet sent to the minister a few months later with a lengthy case for reclamation. First came his argument for the existence of a de facto competition in 1866, then he dug back into earlier reports to argue that Garnier had stolen from Quéruel the idea of building a below-stage frame in iron. He concluded by pointing out that he had devoted enormous time and money to this project, and deserved restitution.[95]

---

[90] Quéruel 1871; the article is dated 7 December 1871.   [91] See Quéruel 1869, 1874b.

[92] 'L'intérêt public ne peut être indifférent à la réussite de cette tentative de réforme que l'on se propose d'inaugurer dans la plus grande scène qui existe'; Quéruel 1874a, 669.

[93] Quéruel drew attention to the use of iron for the below-stage structure, and to some more technical details of the construction.

[94] This exchange is reproduced in F-Pan AJ[13] 453/III: Quéruel, 'Machinerie de la scène du Nouvel Opéra. Note à l'appui de la réclamation adressée à Monsieur le Ministre des Travaux Publics'. Garnier's response to Quéruel is partial, however, since Quéruel, like so many others, could not easily decipher Garnier's notoriously messy handwriting.

[95] Quéruel, 'Machinerie de la scène'.

Whether Quéruel's case was successful remains unclear, but it is hard not to feel some sympathy for him: Garnier had borrowed what he needed from his designs, with a focus on pushing through a final plan, but without taking full account of Quéruel's personal investment in the project. And although Quéruel, too, would later receive his own limited apotheosis as another prophet of staging innovation, any signs of his travails and grievances against the Opéra disappeared from the printed record; the contours of his struggle were steamrollered into the flattened grand narrative of inexorable progress.[96]

Epilogue

At the end of Latour's *Aramis*, the feasibility of the new light transport system is as uncertain as Garnier's unrealised plans for the Opéra machinery. Would either system have worked or were both destined to remain pipe dreams?[97] For Aramis, no matter: Latour's engineer protagonist, frustrated with sociology, tells his mentor that following the system's failed implementation, he is returning to the state-of-the-art and to contemplating its future adoption in new configurations and new locations. It would be possible to trace the aftermath of the story of the Opéra's machinery along the same lines; to the foundation of the Asphaleia Society in Vienna, for instance, dedicated to reorganising theatrical design one hydraulic system at a time; and then to the real hydraulics at the Budapest opera house in 1884, at the Halle Stadttheater in 1886, the Berlin Court Theatre and the Vienna Burgtheater in 1888, and the Wiesbaden Opera in 1894.[98] From there, one could chart the attempts to replace hydraulic power with electricity in moving scenery, as at the Munich's Deutsches Theater in 1896; and so on. That way the historian, like Latour's engineer, gets the vicarious excitement of chasing the next big idea; while the Opéra machinery itself gets pulled within the thrilling world of the once-new, with Garnier's final

---

[96] Gosset 1886, for example, includes a detailed description with plates of Quéruel's hydraulic design (84–7; plate 49); see also G. Moynet 1893, 321–4, along with a description of Quéruel's experiment at the Gaîté, together with the reproduction of Henri Tresca's 1871 report on this to the Société for the Encouragement of National Industry.

[97] See Latour 1993, 277–8, for the full list of possible conclusions that remained in play at the end of the investigation into the later system, many of which could also be applied to the Opéra machinery ('Aramis has been perfected and will be built soon ... Aramis had almost been perfected; more money and more time were all that would have been needed to complete the experiment ... No piece of Aramis has been perfected. There are no repercussions; it is a false innovation ... It is impossible to judge').

[98] On the Asphaleia Society and the development of hydraulics in European theatre machinery see in particular, Pierron 1885; G. Moynet 1893, 214–36; Bourdon 1903, 258–9.

plan recast as a hydraulic fantasy whose imaginary status only intensifies its appeal: worthy of a place in the operatic curiosity cabinet after all.

Might such a final turn suggest, with Abbate, that there is nothing inherently problematic about the scholarly desire for material enchantment? Certainly some of the select corpus of nineteenth-century publications that go behind the stage of the theatre and opera house present their descriptions of showstopping special effects, novel techniques and grand transformations in conjunction with detailed accounts of the mechanics of operatic machinery; all wrapped up into a kind of catch-all backstage sublimity that somehow survived from the romantic era through the Second Empire and into the Third Republic. The yawning chasms above and below the stage; the towering scenery; the bare-armed teams of machinists, breathless and sweating with the exertions of bringing an opera or ballet to life; even the evocative soundscapes of their work: 'the strange commands [and] bizarre cries that come from the under-stage to lose themselves in the flies'; or the 'grinding of pulleys, lifting the counterweights, and the dull thuds that rock the stage floor'.[99] Enough to lure the most spectacle-addicted opera historian out of the stalls and behind the scenes.

Yet while such a move might help to bridge the estrangement between opera and its technologies, in other ways it only risks compounding the original problem, by still treating scholarship as a means to sublimate aesthetic pleasure, and still paying attention to machines and machinists only when remade in mythic form. Better, perhaps, to ground the Opéra machinery within more pragmatic contexts, and the less fanciful the better. The designs for a new cart to transport the Opéra scenery from its off-site store to the stage, for instance, written up in *Le Génie civil* in 1886; or the vexed issue of set and prop storage more generally.[100] Or else new developments in fireproofing; or the working conditions of machinists in comparison with other labourers, and the campaign for pension funds to support injured backstage crew and their families. And not forgetting, of course, all the stuff on, above, below, behind and beside the stage – the pulleys, counterweights, flats, trolleys. Objects that were already old-fashioned in the 1860s, and whose familiarity and longevity rendered them invisible as technologies, yet in many cases remain dominant parts of theatrical machinery to this day. The material history of opera, in other words, just found itself a whole lot more material.

---

[99] 'Des commandements étranges, des cris bizarres partent du dessous pour se perdre dans les frises'; Vizentini 1868, 10; 'ce sont des grincements de treuils, relevant des contrepoids, et des heurts sourds qui ébranlent le plancher'; G. Moynet 1893, 184.

[100] Talansier 1886.

10 | Circuit Listening

ELLEN LOCKHART

Giacomo Puccini was enthusiastic about electricity. To begin with, there were the modern luxuries it made available: electric lighting, the telegraph, the telephone, the radio, the refrigerator – he made use of them all. When he sailed westward across the Atlantic in 1907, on board the SS *Kaiserin Auguste Victoria*, he made a point of counting the electric light bulbs in his cabin – 'I have seventy' – and noting all the other extravagances powered by electricity. There were electric devices on board that he intended to enjoy (heated water, cigar lighters, a Marconi telegraph to supply passengers with news from around the world); and ones he didn't, like the mechanical wooden exercise horses, 'onto which American women climb each day to jostle the uterus'.[1]

But this enthusiasm went beyond Puccini's love of luxury (which was by all accounts profound and lifelong). He was interested in the way that electricity could cause objects to move seemingly of their own volition – interested enough to make repeated forays into amateur inventing, to search for ways that this power might be harnessed not only for domestic pleasures but also for music. First, and most famously, there was the *fonica*: an electric percussion instrument that he designed for use in the final measures of *La fanciulla del West*'s first act. As Puccini imagined it, the *fonica* consisted of three tubular bells pitched at B and E, struck rapidly by electric-powered mallets with heads of sponge. This design was revised before *La fanciulla*'s premiere – perhaps because (as a recent attempt at reconstruction suggests) the *fonica* as Puccini imagined it sounds like the alarm bells at a fire station. But this failure did not prevent him from returning often to dabble in electrical engineering.[2] In 1919, when the annoyances of a nearby peat factory forced the ailing composer out of Torre del Lago, he designed his new home at Viareggio as a complex network of electrical devices and overlapping circuits, over which he presided, a recluse. There was a system of electric bells, and an electric

---

[1] Letter from Puccini to his sister Ramelde, dated 14 January 1907, in Marchetti 1973, 326. Throughout this chapter, translations are mine unless otherwise noted.

[2] On the *fonica* and Puccini's other electric inventions see Fairtile 1999, 332–3.

locking gate controlled by switch from the house, both Puccini's own design. He also designed an electric irrigation system for the grounds, similarly connected by wires to a switchboard of sorts in the house. This was used to douse unsuspecting guests as they traversed his lawns.

Electricity also occasioned what might have been Puccini's only foray into programme music. Among his instrumental works, sandwiched between student essays and a handful of works of dubious authenticity, there is a piece called *Scossa elettrica* (Electric Shock). While no one knows exactly when Puccini wrote it, we know that *Scossa elettrica* began as a piano piece, and was published in this form in 1899. The occasion was an international convention of telegraph operators held in nearby Como, Alessandro Volta's birthplace, to coincide with the centenary of Volta's most famous invention, the battery. Soon thereafter the work was arranged for wind band by one G. Serrao, and it seems to have been performed in this form in Lucca in 1910. Virtually unknown to musicologists even now, it languished forgotten until the late 1970s, when Mario Morini spotted it amongst the pages of *I telegrafisti a Volta*, a brochure (of sorts) published for the centenary convention.[3]

Scossa elettrica would seem to be a notable find for the scholar in search of intersections between the histories of opera and science. After all, the very title of the work seems to promise to depict in music a visceral phenomenon – the shock – that had been a centre of considerable scientific activity in the preceding century. What is more, the Puccini scholar could scarcely hope for a more apt object for musical representation, and not merely because of the composer's side-interests in electrical engineering. Puccini was a composer who specialised in overpowering the listener (aggressively and without their rational consent, if his detractors are to be believed). In this light, one might expect *Scossa elettrica* to be a tone poem in the characteristic form of arias like 'Sì, mi chiamano Mimì', 'Sola, perduta, abbandonata' and, of course, 'Nessun dorma': from the first notes to the last, every parameter building toward a surging, crashing climax.

This chapter begins, then, as a story of frustrated expectations, for the only shocking thing about *Scossa elettrica* is its ordinariness. It is as slight and unassuming a piece as Puccini ever wrote, lasting barely two minutes, unflappably committed to a jolly 2/4 metre (crotchet = 132) and phrases in four bars. A tempo indication labels the piece a 'Marcetta brillante' (brilliant little march), but its quick pace, celebratory tone and pervasive long-short-short rhythmic motive mark its true genre as the *galop*: the easiest of

---

[3] Morini 1979.

the nineteenth-century ballroom dances, performed by couples linked at the hands, galloping frenetically in a circle. Numerous early copper engravings represent dancers of a *galop*, including one attributed to Johann Strauss, *c.*1839, which must refer to the elder Johann Strauss, one of the most prolific composers of the genre in its first decades, but the younger Johann Strauss also wrote many *galops*.

This lineage has troubled at least one Puccini scholar. Julian Budden suggested that 'the mantle of Johann Strauss II sat uneasily on Puccini's shoulders', and the piece 'would hardly merit performance today'.[4] Budden has been proven wrong on the latter count: if the original piano version has not found a place in the concert repertoire, the arrangement for wind band has fared quite well in recent years, garnering several performances in Italy and in the southern states of the USA. He might have been wrong on the first point as well. Puccini slipped on Strauss's cloak (to use Budden's conceit) with the ease of an actor. The piece reveals him to be an accomplished mimic – a veritable Sarah Bernhardt in matters of musical style.

However, metaphors such as this surely miss the point. For *Scossa elettrica* offers a more-or-less unique opportunity to observe Puccini outside the theatre: away from the maximalist traditions and acoustically delimited spaces of the *fin-de-siècle* opera house. It has the proportions of a miniature, but the measureless reach of a commodity, and something of the commodity's knack for advancing and receding simultaneously.[5] Indeed, perhaps the most notable feature of this music is its ability to be at once pompous and weightless – as in the main melody's anacrusis, a helium inhalation that unexpectedly rises all the way to c'', delaying the first oompah bass until the second bar; and as in the successive four-bar phrases, which are similarly most insubstantial in the strongest parts of the metre (see Example 10.1).

One must strain hard against a host of inherited values not to find this piece a little embarrassing. Puccini himself was uneasy about it: 'here is a bit of hogwash for you' ('Eccoti la porcherietta'), he wrote, defensively, straight onto the autograph, as if he suspected that it would one day be unearthed by his canonisers. *Scossa elettrica* supplies a genuine catalogue of embarrassments: civic festivity, scoring for wind band, warm national feeling, and surely a generous commission fee. It was occasional music to commemorate the battery, an invention of a fellow Italian, useful not only

---

[4] Budden 2002, 196–7.

[5] On the recessive and expansive tendencies of the nineteenth-century commodity form, particularly in relation to music, see Willson 2016.

Example 10.1 Giacomo Puccini, *La scossa elettrica*, bb. 1–12

to national and global industry, but also to commodious bourgeois living. Puccini envisioned lines of telegraph operators parading to collect their pensions as his music sounded.[6] So we can add to our litany: bourgeois women of middle age (most telegraph operators were female), open-air parade, the jaunty rhythms of social dance.

But if Puccini was embarrassed by *Scossa elettrica*, he need not have been embarrassed alone. There were other works in this vein, including by an opera composer of something like his stature. Indeed, Puccini's little foray into so-called 'electric' music was only one of many musical works composed in the second half of the nineteenth century to celebrate achievements in electrical science and engineering, in Italy and elsewhere in Europe. A flurry of works greeted the opening of the first telegraphs on the Italian peninsula: for instance, Saverio Mercadante's *Il telegrafo elettrico*, a capriccio for band and fanfarra, was composed for a civic ceremony on 31 July 1852, inaugurating the new line between Naples and

---

[6] The full inscription on one of the piece's two autographs reads: 'Eccoti la porcherietta . . . . [*sic*] che i telegrafisti al suono di questa marcetta arrivino presto alla pensione'. Puccini 2008, [i].

Gaeta.[7] The piece was sufficiently popular to merit two arrangements for pianoforte, published by Francesco Lucca in Milan and Clausetti in Naples that same year. Also in 1852, Lucca published another *Telegrafo elettrico* by the flautist Emanuele Krakamp, this one a waltz scored for flute and piano. The Biblioteca privata Giuseppe Pastore in Lecce holds the manuscript for a *Telegraph Galop* by Fortunato Rayntroph, perhaps inspired by the *Telegraph Galop* of 1844 by Hans Christian Lumbye. These all share a set of family resemblances with Puccini's miniature: most are scored for wind instruments and adapted for keyboard; all deploy the tropes of social dances, and indeed, most are *galops*: quick and jaunty, with oompah basses and cheerful, rhythmic melodies. In this tradition, then, music about electricity and electric instruments does not develop a new set of behaviours or distort itself into strange postures to evoke its object (as in Roger Scruton's notion that programme music must forsake 'its autonomous principles' when bespoke to a foreign thing).[8] Rather, it leaps and patters rhythmically, dancing; and in so doing, it behaves just like a lot of other music for social and civic occasions.

As such, these pieces may be heard to make assertions of kinship: a now-occluded kinship between music and electric science and its technologies. This analogy within musical practice thrived alongside a speculative tradition within aesthetic writings during the middle decades of the century. In what follows, I wish to probe more deeply into this shared history of music and electricity during the period from approximately 1830 until the end of the century. First, I consider the ways in which the first Italian theorists of aesthetics compared the perception of a work of art to the behaviour and sensations of electric current. Many of these writings construed performers and audience as vast batteries through which electric current is discharged. I argue that the language of electricity in these treatises helped to convey a new emphasis on *effect*, in which music is understood as stimulus, rather than as purveyor of *affect* or as mathematical or historical practice. Then I consider how such fantasies of aesthetic connectivity presaged the networks created by the electric telegraph during the Risorgimento years; and how the technology of the telegraph itself required a kind of stimulus-based listening through an attention to rhythmic patterns. These threads are finally drawn together in scenes from two popular Italian pantomime

---

[7] Giuseppe Fagnocchi (1999) alludes to this tradition. The inauguration is recounted in the *Dizionario corografico-universale dell'Italia*, IV/1: *Reame di Napoli* (Milan: Giuseppe, 1852), 407–9.

[8] Scruton 2001.

ballets from the final third of the century, *Il telegrafo elettrico* (1873) and *Excelsior* (1881), in which we arguably uncover the closest cousins of Puccini's miniature homage to Volta.

Circuit Listening

'The aesthetic effect passes from individual to individual like an electric spark': thus did Giuseppe De' Filippi characterise the effect of a very fine melody. The date was 7 January 1847, and the occasion was an address to the Lombard Institute of Science and Literature.[9] De' Filippi was a renowned surgeon and medical doctor, well known for his treatises on inflammation, keratosis and 'the science of life', as well as a popular manual for young doctors. He was from Piedmont but had lived in Milan since the Napoleonic Wars, when he had distinguished himself both as chief army physician and as director of the army band. The address quoted here merited him an entry in F.-J. Fétis's monumental *Biographie universelle des musiciens*, which recounted that De' Filippi had been elected four times to the Institute of Science and Literature, and that the position had been three times revoked by the Austrians, who apparently did not care for him.[10]

De' Filippi's analogy – that a powerful melody could electrify its hearer – was by no means new; it was at least as old as the century. I have written elsewhere about the way this language was used in Italian opera criticism of the 1820s; there, such analogies emerged as a mode of response to operatic performance, and particularly that of the famous soprano Giuditta Pasta.[11] Also derivative is De' Filippi's assertion that melody was more important than harmony or counterpoint, which drew on notions that had been in circulation since the final third of the eighteenth century. One can easily spot Jean-Jacques Rousseau's influence in De' Filippi's suggestion that harmony appeals to the mind, while melody 'gives [musical] sound that spark of life' ('scintilla di vita': also perhaps an allusion to electricity). A nearly identical turn of phrase could be found in Esteban de Arteaga's *Rivoluzioni del teatro musicale italiano* of sixty-two years earlier.[12]

Even so, there are at least two reasons to linger on De' Filippi's formulation. The first of these is its context: De' Filippi's address to the Istituto lombardo di scienze e lettere, which was delivered in lectures on 17 December 1846 and 7 January 1847, and published in its entirety soon

---

[9] De' Filippi 1847, 45. [10] Fétis 1881–9, I [1881]:332–3. [11] Lockhart 2017, 133–50.
[12] Arteaga 1785, 2: 33–4

thereafter in the official journal of the institute. The print version was entitled *Sulla estetica musicale*. It thus forms part of a larger body of mid-century Italian works devoted to the study of aesthetics, a category new to philosophy in the Italian language, but which had flourished in other continental schools since Alexander Baumgarten established the discipline in 1735. De' Filippi's account was almost unique in focusing exclusively on music (there was also Raimondo Boucheron's *Filosofia della musica o estetica applicata a quest'arte*, published by Ricordi in 1842), but he shared both concerns and vocabulary with works like Giambattista Talia's *Saggio di estetica* (1822), Luigi Pasquali's *Istituzioni di estetica* (1827), Girolamo Venanzio's *Callofilia* (1830), Peter Lichtenthal's *Estetica, ossia, Dottrina del bello e delle arti belle*, (1831), Gratiliano Bonacci's *Nozioni fondamentali di estetica* (1837) and Vincenzo Gioberti's *Saggio sul bello, o Elementi di filosofia estetica* (1845).

Most of the treatises, including De' Filippi's, were too indebted to older currents of empiricism to gain currency beyond the Alps (Immanuel Kant and G. W. F. Hegel barely merit a mention in any of them); now, they are merely entries in the vast catalogue of non-canonical nineteenth-century aesthetic theories that are now forgotten. Yet together they formed a new and important chapter in Italian writing on the fine arts; they represented a new willingness to understand the arts in terms of sensory perception and sense-based thinking. In De' Filippi's case, that signified a licence to write about music without first establishing a vast historical narrative stretching from the Greeks and Romans (as earlier Italian writers on music had done, in Padre Martini's model), and without being encumbered by any critical terms or music-theoretical mores; indeed, he opened the treatise by making a virtue of his amateur status.

De' Filippi approached the topic of a musical aesthetics with much the same observation- and physiology-based methods that he had brought to his earlier treatises on inflammation and keratosis. His main credential, asserted in the opening lines, consisted of the ability to reason about the 'physiological causes' of musical effect. What was more, he suggested that his ignorance of music theory aided rather than hindered his ability to define it aesthetically; the opening promised that there would be no recourse to specialist concepts. In place of the jargon of music theory, De' Filippi ostentatiously deployed the languages of physics and anatomy: music is defined as 'the noisy vibration of the atmosphere', organised according to 'proportionality';

the ear is 'the acoustic organ'; hearing is 'the acoustic impression.' For De' Filippi, musical aesthetics comprised one sub-discipline of acoustics (*la parte estetica dell'acustica*), which dealt with the aspect of human intelligence related to 'moral, psychic, physiological, sensory acts'; the other sub-discipline of acoustics concerned sound vibrations and their mechanical perception in the ear, matters that interested him less.[13] The treatise records his search for what he calls the 'physiological reasons why music acts with greater or lesser effect on the living organism'.[14] While De' Filippi had effectively swapped one esoteric apparatus for another, his strategy of considering music via acoustics and the physiology of hearing was not well poised to differentiate one sort of music from any other. In matters of specialist musical knowledge, he was as good as his word: apart from defining melody and harmony, he referred to his object simply as 'music', and did not complicate the matter any further.

Considered 'aesthetically', then, music emerged as a homogeneous substance possessed of a single potency: *effect*.[15] This term, which features in the quotation above ('the aesthetic effect passes from individual to individual') and prominently throughout the treatise as a whole, has been celebrated as the 'scientific' nineteenth-century equivalent of the older notion of music as purveyor of passions or affects. In the context of De' Filippi's treatise the term is peculiarly blank: it resisted the individuating qualities of emotions, and the internal divisions of disciplinary knowledge. In this, De' Filippi was joined by most of his fellow Italian aestheticians, whose continued allegiance to empiricist traditions (compared, for instance, to their German contemporaries) left reflection or imaginative engagement on the part of the listener drastically under-theorised. Note the shrugging reference to 'some emotion or other' in Talia's *Essay on Aesthetics* (1822): he noted that a great variety of stimuli can produce what are 'almost electric shocks [*quasi scintille elettriche*], which cause some emotion or other to burst into flames. This state of the soul, if I am not mistaken, is called enthusiasm, [and it] travels from the heart to the other faculties, and endows them with unusual energy.'[16] In this sense (and as the second half of this quotation implies), the term 'effect' in aesthetics is being treated as akin to the category of energy in physics, also emergent during the first years of the nineteenth century, construing all modes of inter-material and human–object engagement in terms of different quantities of

---

[13] De' Filippi 1847, 24–5.   [14] De' Filippi 1847, 19.

[15] See the evolving uses of the terms around 1800 as considered throughout Dolan 2013.

[16] Talia 1822, 173.

a single potency.[17] The analogy between aesthetic effect and electric current rests on this similarity, the blankness of the energising force; not by accident can such figures be found in nearly all of the first Italian treatises on aesthetics. At least since Luigi Galvani's experiments with frogs' legs, the nervous system itself had been understood to function by means of quantities of electric current circulating within the network of nerves and brain. Galvani's work in bioelectricity was continued by his fellow Italian Carlo Matteucci, who was able to show that biological tissue could create electric current (rather than merely transmitting it), and one could build batteries entirely from animal parts. As Laura Otis and Alison Winter have recently shown, Matteucci's experiments were taken by many to mean that there was an electrical component to all human interactions.[18] In De' Filippi's day, the study of electrophysiology entailed investigating not the kinds of big shocks that had once been analogised within arts criticism – the lightning bolt, the sublime burst that paralyses – but to the measurement, perception and detection of far more subtle, short-lasting bursts of current.[19] Correspondingly, the nervous system was newly analogised in terms of that most efficient instrument of rhythmical electrical pulses, the telegraph.[20]

But I am getting ahead of myself. I would like to linger a little while longer on De' Filippi's formulation, for there was something new in it – or nearly so: a way in which his account of the electrifying effects of a good melody departed from the established model. It is the fact that the electric shock that he described was no longer simply an immediate response to music – a jolt felt by the listener when she is affected by what she hears. Rather, De' Filippi suggested that this shock spread *between* listeners: in other words, an 'electric' impulse of aesthetic stimulation might originate with the singer, but from there it would be conducted around the auditorium, from spectator to spectator; if you got it, you most likely caught it from your neighbour. This image alludes most obviously to the figure of the human chain (or 'series of men', as Galvani called it), in which an

---

[17] A history of the concept of energy within nineteenth-century science is given in Harman 1982; for a consideration of the aesthetic implications of this process in the last decades of the nineteenth century see Crary 1999, particularly chapter 1, 'Modernity and the Problem of Attention'. Crary writes: 'sensation now had empirical significance only in terms of magnitudes that corresponded to specific quantities of energy (e.g., light) on one hand and to measurable reaction times and other forms of performative behavior on the other. It cannot be emphasized too strongly how, by the 1880s, the classical idea of sensation ceases to be a significant component in the cognitive picture of nature' (27).

[18] Winter 1998, 77; and Otis 2001, 19–20.   [19] See Lenoir 1986, 1–54; and Crary 1999, 27.

[20] Otis 2001, 1–48.

electric shock was transmitted through a line of individuals joined at the hand.[21] The most famous of these had been performed by the Abbé Nollet, who sent a shock through a chain of 700 monks, causing them to 'leap into the air with a precision outrivaling the timing of the most perfect corps de ballet'.[22] But the experiment was often repeated by smaller groups, in scientific demonstrations and in salons, with participants linked at the hands and arranged in a large circle – much as they had been in the *galop*.[23] Many factors helped to determine how well a human chain conducted electricity; as these experiments attest, current was thought to travel further in chains built from homogeneous groups.

Such spontaneous human concatenation is strikingly at odds with more familiar notions of nineteenth-century musical attention; these notions have relied – falsely, as I am suggesting here – on a simple listener-to-musical-object relationship. The aesthetic–electric shock runs orthogonal to this relationship, even while intensifying the all-important *effect* belonging to the sounded musical object. A similar figure may be found in Vincenzo Gioberti's *Saggio sul bello*, which compared aesthetic impressions to various forms of airborne contagion (though as the reference to 'the medium of words' suggests, his considerations were confined to poetry): 'aesthetic impressions … communicate themselves agilely to others through the medium of words, like light, caloric, electricity and certain qualities that are advantageous or harmful to organic life propagate themselves through the medium of air, or through rubbing, or by simple contact of bodies'.[24] When Gioberti's colleague Vincenzo de Castro plagiarised him in the *Enciclopedia italiana* later that year, he expunged most of this figure, with its uneasy references to rubbing and 'qualities advantageous or harmful to organic life'. In its place de Castro simply suggested that 'aesthetic impressions' communicate themselves to others 'like an electric shock to a long chain of persons'.[25] Morbid undertones persisted in Cesare della Valle's *Considerazioni sullo stato attuale del teatro italiano* (1856), which suggested that the current enters 'the most susceptible spectators' first, and spreads through the stalls from there; 'a few will suffice' to infect the multitude.[26]

---

[21] 'animal electricity ... manifests itself most conspicuously in muscles and nerves. The peculiar and not previously recognized nature of this seems to be that it flows from muscles to nerves, or rather from the latter to the former, and that it traverses there either an arc or a series of men or any other conducting bodies which lead from nerves to muscles by a shorter and quicker way.' Galvani 2002, 136.

[22] Cohen 1941, 48.   [23] Wosk 2001, 68–9; Pera 1992, 14–15; Fara 2002, 57–8.

[24] Gioberti 1845, 172.   [25] Castro 1845, 1935.   [26] Della Valle 1856, 40–1.

On the whole, though, the electric–aesthetic chain was configured by these theorists as a positive social force, generating brotherhood and shared experience: after all, as De' Filippi suggested elsewhere in his treatise, music was 'one of the most effective means of putting our *microcosm* in accord with the outside world'; it allowed ideas and sensations to 'pass from one individual to the next' in the form of 'original expression'.[27] These positive socialising effects were described by Gratiliano Bonacci in his *Nozioni fondamentali di estetica*, published seven years before De' Filippi's: he praised artworks that communicate 'almost an electric force into the soul', since these artworks 'provoke one to a gay and festive mood, and invite one to take solace amidst parties, games, and dances'.[28] He termed these electrifying works 'grazioso', a third category in his treatise alongside the sublime and the beautiful. For della Valle, the mobile electric impulse is downright democratic, travelling as it does through the stalls – where all the social classes sit shoulder to shoulder – but not in the boxes, where the wealthy and aristocratic remain physically individuated and therefore unaffected. For this reason 'the true judgment [of an artwork] happens in the stalls'.[29] Della Valle was himself a member of the nobility – his title was the Duke of Ventignano – and a tragedian of some renown (he had collaborated with Rossini on *Maometto II*). In his imagining, the aesthetic–electric shock did not merely traverse social classes; it overrode the concerns of individual expertise – overcoming, for instance, the literati's tendency only to 'pay attention to language and to style, philosophers to ideas, dramatic authors to the course of the drama, pedants to Logic, architects to decorations'.[30] Here again, then, aesthetics worked (at least in the first moments of reception) against disciplinary knowledge, and in favour of what della Valle called *theatrical effects*.

This imagery was pervasive in contemporary aesthetic writings in French, English and German, as well as in less formal kinds of music criticism; that is, it was not a uniquely Italian phenomenon. When August Wilhelm Ambros inveighed against those atheist writers who intoned 'enthusiastic, hymnlike drivelings, nay, downright prayers, to electricity, warmth, etc.' he was almost certainly referring not to De' Filippi et al. but to the pre-eminent nineteenth-century aesthetician of music, Eduard Hanslick himself.[31] In *On the Musically Beautiful*, Hanslick could understand the effect of musical performance (or what he suggestively called 'the reproductive act') as one that 'coaxes the electric spark out of its obscure secret place and flashes it across

---

[27] De' Filippi 1847, 24.   [28] Bonacci 1837, 56–8.   [29] Della Valle 1856, 40.
[30] Della Valle 1856, 40.   [31] Ambros 1988, 343.

to the listener'. In this formulation, electricity resides in the dark chambers of the musical work (the 'obscure, secret place') much as a battery might store energy; it is conducted thence during the act of performance, into the hearer, who is thereby energised.[32] Chantal Frankenbach has argued that with this formulation Hanslick unwittingly echoed Viennese music journalists like Joseph Oppenheim, however little he shared their critical hierarchies, which valued Bonacci's *grazioso* and the music of 'gay and festive mood', and the socialising effects of the parterre. She cites Oppenheim's encomium to none other than Johann Strauss, Sr, which asserted that even 'the strictest critic' must 'observe the electric effects of the [music] with a hearty laugh'. Like the Italian aesthetic theorists, Oppenheim suggested that this electricity was to be felt in the parterre, and (perhaps hinting at the paradigm of electromagnetism) most vividly by those seated closest to the stage – and it spread outward from there, a contagion: 'in the front rows of the lower seats, some people who are too close to the magician start to jerk up as if electrified. The musical current infects others very quickly.'[33]

The similarity of Oppenheim's (and others') figures to those I have pointed up in Italian writings around the mid-century may serve as a warning against analyses that rely heavily on local geographic or linguistic context. Yet shared figures such as this could be directed toward specific local ends; they could be inflected differently, or have different resonances, depending on the political context. In the Italian literature, such images of connection between adjacent strangers had obvious significance in the Risorgimento years. They may have implied a certain homogeny of substance within the listeners – as, for instance, Nollet's chains were constructed of people of the same type (monks, soldiers and so on). Participants were further united by shared experience. More than that, though, and as we will consider in greater detail below, the electric links between aesthetes reiterated in microcosm those telegraph lines that were just then being built between Italian cities. The telegraph was an instrument powered by current from a battery, functioning by means of rhythmically controlled bursts of tiny current: short and long pulses that encoded letters according to Samuel Morse's system. At a push, one might compare the labours of the telegraph operator, which decoded those rhythms into messages from a sender, to the act of musical listening as it was construed by De' Filippi and his fellow theorists.

The analogy is not as far-fetched as it might seem. Such images of music-listening circuits rendered the concert hall and opera house akin to another

---

[32] Hanslick 1986, 49.   [33] Frankenbach 2013, 112–13.

Figure 10.1 'The Magnetic Rope' (1853), reproduced in Jeffrey Sconce, *Haunted Media*, 29.

social practice that was just then emergent: the séance. Participants in the séance were usually arranged in a circle, their hands touching their neighbours', in order to facilitate the flow of current around the circle. Together, they aimed to generate enough electric energy to communicate with the departed, which were themselves thought to consist of great bundles of energy. Some séances even 'hard-wired' their human circuits by means of magnetised cables dipped in ionised solutions: Figure 10.1 represents one such 'spirit battery'. As Jeffrey Sconce has shown, the human chains of the séance were understood to engage in a kind of telegraphic activity, attentive to portentous rhythmic knocking thought to emanate from the deceased.[34]

Both the human chains in the concert hall and those of the séance were thought to facilitate an intense collective listening experience, particularly as both environments relied on dim lighting. Of course, in the former case, the sounding object was a musical object, while in the other, listeners sought to hear the spirits of the dead. It is telling, though, that in emphasising the sensory qualities of music this new figure of *aesthetic* electrification drew attention away from those categories – of performer and interpretation – that had prevailed in the earlier model, described above in connection with the singer Giuditta Pasta. The similarities between séance listening, telegraphic listening and concert-hall listening shed strange new light on the

---

[34] Sconce 2000, 21–58.

emergence of the canon during these years; De' Filippi, for instance, avowed a preference for the music of dead composers, particularly Haydn and Beethoven. Robert Schumann laughingly conflated these forms of listening when he requested to hear the opening rhythm of Beethoven's Fifth Symphony at a séance ('the tempo is faster, dear table', he complained).[35]

It might be tempting to suppose that the language configuring audiences as electric circuits attests to new orientation toward science amongst aesthetes: a prelude (as it were) to those more-familiar positivist appeals for a science-based aesthetics heard closer to the end of the century. The reality is more complicated. Within their host works, the passages quoted above often represent rare departures from careful argument. Indeed, even to describe these figurations of audience-circuits as analogies is misleading, for it is by no means clear what process or mechanism is being analogised. These passages suggest that the aesthetic experience is inflected and intensified in ways that are related neither to auditory or visual perception of the artwork nor to its rational cognition. In this sense, the language evokes a category of the ineffable – the experience that in its potency transcends its perceptible cause – which has long been central to accounts of romanticism broadly conceived. Yet it is alert to, even dependent on, factors that do not normally feature in such accounts. Unlike more familiar forms of aesthetic transcendence, it values the work as performed rather than in score, and is alert to practical matters such as noticing, while sitting in the theatre, whether the strangers at one's elbows are attentive; it allows that one can be energised by the well-played dance. It values the *grazioso* alongside the allegro; the music that provokes not a bowed head but a hearty laugh.

But there are other reasons not to interpret this electric imagery as representing a new scientific alertness within the aesthetic discourse. A language of science (of sorts) featured prominently within aesthetic writings from the beginning of the discipline; Baumgarten coined the term to denote what he described as 'the science for directing the inferior faculty of cognition or the science of how something is to be sensitively cognized'.[36] This apparatus persisted in the Italian tradition. Lichtenthal began his *Estetica* of 1834 by distinguishing between aesthetics in practice (that is, the fine arts) and in 'science', by which he meant academic theory: 'Certainly no one could deny Italy the honour of being the richest and most beautiful practical school of aesthetics; but this classic country still

---

[35] Schumann recounted the story in a letter to the conductor Ferdinand Hiller, dated 25 April 1853; quoted in Daverio 1997, 451–2.

[36] Quoted and translated in Guyer 2003, 25.

does not have a single book in which Aesthetics is treated as a science.'[37] Of course, as is clear from the passages just quoted, 'science' was once a far more capacious term: and this is precisely the point. It encompassed the theory and method of any discipline, including those rooted in human perception and feeling – matters not considered unworthy of contributing to 'scientific' understanding until later in the nineteenth century. What we would consider hard science was, in the period under consideration here, deeply invested in analogical modes of thinking.[38] After all, while the first half of the nineteenth century saw the field of inquiry once called natural philosophy splinter into the many fields of 'romantic sciences', these new disciplinary formations did not yet enforce any strict divisions between the subjective and objective, between the arts and the sciences. Take, for instance, the category of acoustics, on which De' Filippi's treatise heavily relies, and which did not feature in earlier empiricist writings on music. For De' Filippi this discipline spanned arts and sciences both: the nature and behaviour of sound waves, but also hearing, as well as music and its apperception.[39] Instead of representing a rapprochement of scientific and aesthetic disciplines, then, the electric imagery considered above can be taken as evidence of an evolving mutual imbrication.

The Battery on the Stage

If this imbrication was not specific to Italy, its aesthetic practice engaged more conspicuously with the achievements of science than did that of any other European nation. And as is attested by Puccini's fleeting encounter with electricity in music on the occasion of Volta's centenary, much of this practice concerned the national achievements in electrical science, the battery, and the instruments of communication that relied on it. Of key importance here were two Italian ballets that depicted scientific invention in music and pantomime dance, positioning Italy at the centre of a narrative of European scientific advancement and global progress. While both might appear quaint and heavy-handed today, they enjoyed great favour with the newly enfranchised Italian audiences, and Puccini would certainly have been aware of these ancestors to his 'porcherietta'.

---

[37] Lichtenthal 1831, vii.

[38] On the history of analogising the nervous system and telegraph, see Otis 2001, 1–48; on the importance of comparison within scientific activity in the first decades of the nineteenth century see a pair of recent essays relating to the polymath Thomas Young: Pesic 2013 and Lockhart 2016.

[39] On the disciplinary history of acoustics see Wittje 2013.

The first was *Il telegrafo elettrico*, a 'historical-fantastical' pantomime ballet choreographed for Trieste in 1873 by the choreographer Luigi Danesi, and remounted to acclaim in Rome and Florence.[40] Its music was written expressly for the purpose (the libretto boasted) by one Giovanni Chiti. The protagonist of *Il telegrafo elettrico* is none other than Volta himself, whose invention was commemorated at its centenary by Puccini's *Scossa elettrica*. A preface to the ballet credits Volta with one of the most 'marvellous, beneficent and practical' inventions in history; the battery was not merely advantageous to the sciences of chemistry, physics and mechanics, but also gave rise to a host of modern practices. Danesi named telegraphy and electric lighting, but also galvanoplasty, electrotherapy, machinery powered by electric motor and 'many other extremely varied applications'.[41] In the ballet proper (the preface asserts), Danesi aimed to demonstrate that Volta would have invented the telegraph as well if his attempts hadn't been cut short by his premature death.

The fact that the real Volta died in 1845 at the age of eighty-two without having come close to inventing the electric telegraph requires the patriotic choreographer to fudge the numbers. Indeed, one can take literally the split generic designation (*ballo storico-fantastico*) to indicate that the pantomime begins with history and ends with fantasy. The Prologue takes place in Como in 1792, and the first two acts – in which Volta demonstrates his battery to Napoleon at the 'Istituto scientifico di Francia' – are set in Paris in 1799. Even this seven-year gap seems to have caused the choreographer some anxiety: in between the Prologue and Act I, Danesi notes, 'the music does not cease with its melodies to represent philosophically the time that lapses from the discovery of the Battery until Volta's appearance at the Scientific Institute of France'.[42] After his return to Como from France in Act III, he suffers from severe and ultimately fatal exhaustion – here the programme conveniently ceases to supply dates – and the final acts, showing Volta's apotheosis, dispense entirely with earthly locales.

More important for our purposes than this historical wishful thinking, though, is the way that the ballet explicitly collapses scientific thinking and aesthetic spectatorship. Volta's invention of the battery is depicted within a kind of abstract/allegorical dream sequence, set apart from the historical

---

[40] Danesi 1873. A copy of the libretto is preserved in the Rolandi collection of the Fondazione Cini in Venice (ROLANDI ROL.0073.39).

[41] 'la telegrafia e l'illuminazione elettrica, la galvano-plastica e la elettroterapia, le macchine elettro-motrici ed altri svariatissime applicazioni'; Danesi 1873, [5].

[42] 'la musica non cessa colle sue melodie di esprimere filosificamente il tempo che trascorre dalle scoperta della Pila, alla comparsa di Volta all'Istituto scientifico di Francia'; Danesi 1873, [9].

Circuit Listening 243

timeframe. In the Prologue, while a magnificent thunderstorm rages, the scientist (a man of 'severe and majestic appearance') conceives of an ambition to 'rob from angry Nature her greatest secret': the 'power of electricity'. His ambition is rewarded in Scene 2 of the Prologue, set in 'The Region of Space' (*La regione della spazia*). This is portrayed here as something like scientific revelation, by means of a pantomime-within-a-pantomime. Volta himself becomes a spectator, while the entire corps de ballet, representing the 'Components of the Battery', is directed by the Queen of Sparks (*La Regina delle Scintille*). Danesi summarised the invention thus:

In this moment the Queen of Sparks appears to him in all her splendid majesty; then she is joined by her companions, who at first reveal themselves to be reticent to reveal the secrets of Electricity to a mere mortal; but, controlled by the will of their queen, they ultimately teach him what elements make up the Battery.[43]

A second scientific dream sequence occurs at the end of Act III, as Volta dies. The Queen of Sparks returns in a brilliant beam of light, to reveal the electric telegraph itself:

Interrogated about the science by the great Italian, she concedes to his desires, showing him that the current of his battery, acting on a metal apparatus, will one day make brothers of all the people of the earth, carrying their communications back and forth with the speed of lightning.[44]

Finally, she shows him a vision of Morse, who would fulfil the promise created by his battery, creating a rhythmic code that would become a new 'universal language'.

As his synopsis makes clear, Danesi was interested above all in the electric connectivity offered by the telegraph: the way that it unified populations and collapsed geographical spaces into a single, vast circuit, inside which circulated a universal language. When the Queen of Sparks invites Volta to touch the metallic apparatus connected to the battery in Act III, the corps de ballet that had previously represented the Components of the Battery now demonstrates 'how Europe, Asia, Africa and America are all one people'. Danesi's description verges here on the ecstatic: 'there

---

[43] 'In questo momento la Regina delle Scintille gli appare in tutta la sua splendida maestà; quindi sopraggiungono le compagne, che in principio si mostrano ritrose a svelare ad un mortale i segreti dell'Elettrico, ma, dominate dalla volontà della loro regina, finiscono col fargli apprendere di quali elementi si componga la Pila.' Danesi 1873, [9].

[44] 'interrogata dalla scienza del grande Italiano, [la regina delle Scintille] risponde alla sua volontà, mostrandogli che la corrente della sua pila, svolgendosi sopra un'apparato metallico affratellerà un giorno tutti i popoli della terra, portando alternativamente le loro comunicazioni colla rapidità della folgore'; Danesi 1873, [12].

are no more distances, there are no more oceans, the electric telegraph has scaled the highest mountains, its universal language has made brothers all the people of the earth!'[45] Observing this nested telegraphic pantomime Volta is similarly joyous – until his battery itself reveals, in 'melancholy dance', that he will soon die.

The notion here is that Volta's electric circuit made a network of the map using a battery. The community that Danesi imagined in *Il telegrafo elettrico* is ultimately a global one, but one built of nations; as he acknowledged in the preface, it was national pride that motivated him to bring Volta's purported role in the invention of the telegraph to the attention of his audience. This audience was, of course, newly nationalised itself: *Il telegrafo elettrico* had its premiere less than two years after the final, Roman chapter in the Risorgimento. Danesi suggested that the unconventional approach of his choreography – a scientific history told through mime, dance and music – was inspired by the new age in which they found themselves: an age in which 'all human faculties are put in the service of a spirit of love'.[46] This spirit of inter-human connection, and the 'incessant progress' to which it must give rise, moved him to base his choreography on what he called 'historic and scientific facts', thus uniting entertainment with instruction.[47]

As such, the ballet *Il telegrafo elettrico* might have been inspired by a canto of the same name, published fifteen years earlier by one Giuseppe Regaldi (with parallel translation into Latin by Giuseppe Gando). Regaldi lauded Volta as a 'new Prometheus' who seized from the gods the vivid electric spark, allowing it to travel 'like desire from city to city' (*va come il desio di villa in villa*). Regaldi's canto was even more explicit than Danesi's ballet in its nationalist aims: the poem ended by beseeching 'electric messengers' inside the telegraph cables to 'carry a word, that shall be a law of love, which will unite all in the bonds of brotherhood, and promise the Italian an honour vindicated in the days to come'.[48] Another work from the same period showed how an electric circuit might stretch 'from city to city': this was the *Manuale di telegrafia elettrica* by Matteucci who had himself recently been appointed Director of the Electrical Telegraphs in

---

[45] 'non vi son più distanze, non vi son più mari, nè mari, il telegrafo elettrico ha superato i passi più ardui, il suo linguaggio universale ha affratellato tutti i popoli della terra!' Danesi 1873, [12].

[46] 'tutte le facoltà dell'uomo sono messe a contributo da quello spirito d'amore'. Danesi 1873, [6].

[47] 'incessante progresso'; 'dati storici e scientifici'. Danesi 1873, [6].

[48] Regaldi 1855. The final verse reads: 'Portino i messi elettrici, / Ovunque d'Eva la famiglia ha sede, / Una parola portion / Che sia legge d'amor, / Che tutti unisca di fraterno vincolo / E all'Italo assecuri / Vendicato l'onor nei dì venturi.'

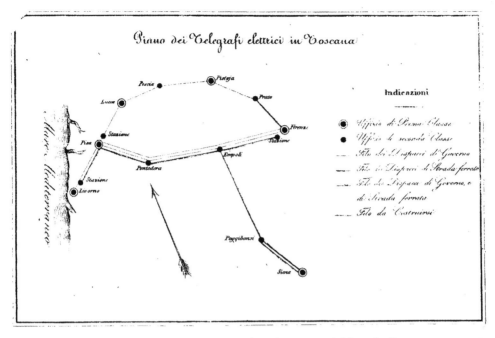

Figure 10.2 'Piano dei telegrafi elettrici in Toscana', Carlo Matteucci, *Manuale di telegrafia elettrica* (Turin: Unione, 1861).

Tuscany.[49] Figure 10.2 shows an early Italian telegraphy map, with a large circuit overlaid on the entire region; such intra-city infrastructure was of obvious use in the key Risorgimento years, and Matteucci was subsequently appointed head of Italian telegraphy in 1860. Similar to Danesi and Regaldi, Matteucci auspiciously credited Volta with making telegraphy possible. Despite his official appointment, though, Matteucci – unlike Volta, but like De' Filippi and the other aestheticians of his day, and like Danesi – was more interested in the excitement of living matter, and the way electric current could link multiple biological bodies together in a single circuit.

We do not know how the pantomime *Il telegrafo elettrico* looked – nor, regrettably, how it sounded, as the music seems to have been lost. Yet some clues might be found in another Italian pantomime from a few years later: Luigi Manzotti's *Excelsior*, which had its premiere at La Scala in 1881 with a new score by Romualdo Marenco. *Excelsior* compresses the action of *Il telegrafo elettrico* to a single act, replacing the Queen of Sparks and the

[49] Matteucci 1851.

Components of the Battery with two allegorical figures of broader significance: Light and Obscurantism. This act, the ballet's third, is divided into two scenes: 'The Genius of Electricity' and 'The Effects of Electricity'. In the former, Volta is shown working on his battery, desiring to 'steal the secret of electricity from nature'. Obscurantism blocking his progress, he has not been able to make it work. Then, Light herself appears, inspiring Volta to discover the spark. Obscurantism seizes the battery and seeks to destroy it, but, as in the earlier ballet, Light reveals the battery's future in the instrument of the telegraph ('The Effects of Electricity'). The second half of the act is a 'Dance of the Telegraph Operators' in Washington's Telegraph Square.

It should come as no surprise at this stage in our narrative that the 'Dance of the Telegraph Operators' is a *galop*. More remarkable, perhaps, is the fact that it calls for a telegraph machine to sound alongside the orchestra, playing simple quavers and crotchets in something like an approximation of Morse code. This music registers quite literally the duality we noted in *Il telegrafo elettrico*, fusing the aesthetic with indices of science and modern industry. First, of course, it serves the requirements of the dance, as effervescent in character and relentlessly predictable in phrase rhythm as the other telegraphic *galops* named at the beginning of this chapter. And alongside, rather less light on its feet, there is a layer of noise provided by the electric bells and telegraph machine: the simple quavers and crotchets approximating the dots and dashes of Morse code (see Example 10.2). These two layers fit so nicely together that we might understand the number merely to make audible sounds that were implied by the other musical tributes to the telegraph considered at the beginning of this chapter: this music confides that there is something buoyant and rhythmical about the telegraph machine itself, something dance-like about its electric jabber. The layer of machine noise in the Dance of the Telegraph Operators makes *Excelsior* an obvious precursor to the *Parade* of Erik Satie and Jean Cocteau, with its lotto-wheels and typewriters. Unlike in the later ballet, though, the cumulative effect is not one of estrangement or even experimental strangeness. Music and science play together nicely here.

And so they might. As Gavin Williams's chapter in this volume makes clear, *Excelsior* was a celebration in music and dance of modern advancement, featuring – alongside the battery and the telegraph – scenes devoted to the steam engine and ocean liner, the Suez Canal, the Mont Cenis Tunnel, the allegorical triumph of Light over Obscurantism, the end of the Spanish Inquisition, and the invention of the telephone. It is, to be sure, a strange roll call for a ballet; as should now be evident, Manzotti was able

Example 10.2 Romualdo Marenco, 'I fattorini del telegrafo. Galop', from *Excelsior* (1881), piano reduction by Michele Saladino (Paris: Ricordi, *c.* 1881)

to draw not only on the precedent of *Il telegrafo elettrico* – surely among the most explicit evocations of scientific history and technology within nineteenth-century theatrical practice – but also on a vibrant theoretical tradition of construing aesthetic activity itself in terms of electric current and circuitry.

We do not know precisely what the dance of the telegraph operators looked like: it is not among the scenes preserved in the 1908 film. But like all of the tableaux in *Excelsior* it involved a vast corps de ballet of hundreds of dancers, circulating in rows through a multi-tiered stage. *Excelsior*'s rows of dancers, which Williams reads as evoking a vast machine, have often been cited as a precedent for those rows of women layered against abstract sets in Busby Berkeley's choreographies. We may now also relate them to the other electrified human chains encountered in this history: the strings of spectators described by De' Filippi, della Valle, Oppenheim and others; the pensioners parading to the vanishing strains of Puccini's *galop* at the Volta centenary; the anthropomorphised components of the battery assembled by the Queen of Sparks in Danesi's *Il telegrafo elettrico*; the chains of telegraph operators spread across Italy and abroad, listening as their machines tap out the rhythms of a quasi-universal language that carries social love and sounds almost like a dance.

The key term, in this summary of the electrical aesthetic in Italy, is connectivity.

Like Danesi's, Manzotti's ballet ends by merging scientific and political utopia: 'all nations gather together and dance joyfully to the glory of the present and the greater glory to come, in the guise of Science'.[50] The final number, representing 'Science: progress, brotherhood, love' (Scienza. Progresso, Fratellanza, Amore), culminates in another vigorous *galop* – the better, no doubt, to facilitate more circling by Manzotti's seriated multitudes. Of course, such exteriorisations of scientific thought as may be found in *Excelsior* and *Il telegrafo elettrico* – wherein multiple athletic dancers are the Components of the Battery, and progress in electrical science is achieved by way of an appearance from the Queen of Sparks – may now seem guilelessly indebted to a mode of allegory that undermines their commitment to the superlative glories of modern life. And the very practice of making science and its consequent luxuries the objects of a ballet may appear as hopelessly bourgeois as counting the light bulbs in one's cabin on a cruise-ship. Yet *Il telegrafo elettrico* and *Excelsior* – both multiply revived and enjoying over 1,000 performances between them in Italy alone – were a primary source of scientific-historical knowledge for many Italians, including Puccini, who saw *Excelsior* in 1886 when it was on a double bill with *Le villi* at La Fenice, and surely remembered it when the local convention of telegraph operators called with a commission. But by the end of the century, as Puccini's scribbled disclaimer in the margins of *La scossa elettrica* attested, the strain of the union was showing. The coded patter of the telegraph bells was already ceding to the full-voiced resonators of the telephone; and as the rich entanglements of subjective and objective knowledge, the multiple overlapping categories and knowledge-generating analogies within the mid-century aesthetic discourse distilled into the more rigid hierarchies of modernism, electricity became a medium for music, rather than music a medium for electricity.

[50] Letellier 2012, xiii.

PART IV

Bodies

11 | *Excelsior* as Mass Ornament
The Reproduction of Gesture

GAVIN WILLIAMS

> Is the view of nature and of social relations which shaped Greek imagination and Greek art possible in the age of automatic machinery, and railways, and locomotives, and electrical telegraphs? Where does Vulcan come in as against Roberts & Co., Jupiter as against the lightning rod, and Hermes as against Crédit Mobilier? (Karl Marx, 1848)[1]

In her 1984 'Cyborg Manifesto', Donna Haraway declared: 'the relation between organism and machine has been a border war' in Western science and politics – which for her primarily amounted to a racist, male-dominated capitalism, as embodied by the notion of technological progress. Her manifesto identified that 'The stakes in the border war have been the territories of production, reproduction and imagination', each of these zones representing its own contentious interface between organism and machine within American post-industrial society: the encroachment of robots in industrial production; the use of test tubes for reproducing the body; the ascendancy of sci-fi imagination in literature and film.[2] And in each case the battles weren't being won by humans. Haraway was instead confident of a machine victory, pushing her towards a notorious conclusion: we are cyborgs.

The historical and cultural coordinates of the present essay are far removed from Haraway's manifesto. My topic, the technophile ballet *Excelsior*, which premiered at Milan's Teatro alla Scala on 11 January 1881, pre-dates Haraway's ironic dream of the cyborg by more than a century; in place of Silicon Valley, I take my bearings from late nineteenth-century Milan's urbanism and nascent industrial culture. Nevertheless, I want to suggest that Haraway's celebration of the cyborg can withstand significant counterpoint with this much earlier Italian ballet, both in terms of its technological plot and of its techno-political gestural vocabulary. My argument will be that *Excelsior* presents us with proto-robotic dance: an anachronistic juxtaposition that can be illuminating because it encourages us to detect in the ballet's unique late nineteenth-century configuration of

---

[1] K. Marx 1904, 310. [2] Haraway 1991, 150.

technology, music and dance more enduring temporalities, temporalities that might begin to suggest an archaeology of gesture for the machine age.[3]

Here we confront a long-standing historiographical default: one that tends to conflate the modern with the machine in the history of music and dance.[4] It is not my intention to increase the brisk scholarly traffic that already runs between these terms. I take my cue instead from an influential study that traces the ebb and flow of operatic gesture throughout the nineteenth century. Mary Ann Smart has described the mutual construction of philosophical and aesthetic discourses and the gestural practices of opera singers, describing a broad shift during the century from musical miming towards 'gestures becoming invisible to music'.[5] While ballet possesses gestural conventions clearly distinct from those of opera, Smart's discursive and cultural approach leads me to seek out more local, flexible interactions between music and movement in which mimetic and anti-mimetic impulses are potentially in constant tension. My interest here will be the historical relationship between gesture in ballet and the prevailing conditions of social production, which in late nineteenth-century Italy were increasingly (though by no means largely) machine-based, yet not what might elsewhere be described as modern.[6] This pre-cybernetic critical-theoretical issue of body, gesture and production will ultimately lead me to revisit Siegfried Kracauer's 1927 essay, 'The Mass Ornament', to suggest alternative ways in which music and movement could enfold an industrial milieu.

Kaleidoscopic Visions

> We had been talking about it for six months; we had known of its highly courageous subject; and after the rehearsals, we had learned all the particulars, the rumoured marvels of Manzotti's creation . . . The only worrying aspect, which put doubt in apprehensive minds, was its libretto. Despite the almost bizarre boldness of its concept, the libretto seemed to be a pandemonium, an impenetrable patchwork, from which nothing could emerge except an unfinished *féerie*, or a revue in the style of Scalvini. However, the pessimists were wrong, and when *Excelsior* was seen and

---

[3] The instigator of archaeological approaches to history was of course Michel Foucault: see Foucault 1971. There have been more recent attempts to adapt Foucault's ideas to media technologies in particular; see Huhtamo and Parikka 2011.

[4] For a recent discussion of this issue, see McCarren 2003. See also Garelick 1999.

[5] Smart 2004, 4. Opera and ballet shared the same performance space: *Excelsior*'s premiere took place following a performance of Filippo Marchetti's *Ruy Blas* (1869), then a stalwart of La Scala's repertory.

[6] See Crepax 2002, 19–125.

Excelsior *as Mass Ornament*   253

admired, all agreed that the topic was not only extremely fine, but that Manzotti had managed to turn it into a real ballet: interesting, wonderful, a choreographic work – or, better, a masterpiece.[7]

Critical hyperbole aside – there would be much of this in the wake of the ballet's premiere – it is not hard to see why the pre-released libretto generated doubts.[8] *Excelsior*'s plot, as outlined by its choreographer Luigi Manzotti, summarises four centuries of humanity's moral progress as manifested in various technological breakthroughs.[9] It opens during the benighted times of the Spanish Inquisition, as a troop of martyrs-to-be trudge, *Don Carlos*-like, across the proscenium; against this gloomy backdrop, Oscurantismo and Luce (Obscurantism and Light), the principal mime characters, emerge, staging an allegorical contest between the forces of good and evil. Luce eventually gains the upper hand, and predicts a future in which all barbarity will come to an end: a utopia of world peace disclosed by the sudden appearance of hundreds of dancers, mimes, children and acrobats. This is the moment captured on the front cover of *Il teatro illustrato* (see Figure 11.1), and was one of *Excelsior*'s most widely discussed special effects.

With this spectacular future in view – a future that was confidently imperial, to judge from the imposing *mise en scène* – *Excelsior* proceeds more-or-less chronologically from sixteenth-century Spain towards the present, though with every new scene the location of the story changes. The next scene features Denis Papin, supposed inventor of the steam engine, who floats along Germany's river Weser by means of a paddle-wheel boat. In Manzotti's loose interpretation of historical record, Papin is attacked and killed by villagers who mistake his invention for sorcery.[10] As though to redeem

---

[7] 'Erano sei mesi che se ne parlava, che si conosceva il soggetto arditissimo e che poscia dalle prove si sapevano tutti i particolari, le supposte meraviglie della creazione manzottiana ... Il solo che prometteva poco e che anzi metteva dei dubbi nella coscienza timorata degli eterni pessimisti, era il libretto, il quale oltre l'arditezza quasi strana del concetto, pareva un pandemonio, un guazzabuglio inestricabile da cui non potesse uscire che una féerie sconclusionata, od una Rivista ad uso Scalvini. Anche costoro ebbero torto e quando l'Excelsior fu veduto e ammirato, tutti convennero che non solamente era il soggetto bellissimo, ma che il Manzotti era riuscito a farne un vero ballo, interessante, splendido, un lavoro, o a meglio dire, un capolavoro coreografico.' Filippi 1881, 1–2.

[8] Manzotti 1881.

[9] The initial consternation was not necessarily generated by the technological theme: as José Sasportes has pointed out, choreographer Luigi Danesi had covered the invention of electricity in his 1873 ballet *Alessandro Volta, o Il telegrafo elettrico*. The cause for concern instead seems to have been over Manzotti's ability to combine the disparate elements into a choreographic whole (Sasportes 1987, 310).

[10] Denis Papin, a French physicist and mathematician, described a mechanism for the basic steam engine in 1690; and, as *Excelsior* claims, he did at some point in the early eighteenth century attempt to propel boats using steam power. Little is known about the circumstances of his

Figure 11.1 Front cover of *Il teatro illustrato* (March 1881).

death, however, and the peasant ambush was Manzotti's embellishment. See McConnell 2004, 42:597–9. See also Hills 1993, 15–16.

Papin's death, Luce appears once again to foretell the steam engine's enormous importance: images of ocean liners and steam trains appear against the backdrop of a New York skyline. The next scene, also characterised by a transatlantic shift, begins at Lake Como, in Alessandro Volta's laboratory; the invention of electricity is about to take place. Once this has been achieved – it is delayed by another mimed contest between Luce and Oscurantismo – sparks fly and the trilling of an electric bell transports us to Telegraph Square in Washington, DC. Here a troupe of ballerina-couriers, dressed in post office uniform and carrying messages, commemorate the electrical telegraph, one of many distant ramifications of Volta's discovery.

The alternation between intimate scenes of mimed narration – focused on the eternal struggle between Luce and Oscurantismo – and large-scale choreographic moments representing humanity at large continues throughout the ballet. *Excelsior*'s structure was the norm in its genre, the late nineteenth-century *ballo grande*, which employed conventional narrative formulae to give coherence to heavily peopled dances and spectacular stage effects.[11] The latter involved, among other things, dramatic lighting, impressive costumes, acrobatics and even onstage animals. Notoriously, Manzotti's next *ballo grande* at La Scala, *Amor* (Love; also 'Roma' spelled backwards), was to incorporate twelve horses, two oxen and an elephant.[12] The final segments of *Excelsior* include spectacular effects inspired by two recent, enormous industrial projects: the nations of the world meet along the Suez Canal, providing the opportunity to display multiple national garbs; and the ballet's *coup de théâtre*, the perforation of the Mont Cenis Tunnel, recently connecting Italy and France through the Alps, giving rise to a sequence that ends with miners from both sides joyfully embracing. Pursuing the theme of international cooperation, the final scene is a ceremonial 'Quadriglia allegorico-fantastico delle nazioni' (Allegorical-Fantastical Quadrille of the Nations) – an apotheosis to Luce, while at the front of the stage Oscurantismo lies eternally vanquished.

Excelsior's optimistic conclusion draws strength from a temporal ambiguity: if the final defeat of Oscurantismo represents a final step in the process of Enlightenment, does this moment lie in the present or in the

---

[11] This structural alternation between dance and mime was standard in the late nineteenth-century *ballo grande*, as it was in the early nineteenth-century *coreodramma*. As Sasportes (2011, 185–233) has pointed out, the distinction became less strict as the century wore on, with choreographers attempting smoother connections between the two – a trend that is reflected in *Excelsior* – and celebrated dancers, such as Enrico Cecchetti, managing to combine the two styles in performance.

[12] See Toelle 2009, 20.

near (yet endlessly receding) future? The powerful contradictions of 'living progress' might seem all too familiar to us now.[13] In Milan in 1881 this ideology had particular local significance, as observed by critics at the ballet's premiere: *Excelsior* was synergetic with the transformation of the city and the excitement for technological display brought about by that year's National Exposition. Over the course of seven months, hundreds of thousands of visitors arrived in Milan by train, then to be transported from the Central Station to the Exposition site by means of a purpose-built railroad.[14] *Excelsior*, throughout this time, remained a fixture onstage at La Scala, providing conspicuous theatrical continuation of Milan's industrial festivities.

There are more deeply-woven threads connecting *Excelsior* and the Exposition – threads that transect meanings only ever latent in contemporary journalistic discourse. To get at these meanings, it is worth pausing over the opening sequence to observe the terms in which reviewers described *Excelsior*'s instantly overwhelming effect. Influential music critic Salvatore Farina praised Manzotti's choreography as 'magnificence without confusion', and summed up the ballet's technological theme and visual style as 'a great phantasmagoria of progress'.[15] Another revered commentator, Filippo Filippi, referred to the ballet's 'first kaleidoscopic impression', and went on to compare its fantastical quality with a magic lantern show.[16] And, in fact, the idea of kaleidoscope was elaborately developed throughout *Excelsior*'s early journalistic reception:

Have you ever looked into a kaleidoscope? If so, imagine Manzotti's choreographic moves taking place within it, inside the kaleidoscope. The thousand combinations of extremely varied colours, the elegance of the moves, the novelty of the ensemble, the importance of invention – everything reveals *Excelsior* as the work of a master.[17]

These anonymous words can begin to revive the sense of animation kindled by the sudden mass choreography, a fascination with colour and geometry in motion.[18]

---

[13] On the pitfalls of synoptic strategies in the history of technology, see L. Marx 2010.

[14] See Lopez 1981, 7–8.

[15] 'grandiosità senza confusione'; 'grandiosa fantasmagoria del progresso'. Farina 1881, 22.

[16] 'prima caleidoscopica impressione'. Filippi 1881, 1–2.

[17] 'Avete mai guardato in un caleidoscopio? Se sì, immaginate le mosse coreografiche del Manzotti quali vi si presentano là dentro, nel caleidoscopio. Le mille combinazioni di svariatissimi colori, l'eleganza delle mosse, la novità dell'assieme, l'importanza delle trovate, tutto, tutto rivela nell'*Excelsior* il lavoro di un maestro.' [unsigned] 1881b, 1.

[18] Another contemporary review described the dazzling effect of sheer numbers on stage, stressing their colourful costumes and geometrical arrangement: 'Then the city disappears, the ruins fade away in an instant and we see a scene that puts a break, for a moment, on the excitement; such is

The kaleidoscope was a multiply determined metaphor in early discussions of *Excelsior*, allowing critics to broach not only choreographic matters, but also the issues of La Scala's stage mechanics and its novel, controversial system of gas lighting. As Jutta Toelle has shown, Milan's foremost theatre was navigating murky financial waters in the last decades of the nineteenth century, drifting between a system of elite patronage and increasing local government control (not to mention the absence of state subsidy).[19] Loosely referencing this context, Farina took the opportunity to complain about the stage illumination, 'those zones of eternal shadow and semi-darkness, that lack of speed and precision', appealing to the municipal council for swift action.[20] The *Gazzetta musicale di Milano* similarly alluded to the theatre's technical deficiencies:

We have mentioned the miracles of La Scala's old mechanism, and we return to this topic to say that ours is no longer an age of miracles, and we should think about how to promote La Scala – let's not say to the summit of its fame, but at least to a level of equality with second-rate stages in Paris and Vienna.[21]

the stupor, the astonishment that it awakens. It is an empyrean of light, in which are gathered more than 400 people, among them ballerine, ballerini, chorus dancers, acrobats, extras and a small contingent of wonderful girls and boys under the age of ten . . . Those configurations, those novelties, those *ideas* are impossible to describe: you must go and see them.' ('Allora la città svanisce, i ruderi si sprofondano in un attimo e si vede una scena che mette freno per un poco all'entusiasmo, tanto è lo stupore, lo sbalordimento che desta. È un empireo inondante di luce, ove stanno aggruppate più di 400 persone, fra ballerine, ballerini, corifei, tramagnini, comparse, e un piccolo esercito di brave ragazzine e di bimbi al disotto dei dieci anni . . . Quegli intrecci, quelle novità, quelle *trovate*, non si possono descrivere, bisogna andare a vederle.') [unsigned] 1881a.

[19] On the economic vicissitudes of La Scala see Toelle 2009, 62–80; and on theatrical illumination in Milan, see Protano-Biggs 2013.

[20] 'quelle zone di ombre e di penombre eterne, quella mancanza di prontezza e di precisione'. Farina 1881, 22.

[21] 'Abbiamo accennato ai miracoli del vecchio meccanismo della Scala; e vi ritorniamo per dire che non è più età di miracoli, e che è doveroso si pensi a mettere il palcoscenico della Scala, non diremo all'altezza della sua fama, ma almeno a pari dei palcoscenici dei teatri di second'ordine di Parigi e Vienna.' Farina 1881, 22. In reviews of *Excelsior*, there was a more general tendency to compare La Scala (whether favourably or not) with other European stages, thus registering the ballet's (and the theatre's) cosmopolitan aspirations. Filippi boasted that 'outside of La Scala there is no other theatre, neither in Italy nor abroad, which can offer equal means of reproduction' ('all'infuori della Scala non havvi altro teatro, nè in Italia nè all'estero, che possa offrire eguali mezzi di riproduzione'), though he went on to admit that 'the only improvement there could be in Paris, in Vienna, in London, or in Berlin is in the scenography and in the machinery, which in La Scala, though much improved, still leave not a small amount to be desired' ('la sola superiorità ci potrebbe esserci a Parigi, a Vienna, a Londra, a Berlino sia nelle scene e nei meccanismi, che alla Scala, benchè progrediti da molto, lasciano ancora, e non poco, a desiderare'). Filippi 1881, 1.

Excelsior's technological theme and stage effects recursively drew back on La Scala itself, drawing attention to its own ageing stage machinery – a shift of attention onto old technology that might explain why the kaleidoscope became a trope during *Excelsior's* initial reception. For the kaleidoscope, much like La Scala's machinery, was itself growing old in 1881. Invented by David Brewster in 1817, the device enjoyed an extended heyday during the first half of the nineteenth century: it was hailed as an infinite source of colourful, symmetrical patterns – patterns that could be traced and reproduced on ornaments, wallpaper and decorative fabrics. As Jonathan Crary has pointed out, the kaleidoscope came to represent an 'industrial mechanical means for the reformation of art according to an industrial paradigm'.[22] Yet by the 1880s, dreams of infinite serial production gave way to soberer reflections, and kaleidoscopic enthusiasms had for the most part largely dropped away. Art historian Arnaud Maillet has shown that attitudes toward the kaleidoscope underwent a general shift, one intimately connected to changing notions about the capacities and limits of factory production.[23] By century's end, the device had become a way of talking about human creativity and innovation as an endless mechanical process, monotonously recombining fragments of sensory stimulation.

Exposition Narratives

This kaleidoscopic way of seeing – an historical gaze inured to industrial enthusiasms – had particular resonance in Milan in 1881. Around the city centre, street lamps were interwoven with trees and exotic plants, while the city's central Public Gardens were converted into a fantastical landscape for the exhibition of machines. Entry to the gardens was granted via a series of kiosks, each inspired by human habitations from around the globe, such as the much admired Russian *izba*; the price of admission was one lira, the cost of a dozen eggs.[24] From any one of the gates dotted around the perimeter, the visitor could proceed into the gardens either on foot or, for an additional fee, on board an electric train – the first of several transportation amusements within the Exposition site that included a hydraulic lift, hot air balloon and hand-cranked unicycle running along an overhead track. Transport-based entertainments were immensely popular, paving the way for the fairground rides of the modern theme park,

[22] Crary 1990, 116.   [23] Maillet 2012, 36–55.   [24] Lopez 1981, 7–8.

Excelsior *as Mass Ornament*   259

while also providing mini-demonstrations of machines on display within the Exposition's halls.[25]

Impressive warehouses of brick and glass, these halls were patent intruders amid the greenery of the Public Gardens and contained rooms dedicated to the fine arts, military uniforms, locomotives, combustion engines and musical instruments, among many other things.[26] One of the most successful exhibits was the so-called Work Gallery (*Galleria del lavoro*): it comprised a series of warehouse-like rooms run by Italian and foreign firms, each manned by workers demonstrating artisanal skills and the use of industrial machines.[27] Diverse commodities-in-the-making included leather wallets, notebooks, artificial flowers, jewellery made of gold and diamonds; visitors could even observe as the Exposition's own weekly illustrated newspaper, *Milano e l'Esposizione*, was being printed. The paper reflexively described the environment in which it was produced:

All the machines are in operation: the bustle is very lively: the workers attend to their work under the eyes of the public as though they were in their factories . . . In the (adjacent) Gallery of Small Industries, here too is working life; here too there are fast wheels, the turning of handles and of leather pulleys: mechanical forces that enhance, extend and collaborate with those of man.[28]

The newspaper's pervasive fascination with the interaction between workers and machinery is keenly expressed here; emphasised too is the public's unusual proximity to the mass production of various items and the dynamics of spectatorship involved. Visitors were cordoned off from the workers by a guardrail that marked a persistent border extending throughout the Work Gallery, visibly demarcating the spectacle of miscellaneous human-machine operations.[29] This guard rail rehearsed and rigidly defined the territories of social production,

---

[25] Della Coletta 2006, 101.

[26] Both the architecture and its contents were typical of Expositions during the second half of the nineteenth century; see Hamon 1992, 3–14.

[27] On the Work Gallery, see [unsigned] 1881c, 11, 26, 146.

[28] 'Tutte le macchine sono in azione: il movimento è vivissimo: gli operai attendono all'opera, sotto gli occhi del pubblico come fossero nella loro officina . . . Nella Galleria delle piccole industrie c'è anche qui vita operaia; anche qui rapidità di ruote, giri di manubri e di cuoi, forze meccaniche che si sviluppano, che si trasmettono e collaborano con quelle dell'uomo.' [unsigned] 1881c, 11.

[29] The majority of visitors to the Exposition belonged to the middle classes; but as Guido Lopez has pointed out, the municipal council coordinated occasional trips to enable workers to visit the Exposition. See Lopez 1981, 8. For an imaginative reconstruction of workers encountering the machinery on display at an earlier industrial exposition (the 1867 Exposition Universelle) see Rancière 2011, 64–88.

preempting the cause of Haraway's 'border war' critique by more than a century. The expressionless stares of these workers may also suggest the tendency of capitalism to reduce people to the status of things, an old Marxist theme. In 1881, visitors were being encouraged to inspect workers alongside machines as comparable objects within a systematic manufacture. Workers, like machines, could be looked upon as objects with a particular capacity for labour: a calculable limit of exhaustion that appeared to represent determinate economic value.

Dancing Machines

A general mood of enervation lingers over both the Exposition and ballet, in spite of their assertive confidence in industry – an ambivalence that would pursue *Excelsior* in its performance afterlife. During the 1880s, the ballet circulated widely in multiple concurrent international tours in Europe and North America.[30] These performances were largely supervised by Manzotti's own students, who assiduously reproduced his choreography by means of transcriptions involving copious colour-coordinated diagrams.[31] If we fast-forward to a major revival of *Excelsior* at La Scala in 1909, the trend continues: the ballet was supervised by Achille Coppini, La Scala's official *coreografo riproduttore* (choreographer-reproducer), whose role consisted in slavishly reviving older choreographic works. The consequent recurrence of *Excelsior*'s dance steps across more than thirty years is noteworthy, for it stands in curious tension with the new production's attempt to update the ballet to reflect more recent technological advances: the ballet now included, for example, an impressive scene dedicated to the airplane, and its *mise en scène* incorporated film projections of the Suez Canal.[32]

Some vintage technologies were preserved for the 1909 revival, however. This much can be seen from costume designs, such as the one worn by

---

[30] Pappacena 1998, 55–72. Pappacena's book extensively reproduces notes and diagrams from one of three surviving choreographic scores: that of Manzotti's student Giovanni Cammorano.

[31] Detailed choreographic scores also served to enforce copyright law; see Lo Iacono 1987. As Lo Iacono points out, the choreographer was traditionally understood to be the author of the ballet work, and, as was customary, Manzotti bought the rights to the score from Marenco. When *Excelsior* became enormously successful, however, Marenco (unsuccessfully) launched a legal challenge for a share in the profits. Embittered by the experience, Marenco went on to write a manifesto, 'Per l'avvenire della musica in Italia' (1889), which has been reprinted in Fusco and Garavaglia 2008.

[32] [unsigned] 1908a, 1005–8.

Excelsior *as Mass Ornament* 261

Figure 11.2 Costume design for 'Il telefono'.

ballerinas sustaining the role of the Telephone (see Figure 11.2). Technological paraphernalia fuse with the ballerina's body: earpieces and speaking tubes are strapped to her arms, and iron breastplates are fashioned into electromagnetic bells. Her ears are covered by electrical headphones (note the decorative sparks jutting from her head) in reference to the dynamic, turn-of the-century occupation of switchboard telephonist.

With this prototypical fem-bot get-up, Haraway's 'border war' takes on literal meaning, the female body becoming the ground for a battle between organism and machine – a site where science fiction, sexual fantasy and technology violently intertwine.[33]

In 1913, film director Luca Comerio shot Coppini's revival of *Excelsior* in a warehouse in Milan: an ambitious project that aimed to capture the ballet in its full ninety-minute duration. The project required 2,000 metres of film stock – a significant length at the time, even measured against contemporary cinematic monuments such as *Quo Vadis* (1912) and *Cabiria* (1913).[34] Like these better-known films, *Excelsior* was intended for theatrical performance with live orchestral accompaniment: Comerio took static shots of the entire proscenium, emulating the audio-visual experience of the theatre. On its release the film was billed as a 'cine-phono-choreographic show', stressing the novelty of this multimedia experiment: the film reimagined the screen as a surface across which bodies moved, their visible choreographies recombining in rhythmic gesture with the ballet's musical score.[35]

Part of this film has recently been restored at Rome's Cineteca nazionale, and may be the closest we will ever come to seeing and hearing a late nineteenth-century Italian ballet. As I have been suggesting, Comerio's 1913 film remained faithful to Manzotti's original choreography, a fact which might be confirmed by comparing the film with the transcriptions drawn up by Manzotti's students in 1881.[36] This stability over more than thirty years is remarkable, but my point here is neither about the standardising effect of dance texts nor about the fixity of the choreographic work during the late nineteenth and early twentieth centuries. Much more specifically, I want to suggest that the film clip is a distant but nonetheless loyal reproduction of *Excelsior* – one now channelled not through the lens of the kaleidoscope, but that of 1910s experimental cinema.

To this end, I would first like to describe in detail an episode from *Excelsior*'s second scene – which, as previously mentioned, follows the initial triumph of Luce over Oscurantismo that gives rise to a series of dances in praise of the former. The transcriptions from the 1880s noted

---

[33] In addition to Haraway, see R. Williams 2005, 50–66.   [34] Bondanella 2009, 8–14.

[35] 'azione cine-fono-coreografica'. See Mosconi 2006, 55–73. Only 350 metres of film survives today, comprising most of the opening scene dedicated to Oscurantismo and three numbers drawn from the second scene starring Luce. The film was restored at Rome's Cineteca nazionale in 2001: music was reunited with the moving image by means of piano accompaniment, synchronising Marenco's score to Manzotti's choreography once more.

[36] For detailed analysis of the dance, see Pappacena 1998, 78–81.

that this scene required the use of an octagonal platform with four levels in order to provide a 'music-box effect'.[37] A ballerina representing Civilisation stands on top, encircled by lesser allegorical figures on the rungs below, while men in armour and white-winged children gather around the platform on the stage.[38] The film replicates this arrangement, also following one 1880s transcription in drastically reducing the gestural range to 'rhythmic articulations with poses and skips'.[39] As the film shows, these poses involve holding a curved arm high above the head, first the left then the right, each movement marking the downbeat of every second bar. To close each eight-bar phrase, the ballerinas at stage level skip through small circles, mirrored by the children who loop round the men. This dyad of poses and circular skips comprises the first choreographic unit, evoking iterative figurines within an elaborate jewellery casket.

Some of the words from the 1880s transcriptions have been mapped onto the piano score in Example 11.1: the onset of 'rhythmic articulations with poses and skips' marks the beginning of the 'Galop', one of the ballet's most famous musical numbers, which enjoyed extensive independent circulation in piano reduction.[40] The Galop is preceded by repeated, emphatic cadences that peter out onto a dominant pedal (bb. 1–28) – which, as the surviving film bears witness, gives the dancers time to assemble the elaborate platform. By the time the melody disintegrates into a ticking octave leap, the ballerinas get into position; then, in time for the pause (in b. 28), they gradually sink to their left in parallel over the platform. Unwound into a momentary slumber, the Galop (bb. 29–44) makes the ensemble spring to life in various stiff poses: an effect enhanced by the contrast between the Galop's rapid pace and the dancers' static upper-body gestures. The music thus informs us as to the nature of an old choreography, their recombination allowing us to recapture the mechanical inspiration of the gesture.

Following a transition based on concentric circles of dancers twisting around the octagonal platform, the next sequence again comprises largely fixed positions and isolated arm gestures. The rate of these gestures doubles to one per bar, creating a more fluid motion, but now only the left arm is

[37] 'effetto carillon'; described in a transcription from the 1880s. This descriptive term, along with those subsequently cited, is taken from (Manzotti's student) Giovanni Cammorano's choreographic score, which is reproduced in Pappacena 1998, 91–118.

[38] These lesser allegorical figures are Valore (Valor), Costanza (Constancy), Invenzione (Invention), Concordia (Harmony) and Fama (Fame). Manzotti 1881, 8.

[39] 'Scansione ritmica con pose e corsette'. Pappacena 1998, 91–118.

[40] Equally well known was the music for the 'Fattorini del telegrafo' (Telegraph Messengers). Music for both scenes was soon circulating in piano reduction: Marenco 1881a, 1881b.

Example 11.1 Romualdo Marenco, 'Galop', preceded by a waltz, from *Excelsior* (1881), piano reduction

"effetto carillon" = "scansione ritmica con pose e corsette"
(music-box effect) (rhythmic articulations with poses and skips)

involved, giving the overall impression of a collective wave. This action is answered by a much slower, more deliberate one: over the course of an entire four-bar phrase the armoured men protractedly raise clubs from the stage floor, while the rest of the cast bend down equally slowly. A complementary four bars provide the opposite movement: the men lower their clubs as the ballerinas and children gradually stretch upwards while shaking their arms and torsos. This interplay of rising and falling gestures within the group was described in the 1880s transcriptions as giving a 'fountain effect', the diffusion of gestures through the whole supposedly resembling a body of water majestically surging up and down.[41]

This is a gestural dynamic we have perhaps seen before: a similar isolation of gesture repeated across the human *mise en scène* was at play at the Work Gallery. There workers also performed beneath eyes trained on the economy of gesture: gazes attuned to the productive output that might be achieved by optimal choreography of workers and machines. The same concern with gestural economy recurs in the focus placed on the ballerinas' arms, forming impressive, rigid postures in the upper body, creating maximum theatrical impact for minimal input from performers.[42] This danced relationship between people and machinery hints at their dream-like synthesis, the inorganic slowness of the fountain effect transforming the onstage multitude into an immense dancing machine.

And so *Excelsior*'s movements might redirect us to the Exposition. For the dance of machines was an impressive effect, one noted by visitors to the Work Gallery and the adjacent Gallery of Machines as engines were turned on first thing in the morning – warming up with majestic, and yet laborious slowness:

At a given signal, the hundred inert parts of many steel devices began to move very slowly; then the movement became, as it went on, very quick and collective . . . And in the air – a clatter, a noise, and a flash of very bright wheels: a display that raised the spirit and made us proud.[43]

The spectacle of machines and industrial clamour was the occasion of excitement and of pride, a context that discloses the politics of gesture: in particular, that formed by the juxtaposition of the Manzotti's fountain effect and Marenco's headlong Galop. Their conjunction in 1881 – the cultural superimposition that sustained the interaction between this music and this dance – was, at base, a mechanical mimicry, one that gave shape to Milan's industrial celebrations and let them be felt.

---

[41] 'effetto fontana'. Pappacena 1998, 91–118.

[42] McCarren (2003, 14–20) discusses in greater depth the confluence between nineteenth-century work-science and the development of modern dance.

[43] 'Ad un dato segnale le cento parti inerti di tanti congegni d'acciaio cominciarono lentamente, lentamente a muoversi, poi il movimento si fece, come avviene, velocissimo e generale . . . E nell'aria un frastuono, un rumore, e un baleno di ruote lucidissime: uno spettacolo insomma che allargava l'animo, che insuperbiva.' [unsigned] 1881c, 22.

Industrial Ornaments

Thus far this chapter has shadowed *Excelsior* from its premiere in the late nineteenth century to its cinematic refractions in the early twentieth. Skip forward a decade or so and Siegfried Kracauer would publish his famous essay 'The Mass Ornament', in which he criticised a cinematic craze for the all-female dancing chorus by singling out the sensation caused by the Tiller Girls: an American dancing troupe whose signature routine consisted of interlocking arms across a single line, with the whole ensemble propelling itself by means of cancanning, scantily-clad legs.[44] Kracauer notoriously invested the Tiller Girls (and their legs in particular) with epoch-defining significance, claiming they incarnated a recent mutation in capitalist production: their kicks mirrored hands in the factory along Taylorist assembly lines, in which bodily gestures had been atomised into meaningless components of an integrated human–machine interface.[45] Thus reconstituted into 'indissoluble girl clusters', these dancers presented a mass ornament: a mobile geometry that conveyed nothing but its own bewitching organisation.[46] The mass ornament communicated the law of a productive system in thrall to the interests of capital, which drove mindlessly towards its own accumulation.[47] Here we might detect the whiff of vintage misogyny, as labouring female bodies came to stand in for a lack of guiding intelligence in human productive forces writ large. Yet the body logics that Kracauer unearthed may deserve renewed attention. Significantly for my purposes, Kracauer looked back to the late nineteenth century for precursors: 'Ballet likewise used to yield ornaments, which arose in kaleidoscopic fashion.'[48]

The after-image of the kaleidoscope evokes once more the metaphor of serial production noted in *Excelsior*'s initial reception. It hints too at the technological legacies that linger on in the ballet's endlessly reproduced geometric routines. While Kracauer's notion of the mass ornament has

---

[44] 'The hands in the factory correspond to the legs of the Tiller Girls.' Kracauer 1995, 79.

[45] An overview of Taylorism, one of the earliest forms of scientific work management, can be found in Banta 1993, 3–35.

[46] Kracauer 1995, 76.

[47] 'Ornament der Masse' was one of the first essays Kracauer wrote following a period in which he studied Marx's economic theories intensely; see Thomas Levin's introduction to Kracauer 1995, 16. Marx based his explanation of capital's self-serving logics on the distinction between dead (accumulated, past) labour and real, living labour – the latter enslaved to the former; see K. Marx 1993, 459–63. As Kracauer put it: 'Like the capitalist production process, the mass ornament is an end in itself.' Kracauer 1998, 78.

[48] 'Auch der frühere Ballett ergab Ornamente, die kaleidoskopartig sich regten.' Kracauer 1927.

itself come in for various critical assaults over the years, I would like to suggest that it can do two things here.[49] First, it allows us to reposition the ballerina-cum-cyborg, a figure that has become prominent in the history of twentieth-century modernism and the avant-garde. To put it crudely, this dancing automaton emerged from middle-class popular cultures long before celebrated avant-garde works such as Satie's *Parade* (1917). Second, rereading Kracauer encourages us to examine anew *Excelsior*'s complex interactions between dance, technological forms and social production. As Christian Sieg has argued, the 'Mass Ornament' essay might best be read now for its 'preconscious logic': one that reproduces choreographically – in a way that is on the verge of emerging into thought and language – an embodied sense of repetitive factory work involving the use of various machines.[50] This preconscious logic lurks around the cusp of awareness and can be glimpsed through the metonymic relations it produces between diverse elements along a continuous social surface. *Excelsior*'s own Milanese superficies are a case in point: for example, the long, straight street (Via Manzoni) that connected La Scala to the city's Public Gardens, where on any given day between May and November in 1881 a related choreography of manufacture and machines was in progress at the Work Gallery. Throughout this time, *Excelsior* remained a fixture onstage at La Scala, clocking up 100 performances at the opera house by the end of the year: the ballet was a semi-permanent urban landmark, which, like the Exposition itself, provided a form of industrial entertainment for thousands of visitors.[51] Viewed from the trampled surface of Milan's pavements, *Excelsior*'s gestures – its music-box effect in particular – come into focus as a motile, musically enhanced extension of a particular urban topography.

When the buzz of the Exposition eventually faded and its makeshift architecture was disassembled, *Excelsior* began its own migrations, which saw it travel well beyond Milan.[52] Yet a trace of the ballet remained at the heart of the city: it took up quasi-permanent residence at the Teatro Gerolamo, a famous puppet theatre located in the streets behind Piazza del Duomo. *Excelsior*'s 1884 premiere in puppet form merited a newspaper review, which claimed that 'The ballet is faithfully reproduced from the

---

[49] On changing attitudes towards Kracauer, see Eksteins 1997; see also Hansen 1992.

[50] Sieg 2010.

[51] On walking and urban psychogeography in Italy in the late nineteenth and early twentieth centuries, see Bruno 1993, 11–23.

[52] For more information on *Excelsior*'s international circulation, see Scholl 2007 and Propokovych, 2008.

beginning to the end,' detailing every one of *Excelsior*'s eleven scenes.[53] 'Those talented wooden heads … know how to represent Manzotti's various characters with admirable art, such that it seems, in their movements, in their gestures, that they possess an unusual intelligence', this review judged, noting too that Marenco's music was accurately reproduced.[54] The anonymous critic leaves to us to guess how those puppets coped with the onset of Marenco's Galop: did wooden arms stretch over wooden heads, double-bluffing the illusion of mechanical-human motion, as puppets pretended to be humans imitating machines?

Excelsior maintained a presence in Milan until the theatre closed in the 1950s, its survival now symbiotically linked to the steady decline of puppetry – a once-celebrated form of mechanical reproduction that had been largely superseded by the mid-twentieth century. At roughly this moment *Excelsior* was picked up in 1952 by film director Alessandro Blasetti, in his potpourri portrait of late nineteenth-century Italy, significantly named *Other Times* (*Altri Tempi*). By now, the ballet had come to represent a curious and unfamiliar past, representing a turning point in its longer reception history.[55] Between the last mechanical displays of puppet theatre and the stereophonic glamour, a silent transition had taken place: a technical shift in the way *Excelsior*'s gestures were transmitted. This transition meant the estrangement of the mass ornament, marking the end of a time when the reproduction of gesture could smoothly connect to the gesture of production.

[53] 'Il ballo è fedelmente riprodotto dal principio alla fine.' This *Perserveranza* review has been cited in Monti Colla n.d. The puppet version of *Excelsior* was also deemed worthy of mention among the theatrical notices in *Il mondo artistico* (9 March 1884), 2.

[54] 'quelle brave teste di legno … sanno rappresentar con arte mirabile i diversi personaggi manzottiani, così da parere, nelle loro mosse, nei loro gesti d'avere una non comune intelligenza'. For more on the Teatro Gerolamo see Leydi and Mezzanotte Leydi 1958, 235–80. On musical ensembles typical of the Teatro Gerolamo, see Dotti 2003.

[55] When choreographer Filippo Crivelli revived the ballet at La Scala in the 1970s, he would describe the work as a 'perfect mechanism' – timeworn but intact – which could be reanimated in such a way as 'to provoke sensations as near as possible to those *Excelsior* must have produced in 1881' (1974).

12 | Automata, Physiology and Opera in the Nineteenth Century

MYLES W. JACKSON

> Without the heart's activity, the action of the brain would be no more than of a mere automaton; the action of the body's outer members, a mechanical and senseless motion. Through the heart the understanding feels itself allied with the whole body, and the man of mere 'five-senses' mounts upwards to the energy of Reason. (Richard Wagner, 1849)[1]

E. T. A. Hoffmann's eerie tale of 'Der Sandmann' (1816) famously recounts the story of a young college student, Nathanael, who unwittingly falls in love with an android named Olympia, a creation of the professor of physics and renowned *Naturforscher* Spalanzani. After seeing her through a telescope, Nathanael is enchanted by her beauty. Spalanzani invites Nathanael and others to a celebration at his house, where Olympia is to make her grand debut as the professor's daughter. Nathanael proceeds to dance with the automaton all night long. His visits become more frequent, while he remains blissfully unaware of the fact that she is not human. One day Nathanael hears a quarrel between Spalanzani and the mechanician Coppelius in the professor's apartment. Coppelius wrestles Olympia away from Spalanzani and runs away carrying the automaton over his shoulder. Nathanael witnesses Olympia's eyes falling from her head and immediately realizes that she is an android. Enraged, he attempts to kill Spalanzani and is subsequently sent to a madhouse. In 1851, Jacques Offenbach attended a performance of a play at the Odéon, *Les Contes fantastiques d'Hoffmann* by Jules Barbier and Michel Carré. It was based in part on Hoffmann's story.[2] After the performance Offenbach spoke to Barbier and Carré with a view to composing an opera based on the play. Barbier ended up writing the libretto to Offenbach's opera some time before 1878, and it premiered at the Opéra-Comique in Paris on 10 February 1881.

Like a number of such automata of the late eighteenth and early nineteenth century (such as the Turkish Chess Player), deception and profit were key to the story. Act II of Offenbach's opera opens with Spalanzani in mercantile mood, hoping that he will recover through her 'the five hundred ducats which the bankruptcy of the Jew Elias costs me! There remains

---

[1] Wagner 1895, 110. [2] Kracauer 2002, 378.

Coppelius, whose deceit, in order to get a sum from me, can claim the rights of paternity, the deuce of a man!'[3] Yet where, if at all, did the android's abilities fall short of the human's? As I have argued elsewhere, a number of physiologists and physicians viewed the human body as a machine during the nineteenth century.[4] They attempted to explain the talents of virtuosi such as Niccolò Paganini and Franz Liszt in a mechanical, deterministic fashion. And as discussed below, when attempting to reproduce human facial expressions by applying electricity to certain muscles and nerves, French physicians and physiologists from the 1860s to the 1890s viewed their unfortunate human subjects as helpless automata, being manipulated at the will of the investigator.

While many had argued initially that affectations brought about by music were distinctly human characteristics, mechanicians successfully created androids that replicated such attributes and gestures while performing. Lest one forget, Hoffmann himself finds distinctly expressive qualities in Olympia's singing and he speaks of her 'charming gaze'.[5] The period also witnessed a shift from surgeons and physicians elaborating the anatomical and physiological processes involved in facial expressions to physiologists and neurologists replicating certain emotional expressions in their patients. Some of these patients became rather famous and were depicted in various genres, including opera. Such links between the body and opera have of course been well documented in the secondary literature.[6] This chapter seeks to deepen existing work on medical history by concluding with an exploration of such a possible connection between the work at the renowned Salpêtrière hospital in Paris and Richard Wagner's *Parsifal*.

Music, Emotions and Affectations

Recent work in the history of science and technology has focused on the theme of emotions and affectations with a view to analysing the complex and historically contingent relationship between musical androids and musicians.[7] During the last quarter of the eighteenth century, music

---

[3] 'Dans les cinq cents ducats que la banquerote / Du juif Élias me coûte! / Reste Coppélius dont la duplicité / Pour avoir de moi quelque somme, / Peut réclamer des droits à la paternité, / Diable d'homme!' (Offenbach 1955, 18–19).

[4] Jackson 2006, 253–66; 2010–11.   [5] Dibbern 2002, 62, 65.

[6] See, for example, Hutcheon and Hutcheon 1996, 2000; Davies 2014.

[7] For a brilliant recent study on the topic, see Voskuhl 2013.

theorists such as Johann Georg Sulzer and Heinrich Christoph Koch underscored the importance of affectations in music, or the ability of musicians to elicit certain emotional responses from the audience both by bodily gesticulations and the phrasing of the music. They had dedicated themselves to analysing the ways in which performers could summon forth listeners' emotions. As Koch argued:

The fine arts in general, and thus also music, possess a unique property which enables them though artistic means to awaken feelings in us. They awaken pleasure through the enjoyment of a good represented through art and fear through an evil brought forth by it. Thus, if the fine arts make use of their special power to have the feelings they arouse inspire noble resolutions, to affect the education and ennoblement of the heart, then they serve their highest purpose and show themselves in their proper worth. If deprived of this noble function, if used to another end, then the fine arts are degraded, they are dishonoured.[8]

In fact, Koch was merely echoing Sulzer's earlier sentiments, which read:

Just as philosophy and science have knowledge as their ultimate goal, so the fine arts have the goal of sentiment. Their immediate aim is to arouse sentiments in a psychological sense. Their final goal, however, is a moral sentiment by which man can achieve his ethical value.[9]

Sulzer linked art, affect and virtue. His 1771 article on sentiments (*Empfindung*) declared both that they dictate behaviour and that the arts are capable of evoking proper sentiments, such as the love of one's country, virtuousness, freedom and humanity.[10] As Adelheid Voskuhl has demonstrated, the cultivation of sentiments was a critical aspect of the Enlightenment ideal of generating a more equitable and social order, indeed a new civic order. Sentiments enabled the creation of new forms of social interactions, which formed the backbone of a new civic society composed of rational, sensible and equal citizens dedicated to replacing the anachronistic estate and court societies.[11] This European culture of sentiment and sensibility, both in the physiological (i.e. the faculty of sensing) and moral senses of the term, was also present in late eighteenth-century opera, including Giovanni Paisiello's sentimental comedy *Nina, o sia La pazza per amore* and Mozart's *Le nozze di Figaro*.[12] Crucially, Voskuhl goes

---

[8] Koch 1782–93, 2:1, in Baker and Christiansen 1995, 144.
[9] Sulzer 1771–4, 2: 54, in Baker and Christiansen 1995, 28.
[10] Sulzer 1771–4, 2: 55–7. See also Voskuhl 2013, 156–7.   [11] Voskuhl 2013, 7.
[12] *Le Nozze di Figaro* is typically seen as being simultaneously sentimental and anti-sentimental. See Castelvecchi 2013, particularly 125–209.

on to argue that mechanicians went to great lengths to generate such bodily practices that cultivated sociability and sentimentality in their androids.

Eighteenth-century musicians' performances were not only meant to be heard: they were meant to be seen, as performers strove to communicate affectations and sentiments to their audiences. Likewise, late eighteenth-century automata builders, including Pierre and Henri-Louis Jacquet-Droz, David Roentgen and Pierre Kinzing, strove to have their androids elicit similar emotions among their audiences by mechanically creating affections.[13] These music-playing automata could move their eyes, eyebrows, head, hands, arms, fingers and torso. They could watch the movements of their hands as well as nod, breathe and even bow.[14] As Voskuhl points out, the definition of sentimentality was metamorphosing from the seventeenth- and early eighteenth-century definition of being sensitive to physical impressions (*sensibilité*) to one denoting intellectualism and affectations: 'the faculty of perceiving moral impressions' and 'the sentiment of humanity, piety, and tenderness'.[15] Sentimentality had become a moral issue, as Sulzer's statement makes clear. Popular philosophers argued that teaching the art of emotion (*Gefühlskunst*) was necessary for humans to be capable of moral action. Questions were then raised about the outward representations of those emotions: acting and mimicry were germane. Similarly, these theories were applicable to the spectators who needed to induce the emotion supposedly conveyed by each affect.[16] The flautist and pedagogue Johann Joachim Quantz stressed in 1752 that 'the performer must aim to put himself into those . . . passions that he is meant to express'.[17] Similar experiences of passions thus linked (acting) performer to (perceiving) audience.[18]

Emotions, Art and Physiology in the Eighteenth and Nineteenth Centuries

Musicians and composers were not the only ones interested in human emotions. During the eighteenth and nineteenth centuries, surgeons and physiologists were attempting to provide a more detailed account of the

---

[13] Voskuhl 2013, 129. For the details of the mechanisms behind how these automata builders and clockmakers were able to produce these effects, see 129–44.

[14] Voskuhl 2013, 128. [15] As quoted in Voskuhl 2013, 148. [16] Voskuhl 2013, 150.

[17] As quoted in Voskuhl 2013, 159.

[18] It should be noted, however, that during this period the tension between subjectivity and appearance often ironised gestures and facial expressions. See Le Guin 2002.

Automata, Physiology and Opera 273

anatomy of human expression. The Dutch physician, surgeon and anatomist Petrus Camper sought to link the science of anatomy with the fine arts of drawing, painting and statuary.[19] Camper's work owed much to Johann Kaspar Lavater's *Physiognomic Fragments on the Promotion of Human Knowledge and Love* (1775–8), the standard text on physiognomy in its explanation of the link between external facial and cranial characteristics and behaviour.[20] The English physician, natural theologian and founder of the Royal Human Society Thomas Cogan, who translated Camper's work into English, called for artists to acquire 'a deeper insight into Nature' with a view, among other things, to observe 'the effects produced by the passions upon the human face'. In particular, Cogan argued that knowledge gleaned by the study of anatomy 'shall enable him to delineate the general situation of the muscles in a placid and inert state, their action in varied positions, and their influence in describing every emotion or passion of the mind'.[21] While previous masters focused their attention only on the workings and positions of the muscles, Cogan encouraged contemporary artists to study osteology and neurology, the latter of which 'is proved to be of high utility in the representation of the emotions of the mind: an attainment confessedly the most difficult, as well as the most interesting and sublime'.[22]

Camper dedicated the first lecture of Book II to the depiction of different passions.[23] He claimed that while the accurate representations of the passion of the mind had been admired since ancient times, artists' depictions throughout history had not been true to nature. Even Giovanni Paulo Lomazzo and Leonardo da Vinci had been more interested in 'the different attitudes of body' than on elaborating upon the 'particular features' of facial expression.[24] Camper praised the work of the seventeenth-century French painter and art theorist Charles Le Brun for his writings on the expressions of the different passions; yet for Camper, Le Brun

reasoned metaphysically concerning the operations of the mind, without attending to the physical causes of the changes produced by these operations. But in my opinion, speculations concerning the manner of the soul's working, or concerning the seat of the soul's working, are of no use to the artist. These belong to metaphysicians, who by the way lose themselves in a labyrinth of terms, or words, with no definitive meaning, without having in the least explained the action of this immortal principle upon the corporeal and mortal frame.[25]

---

[19] Camper 1794.   [20] Lavater 1778.   [21] Cogan, 'Preface' to Camper 1794, iv.
[22] Cogan, 'Preface' to Camper 1794, vii.   [23] Camper 1794, 123–37.
[24] See Lomazzo's *Trattato dell'arte della pittura, scultura et architettura* of 1585 for his brief description of the influences of the passions upon facial muscles. Camper 1794, 126.
[25] Camper 1794, 127–8.

The operations of the mind were only interesting for Camper when they brought about physical manifestations in the body. Or, to put it another way: Camper was not interested in the 'workings of the soul', but rather in 'what changes take place in the body, in consequence of its [the soul's] operations'.[26] Camper underscored the importance of the artist studying the cranial nerves, a conclusion he had drawn after dissecting innumerable human corpses: 'every painter ought to make himself acquainted with the construction and connexion of the nerves productive of these changes' in emotions.[27] He concluded his lecture by discussing the deterministic relationship between the cranial nerves and facial muscle for a myriad of countenances, including expressions of placidity, surprise or wonder, contempt, complacency, friendly greetings, tacit joy, laughter, sorrow, anger and death.[28]

Camper's work was not isolated. In a similar fashion, the Parisian physician Jacques-Louis Moreau de la Sarthe wrote about the structure, use and characteristics of the human face.[29] A collaborator with Lavater, his meticulous physiological treatment of the action and effect of each muscle on facial expression won the praise of numerous physiologists later in the nineteenth century. In 1806, the Edinburgh surgeon, anatomist and theologian Sir Charles Bell published his treatise *The Anatomy and Philosophy of Expression as Connected with the Fine Arts*, demanding that artists study anatomy, or 'that structure by which the mind expresses emotion', since through such a study we become aware 'of the relations and mutual influences which exist between the mind and the body'. Anatomy, specifically the physiology of human facial expression, could 'give the artist a true spirit of observation, [and] teach him to distinguish what is essential to just expression'.[30] Thus, facial expression, as illuminated and captured by the science of anatomy, could be communicated by painters to their audience. His study owed much to Lavater's work on physiognomy and was infused with natural theology. His commitment to understanding God by recourse to nature should come as no surprise as he had collaborated with William Paley on *Natural Theology* of 1803, that seminal work arguing that one can understand God by studying His [sic] creation, Nature. (Charles Darwin would famously rail against *Natural Theology* some fifty-six years later.)

Certainly the claim that artists need to study anatomy was hardly new in the early nineteenth century. Many sixteenth-century artists,

---

[26] Camper 1794, 128.　[27] Camper 1794, 129.　[28] Camper 1794, 133–6.　[29] Sarthe 1806.
[30] Bell 1865, 213, 14.

Automata, Physiology and Opera 275

including most famously Albrecht Dürer, Leonardo da Vinci and Giambattista della Porte, had studied physiognomy and pathognomy, or the external appearance of the passions.[31] Nor was Bell's the first scientific study of emotions. René Descartes's *The Passions of the Soul* (1649) had offered a physiological account of the expressions of emotions, asserting that they could be understood as the product of physico-chemical interactions.[32]

Bell's treatise was novel in his research on the specific nerves responsible for facial expression in humans and animals. Up until his work, physiologists and surgeons had assumed that all parts of the nervous system shared common properties and functions. In essence, all nerves were seen as possessing the dual function of the power of motion and of sensation to the limbs.[33] Bell was able to demonstrate that nerves instead possess distinct and appropriate functions, which correlate with the parts of the brain and spinal cord. By focusing on nerves of the sense organs, Bell recognised that they were not mere modifications of one common property and that the nerve of one sense organ could not be substituted for the nerve of another. He noted that each nerve is limited to receiving a distinct and relevant impression, i.e. the nerve of sight can only give ideas of light and colour, while the nerve of hearing could only generate impressions of sounds.[34] Hence Bell's observations precede Johannes Müller's famous law of specific sense energies by nearly three decades. The cause of the uniqueness of each nerve was the location of its root in a distinct portion of the brain.

Bell also went on to explain how the spinal nerves with two roots could convey both motor and sensation conjointly. By taking the nerve in the arm and tracing it from the arm back to the spinal column, he noticed that the nerve branched into two parts, i.e. its roots. One root gave rise to motion, while the other gave rise to sensation. In short, he found 'that nerves of Sensation [sensory nerves] are distinct from nerves of Motion [motor nerves]: and that to different parts of the Brain and Spinal Marrow, belong distinct and appropriate endowments'.[35]

On this basis, Bell saw emotional expressions as the links between the mind and body:

---

[31] Prodger 1998, 150.   [32] Descartes 1649. See Prodger 1998, 151.

[33] Shaw 1847, 3. See also Charles Bell, *An Idea of a New Anatomy of the Brain, submitted for the Observation of His Friends* (1811).

[34] Shaw 1847, 5.   [35] Shaw 1847, 11.

Since we are dwellers in a material world it is necessary that the spirit should be connected with it by an organised body, without which it could neither feel nor react, nor manifest itself in any way. It is a fundamental law of our nature that the mind shall have its powers developed through the influence of the body; that the organs of the body shall be the links in the chain of relation between it and the material world, through which the immaterial principle within shall be affected.[36]

God created the connection between the mind and external nature, in other words. 'In every intelligent being He has laid the foundation of emotions that point to Him, affections by which we are drawn to Him, and which rest in Him as their object.' Bell chastised those philosophers who were only interested in the workings of the mind for overlooking the relationship between mental operations and the condition of the body: 'as the organs of the five senses serve to furnish ideas of matter, the framework of the body contributes, in certain conditions, to develop various states of the mind'. Emotions, or 'impressions communicated by the external organs of sense', are a product of 'a mutual influence exercised by the mind and frame on each other'. In short, Bell was fundamentally committed to showing how 'the passions of the mind' influenced the muscles of expression by means of the nerves.[37]

Medicine, Emotions and Human Automata

By the second half of the nineteenth century, physicians possessed the tools not only to study the nerves and muscles involved in human emotions, but also the ability to generate those gestures artificially. In 1862, Guillaume-Benjamin-Amand Duchenne de Boulogne published his *Mécanisme de la physionomie humaine*.[38] In this work, Duchenne detailed the use of an electric current to stimulate the facial muscles of his subjects: 'Armed with electrodes, one would be able, like nature herself, to paint the expressive lines of the emotions of the soul on the face of the man. What a source of new observations.'[39] Duchenne's mechanical technique could reproduce qualities that had previously been seen as quintessentially and uniquely belonging to the domain of the human self. A classic example was his reconstruction of feminine aggression typified by Shakespeare's Lady Macbeth, for which he employed the services of one of his female patients

---

[36] Bell 1865, 83.   [37] Bell 1865, 83–4, 90.
[38] Published in English as Duchenne de Boulougne 1990.
[39] Duchenne de Boulougne 1990, 9.

in constructing a series of *tableaux vivants*: 'I tried to represent the expression that Lady Macbeth must have had, when, after assuring herself that Duncan and the guards, whom she drugged, were soundly asleep, and after having given Macbeth the murder signal, she waited while he cut the throat of the king, his host and benefactor.'[40] While not directly addressing musical or operatic performances, he did believe that his experimental techniques could elicit the characteristic signs of human emotions.

Duchenne himself labelled his enterprise 'a new sort of anatomy, to which one can apply the two words by which [Albrecht von] Haller described physiology: it is *animated anatomy*'.[41] The human expressions he was able to generate with electrical current became for him a 'universal and immutable' language and evidence of the Creator's work.[42] The patient did not need to experience the actual emotions: his was a method to produce the superficial signs without the natural cause. Duchenne then linked human expressions, such as attention, reflection, pain, aggression, weeping, joy, laughter (and false laughter), irony, sadness, surprise, doubt, contempt, terror and fright, to name just a few, with the muscles and nerves that produced them.[43] Photographs were able to capture the fleeting expressions of his subjects after their electrical stimulation: 'Photographic figures that represent, as in nature, the expressive traits assigned to the muscles that interpret the emotions, teach a thousand times more than extensive written descriptions.'[44] Darwin took the argument one stage further in his *Expression of the Emotions in Man and the Animals* (1872), drawing upon Bell's and Duchenne's enterprises to argue that expression and its recognition were crucial to survival.[45]

Subjects were chosen because of their docility. In one instance, Duchenne was treating with electricity a nearly blind girl who was afflicted with bilateral optic nerve atrophy. He writes: 'she cannot understand the gestures or the poses that I show her, so that I am obliged to position her and dress her *as if she were a mannequin*'.[46] Duchenne was the operator who dictated the responses of his subjects: 'I am careful . . . not to involve my subject's feelings; I rely only on my judgement and on my artistic feeling. Thus I arrange her head in a particular direction, open or shut the eyes and mouth, ask her to smile or laugh, and so on. In this way I obtain the expression that I want, as I feel it.'[47] Perhaps his favourite

---

[40] Duchenne de Boulougne 1990, 120. See also plate 81.   [41] Duchenne de Boulougne 1990, 10.
[42] Duchenne de Boulougne 1990, 19.   [43] Duchenne de Boulougne 1990, 26–7.
[44] Duchenne de Boulougne 1990, 37.   [45] Gilman 2015, 136.
[46] Duchenne de Boulougne 1990, 105. Emphasis added.
[47] Duchenne de Boulougne 1990, 106.

model was 'the simple old man, who suffered from facial anaesthesia', meaning that the patient could not feel anything done to his face.[48] The old man was, in essence, an empty canvas upon which Duchenne could experiment. The physician seemed to care more about the facial façade than the human behind it. These 'mannequins' were eerily similar to Hoffmann's Olympia. Their bodily responses and indeed their identities were being manufactured and orchestrated by physicians and physiologists.

Duchenne's method of local faradisation, as he called it, was adopted in the Salpêtrière Hospital in Paris, where he spent the later years of his career. He was hired by the young physician and neurologist Jean-Martin Charcot, who had been impressed with Duchenne's work on electrical stimulations of the face. As Charcot's renowned student Sigmund Freud tells us, his mentor was very visually orientated.[49] Indeed, visual representation was critical to Charcot's work on hysteria, as he often took photographs – a technique he learned from Duchenne – of his experimentation on his patients.

Charcot was most famous for his work on hypnosis and hysteria. In 1877 an eighteen-year-old girl, Marie Wittmann, entered the Salpêtrière suffering from convulsions, fainting spells and bouts of paralysis.[50] She would become known as 'Blanche', Charcot's most famous patient and 'a medical diva whose fame spread throughout Europe, where she became known as "the Queen of Hysterics"'. Charcot often chose her to demonstrate the numerous and complex symptoms of hysteria to physicians and medical students alike. She too was considered a mannequin, often photographed, painted, sketched, and even reproduced in sculpture. She was the subject of newspaper articles, plays and novels. As Asti Hustvedt argues, 'If hysteria was not actively "manufactured" at the Salpêtrière, as some claimed, it was most definitely cultivated.' And 'Blanche' was a rather appropriate name, Hustvedt continues, for she was a blank (white) page upon which Charcot could experiment at will.[51] While Duchenne referred to one of his patients as a mannequin, Paul Richer, a physician at the Salpêtrière and professor of artistic anatomy at the École des Beaux-Arts in Paris, went further in speaking of Blanche as 'a mechanical toy' and a 'music box'.

---

[48] Duchenne de Boulougne 1990, 23.   [49] Duchenne de Boulougne 1990, 10.

[50] Hustvedt 2011, 35. For a history of the Salpêtrière, see Micale 1985.

[51] Hustvedt 2011, 35, 49, 43.

Automata, Physiology and Opera

This order [of her symptoms] is so invariable ... that if by ovarian compression one suppresses attack #1 at its onset, attack #2 begins. Allow me a somewhat banal comparison, but one that seems to me to express what happens here: our patient resembles one of those music boxes that play several different tunes, but always in the same order. If we successively stop one, two or three attacks, it is as though we have skipped one, two or three notches in the music box, and if we let the next attack follow its course, it is the following motif, #4, that is carried out. This occurs to such a degree in this patient that we can choose to let one or another of her attacks unfold.[52]

His colleague Joseph Delboeuf concurred. Blanche's passivity, which enabled Charcot's work, reminded Delboeuf of the relationship between piano and pianist: Charcot 'played her as though she were a piano, and ... he played any tune'.[53] There is an implicit gender dimension here, for musical automata of the period were mostly gendered female.[54] This masculine domination becomes explicit when Charcot hypnotised and moulded Blanche into a woman–machine hybrid. Indeed Gilles de la Tourette and Richer labelled her in this state 'an actual automaton who obeys each and every order given by her magnetizer'.[55] They use the words 'to imprint' to describe the physician's actions, and 'operator' to denote his role. Charcot himself claimed that his woman-machine, 'in her utter simplicity', was an instantiation of the man-machine, as imagined by the materialist philosopher Julien Offray de la Mettrie.[56] Catalepsy, or the nervous condition in which muscles remain rigid regardless of external stimuli, was further described by Tourette and Richer in 1889 as a process that

transforms the patient into a perfectly docile automaton, without any stiffness, on which one can imprint, with the greatest of ease, the most varied positions. Moreover, these positions are always harmonious, making our automaton something more than a simple mechanism à la Vaucanson. Her expressions harmonize all by themselves with the gestures that are imprinted, and vice versa.[57]

And one of the pioneers of electrotherapy, François-Victor Foveau de Courmelles, also linked the cataleptic hysteric to the automaton: 'Although at first an inert, plastic mass of flesh and bones ... the cataleptic

---

[52] Richer 1881, 147, as translated in Hustvedt 2011, 54.
[53] Delboeuf, 1886, 258, as translated in Hustvedt 2011, 54.   [54] Wise 2007; Voskuhl 2007.
[55] Richer and Tourette, as translated in Hustvedt 2011, 68.   [56] Charcot 1886–93, 3:337.
[57] Richer and Tourette 1875, 88–89.

subject allows herself to be molded at the will of the operator. She becomes a soft wax figure on which the most fantastic emotions can be imprinted, she is an automaton capable of being animated.'[58] As Roy Porter pointed out: 'hysteria could be fashioned as a disorder, precisely because the culture-at-large sustained tense and ambiguous relations between representations of mind and body, which were in turn, reproduced in the hierarchical yet interactive ontologies of morality and medicine, and, yet again, reflected by the sociological interplay of clinical encounters'.[59] Audiences began to wonder: was Charcot demonstrating and revealing hysteria as actually reflected by his patients' bodies, or was this a false identity, that is, a fake? Were his patients simply acting, producing a fraudulent display of hysteria? The boundaries among the body, mind, self, and machine were blurred, the more so by the credulity and scepticism exhibited by Charcot's witnesses.

As Robert Brain has demonstrated, automatism played an important role in late nineteenth-century physiology more generally, referring both to organic movements, which could be reduced to automatic, machine-like processes, and to the psychological actions of higher animals, which took place without a mind or will.[60] As the Cambridge physiologist Michael Foster – referring to hydra and amoeba – wrote in 1877: 'the great value of automatic processes in a living body depends on the automatism being affected by external influences, and on the simple effects of stimulation being profoundly modified by automatic action'.[61] So, while the processes involved in automatic impulses are independent of external influences, they are subject to and largely modified by those stimuli.

Hence, from the 1860s to the 1880s, the body of the medical subject was reduced to an automaton, under the total control of the physician. And as Brain has demonstrated, this is precisely what the physiologist Étienne-Jules Marey and his cohort accomplished, starting in the late 1860s and lasting well into the early twentieth century. Physiological instruments 'had in Marey's view acquired a degree of autonomy analogous to self-acting machines capable of doing the bidding of humans with little or no reference to their progenitors. Human subjects fell out of the picture.'[62] The logic was brutal: first standardise the body, rendering it a machine, and then make the body disappear altogether.

---

[58] Courmelles 1890, 91.   [59] Porter 1993, 265.
[60] Brain 2008, 399. See also Brain 2016, 5–36 and 95–149.
[61] Foster 1877, 74–5; as quoted in Brain 2008, 404.   [62] Brain 2008, 402.

Epilogue: Wagner's *Parsifal*

Walter Benjamin reminds us that the Salpêtrière, along with Offenbach's cancan, the Eiffel Tower and the giraffes at the zoo, became one of the fashionable sites of belle époque Paris.[63] Tuesday lectures and demonstrations were frequented by the likes of Cardinal Charles Lavigerie, Guy de Maupassant and the lawyer, inventor and politician Louis Lépine. It is not surprising, then, that gestures of hysteria made their way to the theatre stages of Paris.[64] Even opera was influenced by Charcot's work, as 'the greatest divas of opera strove to outdo the now universally famous stars of the Salpêtrière, from Wagnerian Kundry's display of remorse in 1882 to the long vindictive cry in Richard Strauss's *Elektra*'.[65]

The importance of the hysterical body is indeed clearly seen in Wagner's *Parsifal*, and a long scholarly tradition explores their rich interrelation.[66] The period from 1877, when Wagner finished *Parsifal*'s libretto, to the work's premiere in Bayreuth in 1882 is coeval with Charcot's work on hysteria. And in this closing section, I pursue a hypothetical reading of Wagner's final opera in light of the medical discourse given above, expressly with the intention of exploring how far their association can be maintained. We might begin with Friedrich Nietzsche, who, in 1888, famously chastised Wagner for his hysterical depictions on the stage as part of his larger critique of Wagner as an actor:

I place this perspective at the outset: Wagner's art is sick. The problems he presents on the stage – all of them problems of hysterics – the convulsive nature of his affects, his overexcited sensibility, his taste that required even stronger spices, his instability which he dressed up as principles, not least of all the choices of his heroes and heroines – consider them as psychological types (a pathological gallery)! – all of this taken together represents a profile of sickness that permits no further doubt. *Wagner est une névrose* [Wagner is a neurosis]. Perhaps nothing is better known today, at least nothing has been better studied, than the Protean character of degeneration that here conceals itself in the chrysalis of art and artist. Our physicians and physiologists confront their most interesting case in Wagner, at least a very complete case. Precisely because nothing is more modern than this total sickness, this lateness and overexcitement of the nervous mechanism, Wagner is *the modern artist par excellence*, the Cagliostro of modernity. In his art all that the

---

[63] Micale 1985, 724.   [64] For the spectacle of the Salpêtrière, see Marshall 2008.
[65] Corbin 1990, 4:630.   [66] See Hyer 2006 and Bronfen 1996.

modern world requires most urgently is mixed in the most seductive manner: the three great *stimulantia* of the exhausted – the *brutal*, the *artificial*, and the *innocent* (idiotic).[67]

This oft-quoted statement is typically read in the context of discourses of cultural degeneration, of decadence as a wilful corruption of bourgeois health, and of biographical interest in the shifting Nietzsche–Wagner relationship. But the point here is that Nietzsche knew directly of what he spoke: he was very familiar with the goings on at the Salpêtrière; his notes include numerous references to the work of Charles Féré, Charcot's assistant at the Salpêtrière.[68] It is telling, then, that Max Nordau's hyperbolic critique of Wagner's music – 'certainly of a nature to fascinate the hysterical' – later on references the Salpêtrière and Charcot's work directly.[69]

Brian Hyer has suggested in this context that Parsifal's transformation mirrors Charcot's four stages of hysteria, which the French physician documents in 'Description de la grande attaque hystérique' of 1879.[70] First, the 'période épileptoïde' is characterised by severe convulsions and contractions; then the 'période des contorsions et des grands mouvements' follows after an interval of calm. This second phase witnesses extreme physical contortions inevitably ending with the body assuming a stiffened concave pose whereby the spine curves backward. During the third period, one of 'passionate attitudes', the patient hallucinates, and the body assumes a familiar pose, while she acts out scenes depicting dramatic experiences from her life.[71] And in the final period, the patient calms down and becomes melancholic, after which time she regains consciousness.

Parsifal's extended arioso of the second scene of Act II, which lasts an exhausting eight minutes, parallels Charcot's description of the *grande attaque*.[72] In the first stage, *période épileptoïde*, Parsifal experiences 'a fearful change' and 'gestures in horror' after he embraces Kundry and they kiss. He cries out in pain, 'Amfortas! The wounds! The wounds!' And so starts the seizure.[73] The second stage, or the *période des contorsions*

---

[67] Nietzsche 1968. See also M. Smith 2007, 11.

[68] Kennaway 2012b. See also Herrmann 2007, 87–9.   [69] Nordau 1895, 210.

[70] *Période épileptoïde, période des contorsions et des grands mouvements* (Clownisme), *période des attitudes passionnelles* and *période terminale*. See Hyer 2006, 282–309. The next few paragraphs offer a summary of Hyer's argument. For the original article, see Charcot 1879.

[71] While hysteria affected men and women, Charcot and others argued that women were more affected by the ailment.

[72] On this point, see also Bronfen 1998, 180–2.   [73] Hyer 2006, 288.

Example 12.1 Klingsor's 'Zaubermotiv' ('magic motif') from Richard Wagner, *Parsifal*, Act II scene 2, bb. 1025–1034

et des grands mouvements, is signalled by the music's rigid return to the opening themes followed by one-bar iterations of the chromatic 'magic' motif (*Zaubermotiv*) symbolising short, fast muscular contractions when Parsifal realises his wounds are emotional, not physical (see Example 12.1). This phase resolves itself into the string accompaniment to Parsifal's laboured breathing and irregular heartbeat. During the third period of the '*attitudes passionnelles*', Parsifal falls into a trance and hallucinates, and three brief *tableaux vivants*, reminiscent of Duchenne's *tableaux vivants* mentioned above, ensue. In the first, Parsifal gazes at the sacred blood glowing from the grail. Despair is the theme of the second tableau, as Christ cries out to Parsifal from the cross. In the final tableau, Parsifal addresses the saviour as himself begging for atonement of his sins. The *période des attitudes passionelles* ends with an exhausted and vulnerable Parsifal. The terminal stage commences with Kundry's plea to be Parsifal's saviour, and he enters into a hallucination. As Hyer points out, hysteria 'is pantomime, all mimesis' – and Kundry stages the pantomime with 'anatomical precision'.[74]

Wagner's Kundry is a complex and multivalent character. She connects Parsifal and Amfortas through acts of seemingly irresistible seduction; the former withstands her only by identification with the latter's suffering, an act that frees her from the cycle of Schopenhauerean enslavement to sexual desire. Wagner himself referred to her 'sphinx-like' regard of Parsifal as the 'pure fool' as she witnesses Amfortas's torturous wound opening. Among these identities, she is also a hysteric to the extent that her characteristic mode of utterance is laughter. While normative readings of the role speak of Kundry's redemption from her condition, and – outwardly – from Klingsor, one reading sees Wagner close the opera by wishing to cure the hysteria by means of hypnosis and electricity, just as Charcot did to his patients. In the premiere of *Parsifal*, both electricity and elements of hypnosis were used when Parsifal held up the Grail, which was illuminated by electric lighting, and which glimmers entrancingly.[75]

Hysterics fascinated audiences because of the violence of their body language and because their symptoms are artificial. Just as Duchenne's work was the artificial creation of human expressions not based on the experiencing of emotions, the body language generated by the hysterics 'ha[s] no organic lesions'.[76] Thus, Kundry is famously described as a wild animal in the stage directions for Act I scene 1:

Kundry rushes in, almost staggering. She is in wild garb, her shirts tucked up by a snakeskin girdle with long hanging cords; her black hair is loose and dishevelled, her complexion deep ruddy-brown, her eyes dark and piercing, sometimes flashing wildly, more often lifeless and staring.[77]

She does not listen when summoned by Gurnemanz to stand up. Later the third squire compares her to 'a wild beast'.[78] And she informs the squires that 'I never help', asserting her own will to resist.[79]

---

[74] Hyer 2006, 306.   [75] M. Smith 2007, 13.

[76] Bronfen 1998, 225. See also Nietzsche's critique of Wagner's use of hysteria, which he labels as 'artificial'.

[77] '*Kundry stürzt hastig, fast taumelnd herein. Wilde Kleidung, hoch geschürzt; Gürtel von Schlangenhäuten lang herabhängend; schwarzes, in losen Zöpfen flatterndes Haar; tief braunrötliche Gesichtsfarbe; stechende schwarze Augen, zuweilen wild aufblitzend, öfters wie todesstarr und unbeweglich.*' Wagner 1882, Act I.

[78] '[E]in wildes Tier.' Wagner 1882, Act I.   [79] 'Ich helfe nie.' Wagner 1882, Act I.

Automata, Physiology and Opera 285

In the opening of Act II scene 1, Klingsor warns Kundry that she will succumb to his will: 'Are you waking? Ha! To my power you fall again today, at the right time.'[80] While she served the saintly knights, she tries in vain to resist Klingsor, whose power arguably resembles that of the hypnotist:

KUNDRY: I ... will not! ... Oh! ... Oh!
KLINGSOR : You will, because you must.
KUNDRY: You ... cannot ... force me.[81]

Later in the scene she 'breaks into hysterical laughter, which turns to a convulsive cry of woe', reminiscent of Charcot's patients.[82]

By Act III, she has metamorphosed. She is now depicted as 'a body without will, speaking of the desires of those who animate her'.[83] She now exists to serve: she seems to have no self-will:

[Gurnemanz] drags Kundry, quite stiff and lifeless, out of the bushes and carries her to a nearby grassy mound. He does his utmost to restore Kundry's numb circulation. Gradually life seems to return to her. When at last she opens her eyes, she utters a cry. Kundry is in the coarse robe of a penitent, similar to that in Act One, but her face is paler and the wildness has vanished from her looks and behaviour. – She gazes long at Gurnemanz. Then she rises, arranges her clothing and hair and at once sets to work like a serving-maid.[84]

Her only words in Act III plead to Gurnemanz, 'Let me serve ... serve!'[85] He registers her transformation immediately: 'How differently she moves from before.' Later in the act, Parsifal orders her to 'wash my feet, now bathe my

---

[80] 'Erwachst du? Ha! / Meinem Banne wieder / verfallen heut du zur rechten Zeit.' Wagner 1882, Act II.

[81] '[Kundry:] Ich will nicht! Oh... Oh!... [Klingsor:] Wohl willst du, denn du musst. [Kundry:] Du... Kannst mich... Nicht... Halten.' Wagner 1882, Act II.

[82] 'Kundry gerät in unheimliches ekstatisches Lachen bis zu krampfhaftem Wehegeschrei.' Wagner 1882, Act II.

[83] Bronfen 1998, 233.

[84] 'Er zieht Kundry, ganz erstarrt und leblos, aus dem Gebüsche hervor, trägt sie auf einen nahen Rasenhügel, reibt ihr stark die Hände und Schläfe, haucht sie an und bemüht sich in allem, um die Erstarrung von ihr weichen zu machen. Endlich scheint das Leben in ihr zu erwachen. Sie erwacht völlig: als sie die Augen öffnet, stösst sie einen Schrei aus. Kundry ist in rauhem Büssergewande, ähnlich wie im ersten Aufzuge; nur ist ihre Gesichtsfarbe bleicher; aus Miene und Haltung ist die Wildheit verschwunden. - Sie starrt lange Gurnemanz an. Dann erhebt sie sich, ordnet sich Kleidung und Haar und lässt sich sofort wie eine Magd zur Bedienung an.' Wagner 1882, Act III.

[85] 'Dienen... Dienen.' Wagner 1882, Act III.

head',[86] and we are reminded of Wagner's statement from *The Artwork of the Future* (1849), cited in the opening quotation of the chapter: 'Without the heart's activity, the action of the brain would be no more than of a mere automaton.'

Both Offenbach and Wagner, then, were caught up in their different ways in the eternal enquiry into human identities. Hoffmann provided Offenbach with a perfect resource to question his own identity, as a German Jew in nineteenth-century France, a fractured identity that distantly mirrors Olympia being literally torn apart at the end of the first scene of Act II of *Les Contes d'Hoffmann*. Wagner's portrayal of a hysteric mirrored Charcot's demonstrations at the Salpêtrière. In short, theories of the mind, body, self and identity were intricately and inextricably linked with nineteenth-century physiology. Physicians blurred the boundary between human and android by treating their patients as automata, manipulated by their will. The tension generated by the transgression of this boundary was grist to operatic composers' mills. A cultural history of science, medicine and music can begin to illustrate how these critical notions of the body, mind and self were constructed and depicted for audiences of the late eighteenth and nineteenth centuries.

---

[86] 'Wie anders schreitet sie als sonst! … Du wuschest mir die Füsse, nun netze mir das Haupt!' Wagner 1882, Act III.

13 | Wagnerian Manipulation
Bayreuth and Nineteenth-Century Sciences of the Mind

JAMES KENNAWAY

In one of the most striking passages in his 1892 jeremiad *Degeneration*, the physician and critic Max Nordau suggested that Richard Wagner's theory of the *Gesamtkunstwerk* meant that his works could 'degrade man to the undifferentiated sense perceptions of the pholas or oyster'.[1] By reducing human perception to one sense, he argued, the audio-visual spectacle at Bayreuth would amount to an attempt literally to reverse evolution in order to suit the brains of a degenerate audience overwhelmed by the stimulations of the modern world.[2] Far from being an eccentric aside, Nordau's remarks drew on an extensive scientific and medical critique of the multimedia character of the Bayreuth experience focused on its sensory neurophysiological dangers.[3] Many contemporaries made similar arguments, worrying that the all-round sensory experience at Bayreuth was an uninvited attempt to stimulate the nerves, subvert rational thought and leave viewers in a pathological trance state.

This critique of the *Gesamtkunstwerk* as passive brain stimulation can be found not only in Nordau's intemperate book but in a wide range of other critics, authors, scientists and physicians including Eduard Hanslick, Friedrich Nietzsche and later figures such as Bertolt Brecht and Theodor W. Adorno, reflecting anxieties about the unconscious, sexuality, self-control and social order in an uncertain modern world. Wagner may have argued that his *Gesamtkunstwerk* was a return to ancient unity in the arts, but his quintessentially modern innovations, such as the darkened auditorium, the hidden orchestra and his elaborate stage machinery, made his theatre at Bayreuth arguably one of the most extraordinary sensual experiences of the nineteenth century.[4] Debate concerning the vulnerability of audiences to this sensory manipulation was in many ways just as modern, with as much in common with twentieth- and twenty-first-century ambivalence about the impact of cinema, TV and the Internet on the brain and its neurology

---

[1] Nordau 1895, 176. This metaphor was surprisingly common. See Hanslick 1950, 127, and Sydow 1921, 206.

[2] Nordau 1895, 207.   [3] See Kennaway 2005.   [4] See Spotts 1994.

as with traditional operatic criticism.[5] This chapter seeks to show the debt owed to late nineteenth-century sciences of the mind, especially medicine, psychiatry and psychology, in creating the framework for this critique of the ultra-modern Bayreuth media experience.

Popular criticism of Wagner might have generally focused on caricatures of hefty sopranos, stamina-testing longueurs and sheer volume, but it is striking that Wagner's most persistent and thought-provoking critics, far from denying the *Gesamtkunstwerk*'s power, have generally attacked it for being *too good* at manipulating its audience. The supposed power of the *Gesamtkunstwerk* to undermine the self-awareness and attention of those in the audience via brain stimulation was often understood at the time in terms of discourses on drugs and hypnosis.[6] In the 1870s and 1880s hypnotism emerged from its quasi-occult past to be an important part of neurology and psychiatry, becoming a vital means of discussing anxieties about affective contagion and its dangers in the emerging era of mass society. The idea of hypnotism fitted in a broader medical critique of the Romantic aesthetics and ethics of opera in which it almost seemed a duty to be swept away into quasi-mystical ecstasy.[7]

The debate on hypnosis and on the *Gesamtkunstwerk*'s impact on the brain in turn owed much to developing scientific conceptions of the mind. A more materialist physiological model of mind that understood mental life in terms of automatic reflex response to stimuli, restrained by an inhibiting willpower, was influential in the final decades of the nineteenth century.[8] The work of the likes of Henry Maudsley, Théodule Ribot, as well as that of Jean-Martin Charcot and his colleagues at the Salpêtrière hospital in Paris, offered a mechanistic model of how the mind worked which not only laid the ground for broad cultural assumptions underpinning the debate on Bayreuth, but also was often referred to directly.[9] Although this model was later challenged by a less physiological view put forward by William James, Hippolyte Bernheim, Sigmund Freud and others, similar automatic models of the mind have been revived intermittently since, notably with Behaviourism and the rise of twenty-first-century 'neuromania'.[10] Paradoxically, the mechanistic stimulation response model of the mind made willpower the centrepiece of ideas about the regulation of an embodied self. In the face of societies confronted by the

---

[5] Kittler 1999; Adorno 2005; see also A. Williams 1997.   [6] See Kennaway 2012b.

[7] Johnson 1995; Winter 1998; Voskuhl 2007; Castelvecchi 2013, 125–60.

[8] R. Smith 1992; Hacking 1995; N. Rose 2012.

[9] See Maudsley 1883; Ribot 1883; Charcot 1886–93; Herrmann 2007;.

[10] See Peretz and Zatorre 2003;Levitin 2006; Patel 2006; Sacks 2008 .

Wagnerian Manipulation

dislocations of industrialisation, the necessity of individual self-control (especially sexual continence) to maintain health, sanity and social order was repeatedly emphasised. Many described this self-mastery as a kind of 'mental hygiene' that was necessary to ward off the contagious stimulations of modern life. For Nordau, for instance, an inability to pay attention, to control perception with willpower, was the 'disease of the century'.[11] The scientific critique of Bayreuth was a strikingly early example of the very modern discourse of a moral and physiological struggle between the excessive stimulations of multimedia and this conception of individual autonomy.

Such arguments were often echoed in twentieth-century anxieties about cinema and its seemingly hypnotic powers. Among other things, this helps explain why Friedrich Kittler called Nietzsche's writings on Wagner a critique of film *avant la lettre*.[12] Only twelve years separated Wagner's death in 1883 and the official invention of the cinematograph in 1895, and – as commentators from Adorno to Jeongwon Joe have argued – cinema has proved to be arguably one of the most important heirs of Bayreuth's phantasmagorical aesthetic.[13] Certainly Wagner's integrated and technologically sophisticated works were as close to early film as anything in their era; for this reason Adorno spoke – in a famous misreading of Wagner – of 'the birth of film from the spirit of music'.[14] Like Bayreuth, the cinema was marked as modern, degenerate, female and as a threat to masculine, rational autonomy, replete with the same metaphors of hypnosis and passivity.[15] Indeed, Stefan Andriopoulos has written of 'the structural affinity between cinematography and hypnosis around 1900'.[16] More recently, work by Jeffrey Zacks on the neuroscience of film has given a new depth to older concerns about the impact of moving images on the brain.[17]

The critique of Bayreuth as a form of stimulation was predicated on contemporary medical and scientific theories, notably the theory of *dégénérescences* developed by Bénédict Morel in the 1850s that argued that vice and sickness could be passed down by successively weaker generations, and George Beard's neurasthenia diagnosis that saw urban over-

---

[11] Schulte 1997, 179. [12] Kittler 1999, 184. [13] See Gilman and Joe 2010.

[14] 'in ihm ereignet die Geburt des Films aus dem Geiste der Musik.' Adorno 2005, 100–1.

[15] See Kracauer 1963.

[16] 'der strukturellen Affinität von Kinematographie und Hypnose um 1900'. Andriopoulos 2000, 23. This point was seconded by Jean Cocteau, who wrote of film as 'collective hypnosis' ('die kollektive Hypnose'). Kittler 1999, 224.

[17] Zacks 2014.

stimulation as the cause of nervous sickness.[18] The sensory excitement experienced at Bayreuth was regularly portrayed as a form of quintessentially modern technological stimulation likely to lead to the pathological fatigue of neurasthenia. An oft-cited example is the psychiatrist Richard von Krafft-Ebing, who included Wagner's music in a list of dangerous forms of 'abnormal stimulation' associated with modernity.[19] An inability to resist stimulation was also a symptom, since neurasthenics suffered from a weakness of 'memory, attention, judgement, will and the resistance to impressions' as Leon Bouveret put it in his 1890 *La Neurasthénie*.[20] Likewise, fears that excessive stimulation would rob members of the audience of the ability to pay attention were matched by the suggestion that Wagner's music appealed to degenerate spectators, those lacking in attention from an inborn evolutionary flaw. For Nordau, Wagner's 'endless melody' and stage spectacle were signs of degeneration, since the 'degenerate is not in a condition to fix his attention long'.[21]

Until the 1920s most of the medicalised critique of Bayreuth as the site of quasi-hypnotic mind-control was of a conservative bent, fretting about its impact on morals. As is well known, in the twentieth century the notion of Wagner's work as sense manipulation on the brink of hypnosis became part of a left-wing critique of the Culture Industry and 'phantasmagoria', especially in the work of Adorno and Brecht. Bayreuth, with its supposed ability to anaesthetise critical thought and stimulate unconscious desires and libidinal drives, was portrayed as a forerunner of mass consumerist culture and indeed of fascist propaganda. Its mimetic, affective contagion was the antithesis of the critical thinking and political engagement demanded by the nascent Frankfurt School. It is striking that there was a high level of continuity between the medical critique of the late nineteenth century and the political version during the Weimar Republic. In particular, both eras shared anxieties about modern media and the rational self as technology and a developing culture of audience silence and attention combined to radically intensify the passivity of spectatorship.[22]

In what follows, I first consider the pioneering stage technology used in the *Gesamtkunstwerk*, in particular at Wagner's own theatre at Bayreuth, the extravagance of which caused the physician and historian Theodor Puschmann to denounce its 'unprecedented luxury in decoration and

---

[18] Morel 1857.   [19] Krafft-Ebing 1903, 71, 10.

[20] 'Sie äussert sich in verminderter Ausdauer aller Gehirnkräfte, insbesondere des Gedächtnisses, der Aufmerksamkeit, des Urtheils, des Willens und der Widerstandskraft gegen Empfindungen und Gemüthseindrücke.' Bouveret 1893, 34.

[21] Nordau 1895, 199, 21.   [22] Johnson 1995; Sennett 2003.

machinery, only thinkable in the dissipated imagination of a madman' in his 1872 pathography *Richard Wagner: eine psychiatrische Studie.*[23] It then looks at discussion of innovations such as the darkened auditorium and hidden orchestra in the context of contemporary theories of hypnosis and narcosis. Thereafter, it examines the brain stimulation model of the mind that provided the basis for the language of trance used to disparage Wagner's multimedia spectacle, and shows how the fear of loss of autonomy and willpower was directly addressed in attacks on Bayreuth. The conclusion touches on the afterlife of these anxieties within the more political debate on Wagner during the interwar period, and closes by discussing the value of understanding this debate on Bayreuth as an early example of a kind of neurophysiological critique of media that is currently enjoying renewed influence.[24] The furore around suggestions that modern technology is 'rewiring' our brains, occasioned by books such as Susan Greenfield's *Mind Change: How Digital Technologies are Leaving their Mark on our Brains*, has a surprising amount in common with the late nineteenth-century discourse on Wagner.[25] An examination of the medicalised debate surrounding Bayreuth might serve as a reminder for us today of the pitfalls of an appeal to the prestige of science in attempts to explain complex social phenomena in biological reductionist terms.

The *Gesamtkunstwerk* as Hypnotic Media Technology

The creation of a new Wagner theatre at Bayreuth, despite the existence in the city of the Markgräfliches Opernhaus, allowed Wagner to indulge his ideas about stage design and the organisation of a theatre. Although incremental changes in the technical aspects of the theatre laid the groundwork for the innovations of the *Gesamtkunstwerk*, commentators have made clear that it marked a real departure in media technology. Kittler famously described the 1865 premiere of *Tristan und Isolde* as the 'beginning of modern mass media'.[26] Wagner's artistic vision demanded elaborate visual tableaux, especially in the *Ring*, with its gods walking over the rainbow bridge, Alberich turning from a dragon into a frog, Brünnhilde

---

[23] 'unerhörten Luxus in Dekoration und Maschinerien, wie sie eben nur die ausschweifende Phantasie eines in Überschwenglichkeit schwelgenden Wahnsinnigen zu erdenken vermag'. Puschmann 1872, 30.

[24] See, for example, Lehrer 2007 and Andreason 2005.   [25] Greenfield 2014.

[26] Kittler 1987, 208.

being surrounded by a wall of fire, and the burning of Valhalla. Bayreuth's technical director, Carl Brandt, realised Wagner's plans as best he could by using coloured steam, pulsating gas illuminations and even electric lights to give the impression of moving water around the Rhine Maidens on their 'swimming carriages'.[27] Such was the role of this state-of-the-art stage equipment that the critic Eduard Hanslick could write: 'we have seen with astonishment the colossal machinery, the gas apparatus, the steam machines above and below the stage at Bayreuth. Wagner could as little have composed the *Ring* before the invention of the electric light as without the harp or bass tuba.'[28] All this technological novelty was quickly co-opted within a medical and scientific critique of Wagner's work as a potential threat to self-control. Nordau, for instance, described the *Gesamtkunstwerk*'s 'variegated pomp, the most fantastic pictures, and the liveliest impressions of light and colour' as 'besieging' the mind via the eye, just as he and others fretted about the over-stimulation of the ear.[29]

One aspect of the *Gesamtkunstwerk* that marked it as a threat to rational autonomy was its 'illusionist' aesthetic: the radical suspension of disbelief and the denial of the artificial character of the action on stage that the critic Paul Bekker called 'the absolute reality of the unreal'.[30] A crucial element in this illusion was the double proscenium arch suggested by the architect Gottfried Semper, which created a receding perspective to make the stage look bigger, making the illusion more complete by achieving what Semper described as 'the desired separation of the ideal world of the stage from the real world on the other side'.[31] Another aspect of this illusionism was of course the innovation of the hidden orchestra, which was introduced not only to dampen the sound of the instruments so that the singers could be heard but also to add to the visual illusion by obscuring the musicians from view. The fear was often expressed that the hidden orchestra could bypass the conscious mind and influence the audience directly via neural stimulation, using the best possible acoustics.[32] Hanslick, for example, suggested that it had the effect of 'a mild opium jag' (*Opiumrausch*), switching off the rational mind.[33] At the time of the first Bayreuth *Ring* in 1876, the Wagnerian Heinrich Porges gave an insight into the unconscious effect that the production aimed to achieve with these techniques when he wrote that 'it will be as though we were experiencing the magical effects of an

---

[27] Srocke 1988.

[28] Hanslick 1950, 171. In fact electric lighting was first used by Giacomo Meyerbeer in 1849. See Campana 2015, 28–33.

[29] Nordau 1895, 174. See Kennaway 2012a, 63–98.   [30] Adorno 2005, 90. See Kämmerer 1990.

[31] Gutman 1990, 340.   [32] Huysmans 1959, 27.   [33] Hanslick 1950, 170

ideal presence; as though no longer conscious of the music'.[34] This notion of the audience not being conscious of the illusory character of what is affecting them is key to understanding the supposed 'subliminal' effect of the new Bayreuth environment.

The use of light and the darkening of the auditorium also added considerably to the illusionist aesthetic. Audiences at the Paris Opéra had experienced similar things since 1822, but Wagner's use of gaslight at Bayreuth, allowing brightening and dimming to be used as dramatic effects, aroused a good deal of attention. The radical extension of the gradual shift to a brighter stage and a darker theatre that had been going on for decades served to focus attention on the stage and to lull audiences into a receptive state in which they more fully suspended their disbelief. Mark Twain remarked that darkening the Bayreuth auditorium created an effect akin to a 'congregation sat in a deep and solemn gloom', so rapt in attention that they looked as if they had been turned to brass.[35] Tolstoy's 1897 book *What is Art?* also referred to the darkening of the auditorium and the hidden orchestra as proof that 'we have here no question of art, but one of hypnotism'. Comparing it to a spiritualist séance, Tolstoy underscored the comparison with chemically altered mental states by arguing that the experience of sitting in the dark with people rendered 'half-crazy ... can be still more quickly attained by getting drunk or smoking opium'. He went on to link these metaphors of narcosis and hypnosis directly with anxiety about the impact of this fixed attention on the brains and the autonomy of the audience. The stimulation of 'the auditory nerves' and 'the brain' in the dark and 'in company with people who are not quite normal' would mean – he wrote – that the audience would be in an 'abnormal condition and be enchanted by absurdities'.[36]

As we see from these examples, discussions of the manipulative power of the technological innovations at Bayreuth were often put in terms of specific scientific and medical theories of trance states and self-control. The idea of possession, of the loss of self, may seem distant from modern concerns, but beneath the language of medicine, it is in fact a persistent anxiety of modernity. The eighteenth and nineteenth centuries saw a radical recasting of trance states from a spiritual and religious context to that of medicine, and a fascination with sleepwalkers and hypnotised subjects as a form of victory of lower forces in the brain over higher, more rational principles. The late nineteenth-century debate on hypnosis, in particular, became the focus of the expression of anxieties, in scientific

---

[34] Porges 1983, 7–8. [35] Twain 1917, 211. [36] Tolstoy 1904, 140–1, 143.

circles and beyond, about the fragility of the rational self. Its roots lay in Mesmerism, the semi-occult medical practice developed by Franz Anton Mesmer in the late eighteenth century that suggested that an invisible animal magnetic force surrounding us could be manipulated by a 'magnetiseur', putting patients into a trance state and thereby solving various health problems. From the 1840s the Scottish surgeon James Braid attempted to move the medical study of trance states away from the speculative hocus-pocus that had become associated with Mesmerism.[37] It was often suggested that music and hypnosis were closely linked, both in Mesmerist and more scientific circles. Both dealt with untouchable forces, and there were numerous reports of unmusical people suddenly developing talent during a trance, while in complementary fashion musicians were often believed to be particularly susceptible to hypnotism.[38]

As it turns out, the work that laid the foundations for the widespread accusation that the *Gesamtkunstwerk* was hypnotic in its effects took place primarily in France, with competing models asserted at the Salpêtrière and in the provincial city of Nancy, both of which directly influenced discussions of artistic culture. In Paris, Jean-Martin Charcot and his colleagues conducted many experiments, often performed in front of an audience, which seemed to demonstrate that direct sensory stimulation, including from tuning forks, gongs and songs, could induce cataleptic fits among hysterical women.[39] For instance, the physician and artist Paul Richer wrote in his 1881 *Études cliniques sur la grande hystérie ou hystéro-épilepsie* about 'the influence of music on hysteria', which he linked to 'catalepsy, lethargy and somnambulism'.[40] Like his Salpêtrière colleagues, Richer was adamant that hypnotic states, including those induced by sound and music, were essentially neurological reflex actions among hysterics and little to do with the conscious mind. As the German physiologist Rudolf Heidenhain put it in 1880, hypnosis was the result of brain stimulation – 'the inhibition of the activity of the ganglion-cells of the cerebral cortex' caused by the 'gentle prolonged stimulation of the sensory nerves of the face, or of the auditory . . . nerve' – that is, exactly the mechanism many suspected to be at work at Bayreuth.[41] This research on trance states had

---

[37] [unsigned] 1847a, 602; Braid 1843, 56.   [38] See Braid 1843, 193–6; Tuckey 1893.

[39] Binet and Féré 1905, 88–9, 93. See also Regnard 1887, 260–3 and Didi-Huberman 2003, 209–13.

[40] 'Il est donc rationnel de penser que l'influence de la musique sur les accès d'hystérie se borne aux accès convulsifs sans perte de connaissance, et aux variétés de l'attaque dans lesquelles la sensibilité spéciale persiste quelquefois, comme dans la catalepsie, la léthargie et le somnambulisme.' Richer 1881, 600.

[41] Heidenhain 1880, 49.

significant cultural influence on discussions of music, but became a significant context in the reception of the *Gesamtkunstwerk* only in the final decades of the nineteenth century; it is not mentioned in Puschmann's otherwise very thorough 'psychiatric study' of Wagner from 1872, for instance.

Later, though, it came naturally to many observers to draw on the Salpêtrière model of hypnosis when describing the behaviour of some of Wagner's characters, notably Kundry.[42] Physicians at the Salpêtrière themselves contributed to the cultural and the literary impact of such theories. Charles Richet, for one, wrote a novel entitled *Sœur Marthe* (1889), in which the eponymous protagonist is frozen in catalepsy because of music.[43] Drawing on the same research, Wagner's hypnotic music dramas were compared to the clinical demonstrations at the Salpêtrière. The nineteenth-century American critic James Huneker described Wagner in no uncertain terms as the 'Klingsor of Bayreuth [who] hypnotizes his hearers with two or three themes not of themselves remarkable, as Charcot controls his patients with a shining mirror', and Nordau followed suit, arguing: 'this music was certainly of a nature to fascinate the hysterical. Its powerful orchestral effects produced hypnotic states (at the Salpêtrière hospital in Paris the hypnotic state is often induced by suddenly striking a gong).'[44] Nietzsche compared Wagner's work to hypnosis several times, and his debt to French theories of trance states, especially those of Charles Féré, has been well documented.[45] In *The Case of Wagner*, to give just one example, he described the *Lohengrin* overture as a study of 'how to hypnotise with music'.[46] Charcotian conceptions of the mind and of hypnosis thus became a lens through which to understand the modern media experience of Bayreuth far beyond medical circles, providing a model of passive stimulation that suited a wide variety of agendas.

However, the Salpêtrière view of trance states was certainly challenged at the time. The Swedish writer and physician Axel Munthe, who had worked there, later declared: 'almost every single one of Charcot's theories on hypnotism has been proved wrong'. The women observed, he suggested, were examples of 'post-hypnotic suggestions' or 'mere frauds ... delighted to perform their various tricks in public'.[47] The theory of the Nancy neurologist Hippolyte Bernheim, who asserted that hypnosis was essentially a matter of suggestion, not neurological disease, and that it was

---

[42] Nietzsche described Wagner's heroines as a 'hysterical-hypnotic type' 'hysterisch-hypnotische Typus.' Borchmeyer and Salaquarda 1994, 2:1041. See also Pfohl 1889, and Myles Jackson's chapter in this volume.

[43] Epheyre 1890, 54. See also l'Isle-Adam 1986.   [44] Nordau 1895, 200–1.   [45] Lampl 1986.

[46] Nietzsche 1969, VI.3, § 7.   [47] Munthe 2004, 215, 207.

something that could potentially be experienced by anyone, not just hysterics, became the standard view. This explanation for the supposed quasi-hypnotic power of the *Gesamtkunstwerk* resonated much less with Wagner's critics than Charcot's more mechanistic view. Although Nietzsche denounced Wagner's theatricality as a means of 'strengthening gestures, suggestion, the psychological-picturesque', and others explained Klingsor's power over Kundry in terms of suggestion, without the brain's 'stimulus and response' model of the mind, the whole idea of hypnosis became a less effective stick with which to beat the *Gesamtkunstwerk* in this more sceptical environment.[48] However, although new subjective and individual paradigms for understanding hypnotism and parallel developments such as William James's work on ideomotor actions offered little to critics of Wagner, the sense that Bayreuth might have hypnotic dangers remained fixed in the public imagination.

Stimulation, Willpower and the Sciences of the Mind

The critique of the *Gesamtkunstwerk* as a hypnotic form of stimulation was thus based on particular medical understandings of trance states. At a deeper level, it also relied on contemporary neurological understandings of the brain and the mind. A model of the mind as a kind of machine that responded to stimuli and which attempted to explain mental states as a form of higher reflex was an ideal foundation for a critique of media stimulation. It made the physical and moral reactions of the audience to media a matter of objective physiology to be analysed by a physician rather than something related to subjective experience. Medicalised critiques of culture based on the development of this neurological conception of mind go back to the Scientific Revolution, as George Rousseau has shown.[49] By the eighteenth century neurophysiology had become, in Philipp Sarasin's words, an 'apparatus of the Subject' – a powerful new way of explaining human behaviour and self-understanding.[50] The work of physicians and scientists from Robert Whytt in the 1750s to Johannes Peter Müller in the 1830s on reflex action laid the foundations for nineteenth-century theories that sought to explain human actions and mental states in terms of automatic response.[51]

---

[48] 'eine Theater-Rhetorik, ein Mittel des Ausdrucks, der Gebärden-Verstärkung, der Suggestion, des Psychologisch-Pittoresken'. Nietzsche 1969, VI.3 §8. Preyer 1890, 118.

[49] G. Rousseau 2004.   [50] Sarasin 2007, 54.

[51] Whytt 1768; J. Müller 1835–40, 1:688–701. See Clarke and Jacyna 1987, 470–1.

In the context of such neurological conceptions of the mind, the concept of willpower took on increasing importance in conceptions of mental health, becoming an important part of the new dietetics, moral therapy and psychological medicine, as bourgeois values of restraint were institutionalised in psychiatric thinking. If the experience of the world is a matter of stimulation, then it was vital to control one's responses for the sake of hygiene and order. This development can be seen in the 'Moral Therapy' tradition in Britain, as well as the continental Romantic psychological medicine such as Ernst von Feuchtersleben's *Dietetics of the Soul* and Etienne Jean Georget's work in the 1820s on 'lesions of the will', all of which emphasised the role of the psyche in the creation and treatment of mental illness.[52] Subsequent medical sources often retained an interest in willpower and self-control despite a more somatic approach to mental health, as one can see in work such as Henry Maudsley's *Body and Will*, Theo Hyslop's *Mental Physiology*, Friedrich's *Maladies of the Will* and Karl Birnbaum's *Pathological Weakness of the Will*.[53] Many medical observers argued that willpower's principal purpose was to regulate imagination and sensuality, and to maintain a 'state of inhibitory perfection'.[54] The French psychologist Théodule Ribot, whose journal Nietzsche knew well, spoke for many when he described the will as a 'power of arrestation, or, in the language of physiology, an inhibitive power'.[55] This conception of the will as a regulator of desires gave it a central role in thinking on crime and morality, providing an apparently objective basis for a medical and scientific replacement for moral and legal strictures, reflecting the level of continuity from older religious and moral models of self-control. There was a wide consensus that the stimulations of the modern world made particularly high demands on the will; the mind's grasp over the body seemed increasingly 'tenuous but imperative', as Roger Smith has argued.[56]

Critiques of the supposed modern sensory overload involved in the *Gesamtkunstwerk* were often directly related to a dangerous loss of self-control, as noted above. Nietzsche is only the most famous commentator to allude to Wagner's destructive impact on the will and autonomy of the audience, as well as the failure of willpower at the heart of the composer's philosophy.[57] Indeed, he wrote repeatedly about Wagner as a threat to

---

[52] Laffey 2003; Feuchtersleben 1838; Georget 1825.

[53] Maudsley 1883; Friedrich 1885; Hyslop 1895; Birnbaum 1911. See also Jacyna 1981; Daston 1982; Hagner 1999.

[54] Clouston 1906, 80. See Taylor 1989, 303.   [55] Ribot 1894, 10.   [56] R. Smith 1992, 1–2.

[57] Nidesh Lawtoo (2008) perceptively links Nietzsche's hostility to the *Gesamtkunstwerk*'s hypnotic powers to Plato's rejection of mimesis as form of enthusiasm or possession, an intolerable loss of self-control by the actors and, via affective contagion, of the audience, too.

willpower, as 'a typical decadent, who lacks any kind of "free will"', and whose work involves a 'dissolution of the will'.[58] This threat to selfhood, Nietzsche argued, was closely linked to the multimedia theatrical character of Wagner's work. The 'restlessness of the visual element' was connected to the 'convulsive nature of his effects, his over-stimulated sensibility', he suggested.[59] The result is mass culture with a degraded self: 'in the theatre one is honest only as mass; as an individual one lies', he wrote in *The Gay Science* – 'One leaves one's self at home when one goes to the theatre.'[60]

Like hypnosis and phantasmagoria, drugs appeared to operate at the boundary of the physiological and the psychological where their external, chemical forces seemed able to undermine willpower. Drug addiction was widely understood as a 'disease of the will', both a symptom and a cause of weak willpower, since only people lacking in will would be seduced by drugs, and those drugs would then destroy their remaining self-control.[61] This was perhaps the principal reason for the frequency with which Wagner's works were compared to narcotics.[62] Nietzsche repeatedly turned to drug references in his critique of Wagner, labelling Wagner's art an 'opiate of the senses' and discussing its 'opium-like and narcotic effects'.[63] Similarly, Hanslick compared Wagner's work to 'the hashish dream of the ecstatic female', while the Nobel Prize-winning German novelist Paul Heyse talked in 1872 of Wagnerian 'hashish-obfuscation' (*Haschisch-Benebelung*).[64] Another reason was the connection between Wagnerian music and an addiction to stimulations (be they media effects or narcotics) in degeneration theory: degenerates 'crave for a stimulus', as Nordau noted.[65] Wagner's works were for some writers symptomatic of this kind of physiological craving. For instance, in his book on music and nerves, the German psychologist Ernst Jentsch wrote of Wagner's modern 'effects', which he linked to 'the constantly growing dependency on narcotics'.[66] Theories of willpower, degeneration and addiction thus

---

[58] 'ein typischer décadent, bei dem jeder "freie Wille" fehlt', 'Disgregation des Willens'. Nietzsche 1969, VI.3 § 7.

[59] 'die Unruhe ihrer Optik'; 'das Convulvische seines Affektes, seine überreizte Sensibilität'. Nietzsche 1969, VI.3 § 7, § 5.

[60] 'Im Theater ist man nur als Masse ehrlich; als Einzelner lügt man, belügt man sich. Man lässt sich selbst zu Hause, wenn man in's Theater geht.' Nietzsche 1969, V.2 § 368.

[61] See Harding 1988.   [62] Mayer 1978.

[63] 'Opiaten der Sinne.' Nietzsche 1969, VI.3 § 1; Wohin Wagner gehört. 'die opiatischen und narkotischen Wirkungen'. Borchmeyer and Salaquarda 1994, 2:788–9.

[64] Hanslick 1950, 172. 'Haschisch-Benebelung'. Heyse 1984, 1:465.   [65] Nordau 1895, 41.

[66] 'Affektshunger also aus dem beständig wachsenden Hange zu den narkotischen Genussmitteln.' Jentsch 1904, 2:83.

provided a key context and a rich source of metaphor to express fears about Bayreuth's apparent threat to autonomy.

Another constant theme in medical discussions of self-control and autonomy was sexuality. The German physician Eduard Reich, for instance, wrote at length about the 'nervous strength' needed to maintain 'moral hygiene' in the face of sexual passion.[67] The *Gesamtkunstwerk*'s supposed quasi-hypnotic over-stimulation of the sensorium was often depicted as a threat to the rational inhibition of sexuality on which decency, health and public order were understood to depend. While some of the discussion on this subject was end-of-the-pier stuff about what people were getting up to in the darkened auditorium (Nordau fretted about the 'hidden enjoyment' of illicit delights), other critics feared that the over-stimulation of the *Gesamtkunstwerk* would undermine sexual morals and health.[68] In an 1896 discussion of the effects of Wagner on female patients, the American physician Frank Parsons Norbury wrote that the impact of 'sensory fatigue' from 'continuous stimulation of the organs of hearing, of vision, of touch' might lead to the disturbance of 'emotional control' through the effect on 'inhibiting centres', leading to neuritis, insomnia and hysteria, all of which he linked to 'disturbances of the organ peculiar to her sex ... and undue sexual excitement'.[69] Nietzsche picked up on this theme, suggesting that Wagner 'hypnotises the mystical-erotic females by making his music put the spirit of the magnetiseur into her spine (one can observe the physiological effects of the *Lohengrin* prelude on the secretions)'.[70] In literature, too, there are many examples of the *Gesamtkunstwerk* overwhelming the self-control of members of the audience and leading to sexual vice and destruction.[71]

The association of lack of willpower with women and sexuality reflected the widespread assumption that the ideal autonomous subject was implicitly (and often explicitly) masculine, and anxiety about willpower was linked to a sense of crisis in masculinity.[72] From the start, discussion between Wagner, his adherents and opponents had frequently been gendered.[73] The composer's whole aesthetic was in many ways a conscious attempt to impose a serious, German masculine character on opera, an

---

[67] 'Kraft in den Nerven', 'moralischen Hygiene'. Reich 1868, 153. [68] Nordau 1895, 14.

[69] Norbury 1896, 112–13.

[70] 'er hypnotisiert die mystisch-erotischen Weibchen, indem seine Musik den Geist eines Magnetiseurs bis in ihr Rückenmark hinein fühlbar macht (– man beobachte das Lohengrin Vorspiel in seinen physiologischen Einwirkungen auf die Sekretion und –.' Borchmeyer and Salaquarda 1994, 1025.

[71] See Kennaway 2012c. [72] See Mosse 1996. [73] McClatchie 1998.

artform that – for many – had often seemed dangerously Italian and effeminate. On the other hand, the phantasmagorical character of Wagner's work, the sensual power of its sound and of visual aspect led many critics who distrusted the manipulative power of the *Gesamtkunstwerk* to question the masculinity of its creator and those who took pleasure in experiencing it, reflecting the assumption that passive weakness of will was essentially feminine or homosexual.[74] In this context Wagner's critics were not shy about making insinuations about the composer's close male friendships and fondness for silk.[75] Contemporary science provided support for the idea that manly willpower was under threat from modern culture. Gustav le Bon, for instance, argued that crowds are essentially feminine in their behaviour.[76] Thus, having overcome the female models of Italian opera (a 'harlot') and French opera (a 'coquette') – as Wagner put it in his essay *Opera and Drama* (1851) – he faced criticism that his work was effeminate from a new angle, that of physical stimulation.[77]

Conclusion

In some ways, the critique of Wagner's work as a matter of physical stimulation was simply a question of fashionable theories being applied to one of the most prominent cultural phenomena of the day. After all, Nordau was happy to suggest that degeneration theory explained almost all European culture of the 1890s, seemingly irrespective of its content. On the other hand, there are vital ways in which the *Gesamtkunstwerk* fitted perfectly with medical thinking about the perils of excessive stimulation of a passive nervous system. The visual aspect played a significant role. The French physician Pierre Bonnier and his brother Charles talked of Wagner's visual powers 'doing away with the autonomy of the audience'.[78] And about the only positive thing that Nordau could bring himself to say about Wagner's conception of the unity of the arts was that Charles Féré's work suggested that 'the ear hears more keenly when the eye is simultaneously stimulated'.[79] The technological control of light and dark, and the manipulation of perception involved in Wagner's 'illusionist' aesthetic and hidden orchestra also left Bayreuth open to medical critiques of its

---

[74] See Scott 2003, 33–59.

[75] See Spitzer 1906, especially 57–8; 1880, 120–1; Dreyfus 2010, 175–217.

[76] Huyssen 1986, 52. [77] Wagner 1852, 1:186–90. [78] Crary 1999, 253.

[79] Nordau 1895, 175.

intentions. It has also often been argued that Wagner's music aims at overwhelming the audience – he was 'the most impolite genius in the world', in Nietzsche's words.[80] The sheer volume of his enlarged orchestra, the lush instrumentation and in particular his innovative harmony were often depicted as hypnotic or narcotic in character, as noted above. Together, these characteristics rendered the audience passive receivers of stimulation, at least in interpretations that took seriously contemporary theories of the mind.

It is striking that the language of hypnosis, drugs and willpower continued to be widely used in the very different intellectual climate of the Weimar Republic even after such theories had become discredited. It turns out that metaphors and frameworks taken from nineteenth-century theories of brain stimulation were co-opted into the terms of a Marxian false consciousness and its concomitant Culture Industry, which also posited a neutrally manipulated, passive consumer of culture. Adorno and Brecht would speak explicitly in these terms; for the former, Wagner's hidden orchestra is a 'phantasmagorical medium' with the power to impose 'visual attentiveness' and 'manage perception'; for Brecht, by 'melting' the different arts into one mixture, the *Gesamtkunstwerk* would also 'melt down' the spectator, making him or her 'passive', an experience that equated to 'unworthy stimulation' and 'hypnotism'.[81]

Since then, discussions of mass manipulation have tended to draw on similar theories of stimuli and response. For instance, the emergence of the concept of brainwashing in the 1950s, which revived many themes familiar from the debate on Bayreuth, drew directly on Neo-Pavlovian concepts of conditioned response. Even if recent revivals in physiological explanations of human actions and in the concept of willpower (linked to neo-liberalism and increasingly neuro-pharmacological paradigms in contemporary psychiatry) are perhaps laying the foundation for a new discourse of media and stimulation, today theories of the Culture Industry and false consciousness are generally treated historically.[82] However, alongside scepticism about reductionist conceptions of the mind and gendered ideals of

---

[80] 'das *unhöflichste* Genie der Welt'. Nietzsche 1969, VI.3 90.

[81] Crary 1990, 24. 'Solange eine 'Gesamtkunstwerk' bedeutet, daß die Gesamte ein Aufwachsen ist, solange also Künste 'verschmelzt' werden sollen, müssen die einzelnen Elemente alle gleichermaßen degradiert werden, indem jedes nur Stichwortbringer für das andere sein kann. Der Schmelzprozeß erfaßt den Zuschauer, der ebenfalls eingeschmolzen wird und einem passiven (leidenen) Teil des Gesamtkunstwerks darstellt. Solche Magie ist natürlich zu bekämpfen. Alles, was Hypnotisierversuche darstellen soll, unwürdige Räusche erzeugen muß, benebelt, muß aufgegeben werden.' Brecht 1997, 6:107–8.

[82] See, for example, Tierney and Baumeister 2012.

selfhood, it is important not to lose sight of the real lesson in the debate on Bayreuth's hypnotic powers and their medical, moral and political implications: the need for critical thinking in media. As Umberto Eco put it in a discussion of television, 'A democratic civilization will save itself only if it makes the language of the image into a stimulus for critical reflection – not an invitation for hypnosis.'[83] While he was not speaking of Bayreuth, the concerns to which he gives voice would seem wholly applicable to discourses of sensory manipulation surrounding Wagner's art, even after discounting the hyperbolic language of many of the composer's contemporary critics.

[83] Eco 1979, 15.

14 | Unsound Seeds

ALEXANDER REHDING

> In the wax museums and anatomical display cabinets of speculative
> sideshow owners there are certain sections that are hung with curtains
> bearing the words 'Admission for adults only' or 'customers with weak
> nerves are warned not to visit this room' and that contain some monstrosity
> as the actual main attraction of the otherwise very harmless collections.[1]

With this image of a curtain hiding and at the same time heightening some
terrible secret, Max Kalbeck began his review of the first Viennese performance of Richard Strauss's *Salome*. Theodor W. Adorno picked up the image
of the curtain in the context of Strauss's fabled skill at composing non-
musical events, when he identified the opening flourish of Strauss's *Salome*
as the swooshing sound of the rising curtain.[2] If this is so, the *succès de
scandale* of the opera was achieved, in more than one sense, as soon as the
curtain rose at Dresden's Semperoper on 10 December 1905.

Critics of the premiere noted that the opera set 'boundless wildness and
degeneration to music'; it brought 'high decadence' onto the operatic stage;
a 'composition of hysteria', reflecting the 'disease of our time', *Salome* is
'hardly music any more'.[3] The outrage did not end there. A few months
after the premiere the ageing Felix Draeseke published the polemic
Confusion in Music, in which he analysed the phenomenon of *Salome*
and the culture that allowed this to happen.[4] Embracing a Spenglerian
cultural pessimism, Draeseke dwelt on the widespread fears that we had
reached the end of music as we know it. Piquantly, Draeseke could hardly
be counted as conservative; rather, as a member of the nineteenth-century
Fortschrittspartei around Liszt and Wagner, he had garnered impeccable
progressive credentials. Draeseke's polemic in turn encouraged other
critics to add their views on *Salome* and the state of contemporary music
in general, and soon a sizeable – and surprisingly coherent – body of

---

This chapter is dedicated to Eric Zakim, with thanks for the countless discussions on musical
degeneracy.

[1] Kalbeck 1990, 336–42.   [2] Adorno 1966, 115n.

[3] Brandes 1905, 1291; Gräner 1905, 437; Brandes 1905, 1293; Gräner 1905, 439, 438. Translations
are my own, except where otherwise noted. See also Messmer 1989.

[4] Shigihara 1990 offers a useful anthology of early responses to *Salome*.

mostly conservative music criticism emerged that diagnosed the ills befalling the patient that was music.

This medical metaphor is no coincidence. A biological, or rather *vitalistic*, model of the musical work and music history informed most critics' observations and conclusions. One of the respondents, Hugo Riemann, spelled out what this debate was really about when he foregrounded the catchphrase of *degeneration* in the debate. This term had been loosely bandied about right from the very outset of the critical responses to the opera, but it was left to Riemann to thematise this term in his polemic 'Degeneration and Regeneration'.[5] Pseudo-scientific terminology was all the rage in turn-of-the-century music criticism, and a scintillating term such as *degeneration*, borrowed as it was from the unholy trinity of nineteenth-century criminal pathology, evolutionary biology and social Darwinism, thrived on overtones of scientific precision – so much so that it seemed unnecessary to define the term in any greater detail. The identification of degenerate elements of music, fantastical as the whole enterprise was, promised the possibility not only of objectively analysing a cultural situation but also appeared to suggest ways to cure music of its ills. We should therefore raise the curtain of *Salome* once again, a century later, to get a sense of how the critical discourse of musical degeneracy was elaborated around that most scandalous of Strauss's operas.

***

But wait. It would not be in the spirit of the culture of degeneracy, characterised as it is by excess, licentiousness and luxuriousness, that we jump into a discussion *in medias res*. What follows is less an analysis of Strauss's score than a reconstruction of the broader discourse of musical degeneracy that will, somewhat self-indulgently, weave in and out of the critical and analytical commentary surrounding Strauss's scandal-ridden opera, behind which, needless to say, Wagner's long and dark shadow always looms large. The battle-cry of 'degeneracy' functions, in many ways, as a conduit metaphor, as a term whose very pronouncement unlocks a certain mode of thinking. The utterance of 'degeneracy' forcefully steers associations in one particular direction and opens up a force field leading irresistibly into the powerful realm of cultural pessimism.

What, then, is cultural degeneracy? The bare-bones history of degeneration can be told relatively swiftly: originally developed as a physiological concept in mid-nineteenth-century France, the medical term

---

[5] Riemann 1908; reprinted in Shigihara 1990, 245–9.

dégénérescence is primarily associated with Bénédict Morel, who was interested in the hereditary qualities of organic abnormalities. In the public imagination this concept soon extended to the larger social body of the nation, mixing it with racial theories, above all Arthur de Gobineau's essay on the inequality of races. Italian criminologist Cesare Lombroso picked up Morel's concept and applied it to his study of hereditary criminality. In Lombroso's hands degeneration became synonymous with 'atavistic regression', the return to a previous evolutionary stage (which, in the context of the nineteenth-century ideology of progress, fed directly into major cultural fears). It was Max Nordau, finally, who transferred the concept entirely to the study of culture in his vastly popular study *Entartung* (1892), dedicated to Lombroso. Nordau's *Entartung*, an international bestseller, was a thundering diatribe, dressed up in scientific garb, against contemporary artistic movements and cultural heroes of the age, including Tolstoy, Ibsen, Nietzsche, Zola and above all Wagner.[6]

For our purposes, degeneracy is best understood as perennial negation, a brightly flashing 'Un-' slapped in front of whatever organic or moral authority one may want to invoke: unnatural, unhealthy, unwholesome, unviable, untenable, untrustworthy, impure, immoral, incorrect, dishonourable, corrupt, contagious, dangerous. It is this slippage that makes the concept so powerful. The epistemological idea on which cultural degeneracy thrives, and which makes this slippage possible, inverts Spinoza's principle of *omnis determinatio negatio est* ('every definition is negation'). No longer does a series of progressive negations lead to one positive definition, but here only the negation – degeneration – is given, encouraging the reader to infer the implied positives. This opens up enormous interpretative scope. In combination with the clear and present danger that is assumed to emanate from degenerate objects or processes, it is not difficult to see how withholding the positive answer while dangling the sensationally toxic negative in front of our eyes (or ears) will lead to the kinds of behaviour psychoanalysts describe as neurotic.

Breathing Life into Music

Before musical scientists could apply their cultural stethoscopes on music's body and pronounce the chilling diagnosis of degeneration over it, indeed, before music could even stretch out on the doctor's examination table, the

---

[6] Pick 1989.

patient first had to have received the kiss of life. This was by no means self-evident, as the notion of music as an organism would have been quite unthinkable before the massive intellectual and social transformations of the 1800s.[7] It fell to the romantic generation to breathe life into music and to endow it with aesthetic autonomy and vital functions in one fell swoop.[8] Like other newly vivified fellow organisms – labour, language and love[9] – this warm and pulsating music became a force to be reckoned with.

The theologically inspired philosopher Karl Christian Friedrich Krause, for one, proclaimed in 1831 that 'music itself is determinate life, and it represents the full life of emotions in its peculiar life, in the life of tones'.[10] Krause was too precise an analytical thinker to let himself get away with the conflation between the two conditions he assigned to music: music was both considered to be the metaphorical analogue of life, and to be a living organism in its own right. As this pesky difference between metaphor and essence, however, hampered the full flourishing of the grand metaphysical systems that the romantics were busy constructing around the idea of music, it quickly fell by the wayside.

Over the last 200 years it has become such an ingrained part of talking about music to think of the history of music as an evolution of musical styles or as a series of works that engender one another in a cogent, indeed necessary succession, that the notion of music not only 'representing life' but 'being life' has created a reality for itself.[11] Even nowadays, while most of us would deny that music has a 'life' in any biologically meaningful sense, far fewer object to historical accounts of music in terms of budding, flourishing, birth, maturity or death.

At the risk of stating the obvious: despite music's newly gained identity as a life-force in its own right, the problem with this 'life' of music is that a composition still had to be created by a composer before it could exist. (Scholars beholden to the Idealist tradition sometimes seem to play down this problem by acknowledging that music's autonomy is only 'relative' and otherwise to ignore the vast consequences of this fact.)[12] Of course, referring to musical creations themselves in humanising terms was common practice. Even in the 1910s, Ferruccio Busoni and Hans Pfitzner still

---

[7] The famous chapter nineteen of Jean-Jacques Rousseau's *Essay on the Origin of Language* – titled 'How music has degenerated' – is a rare exception. See Rousseau 2009.

[8] See, among many others, Chua 1999.   [9] See Foucault 1971.

[10] Krause 1839, 19. The unfinished, posthumously published manuscript was written in 1831 but is based on lectures Krause gave between 1824 and 1829.

[11] For an impressive analysis of evolution and progress in music historical texts, see Allen 1953.

[12] See Dahlhaus 1989.

quibbled about what exactly it meant for music to be described as an 'infant', though no one doubted the veracity of this image.[13] It had become much more than a mere metaphor. But even if one believed, as did Pfitzner, that in his day music had grown up to become a strapping – German – lad, an important difference remained: composers could create musical compositions, which could then live on as autonomous works, but, put bluntly, no musical work has ever been reported giving birth to a composer.

In the context of Darwinism this was actually a serious scholarly discussion. In 1900, Oswald Koller made a sustained attempt to transfer the principles of sexual selection to music history. For him, the musical organism was always 'the product of two factors', effectively its two genetic parents: it carried the general traits of its age, 'style', which Koller gendered as paternal, and the particular traits of its creator, 'individuality', which carried maternal traits.[14] The reason for his gendered choice was that the composer is the 'receptacle' of traditions from generations past, whereas 'present circumstances' constitute the fertilising elements. Koller was aware that these dual influences, one personal and the other historical and interpersonal, were qualitatively different from biological parents. He nonetheless tried to push the simile as far as he possibly could: 'Every new work has a fertilising effect not only for contemporaries and descendants, but also on its creator himself.'[15] We need not buy into Koller's exuberant, and sometimes tortured, attempt to argue away the asymmetry between composer and work, to see how important this biologistic strain of thinking was at the turn of the century.

It was precisely this asymmetry that Krause had originally articulated in his distinction between 'representing life' and 'being life'. The asymmetrical relation between composer-as-creator and work-as-autonomous-organism added an awkward level of complication in the genealogies of musical evolution. The two formed two strands in a lopsided double helix of an evolutionary music history that had a habit of tying themselves in knots which were difficult to disentangle.

∗∗∗

[13] See Busoni 1916. Music is described as a young child starting on p. 7. And see Pfitzner's *Futuristengefahr* (1917), reprinted in H. Pfitzner 1926, 185–223. The image of music as a growing boy is found on p. 193.

[14] Koller 1901, 40. This was hardly a singular occurrence: similar attempts are found in other European contexts, such as in the work of Jules Combarieu in France, and Edmund Gurney in England.

[15] Koller 1901, 41.

In a world where music was a life form, music history had to solve its own chicken-and-egg problem: composer and work became so inextricably joined that music history was running the risk of turning into biography. Few music historians were as clear-sighted as Franz Stoepel, who took the most radical, and admirably logical, step in solving this problem by strictly uncoupling the history of music from that of musicians, presenting both in separate sections of his *Grundzüge der Geschichte der modernen Musik* (1821).[16] More commonly, only one side was foregrounded. Or both were conflated, as Guido Adler prescribed in his foundational methodology for musicology: the purpose of music history is to understand 'the developmental process of music in works and their creators'[17] where all differences between these two aspects are brushed aside.

The problem leading to Adler's indifference can be traced back right to the earliest scholarly music histories written on the continent in the 1830s. The German music historian Raphael Georg Kiesewetter led the way along the road to the great-man history of music. He rejected any division of music history according to world-historical periods, or stylistic periods, in favour of epochs named after outstanding composers, as the 'most natural order', offering 'the most reliable survey'. The composers that gave their name to their age were those who had 'left the greatest imprint on the creation of art and the taste of their contemporaries and ... evidently advanced art to a higher degree of perfection'.[18]

His equally influential Belgian colleague and vociferous opponent François-Joseph Fétis, meanwhile, moved away from the figure of the composer and concentrated on the gradual unfolding of the potential inherent in the scalar material. Fétis recounted his creed: 'I believed ... in one scale given by nature as the basis of all music.'[19] The grand system Fétis had created in his concepts of the progression of stages of tonality, from *unitonique* to *omnitonique*, predicting the completion and demise of tonality was the closest music theory should come to a morphology of music history.

At face value, Fétis and Kiesewetter seem poles apart, and the extensive polemics between them, first and foremost about the nature of tonality, only serve to confirm this impression. (It might be tempting to construe this polarity in terms of differences between Francophone and Germanic cultures, but the Idealist Fétis considered himself intellectually an out-and-out German.)[20] Below the polemical surface, however, the

---

[16] Stoepel 1821.   [17] Adler 1919, 13.   [18] Kiesewetter 1834, 10.   [19] Fétis 1869, 1:i.
[20] See Schelhous 1991.

historiographical basis of each can accommodate the tenets of the other. Kiesewetter in fact also conceived of music as an abstract evolving force shaped by composers, whose principles can be captured by a system of rules. Thus, in Kiesewetter's view, the Greeks had fundamentally misunderstood this system, as they had not understood harmony and polyphony – as a consequence, their 'amiable' musical child was stillborn.[21] And Fétis, whose first major work was, not coincidentally, a *Universal Biography of Musicians* (1835–44), held fast to the belief that each new stage of tonality was ushered in by one great composer: Monteverdi, Mozart and – much to Fétis's annoyance – Berlioz.

The difference between Kiesewetter's biographical and Fétis's structural approaches, then, turns out to be one of degree, or rather of hierarchy: are composers determined (or constrained) by the 'state of the musical material', or do they, conversely, determine (or control) this state? Their answers determined how they viewed the problem of degeneration: as Fétis argued, 'the greatest composers, whose genius was determined by the nature of the harmonic elements that they had at their disposition, could not extract themselves from the rigid despotism of this tonal unity'.[22] Kiesewetter, who in 1834 did not believe that music's time was up yet, would hold against this attitude that 'wherever art decayed, it decayed at the hands of the artist'.[23]

More generally, the dichotomy between Kiesewetter and Fétis represented opposite responses to the problem of understanding the cause and nature of progress. This great blank in the historical understanding in the nineteenth century was usually filled with the figure of the creative genius. No matter what role was assigned to the genius – whether it consisted in being a godlike 'second maker' (Shaftesbury), in giving 'nature's rule to art' (Kant), or in representing the manifestation of the world spirit (Hegel) – the genius was designated the virtually ubiquitous placeholder in art and the history of art.[24] The role of the genius was to bring individual achievement into alignment with the notion of a pre-ordained plan of the whole. However conceived, the concept of the genius managed to fill the gaping hole between the startling phenomenon that some individuals were responsible for historical deeds or new artworks, often in a haphazard and apparently meaningless way, and the comforting thought that (music) history would unfold in a logical underlying progression, even if its course was not always immediately apparent. With this sleight-of-hand, the

---

[21] Kiesewetter 1834, 1.   [22] Fétis 1849, 151.   [23] Kiesewetter 1834, 100.

[24] For a useful survey of the genius concept, see Schmidt 1985.

contention that music 'represented life' (was a creation) and simultaneously 'was life' (was a creature, an organism) in its own right, convinced generations of musical thinkers at all levels.

By means of the genius, then, the awkward problem of music's compromised autogenetic prowess – its 'relative autonomy' – could be solved in an elegant way: the composer would become something that was both mother and midwife in a creative process that was at liberty to transgress certain rules with impunity. If lesser spirits were to commit them, these transgressions would have to be considered offences, but the genius was a seal of approval, vouchsafing compliance with the dictates of nature or history. Appealing to the genius implied no less than a leap of faith across this divide between 'representing life' and 'being life'.

***

The genius was designated to close this epistemological gap: he would create innovative works, it was asserted, of unprecedented exemplary quality.[25] As these works followed the exigencies of nature, their startling newness notwithstanding, the succession of these works would constitute a cogent historical narrative describing the gradual and inevitable evolution of music. Thus the unity of individual aesthetic value and general historical narrative could be preserved seamlessly. In this way, the genius and his works would simultaneously reaffirm a whole string of idealist beliefs: the equation between beauty and truth, progress and perfection, and ultimately the meaning of history as a succession of autonomous artworks.

The admiration the genius elicited from the masses or posterity was taken as the token of the unimpeachable moral quality of these works, and the educational value of a history constituted of such works. But what if the genius was not the shining beacon he was thought to be? The free rein the genius had been granted came under increasing scrutiny, as these idealist certainties fell apart in the nineteenth century. Scepticism was not unwarranted: if direct knowledge of the workings of nature or history was foreclosed to lesser individuals, that is, most of us, how could one know that the genius was not leading us astray? The story of degeneration in music can be understood as an expression of this suspicion.

Immanuel Kant wrote a note of caution into his influential reflections on genius: 'But since [the genius] also can produce original nonsense, its products must be models, i.e. exemplary; and they consequently ought

---

[25] I consciously use masculine pronouns for the genius. See Battersby 1989.

not to spring from imitation, but must serve as a standard or rule of judgment for others.'[26] Kant was blithely unconcerned about the wider ramifications of this point; for him the problem of nonsense was a closed system in its own right: nonsense would be recognised either by not being original or, retroactively, by its inability to have given 'nature's rule to art' – that is, nonsense would not function as a model and would not produce artistic progeny. The proof, for Kant, was in the pudding, and the problem of nonsense would automatically take care of itself.

Later commentators, by contrast, were not convinced that original nonsense could never become a model. This thought would become one of the main fears within the discourse of degeneracy: What if art was following false idols, and unknowingly strayed from the path of *good* art? How would we even know we are on the right track? What is the difference between good, 'healthy' originality, and nonsensical innovation? As we will see, a number of critics of degeneration would invest a lot of energy trying to find ways to discriminate between true geniuses and false idols.

Insofar as the discourse of musical degeneration never questions the 'life' of music (and could not possibly do so) it partakes of the very idealist convictions that it claims to examine with scientific impartiality. It is here that we return to our dual approach to the phenomenon of degeneration as, on the one hand, the attempt to elevate cultural pessimism onto a scientific pedestal, and on the other, a fictionalisation of science in the service of upholding these cherished idealist values. No matter what biological model we discover underlying approaches to degeneration, and no matter what intellectual expressions we determine as requirements – physiognomy, Spencerianism, etc. – the constant factor between all of them is the conviction that some invisible underlying state of culture can be read out of artistic products. The signs of artistic decay are invariably read as symptoms of something much bigger. The relation between the composer and his creation is central to this concern, as we shall see, and it determines the way in which degeneration is imagined.

In the following, we will explore three of these main lines in which musical degeneration has been imagined, using Strauss's *Salome* as a reference point. First, if the work of art is imagined as a fully autonomous entity that exists independently of its creator and creates its own historical trajectory then degeneration may set in with a fault in the 'genetic code' of the work of music. The consequences, the argument continues, will be felt

---

[26] See also Lewis 2005.

in subsequent generations if the evolution of such work strays away from a healthy development and leads in the wrong direction. (Underlying this construction is invariably a tacit conviction that a 'right' direction exists.) Second, if the individual work of art is considered as a vehicle of moral and sensuous pleasure, the main point of concern becomes the relationship between surface and deep structure. The sensuous, sounding surface – stimulating the nerves – was often seen as a danger to the spiritual content of the work of art. Not only was the composition believed to reflect the nervous disposition of the composer, but it could also gravely affect the nervous state of its listeners. And third, we will return to the figure of the genius as a surface onto which cultural fears and aspirations were projected.

All this invests a metaphor with great power. If we have to appeal to the laws of literature in order to understand the full power of the discourse of degeneration, then its force is driven by the search for closure, the quest for an ending – ideally one that is in consonance with the kind of life that music had been assigned in the first place. For all its scientific posturing, the discourse of degeneration is ultimately about the force of narrative. And the tales we hear are inescapably moralising.

Evolutionary Models

The vehement critical reaction Strauss's *Salome* elicited is useful from our perspective, as it brings out the tacit critical assumptions and pedigreed critical dogmas more clearly than in any other musical work of the time. Both supporters and detractors of *Salome* were caught up in the nine-teenth-century doctrine of organicism, in which nature metaphors abound. One enthusiastic critic of the premiere compared the opera with a 'flower of the rarest, erotic kind'. He emphasised that this 'erotic flower,' like the opera itself, was a 'product of *nature*'.[27] (Intriguingly, others mis-read the extravagant image as 'exotic flower'.) Most other critics disagreed. Granted that *Salome* was a product of nature, it was a musical organism gone wrong:

That which blossoms and grows in the artist through nature's touch, organises itself according to a peculiar law, emerging together with the embryo of the work of art, is a product of nature, almost without any human contribution. The science of harmony, of counterpoint, the entire theory of composition exhausts itself in the

---

[27] Hermann Boehringer, cited in Messmer 1989, 45.

Unsound Seeds 313

focus of artistic creation and even in the slower work of elaborating, the artistic idea imperceptibly flows back together with nature. And nature never repeats itself.[28]

If there is such a 'peculiar law' in music, where is its embryonic seed located? Musical thinkers were divided between the three principal elements of music: melody, rhythm and harmony. A. B. Marx, Ernst Kurth and Jean-Jacques Rousseau, albeit coming from very different perspectives, would all appeal to the emotional force of melody. Krause, whom we encountered earlier, found himself in the diverse company of Margaret Glyn and Friedrich Schelling in choosing rhythm as music's heartbeat.[29] Harmony, finally, with its traditional associations with physics, was harder to add to music's biological functions, but it came to play a vital role nonetheless, particularly when it came to explaining evolutionary models of music.[30]

Before we return to *Salome*'s exotic-erotic flower, let us explore a little further how the element of harmony was construed to unfold historically. A favourite demonstration, something of a learned musical parlour game, was the evolution of the *Tristan* chord.[31] Donald Tovey, for instance, identified the origin of *Tristan*'s opening, shown in Figure 14.1, as a half-cadence with modal bent, as it might have been written during the sixteenth century, and showed how the music evolves following a route towards elaboration, cogently tracing the rules of voice-leading.

Tovey identified this development as an evolution from simple harmonic progressions to advanced chromatic passages. This evolution is an elaboration toward ever more intricate musical structures laid out over an imagined chronology. It is tempting to imagine this entirely hypothetical model as the musicological equivalent of Ernst Haeckel's visually stunning, and scientifically dubious, parallel tables of human evolution (see Figure 14.2), where the developmental stages of embryos from different species are juxtaposed, suggesting that their early stages are virtually indistinguishable from one another, only gradually evolving into their characteristic shape.

All this is in support of Haeckel's highly influential and irresistibly romantic thesis that ontogeny replicates phylogeny, that 'the history of

---

[28] Karl Schmalz, 'Annus Confusionis. Eine Trilogie', in Shigihara 1990, 282. The quotation is a passage by the music critic Paul Marsop.

[29] A. B. Marx 1884, 443; Krause 1839, 169; Glyn 1909.

[30] For some pathos-ridden rhetoric see Heller 1930, 14.

[31] Tovey [1911] 1944, 68. For another model see Schering [1935] 1941, 132.

314 ALEXANDER REHDING

Evolution of the opening of Wagner's Prelude to *Tristan und Isolde*

Ex. 19 — Three concords (tonic, first inversion of subdominant, and dominant of A minor, a possible 16th-century cadence in the Phrygian mode)

Ex. 20 — The same chords varied by a suspension (*)

Ex. 21 — Ditto, with the further addition of a double suspension (*) and two passing notes (††)

Ex. 22 — Ditto, with a chromatic alteration of the second chord (*) and an 'essential' discord (dominant 7th) at (†)

Ex. 23 — Ditto, with chromatic passing notes (**) and appoggiaturas (††)

Ex. 24 — The last two chords of Ex. 23 attacked unexpectedly, the first appoggiatura (*) prolonged till it seems to make a strange foreign chord before it resolves on the short note at ♯, while the second appoggiatura (†) is chromatic.

Ex. 25 — The same enharmonically transformed so as to become a variation of the 'dominant ninth' of C minor. The G♯ at * is really A♭, and ♯ is no longer a note of resolution, but a chromatic passing note.

Figure 14.1 Tovey's evolutionary model of music, from a modal turn of phrase to the *Tristan* chord, from 'Harmony', *Encyclopaedia Britannica* (1911).

Unsound Seeds 315

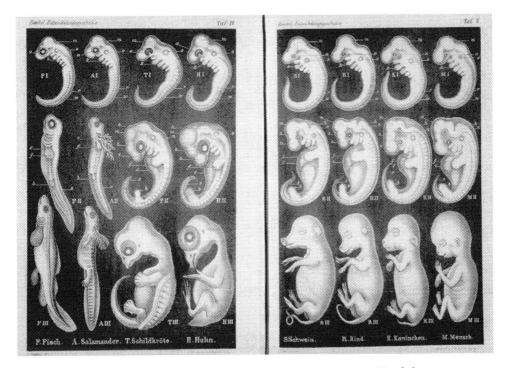

Figure 14.2 Parallel evolution of embryos from various species. From Ernst Haeckel, *Anthropogenie* (1874), table iv/v.

the individual is the abbreviated history of the species'. He declared that the embryonic stages of higher-evolved species correspond to the former fully developed stages of its ancestral species – in other words, that each individual has to undergo a fast-forwarded summary of the entire history of evolution.[32]

Tovey's model also carried the same evolutionary idea with it, where each apparently historical stage in the evolution towards the *Tristan* chord represents one stepping stone which carries all the previous stages in itself and is in turn superseded by a more complex manifestation. Putting his organicist cards on the table, Tovey explains his ambition to show that the laws of harmony 'are true to the nature of art and are no mere rules of a game'.[33] On one level, such evolutionary tables could be seen as exemplifications of the principle with which Adler began his programmatic exposition of a stylistic history of music:

---

[32] See Gould 1977, 1981. [33] Tovey 1944, 44.

The development of musical art is organic. In continuous succession one evolutionary moment links up with the next to bring the organism to completion. The individual phenomena can be viewed from different perspectives. For the purpose of historical depiction, that which shows the phenomena in their temporal succession offers the most readily intelligible perspective.[34]

The unilinearity from one historical level to the next suggested in these constructs makes an impressive plea – visually more so than aurally – for the organic evolution of the chromatic harmony of *Tristan*. The *Tristan* chord is shown to carry within it the whole history of Western harmony from humble beginnings to its most complex flowering. In this representation nothing appears illogical, wilfully contrived or artificial – it follows in a stringent progression.

The *Tristan* chord is, of course, not just any chord. This enigmatic harmonic–contrapuntal complex stood emblematically for the pinnacle of musical modernity – or the beginning of the end of harmonic tonality.[35] While not explicitly claimed by either author, it is almost impossible not to read such an evolutionary table as a powerful visual argument against the widespread assertions that Wagner's music constituted the main degenerative force in late nineteenth-century culture.[36] As if to liberate Wagner's music from the taint of *fin-de-siècle* decadence, Tovey added mischievously that Wagner's sense of key was no different from Beethoven's (whose vigour and 'health' was never in any doubt), except carried out on a broader temporal span.

As far as stylistic history is concerned, however, Tovey's idea of evolution is distinctly dubious. The actual argument presented here lies in the continuity and cogency suggested in the presentation. The historical trajectory providing the explanatory logic for Wagner's famous opening bars is clearly constructed backwards, beginning with the *Tristan* opening, not culminating in it. After all, only by means of this teleology can the historical narration protect the work against accusations of degeneration, real or imaginary. Like Haeckel's example, the evolutionary progression from modal polyphony towards *Tristan* is nothing but a theoretical systematisation spread out over quasi-historical instantiations, amounting to an arbitrary succession of stylistic stages. Likewise, the assumed succession of musical styles, progressing towards ever-clearer distinction and individuality, and culminating and concentrating in a single work is a

---

[34] Adler 1880, col. 690.   [35] Kurth 1920.

[36] A wonderful example is Edmund Gurney's vividly synaesthetic description of *Tristan* in 'Wagner and Wagnerism', in *Tertium Quid* (1899), 2:19. See also Kennaway 2012a.

questionable historiographical assumption, albeit one that perfectly replicates the basic idea of ontogeny-as-phylogeny. In this way, the organic work of art functions as both a representative of a distinct style and as an autonomous living organism in its own right.

***

Unfortunately for Strauss, his critics felt that none of this applied to *Salome*. According to organicist dogma, it was nature that warranted the character of art, and in so doing nature set absolute limitations to art. The ways in which nature apparently indicated these limitations reflected the staples of nineteenth-century music theory: according to the critics, nature constituted itself variously in the harmonic series, in closed forms, in the rules of counterpoint, or indeed in the healthy sentiment of the nation.[37] And Strauss seemed to fall foul of all these authorities in some respect.

The problem was identified in his colourful orchestration, his overly refined handling of timbre, and ultimately his provenance from the dreaded genre of programme music:

The combination of instrumental colours went hand in hand with the dissolution of form. And colour without form?! Perhaps the germ of such sudden decay must be sought in this untenable state [i.e. the impossibility of colours to hold up without form]. In any case, the germ of decay was that one began alienating autonomous music from its very own primordial essence . . . Nothing good could come of this.[38]

If the very own *Ur*-essence of music resided in autonomous forms, then this musical essence was denied by Strauss's composition. However, another aspect is implied in this critic's assessment of the situation: when he uses the organicist metaphor of 'the germ of decay' he adds a historical dimension to the argument. The germ is not merely the musical idea but an expression of cultural pessimism. What is at stake is no less than the future of music. From this angle, programmatic elements that Strauss composed out in his score – such as the initial rustling of the rising curtain – become signs of the Decline of the West.

Draeseke went one step further: in *Salome* 'there are moments that cannot be explained in purely musical terms and that I therefore cannot assess as music'.[39] Strauss had committed the cardinal sin of overstepping the boundaries of what was considered music. A particular thorn in the critics' side was the double-bass solo during Jochanaan's off-stage

---

[37] Arno Kleffel, 'Ueber Konfusion in der Musik', in Shigihara 1990, 145; P. Pfitzner 1905, 903.

[38] Schmalz, in Shigihara 1990, 286.

[39] Felix Draeseke, 'Offene Antwort an Richard Strauß', in Shigihara 1990, 173.

execution. Strauss's performance instruction indicates: 'Instead of pressing down [the string], this tone is to be played by tightly holding the string between thumb and index finger; a short sharp attack with the bow so as to create a sound that resembles the suppressed sighing and moaning of a woman.'[40] Zooming in on this moment, one critic commented sarcastically:

So that's what all the fuss is about. If this entire development began by creating means and forms that were adequate to great contents, then it ended by characterising possible and impossible things: in particular, music became more and more characteristic, until it comprised the ugly and the sick . . . – and lost its character altogether.[41]

Here again, degeneration of a purported musical essence is telescoped into the historical dimension, heralding the end of music at large. The problem of degeneration is, on one level, one of musical progress-as-procreation. Here the metaphors of reproduction that abound in the debate – 'erotic flower', 'germ cell', 'embryo' – come to full effect: after all, it is sex that is at the core of the opera.

Non-reproductive sex, to be specific: Herod's lust for his step-daughter, Herodias' sublimated desire for power, Salome's necrophilia, Narraboth's masochistic longing for Salome, the little page's homosexual feelings for Narraboth. And behind all this, as the more reactionary critics eagerly reminded their readers, lay the sexual perversion of playwright Oscar Wilde.[42] No surprise, then, that sexual reproduction was seen as a danger – or as an opportunity – in the critical responses to *Salome*. Ferruccio Busoni made this genealogical thought more explicit than anyone else, albeit in unreservedly positive terms:

In art everything changes step by step. With this *Salome* such a step may have been taken on the top of other manifestations which will hurry on to the ascent of a new and higher step. Every son has the stuff of his ancestors in him – by his side flourish a hundred other species.[43]

What Busoni celebrated here encapsulated the worst fears of the detractors of *Salome*, for it might indeed herald no less than the end of music – at least a music that works on the basis of triads and counterpoint and complies with the 'healthy sentiment of the nation'. Added to these limitations set by nature are those from Idealist aesthetics:

---

[40] Strauss 2009, 294.   [41] Schmalz, in Shigihara 1990, 285.
[42] See for instance, Adam Röder, quoted in Puffett 1989, 133.   [43] Busoni in Puffett 1989, 140.

Topics of a more or less explicitly sexual nature are nothing unusual in modern art but rather tend to represent the norm. The limitations should not be set by moral but by artistic interests. Sex may well find its place in rustic anecdotes and cheap novels, in the variety show – as much as is allowed by the police, this has nothing to do with art. From the artist, however, we demand the highest sensitivity – not out of prudishness but for the sake of art itself. One loves to talk about modern liberated art, which does not close off anything human or natural. Nothing may be closed off but it closes itself off from anything that cannot be spiritualised, anything that remains animalistic. Schiller – who will surely be a philistine for the new composers of decadence – demarcates this boundary by calling on the artists: 'The dignity of humankind is laid in your hands. It is yours to preserve!'[44]

This critic spelled out what others assumed tacitly: the categories on which *Salome* was assessed are ultimately derived from German Idealism. While in German philosophy the unity of goodness, truth and beauty had come under suspicion at least since Nietzsche, this dubious triumvirate still ruled strong in the field of music criticism (or was invoked when it seemed convenient). Even though this Idealism had acquired a distinct Darwinian tinge in the later nineteenth century, it was on the basis of this surviving Idealism that several critics made a direct connection between the ethical import of the work and its technical features.

***

Let's take a step back from Strauss's *Salome* again, to consider the wider implications. For the conclusion that Strauss had somehow overstepped a mark and had turned 'good' progress into 'bad' degeneration is, of course, an arbitrary decision. Busoni's glowing assessment has no greater or lesser validity than the abject dismissal of the conservative critics, and the moral dimension attached to their aesthetic judgment is, at bottom, just as metaphorical – just as meaningful or meaningless – as the evolutionary trajectory critics drew to bolster their respective positions.

For an object like music, whose commentators steadfastly refuse to decide whether it 'represents' life or 'is' life, the imagined processes of evolution, based on graphic chains of metamorphoses, need not in principle continue in one direction only. Even the nineteenth century itself, though overawed by the idea of evolution, knew that such graphic evidence could easily be manipulated. The French caricaturist J. J. Grandville latched

---

[44] Georg Göhler, 'Richard Strauß', in Shigihara 1990, 212.

Figure 14.3 J. J. Grandville, 'L'homme descend vers le brute', *Magasin pittoresque* 14 (1843), p. 108.

on to the reversibility of these images, showing (Figure 14.3), how the developmental chains could overshoot the goal and go the other way: from a child, via the adult stage, and gradually metamorphose into an ape-like brute in chains.[45] It is difficult to tell whether Grandville is making a commentary on social decline or physiological degeneration, but in nineteenth-century French discourse, as Daniel Pick has shown, the differences were negligible.[46] The graphic evidence documents this process of degeneration with equally compelling force as Tovey showed musical progress as a forward-propelled process.

Musical degeneration is always based on an interpretative act. The paradigmatic trajectory of organic process describes a succession of germination, flourishing and decay. Always interested in endings, degeneration does not accept the period of decay as an inevitable part of this trajectory but regards it as irreconcilable with the mantra of progress – 'up and up and up, and on and on and on'[47] – and treats it as the symptom of a disease that has befallen the organism.

This idea of identifying a turning point beyond which history cannot progress is at the heart of the discourse of musical degeneracy. No one has put this thought more concisely than the music historian August Wilhelm Ambros, who was the first to assign the composers of the 'New German School', Wagner and Liszt, a place in history in 1860:

---

[45] See Blindman 2002.   [46] Pick 1989, 37–44.   [47] Pick 1989, 13.

The direction of these artists memorably signifies the point toward which historical evolution has moved music at large. Of course, excessive rigour in follow-up efforts will lead to doom, and in any development there is a certain point, which is its actual, true 'point of life', beyond which any further development turns into *degeneration*, and will eventually fall into the abyss of aimlessness.[48]

The art of the music-historian-as-diagnostician was to identify this turning point in history, when progress turns into degeneration, and to establish criteria on the basis of which such pronouncements can be made authoritatively. There was little dispute about the existence of such a turning point, but it was much harder to gain consensus on the moment when this turning point was reached – and why.

The basis on which this music is judged as degenerate (or, conversely, as 'healthy') is much more difficult to determine. Most arguments hark back to a simpler age when, as in the eighteenth century, aesthetics could draw on a *sensus communis* and a unified, authoritative notion of taste, and before evolutionary thought introduced a stringent historical dimension into musical thinking. Eighteenth-century aestheticians availed themselves of a notion of 'correct music' that could become the normative basis of judgment.[49] In the nineteenth century, however, such consensus was much harder to achieve, and democratic tendencies were often blamed for the disintegration of taste. As a consequence, the rhetorical volume had to be cranked up to retain an authoritative sense of unity in matters of taste.

For example, the respected Italian physiologist Paolo Mantegazza turned his medical authority to a blistering cultural critique in which he argued that there can be no debate over matters of taste. For him, this was not a question of opinion, taste, aesthetics or even physiology, but of plain pathology:

Whoever loves the baroque and confuses it with the sublime, whoever seeks out the grotesque and considers it to be great, whoever cannot separate the ornate from the graceful, the common from the plain, the new from the beautiful – this person is a degenerate, a mentally sick man, his aesthetic sense is diseased.[50]

This abject condemnation was brought about by the abomination of a woman combining a green dress with a yellow scarf. With the benefit of hindsight, the stern health warnings of Mantegazza and other men of science can merely seem like a historical and hysterical curiosity, but we do well not to dismiss these questionable pronouncements too lightly. Learned men pronounced apparently eternal truths from the bully pulpit

---

[48] Ambros 1860, 174.   [49] See Hentschel 2006.   [50] Mantegazza 1891, 135.

of science in a world that appeared to be changing all too rapidly and to be leaving behind any sense of stable common ground. For some, at any rate, there was considerable comfort to be gained from hearing that there was an absolute and non-negotiable line between good and bad, sublime and baroque, ornate and graceful, or right and wrong – particularly if it was couched in the clearly marked terms of sickness and health.

The danger of cultural degeneracy always lay in its contagious effects. Its excess could hardly be contained and always threatened to spill over into other areas: from music into noise, from one work into a whole historical trajectory, and from sound into amorality. What was at stake was always the stability of the (implied) definition of the good, true and beautiful. By the late nineteenth century it was hardly possible to define these in positive terms, but they could still be captured negatively – or so it seemed – as degenerate deviations from these implied positives that would in this way define and circumscribe that which was asserted to be self-evidently and emphatically normal. But how would unassuming listeners protect themselves from the dangerous effects of such degenerate music?

Pathogenic Sonorities

The discourse of degeneracy is complicated by the fact that there is another dimension cutting across the (quasi-)temporal axis of the evolutionary models we just examined. The evolutionary chains are often not merely to be read diachronically, as developmental chains that unfold (and inescapably decline) over time, but also 'in depth'. This second axis is based on the belief that appearance can provide important insights into underlying ethical qualities. We already saw this in the invocation of Schiller's artistic ideals, forging connections between sounding surface and underlying morals. This idea of the unity of the beautiful and the good – often called *kalokagathia* – was revived in the eighteenth century, particularly by the Earl of Shaftesbury, and it was eagerly adopted by other scholars, most famously the physiognomist Johann Kaspar Lavater.

Physiognomy concerned itself with the interpretation of physical features in terms of its relation to the underlying moral character. Lavater was well known for another brand of developmental chains that bear some resemblance to the later evolutionary models of Haeckel and his colleagues, and no less visually stunning than those, though they actually signified something rather different. Take Lavater's famous transformation from a frog to Apollo

Unsound Seeds   323

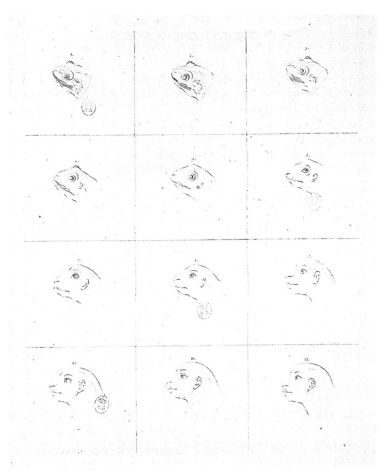

Figure 14.4a Johann Kasper Lavater, *Physiognomische Fragmente* (1775–78), [Vom Frosch zum Apollo Belvedere], Tables LXXVIII/LXXIX. Image used courtesy of Bibliothèque nationale de France.

in Figure 14.4a, as an imagined spectrum from the very ugly to the epitome of perfect beauty. These kinds of chains were closer in outlook to the medieval *scala naturae*, the immutable hierarchy of the Great Chain of Being, than to any evolutionary process, and they served as an illustration of the various levels of moral standing that are attainable by various creatures.

In the context of a culture, however, that became obsessed with evolutionary biology, or rather its popular reception, a parallel reading of these images with the diachronic evolutionary tables was almost invariably imposed. Grandville, for one, irreverently inverted the image (Figure 14.4b), in exactly the same way he had prognosticated

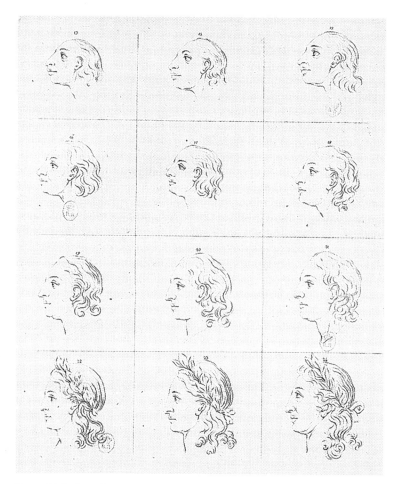

Figure 14.4a (cont.)

the degenerative evolution from human to ape, suggesting a parallelism between these two very different kinds of evolutions. By turning the succession back to front, his caricature exposes the merely visual appeal on which the supposed coherence hinges in such chains of images. And of course, the discourse of degeneration conflated precisely the temporal dimensions of evolution and the 'depth' dimension of an underlying morality that could apparently be read out of anatomical features.

The circle around Italian criminologist Cesare Lombroso, much-revered dedicatee of Max Nordau's *Entartung*, gained fame and notoriety for their large-scale quantitative studies measuring facial features of criminals and comparing them with those of law-abiding – emphatically 'normal' – citizens in order to gauge whether physiological abnormalities could serve as

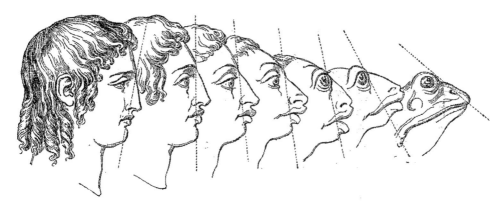

Figure 14.4b J. J. Grandville, [L'homme descend vers la grenouille], *Magasin pittoresque* 15 (1844), p. 272.

predictors for socially abnormal and criminal behaviour. It would be wrong to assume that the discourse of degeneration simply inverted the idea of *kalokagathia* and posited that the ugly was coterminous with the morally repugnant – things were never *that* straightforward. Rather, Lombroso sought to prove that there is one model of anatomical normalcy and that any deviations from this normal standard would signify underlying flaws of character.

A firm believer in the ontology-replicates-phylogeny parallelism, Lombroso argued that anomalous physiological features were not markers of disease or hereditary traits, but rather signs of 'atavism,' a regression to an earlier stage in our evolutionary past. With the word 'stigmata', which Lombroso used to refer to these physiological atavisms, he chose an etymologically correct but culturally loaded term.[51] These stigmata linked modern humans with their developmental ancestors – and here the idea of ontogeny-replicates-phylogeny allowed Lombroso to freely lump together apes, savages and children. As the stigmata gave visible proof that these individuals had reverted to earlier evolutionary – less civilised – stages, it seemed self-evident that they would have regressed in their social behaviour as well. Following this logic, the deviations from anatomical normalcy could thus help scientists to read an innate propensity toward crime and antisocial behaviour out of the physiological make-up of individuals afflicted with such stigmata. In the words of Stephen Jay Gould, Lombroso's 'born criminal pursues his destructive ways because he is, literally, a savage in our midst – and we can recognise him because he carries the morphological signs of an apish past'.[52]

---

[51] Lombroso 2006.   [52] Gould 1977, 120.

In the field of music, especially non-representational music, the connections between moral comportment, anatomy and heredity were somewhat less straightforward – largely because the double notion of music 'as life' and 'representing life' made concepts of evolution and heredity more complicated. Only few musicians made attempts to transfer an explicit notion of 'atavism' to the realm of music history.[53] But this did not deter scholars from observing the musical surface very closely to get a clearer view of what lurked behind it.

∗∗

What had been conceptualised in the evolutionary models as a process of decline unfolding in the diachronic domain was being reconfigured in this discourse into the synchronic dimension of depth and surface. Criticism was expected to look behind the sounding surface and to penetrate the deep structure of the musical work. In Kurth's immortal words: 'The gaze into music is veiled by sounds.'[54] The 'correctness' of the music was judged according to that which did not simply meet the ear.

The idea that composers were fascinated by the surface of music, which would somehow constitute a danger, was widespread among *fin-de-siècle* music critics and aestheticians. The general consensus was that a focus on the surface, a process of externalisation, obscured the deep structure of the music and, more broadly, that the sensuous features of music might take over from the deep intellectual pursuit that characterised particularly the tradition of instrumental music.[55]

Even where there was no explicit concept of a Schenkerian *Ursatz*, musical and cultural critics saw certain dangers emanating from too much focus on the sounding surface. The sensuous dimension of orchestration, which had stubbornly resisted structural analysis throughout the nineteenth century, was a central concern in this respect. The idea that instrumental timbre might be used to paper over structural flaws was widely accepted. Kurth, the first music theorist to analyse Strauss's *Salome*, argued that 'considerable mollification of the harshnesses [of harmonic clashes] is always found in the instrumentation'.[56]

Some critics saw a genuine threat emanating from instrumental sounds:

---

[53] See for instance, Koller 1901, 42.   [54] Kurth 1920, 3.   [55] See Watkins 2011.
[56] Kurth 1920, 136.

The study of instrumental sounds belongs in the chapter of musical stimuli, that is, based on their effects on the nervous system. This can, under certain circumstances, attain a degree that the stimulus becomes pathological. In more recent times especially, pathological stimuli play a major part in music, and there is many an artist who works with instrumentation almost exclusively.[57]

Some critics prescribed sonically 'neutral' piano arrangements to spare overly sensitive nerves. In this line of thought, the purest music is silence, unencumbered by sounds.

The idea that instrumental sounds are somehow 'pathological' resonated with music critics of the earlier nineteenth century, and was famously highlighted by Eduard Hanslick.[58] 'Pathological' listening wallows in sounds and excites the nerves. He set up his own strategy of formal appreciation of musical works in sharp opposition to the 'pathological listening' which reacted to the glittering acoustical surface of musical works, ignoring the underlying structural features. Hanslick's example shows as well that the criticism of 'pathological' music is not only focused on the relationship between the genius composer and musical evolution, but expands the circle of influence to the relationship between music and listener.

∗

The term 'pathological' is not randomly chosen: it allows, on the one hand, a connection to the scientific advances of musical perception, and on the other, it raises the frightful possibility of music no longer appealing to traditional 'ethos' (character), but instead attaching itself to 'pathos' (experience).[59] In other words, music would no longer be a spiritual force, as especially idealists had demanded, but rather a force that worked directly on the body.

In the final analysis, the squeamishness about the sensuous surface of music leads us back down the road to sensuousness and eroticism. The attitude of the Victorian period toward sexuality is famously complex. The Darwinian line that was promoted in certain circles about the function of music in sexual selection did not help those who felt uncomfortable with the sensuous dimension of music. Darwin himself had

---

[57] Schaeffer 1877, 8.

[58] For instance, in his *Vorlesungen über Musik* (1826), Hans Georg Nägeli suggests performing symphonies as piano duets to prevent sensual stimuli from impinging too much on the perception of music. See Sponheuer 1987, 173.

[59] See, for instance, Painter 1995, 238.

suggested, based on his speculations on birdsong, that music was an important part of rituals of sexual attraction. Koller, the most outspoken Darwinian among the musicologists, applied this idea more rigorously than anyone:

> In the competition for females it is not only the strongest males that remain victorious but also those that stand out over and above all other competitors on account of exceptionally decorative colours, plumage, song, etc. The parallel in music, it seems, is the observation that here, too, the splendour of the exterior means of expression, in the form of virtuosity, catchy instrumentation, new surprising effects, etc. is continuously augmented and intensified.[60]

Koller argued that this principle of 'sexual selection' in the musical domain was responsible for a natural tendency toward progressively coarsening audience tastes. But here Koller followed Spencer rather than Darwin: according to the latter's musical rule of the 'survival of the fittest', compositions lacking in splendour and appeal would 'die out' by no longer gaining favour with audiences and eventually not being performed.

Koller came close to naturalising market capitalism in the concert hall. His cheerful Spencerianism is perhaps an indication of anti-elitist, democratic tendencies inherent in his thought. How valid these are in practice is another question, as Koller seems to imagine audiences as unsusceptible to manipulation. However, his optimism seems wilfully to repress a problem that loomed large in more pessimistic commentators' minds: the lowering of standards to please audiences, in the service of a musical kind of sexual selection. More sensual music leads down the road of immediate sensual effects without reflection.

In this respect, Strauss's orchestral technique was deemed particularly suspicious, as it threatened to supplant the intelligibility of the formal aspects of his music. For one critic, this has grave consequences:

> The iridescent beauty of the orchestra is admirable but its incapability of creating a single fully shaped musical idea from this chaos of colours is deplorable ... The only thing we do not get is redeeming melody, redeeming music. From the rotting vaults of the drama this shapeless windy music blows up dust and dirt that cause the listener to suffocate.[61]

As seen before, beauty – and any ensuing ethical qualities – are bound up with form. Strauss's orchestral counterpoint particularly arouses suspicion:

---

[60] Koller 1901, 48.   [61] Gräner 1905, 438.

The reckless brutalities of the contrapuntal voice-leading, in strange opposition to the refined, sophisticated instrumentation, the contorted progressions, the frequent use of melodically vacuous passages and trills, the merely external, sensual, splendid [but] screaming orchestral colours: all these feature in Strauss's compositions bear witness to a disturbed psychological state, which has lost a sense of the true beauty of clear, pure form and controlled power within bounds.[62]

Other critics harboured the same fears that counterpoint and orchestration might team up against musical form. Some responded by charging ahead and denying Strauss any artistic qualities:

This kind of contrapuntal work is child's play. The fact that Strauss immediately becomes banal whenever, for the sake of contrast, he works without it, confirms the suspicion that this bold technique is only needed, out of embarrassment, as a shroud to cover up his lack of invention.[63]

Even though Strauss's technique was supposedly mere child's play, it took another seven years before anyone seriously engaged analytically with the music. Kurth provided the theoretical framework in which harmony, counterpoint and orchestration were brought together in forever historically changing constellations.

Kurth's concept of 'disalteration' suggests that a pitch in a triad is chromatically altered in two different ways simultaneously. From this perspective, shown in Figure 14.5, the opening gesture, with the sweeping clarinet run over a non-standard exoticist scale, becomes a simple C♮-minor plagal cadence, with the F♮-minor subdominant disaltered to comprise D and C♮. It *sounds* like a non-functional dominant-seventh chord in second inversion but its actual function would be veiled by this disalteration. Likewise, bar 3 becomes a sustained C♮-minor chord with a doubly-altered fifth (A and G♮). By this means, Kurth's analysis lifts 'the shroud that covers up' the opening passage.

Kurth recognised that disalteration bore within it the seed of the destruction of tonality. In the most extreme case, from Schoenberg's *Harmonielehre*, a dominant ninth chord can simply be 'disaltered' into a whole-note scale. Kurth explored how disaltered chords shift the focus away from harmonies towards voice-leading, from the vertical to the horizontal dimension. The voice-leading from disaltered chord to disaltered chord was often associated with harsh clashes but, as Kurth assured his readers, these contrapuntal harshnesses were mollified by means of orchestration. Put more ominously, Strauss's luscious, beguiling orchestration would function as the veil that

---

[62] Gräner 1905, 436–7.   [63] Göhler, 'Richard Strauß', in Shigihara 1990, 216.

Denkt man sich in der einfachen Kadenz:

im fis-Akkord die Quinte Cis disalteriert, so resultiert:

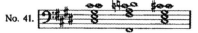

Eine dieser Kadenz zugehörige Skala:

ergibt den melodisch höchst interessanten Klarinettenlauf des 1. Taktes. Im nächstfolgenden Takte wird unter dem in den Streichern tremolierten Cis-moll-Akkord der Ton Gis chromatisch umspielt, ohne selbst nochmals angeschlagen zu werden, die Harmonie, auf der das Motiv ruht, ist also Cismoll mit disalterierter Quinte. Analog ist der in Quintolen geschriebene Lauf des nächsten Taktes über der Akkordfolge:

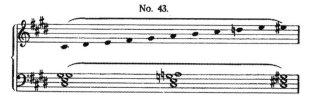

Figure 14.5 Ernst Kurth's analysis of the opening bars of *Salome*, from *Die Voraussetzungen der theoretischen Harmonik* (1913), p. 138.

rendered inaudible the degeneration that had found its way into the harmonic and contrapuntal structures of his music.

***

We cannot know whether Kurth's principle of 'disalteration' in fact offered the music-theoretical representation, the technical basis of degeneration, that the critics in the wake of Draeseke's polemic had imagined, or indeed whether his notion of 'disalteration' is really the altered gene that causes the musical embryo to go astray from form, beauty and morality. Kurth refrained from engaging in the kind of cultural criticism that had surrounded the opera just a few years previously. (Schoenberg's extended tonality, by contrast, was regarded as another harbinger of doom.) However, Kurth's explanations *do* provide a model that goes a long way to tying together various threads (or threats) that were articulated somewhat sketchily in the responses to Strauss's *Salome*. Kurth's developmental history of musical parameters – which, significantly, was devoid of any of the pessimistic outlook that characterised the critical discourse around *Salome* – helps us understand why Strauss's rich orchestration and his programmatic proclivities were regarded with such horror in the critical context of organicism. Put polemically, if skilful orchestration could function as a shroud to cover up the underlying decaying structure, if the limitations set by nature could thus be surreptitiously expanded, then music might be in a worse state than meets the eye: the fear of degeneration reveals itself in the last instance as a formalist fear of sound.

This fear of sonic phenomena, of appearances, may be reflected on the various veils, shrouds and curtains that pervade both the opera and the critical language in which it is, well, clothed. Cultural historian Aleida Assmann reminds us that veils and curtains essentially fulfil the same function: both can conceal and reveal a secret.[64] In that sense, the opening few bars representing the rising curtain are no less revelatory than the sexual core of the opera, Salome's dance of the seven veils. Both harbour secrets that ought not to be revealed.

Or do they? Is it not the veil, the curtain, that only *makes* the secret? What matters is the concealment giving rise to our expectations of a revelation, more so than the object that is to be revealed. To return to the image with which we started, the advisories and warning signs serve to *alert* us to some monstrosity that is to follow, and that we might otherwise not even have noted. From this angle, the critics' real fear turns out to be the (no less monstrous) situation where the lifted veil reveals that nothing had been hidden in the first place.

In the critical discourse around Draeseke's polemic, however, the veil had been turned into the antiseptic linens of the hospital bed to which the patient modern music had been confined. With its belief in organicism and a normative notion of beauty, the concept of degeneracy mainly served to identify the musical object in negative terms: *Salome* emerges as the product of a misguided musical progress, the parameters of which are defined by its deviation from the purportedly natural limitations. The diagnosis of musical degeneration in *Salome* is a reconstruction of an elusive idea of what might constitute 'healthy music'. This diagnosis is premised on a self-evident understanding of healthy music. It is only an

---

[64] Assmann 1997.

apparent paradox that this interest in 'healthy music' emerged at precisely the time when *Salome* was pronounced irrecoverably sick.

Only outside of this heated polemical context was it possible to take a broader stance on the meaning of degeneration, the 'dark side of progress', as a *necessary* by-product of the nineteenth-century ideology of progress.[65] The *Edinburgh Review*, surveying the recent philosophical literature on the topic, observed sagely: 'Degeneration is a necessary accompaniment of progress. We must look upon it with no teleological disfavour but as a normal manifestation of evolutionary change, set up in response to environmental conditions.'[66]

The contentious case of Strauss's *Salome* clearly shows the stakes: in the relentless forward surge of progress and the transcendental homelessness that characterised the modern condition, it became more important than ever to assert stability and control over a world that had apparently lost any sense of stable values. By emphatically excluding artworks such as *Salome*, by branding them with the Cain's mark of degeneracy, cultural critics asserted their authority in demarcating a space for 'normality' – though couched in the unassailable scientific metaphors of 'health' and 'nature' – to give them a sense of the cultural stability that they so sorely lacked.

Hearing the End

In *Der Fall Wagner* Nietzsche interpolated a proclamation in French, '*Wagner est une névrose.*' He could expect his educated contemporaries to hear the resonances: the French psychiatrist Moreau de Tours had made a similarly terse pronouncement: 'Le génie est une névrose.'[67] For Moreau, madness and genius were congeneric, '*in radice convenient*'.[68] This judgment was eagerly picked up all over Europe: the psychological literature on the genius at the turn of the century was legion. But what exactly does it mean when genius and madman 'come together at the root'? Obviously, the common ground between genius and the madman lay in the deviation from the norm: both had a penchant for thinking 'outside the box', and this could lead to culturally useful results in the case of the one or not, in the case of the other. Beyond that, there was no agreement on how to relate degeneracy and genius. For every Lombroso, arguing that madmen and

---

[65] Chamberlin and Gilman 1985.   [66] [unsigned] 1911a, 138–64.

[67] Moreau 1859, 464. This statement was eagerly taken up and quoted by Lombroso.

[68] Moreau 1859, 493.

geniuses were closely related, there was a Nordau, who pronounced them irreconcilably opposed.

The two positions reflected their own underlying biases. Lombroso's examination always began with the physiology of the creator, showing large overlaps between the insane and the genius.[69] He saw non-causal parallels between 'healthy geniuses', 'insane geniuses' and the 'insane without any special gifts'. To Nordau, however, that there might be any form of overlap of these groups was anathema. Analysing cultural creations to infer the mental state of their creators would simply not allow for such a possibility.

It was common in psychologists' circles to analyse the creative artworks of their patients and to examine them for clues as to their psychic make-up. But in a world where the creations flowing from the geniuses' nibs develop a life of their own and affect the world around them, the stakes are particularly high. The logic of musical degeneracy posited a closed circle: 'A lack of chastity in artistic creation will always be avenged by diseases of the art, which have a dangerous effect back on the artist.'[70] What exactly these 'diseases of the art' are and how exactly they afflict their environment remained unclear; the boundary between metaphor and reality remained tantalisingly undefined.

In its ill-defined boundaries, however, degeneracy in music could hardly be contained: music affected health and sickness of individuals in mysterious ways, as it did society at large. There is no distinction between individual and collective (whether it be identified biologically as race or sociologically as community), though given the strong organicist overtones of the discourse of degeneracy, these conflations should come as no surprise. The burden was firmly on the composers. Musing on the agency of the individual composer, Adler underlined: 'Every being carries the germ of decay in him, and the greatest deed of a human is not seldom the cause of his fall.'[71] Pure organicist lore, this rule has little to do with biology or evolution – or with history, for that matter. It is nothing other than Aristotle's *harmartia*, the 'fatal flaw' of the tragic hero.

As we saw, the laws of degeneration are invariably the laws of literature; its fears are based on the poetic justice that its practitioners fear the real world has denied them. No wonder that listening to *Salome* on the radio motivates a character in Alfred Döblin's novel *Hamlet* to move to Paris and to degrade into prostitution. No wonder that George Du Maurier's wholly unmusical Trilby, whose singing enchants her fawning audiences as

---

[69] See Lombroso 1864 and especially 1894.   [70] Raff 1854, 183.   [71] Adler 1911, 28.

Svengali extends his dark powers over her, became the best-selling novel of the 1890s. No wonder that it is the self-absorbed twins of Thomas Mann's *Wälsungenblut*, like those of Elimir Bourges's *Crépuscules des Dieux*, who are inspired by Wagner's music to consummate incest as an act of higher purity.

Despite all the cultural fear-mongering, in real life music has never effected such moral decrepitude. The discourse of degeneration adopts the persona and the authority of the scientist, and puts him (there is little ambiguity about the gender) in power over the narrative. He decides when the story is over and how it ends – as long as he abides by the rules of poetic justice. As a man of science, who can get below the sounding surface, he is in a position to tell us what the rest of us cannot hear but which may be of baleful influence to the rest of us. And as a poetic figure, his stories will always follow the same moralising archetypes, asserting order over a world that has become complicated and unstable. He tells us, in categorical terms that allow no objections, how to separate right from wrong, beautiful from ugly, healthy from unhealthy. Audiences at the time would ignore these health warnings at their own peril. What the frightened – and titillated – public rarely realised was that those pronouncements were, in the most literal of senses, works of science fiction.

Bibliography

[unsigned]. 1786. *Auf die Luftreise Herrn Joseph Freyherr von Lütgendorf den 24. May 1786 in der Reichstadt Augsburg geschehen wird.* Augsburg: Phil. Joseph Fill.

[unsigned]. 1824. 'Naturwissenschaft'. *Allgemeine Deutsche Real-Encyclopädie für die gebildeten Stände (Conversations-Lexikon).* 10 vols. Leipzig: Brockhaus.

[unsigned]. 1831. 'Opéra'. *Le Figaro.* 23 November, 2–3.

[unsigned]. 1835. 'Review of *Die Musik und Poesie*'. *Allgemeiner musikalische Zeitung* 37/47 (November), 779.

[unsigned]. 1836. 'Review of *Die Musik und Poesie*'. *Allgemeiner musikalischer Anzeiger* 8/17 (28 April), 65.

[unsigned]. 1838. 'Theatricals'. *Actors by Daylight* 25 (18 August), 197.

[unsigned]. 1840. 'Peter Joseph Schneider'. In *Musikalisches Conversations-Lexikon: Encyklopädie der gesammten Musik-Wissenschaft*, ed. August Gathy. Hamburg: G. W. Niemeyer.

[unsigned]. 1847a. 'Jenny Lind and Hypnotism'. *Medical Times* 16 (18 September), 602.

[unsigned]. 1847b. 'Lunacy Relieved by Musical Exercises'. *The Eclectic Review* 21/2, 206–20.

[unsigned]. 1854. 'Das menschliche Ohr'. *Unterhaltungen am häuslichen Herd* 2, 475–7.

[unsigned]. 1878a. 'A Fourth without Noise'. *The New York Times.* 4 July, 5.

[unsigned]. 1878b. 'Physicians Making a Complaint: A Petition Presented to the Grand Jury – The Metropolitan Railway Asked to Prevent the Intolerable Din of its Trains'. *The New York Times.* 3 July, 8.

[unsigned]. 1878c. 'Ueber die missbräuchliche Anwendung der Dampfpfeife', *Zeitung des Vereins Deutscher Eisenbahn-Verwaltungen* 18/11, 154–5.

[unsigned]. 1881a. 'Corriere dei teatri'. *L'illustrazione italiana.* 18 January.

[unsigned]. 1881b. 'Scala: Excelsior'. *La gazzetta dei teatri* 16 (13 January), 1.

[unsigned]. 1881c. *Milano e l'Esposizione.* Milan: Treves.

[unsigned]. 1882. *Trewman's Exeter Flying Post.* 13 September, 1.

[unsigned]. 1883a. 'Music'. In *The Cyclopædia of Education*, ed. Henry Kiddle and Alexander Jacob Schem, 603–12. 3rd edn. New York: E. Steiger.

[unsigned]. 1883b. 'Noise Nuisance'. *The Cincinnati Lancet and Clinic.* 22 September, 264.

[unsigned]. 1885a. Advertisement. *Book-Lore: A Magazine Devoted to Old-Time Literature* 2 (July).

Bibliography

[unsigned]. 1885b. Advertisement. *The Sword and the Trowel* 21 (December). Appendix.

[unsigned]. 1888. 'Noise and Vibration'. In The *American and English Encyclopedia of Law*, ed. John Houston Merrill. 31 vols. Northport, NY: Edward Thompson Company.

[unsigned]. 1889. 'Noise'. *All the Year Round*, 3rd series, no. 46 (16 November 1889), 474–6.

[unsigned]. 1891. 'Stated Meeting, November 20, 1891'. *Proceedings of the American Philosophical Society* 22 (January–June), 149–62.

[unsigned]. 1892. 'Sarah Bernhardt ipnotizzata'. *Magnetismo e ipnotismo. Rivista psicologica mensile. Neurologia, neuropatologia, elettroterapia, psichiatria, criminologia* 3/5 (May), 77.

[unsigned]. 1893. 'Emma Seiler, Scientist and Musician'. *The Review of Reviews* 8 (November), 591–2.

[unsigned]. 1894a. 'Mr. Frederic W. Root'. *The Musical Herald*. 1 August, 227–30.

[unsigned]. 1894b. 'The Lesson of Bayreuth'. *Musical Standard*. 4 August, 79–80.

[unsigned]. 1894c. 'The Opera'. *Saturday Review of Politics, Literature, Science and Art*. 23 June, 661–2.

[unsigned]. 1895. 'Jean de Reszke Talks of Training'. *Chicago Daily Tribune*. 17 May, 37.

[unsigned]. 1896. 'Lohengrin in German'. *New York Herald*. 3 January, 7.

[unsigned]. 1897. 'Theories about Sleep'. *The Spectator* (London). 16 October, 12–13.

[unsigned]. 1898. 'La semaine à la Bodinière'. *Le Figaro* 4 December.

[unsigned]. 1899. 'Ammoniaphone'. *The International Cyclopaedia: A Compendium of Human Knowledge* 1:392. Rev. edn. New York: Dodd Mead and Company.

[unsigned]. 1900a. 'Jean de Reszke's Voice is Dying'. *The Argonaut*. 6 August, 10.

[unsigned]. 1900b. 'Royal Opera'. *The Times*. 13 June, 6.

[unsigned]. 1900c. 'Royal Opera'. *The Times*. 5 July, 6.

[unsigned]. 1901a. 'Jean de Reszke as Lohengrin'. *The World*. 1 January, n.p.

[unsigned]. 1901b. 'Jean de Reszke's Latest Triumph'. *The Argonaut*. 14 January, 11.

[unsigned]. 1901c. 'Jean de Reszke's Return'. *The Sun*. 1 January, 3.

[unsigned]. 1901d. 'Last Plays of the Century in the New York Theatres'. *The Morning Telegraph*. 1 January, 3.

[unsigned]. 1901e. 'Lohengrin at the Opera. The De Reszke Brothers Make their Final Appearance'. *New York Times*. 30 March, 8.

[unsigned]. 1908a. 'Il nuovo Excelsior quest'anno alla Scala'. *La lettura* 8/12, 1005–8.

[unsigned]. 1908b. 'Neglect Imperils Pupils: Supt. Maxwell Says Growths in Children's Throats Lead to Depravity'. *New York Times*. 17 November, 6.

[unsigned]. 1911a. 'Degeneration and Pessimism'. *Edinburgh Review* (1911), 138–64.

[unsigned]. 1911b. 'Esprit malveillant'. *Traité sur l'obsession: L'Obsession a pour base la suggestion*. Lyon: Association typographique.

Abbate, Carolyn. 2001. *In Search of Opera*. Princeton, NJ: Princeton University Press.

2017. 'Sound Object Lessons'. *Journal of the American Musicological Society* 69/3, 793–829.

Abbott, Walton. 1924. 'Still on the Larynx'. *Musical Times* 65 (1 October), 932–3.

Abert, Hermann. 2007. *W. A. Mozart*, trans. Stewart Spencer, ed. Cliff Eisen. New Haven, CT: Yale University Press.

Abrams, M. H. 1957. 'The Correspondent Breeze: A Romantic Metaphor'. *The Kenyon Review* 19/1, 113–30.

1971. *The Mirror and the Lamp: Romantic Theory and the Critical Tradition*. Oxford: Oxford University Press.

Adler, Guido. 1880. 'Die historischen Grundklassen der christlich-abendländischen Musik bis 1600'. *Allgemeine Musikzeitung* 15, cols. 689–93, 705–9, 721–6, 737–40.

1885. 'Umfang, Methode und Ziel der Musikwissenschaft'. *Vierteljahrsschrift für Musikwissenschaft* 1 (1885), 5–20. Translated with an introduction by Erica Mugglestone as 'Guido Adler's "The Scope, Method, and Aim of Musicology" (1885): An English Translation with an Historico-Analytical Commentary'. *Yearbook for Traditional Music* 13 (1981), 1–21.

1911. *Der Stil in der Musik*. Leipzig: Breitkopf und Härtel.

1919. *Methode der Musikwissenschaft*. Leipzig: Breitkopf und Härtel.

Adorno, Theodor W. 1966. 'Richard Strauss – Part II'. *Perspectives of New Music* 4/2, 113–29.

1989. *Introduction to the Sociology of Music*. New York: Continuum.

2005. *In Search of Wagner*, trans. Rodney Livingstone. London: Verso.

Ahrens, Christian and Gregor Klinke, eds. 1996. *Das Harmonium in Deutschland: Bau, wirtschaftliche Bedeutung und musikalische Nutzung eines 'historischen' Musikinstrumente*. Frankfurt am Main: Edwin Bochinsky.

Aikin, William Arthur. 1900. *The Voice: Its Physiology and Cultivation*. London: Macmillan.

Albright, Daniel. 2014. 'Verdi'. In *Berlioz, Verdi, Wagner, Britten. Great Shakespeareans: Volume XI*, ed. Daniel Albright, 77–134. London: Bloomsbury.

Albury, William R. 1974. 'Physiological Explanation in Magendie's Manifesto of 1809'. *Bulletin of the History of Medicine* 48/1, 90–9.

1977. 'Experiment and Explanation in Bichat and Magendie'. *Studies in the History of Biology* 1, 47–131.

Allen, Warren Dwight. 1953. *Philosophies of Music History*. New York: Dover.

Ambros, August Wilhelm. 1860. 'Die neu-deutsche Schule'. In *Culturhistorische Bilder aus dem Musikleben der Gegenwart*, 129–92. Leipzig: Breitkopf und Härtel.

1988. *The Boundaries of Music and Poetry: A Study in Musical Aesthetics*, translated in *Musical Aesthetics*, Vol. II: *The Nineteenth Century*, ed. Edward A. Lippman. Stuyvesant, NY: Pendragon Press.

Andreason, Nancy. 2005. *The Creating Brain: The Neuroscience of Genius*. New York: Dana Press.

Andrée, Carl-Maximilian. 1810. *Neuester Zustand der vorzüglichen Spitäler und Armenanstalten in einigen Hauptorten des In- und Auslandes: Paris*. Leipzig: Barth.

Andries, Annelies. 2018. 'Modernizing Spectacle: The Opéra in Napoleon's Paris (1799–1814)'. PhD diss., Yale University.

Andriopoulos, Stefan. 2000. *Besessene Körper: Hypnose, Körperschaften und die Erfindung des Kinos*. Munich: Wilhelm Fink Verlag.

Armstrong, Tim. 1998. *Modernism, Technology, and the Body: A Cultural Study*. Cambridge: Cambridge University Press.

Arnauld, Pierre. 2009. 'Extases musicales et prise du regard. Mucha et la culture de l'hypnose'. In *Alfons Mucha*, catalogue de l'expostion, 25–30. Montpellier–Paris: Musée Fabre-Somogy.

Arteaga, Stefano. 1785. *Le Rivoluzioni nel teatro musicale moderno dalla sua origine fino al presente*. Venice: Palese.

Arthur, Timothy Shay. 1872. 'Weak Nerves'. *The Children's Hour* 11 (January), 10–13.

Assmann, Aleida. 1997. 'Der Schleier: Geheimnis in den Bildvorstellungen der Spätantike'. In *Schleier und Schwelle, Vol. 2: Geheimnis und Offenbarung*, ed. Aledia and Jan Assmann, 181–203. Munich: W. Fink.

Attali, Jacques. 1985. *Noise: The Political Economy of Music*. Minneapolis: University of Minnesota Press.

Atwell, B. W. 1868. *Principles of Elocution and Vocal Culture*. Providence, RI: Bangs Williams News Co.

Ault, Jr, Cecil Thomas. 1983. 'Design, Operation and Organization of Stage Machinery at the Paris Opera: 1770–1873'. PhD diss., University of Michigan.

Baber, E. Cresswell. 1888. 'Laryngology, Rhinology, and Otology'. *The London Medical Recorder* 1 (July), 297–9.

Bablet, Denis. 1983. 'Introduction générale: Adolphe Appia, Art, Révolte et Utopie'. In Adolphe Appia, *Œuvres complètes*, ed. Marie L. Bablet-Hahn. [Lausanne]: L'Âge d'Homme.

Baker, Evan. 2013. *From the Score to the Stage: An Illustrated History of Continental Opera Production and Staging*. Chicago, IL: University of Chicago Press.

Baker, Nancy Kovaleff, and Thomas Christiansen, eds. 1995. *Aesthetics and the Art of Musical Composition in the German Enlightenment: Selected Writings of Johann Georg Sulzer and Heinrich Christoph Koch*, trans. Nancy Kovaleff Baker and Thomas Christiansen. Cambridge: Cambridge University Press.

Balzac, Honoré de. 1837. 'Gambara: Étude philosophique'. *Revue et gazette musicale de Paris* 4/30 (23 July), 347–51; 4/31 (30 July), 355–62; 4/32 (6 August), 362–9; 4/33 (13August), 371–7; 4/34 (20 August), 380–2.

    2001. *The Unknown Masterpiece and Gambara*, trans. Richard Howard. New York: New York Review of Books.

Banta, Martha. 1993. *Taylored Lives: Narrative Productions in the Age of Taylor, Veblen, and Ford*. Chicago, IL: University of Chicago Press.

Bapst, Germain. 1893. *Essai sur l'histoire du théâtre: La Mise en Scène, le décor, le costume, l'architecture, l'éclairage, l'hygiène.* Paris: Hachette.

Barnes, William. 1874. *How to Improve the Voice: A Treatise.* London: John Guest.

Barr, Thomas. 1884. *Manual of Diseases of the Ear.* Glasgow: James Maclehose & Sons.

　1896. *Manual of Diseases of the Ear.* 2nd edn. Glasgow: James Maclehose.

Barraclough, Arthur. 1876. *Observations on the Physical Education of the Vocal Organs.* London: Cramer and Co.

Barraqué, Jean. 1962. *Debussy.* Paris: Seuil.

Barrington, Emilie I. 1890. 'Voice-Figures'. *Werner's Voice Magazine* 12/3 (March), 79.

Barthes, Roland. 1977. *Image-Music-Text,* trans. Stephen Heath. New York: Hill & Wang.

　1988. 'Is Painting a Language?' *The Responsibility of Forms,* trans. Richard Howard. New York: Hill and Wang.

Battersby, Christine. 1989. *Gender and Genius: Towards a Feminist Aesthetics.* London: Women's Press.

Baudelaire, Charles. 1972. *Selected Writings on Art and Literature,* trans. P. E. Charvet. Cambridge: Cambridge University Press.

Becker, Carl Ferdinand. 1839. *Systematisch-chronologische Darstellung der musikalischen Literatur nebst einem Anhang: Choralsammlungen aus dem 16., 17., und 18. Jahrhundert: Nachtrag.* Leipzig: Robert Friese.

Behnke, Emil. [1880] *The Mechanism of the Human Voice.* 11th edn. London: J. Curwen and Sons.

Bell, Charles. 1811. *An Idea of a New Anatomy of the Brain, Submitted for the Observation of His Friends.* n.p.

　1865. *The Anatomy and Philosophy of Expression as Connected with the Fine Arts.* 5th edn. London: Henry G. Bohn.

Benjamin, Walter. 2008. 'Theory of Distraction'. In *The Work of Art in the Age of its Technological Reproducibility and Other Writings,* trans. Howard Eiland, ed. Michael W. Jennings, Brigid Doherty and Thomas Y. Levin, 56–7. Cambridge, MA: Harvard University Press.

Bennett, Joseph. 1897. 'Facts, Rumours, and Remarks'. *The Musical Times and Singing Class Circular* 38, 454.

Bergeron, Katherine. 2010. *Voice Lessons: French Mélodie in the Belle Époque.* New York: Oxford University Press.

Berlioz, Hector. 1967–2005. *New Edition of the Complete Works.* 26 vols. Kassel: Bärenreiter.

　1969. *The Memoirs of Hector Berlioz including his travels in Italy, Germany, Russia and England,* trans. and ed. David Cairns. London: Gollancz.

　1995. *Correspondance générale,* ed. Pierre Citron and Hugh McDonald. 8 vols. Paris: Flammarion.

1998. *The Art of Music and Other Essays*, trans. and ed. Elizabeth Csicsery-Rónay. Bloomington: Indiana University Press, 1998.

Bertati, Giovanni. 1783. *Die eingebildeten Philosophen: Eine Singspiel in zwey Aufzügen*, trans. Gotlieb Stephanie. [Salzburg]: Franz Prodinger.

1784. *I filosofi immaginari: Dramma per musica*. Naples: n.p.

Bijsterveld, Karin. 2008. *Mechanical Sound: Technology, Culture, and Public Problems of Noise in the Twentieth Century*. Cambridge, MA: MIT Press.

Binet, Alfred, and Charles Féré. 1905. *Animal Magnetism*. London: Kegan Paul, Trench, Trübner and Co.

Birnbaum, Karl. 1911. *Die krankhafte Willensschwäche*. Wiesbaden: Bergmann.

Björnström, Fredrik Johan. 1889. *Hypnotism: Its History and Present Development*. New York: The Humboldt Publishing Co.

Blindman, David. 2002. *Ape to Apollo: Aesthetics and the Idea of Race in the Eighteenth Century*. London: Reaktion Books.

Bloch, Gregory. 2007. 'The Pathological Voice of Gilbert-Louis Duprez'. *Cambridge Opera Journal* 19/1, 11–31.

Bloch, Iwan. 2010. *Marquis de Sade: His Life and Works*. Amsterdam: Fredonia Books.

Bloom, Peter. 1998. *The Life of Hector Berlioz*. Cambridge: Cambridge University Press.

Bockholdt, Rudolf. 1979. *Berlioz-Studien*. Tutzing: Schneider.

Boenninghaus, Georg. 1908. *Lehrbuch der Ohrenheilkunde für Studierende und Aerzte*. Berlin: S. Karger.

Bois, Jules. 1903. 'Victor Maurel en Sorbonne'. *Gil Blas*. 1 October.

Bolongaro-Crevenna, Hubertus. 1963. *L'arpa festante: Die Münchner Oper, 1651–1825*. Munich: Georg D. W. Callwey.

Bonacci, Gratiliano. 1837. *Nozioni fondamentali di estetica*. Fuligno: Tomassini.

Bondanella, Peter. 2009. *A History of Italian Cinema*. London: Continuum.

Bonds, Mark Evan. 2006. *Music as Thought: Listening to the Symphony in the Age of Beethoven*. Princeton, NJ: Princeton University Press.

Borchmeyer, Dieter, and Jörg Salaquarda, eds. 1994. *Nietzsche und Wagner: Stationen einer epochalen Begegnung*. Frankfurt-am-Main: Insel Verlag.

Born, Georgina. 2010. 'For a Relational Musicology: Music and Interdisciplinarity, Beyond the Practice Turn'. *Journal of the Royal Musical Association* 135/2, 205–43.

Boulez, Pierre. 1985. *Points de Repère, Textes réunies et présentés par Jean-Jacques Nattiez*, 227–35. 2nd edn. Paris: Christian Bourgois, Seuil.

1986. 'Berlioz and the Realm of the Imaginary'. *Daedalus* 115/4, 175–84.

Bourdon, Georges. 1903. *Les Théâtres anglais*. Paris: Charpentier.

Bouveret, Leon. 1893. *Die Neurasthenie (Nervenschwäche)*. Leipzig: Franz Deuticke.

Bowick, T. Gilbert. 1884. 'Italy; Its Atmosphere and Its Music'. *The Lamp* 27, 123.

Brago, Michael. 1984. 'Haydn, Goldoni and *Il mondo della luna*'. *Eighteenth-Century Studies* 17, 308–32.

Braid, James. 1843. *Neurypnology, or the Rationale of Nervous Sleep*. London: John Churchill.

Brain, Robert. 1998. 'Standards and Semiotics'. In *Inscribing Science: Scientific Texts and the Materiality of Communication*, ed. Timothy Lenoir, 249–84. Stanford, CA: Stanford University Press.

2008. 'The Pulse of Modernism: Experimental Physiology and Aesthetic Avant-gardes circa 1900'. *Studies in the History and Philosophy of Science* 39/3, 393–417.

2016. *The Pulse of Modernism: Physiological Aesthetics in Fin-de-Siècle Europe*. Seattle: The University of Washington Press.

Brandes, Friedrich. 1905. 'Richard Strauß' Salome'. *Signale für die musikalische Welt* 63, 1289–93.

Brant, Clare. 2011. 'The Progress of Knowledge in the Regions of Air?: Divisions and Disciplines in Early Ballooning'. *Eighteenth-Century Studies* 45/1, 71–86.

Brecht, Bertolt. 1997. 'Anmerkungen zur Oper *Aufstieg und Fall der Stadt Mahagonny*'. In *Ausgewählte Schriften in sechs Bänden*. Frankfurt-am-Main: Suhrkamp.

Bressani, Martin, and Peter Sealy. 2011. 'The Opéra Disseminated: Charles Garnier's *Le Nouvel Opéra de Paris* (1875–1881)'. *Studies in the History of Art* 77, Symposium Papers LIV: *Art and the Early Photographic Album*, 195–219.

Bretzner, Christoph Friedrich. 1786. *Die Luftbälle, oder der Liebhaber à la Montgolfier*. Leipzig: Friedrich Gotthold Jacobaer.

Bretzner, Christoph Friedrich, and Ferdinand Fränzl. 1788. *Gesänge aus dem Singspiele: Die Luftbälle, oder Der Liebhaber à la Montgolfier*. Hamburg: J. M. Michaelsen.

Brittan, Francesca. 2006. 'Berlioz and the Pathological Fantastic: Melancholy, Monomania, and Romantic Autobiography'. *19th-Century Music* 29/3, 211–39.

2007. 'Berlioz, Hoffmann, and the Genre Fantastique in French Romanticism'. PhD diss., Cornell University.

Bronfen, Elisabeth. 1996. 'Kundry's Laughter'. *New German Critique* 69, 147–61.

1998. *The Knotted Subject: Hysteria and Its Discontents*. Princeton, NJ: Princeton University Press.

Brown, Andrew. 1970. *Aeolian Harp: The Aeolian Harp in European Literature, 1591–1892*. Cambridge: Bois de Boulogne.

Brown, Bill. 2001. 'Thing Theory'. *Critical Inquiry* 28/1, 1–22.

Browne, Lennox, and Emil Behnke. [1883] 1886. *Voice, Song, and Speech: A Practical Guide for Singers and Speakers*. 4th edn. New York: G. P. Putnam's Sons.

Bruno, Giuliana. 1993. *Streetwalking on a Ruined Map: Cultural Theory and the City Films of Elvira Notari*. Princeton, NJ: Princeton University Press.

Buch, David J. 2004. '*Die Zauberflöte*, Masonic Opera, and Other Fairy Tales'. *Acta Musicologica* 76, 193–219.

2008. *Magic Flutes and Enchanted Forests: The Supernatural in Eighteenth-Century Opera*. Chicago, IL: University of Chicago Press.

Buchanan, Thomas. 1828. *Physiological Illustrations of the Organ of Hearing*. London: Longman, Rees, Orne, Brown and Green.

Budden, Julian. 2002. *Puccini: His Life and Works*. New York: Oxford University Press.

Buffenoir, Hippolyte. 1874. 'Ouverture du Grand Opéra: Hymne Lyrique dédié à M. Charles Garnier, Architecte'. Fonds Garnier, Bibliothèque de l'Opéra, 'Odes et poèmes dédiés à Gamier et au Nouvel Opéra', pièce 99/2.

Burdekin, Russell. 2015. 'Pepper's Ghost at the Opera'. *Theatre Notebook* 69, 152–64.

Burke, Kenneth. 2007. 'Appendix: Additional References to Shakespeare in Burke's Writings'. In *On Shakespeare*, ed. Scott L. Newstok, 211–66. West Lafayette, IN: Parlor Press.

Burnett, Charles H. 1877. *The Ear: Its Anatomy, Physiology, and Diseases. A Practical Treatise for the Use of Medical Students and Practitioners*. Philadelphia, PA: Henry C. Lea.

Busoni, Ferruccio. 1916. *Neue Ästhetik der Musik*. 2nd edn. Leipzig: Insel.

Butcher, Peter, Annie Elias and Lesley Cavalli. 2007. *Understanding and Treating Psychogenic Voice Disorder: A CBT Framework*. Chichester: John Wiley & Sons.

C.D. 1858. 'Richard Wagner's Lohengrin'. *Niederrheinische Musik-Zeitung* 6/38, 297–301.

Cabanès, Augustin. 1926. *Les Cinq Sens*. Paris: E. Le François.

Cahan, David, ed. 1995. *Science and Culture: Popular and Philosophical Essays*. Chicago, IL: University of Chicago Press.

Campana, Alessandra. 2015. *Opera and Modern Spectatorship*. Cambridge: Cambridge University Press.

Camper, Petrus. 1794. *The Works of the Late Professor Camper on the Connexion Between the Science of Anatomy and the Arts of Drawing, Painting, Statuary, etc. etc. in Two Books*, trans. Thomas Cogan. London: C. Dilly.

Canguilhem, Georges. 1955. *La Formation du concept de réflexe aux XVIIe et XVIIIe siècles*. Paris: PUF.

1993. 'Le cerveau et la pensée'. In *Georges Canguilhem: Philosophe, historien des sciences*, 203–22. Paris: Albin Michel.

2002. *Etudes d'histoire et de philosophie des sciences concernant les vivants et la vie*. 7th edn. Paris: Vrin.

Carbonnelle, Henri. 1903. 'Une séance d'hypnotisme chez Rodin'. *Gil Blas*. 27 November.

Carpani, Gioseppe. 1822. 'Intorno alla musica di Gioachino Rossini'. *Biblioteca italiana*. June. 287–318.

Carroy, Jacqueline. 1991. *Hypnose, suggestion et psychologie. L'invention de sujets*. Paris: Presses universitaires de France.

Carter, Scott A. 2013. 'Forging a Sound Citizenry: Voice Culture and the Embodiment of the Nation, 1880–1920'. *The American Music Research Center Journal.* 1 January). 11–34.

Castelvecchi, Stefano. 2013. *Sentimental Opera: Questions of Genre in the Age of Bourgeois Drama.* Cambridge: Cambridge University Press.

Castro, Vincenzo de. 1845. 'Fantasia'. In *Enciclopedia italiana e dizionario della conversazione.* Venice: Tasso.

Cather, Willa. 1970. 'Lohengrin and Walküre'. In *The World and the Parish: Willa Cather's Articles and Reviews,* ed. William M. Curtin. 2 vols. 2, 619–22. Lincoln: University of Nebraska Press.

Chamberlayne, Elizabeth A. 1895. 'Correspondence'. *Musical News.* 5 October). 277.

Chamberlin, J. Edward, and Sander L. Gilman, eds. 1985. *Degeneration: The Dark Side of Progress.* New York: Columbia University Press.

Charcot, Jean-Martin. 1879. 'Description de la grande attaque hystérique'. *Progrès Médical* 7 (11 January), 17–20.

1886–93. *Oeuvres complètes.* 9 vols. Paris: Lecrosnier et Babé, Bureaux du progrès médical.

Charle, Christophe. 2007. 'Opera in France, 1870–1914: Between Nationalism and Foreign Imports'. In *Opera and Society in Italy and France from Monteverdi to Bourdieu,* ed. Victoria Johnson, Jane F. Fulcher and Thomas Ertman, 243–66. Cambridge: Cambridge University Press.

Cheek, David B. 1958. 'Hypnosis: An Additional Tool in Human Reorientation to Stress'. *Northwest Medicine* 57/2, 177–82.

Chladni, Ernst F. F. 1787. *Entdeckungen über die Theorie des Klanges.* Leipzig: Weidmann.

Chua, Daniel. 1999. *Absolute Music and the Construction of Meaning.* Cambridge: Cambridge University Press.

Clancy, Hannah, David Gutkin and Luci Vágnerová. 2016. 'A Chronology'. In *Technology and the Diva,* ed. Karen Henson, 1–10. Cambridge: Cambridge University Press.

Clark, James Henry. 1856. *Sight and Hearing: How Preserved, and How Lost.* New York: C. Scribner.

Clarke, Edwin, and L. S. Jacyna. 1987. *Nineteenth-Century Origins of Neuroscientific Concepts.* Berkeley: University of California Press.

Clewell, Tammy, ed. 2013. *Modernism and Nostalgia: Bodies, Locations, Aesthetics.* Basingstoke: Palgrave Macmillan.

Clouston, Thomas. 1906. *The Hygiene of Mind.* London: Methuen & Co.

Cobrin, Pamela. 2006. 'Dangerous Flirtations: Politics, the Parlor, and the Nineteenth-Century Victorian Amateur Actresses'. *Women & Performance: A Journal of Feminist Theory* 16/3 (November), 385–402.

Cohen, I. Bernard. 1941. *Benjamin Franklin's Experiments: A New Edition of Franklin's Experiments and Observations on Electricity.* Cambridge, MA: Harvard University Press.

Conati, Marcello, and Mario Medici, eds. 2015. *The Verdi–Boito Correspondence*, trans. William Weaver. Chicago, IL: University of Chicago Press.

Cone, Edward T. 2010. *Hearing and Knowing Music*. Princeton, NJ: Princeton University Press.

Connor, Steven. 2000. *Dumbstruck: A History of Ventriloquism*. Oxford: Oxford University Press.

Cook, Harold. 1997. 'From the Scientific Revolution to the Germ Theory'. In *Western Medicine: An Illustrated History*, ed. Irvine Loudon, 86–101. Oxford: Oxford University Press.

Cook, Nicholas. 2002. *Very Short Introduction to Music*. New York: Oxford University Press.

Corbin, Alain. 1990. 'Backstage'. In *A History of Private Life*, ed. Michelle Perrot, trans. Arthur Goldhammer. 4 vols. 4:451–667. Cambridge, MA: Harvard University Press.

Corvée, Flore. 1845. *Mémoires de Mlle Flore (Corvée), artiste du théâtre des Variétés*. 3 vols. Paris, Comptoir des imprimeries unies.

Coudroy-Saghaï, Marie-Hélène. 1988. *La Critique parisienne des 'grands opéras' de Meyerbeer: 'Robert le Diable', 'Les Huguenots', 'Le Prophète', 'L'Africaine'*. Saarbrücken: Musik-Edition Lucie Galland.

Courmelles, François-Victor Foveau de. 1890. *L'Hypnotisme*. Paris: Hachette.

Crary, Jonathan. 1990. *Techniques of the Observer: On Vision and Modernity in the Nineteenth Century*. Cambridge, MA: MIT Press.

1999. *Suspensions of Perception: Attention, Spectacle and Modern Culture*. Cambridge, MA: The MIT Press.

Crepax, Nicola. 2002. *Storia della industria in Italia: uomini, imprese e prodotti*. Rome: Mulino.

Crivelli, Filippo. 1974. 'Excelsior oggi'. *Teatro alla Scala: Stagione d'opera e balletto 1974/5*. n.p.

Crowe, Michael. 1986. *The Extraterrestrial Life Debate, 1750–1900: The Idea of a Plurality of Worlds from Kant to Lowell*. Cambridge: Cambridge University Press.

Cruz, Gabriela. 1999. 'Giacomo Meyerbeer's L'Africaine and the End of Grand Opera'. PhD diss., Princeton University.

2017. 'The Flying Dutchman, English Spectacle and the Remediation of Grand Opera'. *Cambridge Opera Journal* 29/1, 5–32.

Cunningham, Andrew, and Nicholas Jardine, eds. 1990. *Romanticism and the Sciences*. Cambridge: Cambridge University Press.

Curtis, Holbrook. 1894a. 'The Effects on the Vocal Cords of Improper Method in Singing'. *New York Medical Journal* 65 (20 January), 70–4.

1894b. 'Why the Singer Can Sing'. *Werner's Magazine* 16/11 (November), 389.

1896. *Voice Building and Tone Placing, Showing a New Method of Relieving Injured Vocal Cords by Tone Exercises*. New York: D. Appleton.

1897. 'The Tonograph'. *Scientific American*. 29 May. 345–6.

Czermak, Johann N. 1869. *Populäre physiologische Vorträge, gehalted im akademischen Rosensaale zu Jena in den Jahren 1868–1869*. Vienna: K. Czermak.

Czolbe, Heinrich. 1855. *Neue Darstellung des Sensualismus: ein Entwurf*. Leipzig: Hermann Costenoble.

1865. *Die Grenzen und der Ursprung der menschlichen Erkenntniss im Gegensatze zu Kant und Hegel*. Jena and Leipzig: Hermann Costenoble.

Dabney, Robert. 1876. *The Sensualist Philosophy*. Edinburgh: T. & T. Clark.

Dahlhaus, Carl. 1989. *The Idea of Absolute Music*, trans. Roger Lustig. Chicago, IL: University of Chicago Press.

Daly, César. 1861. 'Concours pour le Grand Opéra de Paris: Deuxième Partie'. *Revue générale de l'architecture et des travaux publics* 19, cols. 76–133.

Danesi, Luigi. 1873. *Il telegrafo elettrico, ballo storico-fantastico in un prologo e 5 atti, composto espressamente per il Teatro Comunale di Trieste del cavaliere Luigi Danesi*. Trieste: Appolonia & Caprin.

Darnton, Robert. 1968. *Mesmerism and the End of the Enlightenment in France*. Cambridge, MA: Harvard University Press.

Darwin, Charles. [1872] 2009. *The Expressions of the Emotions in Man and Animals*. 2nd edn rpt. London: Penguin.

Daston, Lorraine. 1982. 'The Theory of Will versus the Science of Mind'. In *The Problematic Science: Psychology in Nineteenth-Century Thought*, ed. William Woodward and Mitchell Ash, 88–115. New York: Praeger.

Daverio, John. 1997. *Robert Schumann: Herald of a 'New Poetic Age'*. Oxford: Oxford University Press.

Davies, James Q. 2014. *Romantic Anatomies of Performance*. Berkeley: The University of California Press.

Davies, James Q., and Ellen Lockhart, eds. 2016. *Sound Knowledge: Music and Science in London 1789–1851*. Chicago, IL: University of Chicago Press.

Davis, Lennard J. 2008. *Obsession: A History*. Chicago, IL: University of Chicago Press.

De' Filippi, Giuseppe. 1847. 'Sulla estetica musicale'. *Giornale dell' I.R. Istituto Lombardo di scienze, lettere ed arti e biblioteca italiana* 16, 19–50.

de Rochas, Albert. 1900. *Les Sentiments, la musique et le geste*. Grenoble: Librairie Dauphine.

de Valenti, Ernst Joseph Gustav. 1826. *System der höhern Heilkunde für Ärzte, Prediger und Erzieher*. 2 vols. Elberfeld: Wilhelm Hassel.

1831. *Medicina clerica, oder Handbuch der Pastoral-Medizin*. Leipzig: F. R. Köhler.

de Vries, Marc J. 2005. *Teaching about Technology: An Introduction to the Philosophy of Technology for Non-Philosophers*. Dordrecht: Springer.

Dechambre, Amédée, ed. 1875. *Dictionnaire encyclopédique des sciences médicales*. Paris: Typographie Lahure.

Delamarre, [Théodore]. 1860. 'La Nouvelle salle de l'Opéra'. *La Patrie*. 1 May.

Bibliography

Delboeuf, Joseph. 1886. 'Une visite à la Salpêtrière'. *Revue de Belgique* 54, 139–47 and 258–78.

Deleuze, Gilles. 1997. *Cinema 2: The Time-Image*, trans. Hugh Thomlinson and Robert Galatea. Minneapolis: University of Minnesota Press.

Della Coletta, Cristina. 2006. *World's Fairs Italian Style: The Great Exhibitions in Turin and Their Narratives, 1860–1915*. Toronto: University of Toronto Press.

Della Valle, Cesare. 1856. *Considerazioni sullo stato attuale del teatro italiano*. Naples: Gioja.

Descartes, René. 1649. *Les Passions de l'âme*. Paris: Henry Le Gras.

Dibbern, Mary. 2002. *The Tales of Hoffmann: A Performance Guide*. Hillsdale, NY: Pendragon Press.

Didi-Huberman, Georges. 1982. *Invention de l'hystérie: Charcot et l'iconographie photographique de la Salpêtrière*. Paris: Macula.

    2003. *Invention of Hysteria: Charcot and the Photographic Iconography of the Salpêtrière*, trans. Alisa Hartz. Cambridge, MA: MIT Press.

Dincklage, Emmy von. 1879. 'Über den Lärm'. *Nordwest* 2/51, 413–14.

Dodd, George. 1853. 'The Harmonious Blacksmith'. *Household Words* 8 (24 December), 402.

Dolan, Emily. 2008. 'E. T. A. Hoffman and the Ethereal Technologies of "Nature Music"'. *Eighteenth-Century Music* 5, 7–26.

    2013. *The Orchestral Revolution: Haydn and the Technologies of Timbre*. Cambridge: Cambridge University Press.

Dolan, Emily I. and John Tresch. 2011. 'A Sublime Invasion: Meyerbeer, Balzac, and the Opera Machine'. *Opera Quarterly* 27/1, 4–31.

Dotti, Anna. 2003. '*I promessi sposi* per marionette della Compagnia Carlo Colla e Figli: breve storia e drammaturgia'. *Musica/Realtà* 70–72, 139–41.

Douglas, Walter Johnstone. 1925. 'His Principles of Singing'. *Music & Letters* 6/3, 202–9.

Dowbiggin, Ian Robert. 1991. *Inheriting Madness: Professionalization and Psychiatric Knowledge in Nineteenth-Century France*. Berkeley: University of California Press.

Draeseke, Felix. 1990. 'Offene Antwort an Richard Strauß'. In '*Die Konfusion in der Musik*': *Felix Draesekes Kampfschrift von 1906 und die Folgen*, ed. Susanne Shigihara, 173–4. Bonn: Gudrun Schröder.

Dreher, Eugen. 1875. *Die Kunst in ihrer Beziehung zur Psychoogie zur Naturwissenschaft. Eine philosophische Untersuchung*. Berlin: Gustav Hempel.

Dreyfus, Laurence. 2010. *Wagner and the Erotic Impulse*. Cambridge, MA: Harvard University Press.

du Bois-Reymond, Emil. 1848. *Untersuchungen über thierische Elektrizität*. Berlin: G. Reimer.

Dubois, Dominique. 2006. *Jules Bois (1868–1943): le reporter de l'occultisme, le poète et le féministe de la belle époque*. Marseille: Arqa.

Duchenne de Boulogne, G.-B. 1990. *The Mechanism of Human Facial Expression*, ed. and trans. R. Andrew Cutherbertson. Cambridge: Cambridge University Press, 1990. Originally published in 1862 as *Mécanisme de la physionomie humaine, ou Analyse électro-physiologique de l'expression des passions applicable à la pratique des arts plastiques*. Paris: Chez Ve Jules Renouard.

Duval, J. Georges. 1876. 'Inauguration du Nouvel-Opéra'. In *L'Année théâtrale: Nouvelles, Bruits de Coulisses, Indiscrétions, Comptes Rendus, Racontars, etc.* 2, 43.

Earle, Pliny. 1841. *A Visit to Thirteen Asylums for the Insane in Europe.* Philadelphia, PA: Dobson.

Eco, Umberto. 1979. 'Can Television Teach?' *Screen Education* 31, 15–24.

Edgerton, David. 2006. *The Shock of the Old: Technology and Global History since 1900*. London: Profile Books.

Eidenbenz, Céline. 2011. 'L'Hypnose au Parthénon. Les photographies de Magdeleine G. par Fred Boissonnas'. *Études photographiques* 28, https://etudesphotographiques.revues.org/3227.

Eksteins, Modris. 1997. 'Rag-Picker: Siegfried Kracauer and the Mass Ornament'. *International Journal of Politics, Culture and Society* 10/4, 609–13.

Ellenberger, Henri F. 1970. *The Discovery of the Unconscious: The History and Evolution of Dynamic Psychiatry*. New York: Basic Books.

Ellis, Alexander. 1885. 'On the Musical Scales of Various Nations'. *The Journal of the Society of Arts* 1688, 485–527.

Ellis, Katharine. 2015. 'Olivier Halanzier and the Operatic Museum in Late Nineteenth-Century France'. *Music & Letters* 96/3, 390–417.

Epheyre, Charles [Charles Richet]. 1890. *Soeur Marthe*. Paris: Ollendorff.

Erdan, Alexandre. 1860. *La France mystique. Tableau des excentricités religieuses de ce temps*. Amsterdam: Meijer.

Erhard, Julius. 1859. *Rationelle Otiatrik nach klinischen Beobachtungen*. Erlangen: Ferdinand Enke.

Esmail, Jennifer. 2013. *Reading Victorian Deafness: Signs and Sounds in Victorian Literature and Culture*. Athens: Ohio University Press.

Esquirol, Étienne. 1816. 'Folie.' In *Dictionnaire des sciences médicales*. 58 vols. Paris: Panckoucke.

   1838. *Maladies mentales et des asiles d'aliénés*. 2 vols. Paris: Ballière.

Fagnocchi, Giuseppe. 1999. *Lineamenti di storia della letteratura flautistica: Con un sommario della storia dello strumento*. N.p.: Mobydick.

Fairtile, Linda B. 1999. *Giacomo Puccini: A Guide to Research*. New York: Garland.

Fara, Patricia. 2002. *An Entertainment for Angels: Electricity in the Enlightenment*. Cambridge: Icon.

Farabegoli, Giorgio. 2016. 'Barbieri's Automatic Electric Organ at Aielli'. *The Gaplin Society Journal* 69, 59–71.

Farina, Salvatore. 1881. 'Scala: *Excelsior, del coreografo Manzotti; Ruy Blas. Teatro dal Verme'. Gazzetta musicale di Milano* 36 (16 January), 22.

Farkas, Márta. 1967. 'Paisiello: *I filosofi immaginari'. Studie Musicologica Academiae Scientiarum Hungaricae* 9, 301–42.

Fatouville, Nolant de. 1721. *Le Théâtre Italien de Gherardi, ou le recueil Général de tous les Comédies Françoises jouées par les Comédiens Italiens du Roy, pendant tout le temps qu'ils ont été au service de sa Majesté.* Amsterdam: Michel Charles le Cène.

Favia-Artsay, Aida. 1991. 'White Gold in the Golden Age: Recalling the Sound of the De Reszke Brothers and One Possible Reason for its Splendor'. *Opera Quarterly* 8/1, 44–61.

Feaster, Patrick. 2007. 'The Following Record: Making Sense of Phonographic Performance, 1877–1908'. PhD diss., Indiana University.

Fegejo, Polisseno [Carlo Goldoni]. 1750. *Il mondo della luna, dramma per musica.* Venice: Modesto Fenzo.

Ferré, Frederick. 1988. *Philosophy of Technology.* Englewood Cliffs, NJ: Prentice Hall.

Fétis, François-Joseph. 1835–44. *Biographie universelle des musiciens et bibliographie générale.* 8 vols. Mayence: Schott.

    1849. *Traité complet de la théorie et pratique de l'harmonie.* Paris: Brandus.

    1869. *Histoire générale de la musique.* 4 vols. Paris: Firmin-Didot.

    1881–9. *Biographie universelle des musiciens et bibliographie générale de la musique.* 2nd edn. 10 vols. Paris: Firmin-Didot.

Feuchtersleben, Ernst von. 1838. *Zur Diätik der Seele.* Vienna: Armbruster.

Feuerbach, Ludwig. 1986. *Principles of a Philosophy of the Future*, trans. Manfred Vogel. Indianapolis, IN: Hackett Publishing.

Filippi, Filippo. 1881. 'Excelsior: Nuovo ballo del Manzotti alla Scala'. *Il mondo artistico* 2–3 (20 January), 1–2.

Finck, Henry T. 1909. *Success in Music and How it is Won.* New York: Charles Scribner.

Finger, Stanley, and David A. Gallo. 2004. 'The Music of Madness: Franklin's Armonica and the Vulnerable Nervous System'. In *Neurology of the Arts: Painting, Music, Literature*, ed. F. Clifford Rose, 207–36. London: Imperial College Press.

Fischer, Peter. 1996. 'Zur Genealogie der Technikphilosophie'. In *Technikphilosophie*, ed. Peter Fischer, 255–335. Leipzig: Reclam.

Flaubert, Gustav. 2005. *November: Fragments in a Nondescript Style*, trans. Andrew Brown. London: Hesperus.

Fodéré, François Emmanuel. 1817. *Traité du délire, appliqué à la médecine, à la morale et la législation.* 2 vols. Paris: Croullebois.

Foster, Michael. 1877. *Textbook of Physiology.* London: Macmillan and Co.

Foucault, Michel. 1971. *The Order of Things.* New York: Random House.

    2013. 'Birth of the Asylum'. In *History of Madness*, 463–511. London: Routledge.

Frankenbach, Chantal. 2013. 'Waltzing around the Musically Beautiful: Listening and Dancing in Hanslick's Hierarchy of Musical Perception'. In *Rethinking Hanslick: Music, Formalism, and Expression*, ed. Nicole Grimes, Siobhán Donovan and Wolfgang Marx, 108–32. Rochester, NY: University of Rochester Press.

Franklin, Peter. 1991. 'Distant Sounds – Fallen Music: *Der ferne Klang* as "Woman's Opera"?' *Cambridge Opera Journal* 3/2, 159–72.

2013. 'Lost in Spaces: Recovering Schreker's Spectacular Voices'. *Opera Quarterly* 29/1, 19–30.

Freud, Sigmund. 1989. *Civilization and Its Discontents*. In *The Freud Reader*, ed. Peter Gay, 722–71. New York: W. W. Norton.

Frey, Lea. 1997. 'Die Zauberflöte'. *The Aria Database*. www.aria-database.com/translations/magic_flute.txt

Friedrich. 1885. *Die Krankheiten des Willens*. Munich: Verlag der G. Friedrich'schen Buchhandlung.

Frigau Manning, Céline. 2016. 'L'Art de la mort volontaire: l'opéra italien et ses suicidés romantiques sur la scène parisienne du XIXᵉ siècle'. *European Drama and Performance Studies* 7, 157–70.

Fritzsche, Peter. 1998. *Reading Berlin 1900*. Cambridge, MA: Harvard University Press.

2015. 'The City and Urban Life'. In *The Fin-de-Siècle World*, ed. Michael Saler, 29–44. London: Routledge.

Fusco, Gennaro, and Luca Federico Garavaglia. 2008. *Romualdo Marenco: la riscoperta di un pioniere*. Milan: Excelsior.

Gallini, Clara. 1983. *La sonnambula meravigliosa. Magnetismo e ipnotismo nell'Ottocento italiano*. Rome: Feltrinelli.

Galvani, Luigi. 2002. *De viribus electricitatis*. Translated in *Literature and Science in the Nineteenth Century: An Anthology*, ed. Laura Otis, 135–40. New York: Oxford University Press, 2002.

Gangadhara Somayaji, K. S. 2015. 'The Story of Progress of Otology'. *Archives of Medical and Health Science* 3/2, 340–5.

García, Manuel. 1854–5. 'Observations on the Human Voice'. *Proceedings of the Royal Society of London* 7, 399–410.

Garelick, Rhonda K. 1999. *Rising Star: Dandyism, Gender, and Performance in the Fin de Siècle*. Princeton, NJ: Princeton University Press.

Garnier, Charles. 1871. *Le Théâtre*. Paris: Hachette.

1878–81. *Le Nouvel Opéra de Paris*. 2 vols. With 6 atlas folios of plates and photographs. Paris: Ducher.

Gauld, Alan. 1992. *A History of Hypnotism*. Cambridge: Cambridge University Press.

Gellerman, Robert. 1996. *The American Reed Organ and the Harmonium*. Vestal, NY: Vestal Press.

Georget, Etienne Jean. 1825. *Examen medical des procès criminals des nommes Leger Feldtmann, Lecouffe, Jean-Pierre et Papavoine*. Paris: Migneret.

Gerhard, Anselm. 2000. *The Urbanization of Opera: Music Theater in Paris in the Nineteenth Century*. Chicago, IL: University of Chicago Press.

Gerhard, Wilhelm. 1826. *W. Gerhard's Gedichte*. 4 vols. Leipzig: Barth.

Gillespie, Richard. 1984. 'Ballooning in France and Britain, 1783–1786: Aerostation and Adventurism'. *Isis* 75/2, 248–68.

Gillmore, Q. A. 1876. *A Practical Treatise on Roads, Street, and Pavements*. New York: D. Van Nostrand.

Gilman, Sander L. 2015. *Illness and Image: Case Studies in the Medical Humanities*. New Brunswick, NJ: Transaction Publishers.

Gilman, Sander, and Joe Jeongwon, eds. 2010. *Wagner and the Cinema*. Bloomington: Indiana University Press.

Gioberti, Vincenzo. 1845. *Saggio sul bello, o Elementi di filosofia estetica*. Naples: Fibreno.

Gleichmann, Johann Andreas. 1820. 'Ueber die Erfindung der Aeoline oder des Aeolodikon'. *Allgemeine musikalische Zeitung* 22 (July), 505–8.

Glyn, Margaret H. 1909. *Analysis of the Evolution of Musical Form*. London: Longman's, Green & Co.

Goehr, Lydia. 2007. *The Imaginary Museum of Musical Works: An Essay in the Philosophy of Music*. 2nd edn. Oxford: Clarendon Press.

Goehring, Edmund. 2004. *Three Modes of Perception in Mozart: The Philosophical, Pastoral, and Comic in* Così fan tutte. Cambridge: Cambridge University Press.

Goethe, Johann Wolfgang von. 2014. *Schriften zur Morphologie*, ed. Karl-Maria Guth. Berlin: Hofenberg.

Göhler, Georg. 1990. 'Richard Strauß'. In *'Die Konfusion in der Musik': Felix Draesekes Kampfschrift von 1906 und die Folgen*, ed. Susanne Shigihara, 200–22. Bonn: Gudrun Schröder.

Goldsmith, Mike. 2012. *Discord: The Story of Noise*. Oxford: Oxford University Press.

Goldstein, Jan E. 1987. *Console and Classify: The French Psychiatric Profession in the Nineteenth Century*. Chicago, IL: University of Chicago Press.

Görgen, Bruno. 1820. *Privat-Heilanstalt für Gemüthskranke*. Vienna: Franz Wimmer.

Gosset, Alphonse. 1886. *Traité de la construction des théâtres*. Paris: Librairie Polytechnique Baudry.

Gould, Stephen Jay. 1977. *Ontogeny and Phylogeny*. Cambridge, MA: Harvard University Press.

  1981. *The Mismeasure of Man*. New York: W.W. Norton.

Gräner, Georg. 1905. 'Richard Straußens "Salome"'. *Die Schaubühne* 1, 436–9.

Greenblatt, Stephen. 2001. *Hamlet in Purgatory*. Princeton, NJ: Princeton University Press.

Greenfield, Susan. 2014. *Mind Change: How Digital Technologies are Leaving Their Mark on our Brains.* London: Rider.

Gruber, Josef. 1870. *Lehrbuch der Ohrenheilkunde mit besonderer Rücksicht auf Anatomie und Physiologie.* Vienna: Carl Gerold.

Guislain, Joseph. 1826. *Traité sur l'aliénation mentale et sur les hospices des aliénés.* Amsterdam: Hey et Fils.

Gurney, Edmund. 1899. 'Wagner and Wagnerism'. In *Tertium Quid.* 2 vols. II:1–46. London: Kegan Paul, Trench & Co.

Gutman, Robert. 1990. *Richard Wagner.* Fort Washington, PA: Harvest.

Guyer, Paul. 2003. 'History of Modern Aesthetics'. In *The Oxford Handbook of Aesthetics*, ed. Jerrold Levinson, 25–60. Oxford: Oxford University Press.

Hacking, Ian. 1995. *Rewriting the Soul: Multiple Personality Disorder and the Sciences of Memory.* Princeton, NJ: Princeton University Press.

Hadamowsky, Franz. 1966. *Die Wiener Hoftheater (Staatstheater) 1776–1966.* Vienna: Prachner.

Hadlock, Heather. 2000. 'Sonorous Bodies: Women and the Glass Harmonica'. *Journal of the American Musicological Society*, 53/3, 507–42.

Hagner, Michael, ed. 1999. *Ecce Cortex: Beiträge zur Geschichte des modernen Gehirns.* Göttingen: Wallstein Verlag.

Hagner, Michael, and Bettina Wahrig-Schmidt, eds. 1992. *Johannes Müller und die Philosophie.* Berlin: Akademie.

Hallion, Richard P. 2003. *Taking Flight: Inventing the Aerial Age from Antiquity through the First World War.* Oxford: Oxford University Press.

Hamon, Philippe. 1992. *Expositions: Literature and Architecture in Nineteenth-Century France.* Berkeley: University of California Press.

Hankins, Thomas L., and Robert J. Silvermann. 1995. 'The Aeolian Harp and the Romantic Quest of Nature'. In *Instruments and the Imagination*, 86–112. Princeton, NJ: Princeton University Press.

Hansen, Miriam. 1992. 'Ambivalences of the "Mass Ornament": King Vidor's *The Crowd*'. *Qui parle* 5/2, 102–19.

Hanslick, Eduard. 1950. *Vienna's Golden Years of Music.* New York: Simon and Schuster.

1986. *On the Musically Beautiful*, ed. and trans. Geoffrey Payzant. Indianapolis: Hackett Publishing.

Haraway, Donna. 1991. *Simians, Cyborgs, and Women: The Reinvention of Nature.* New York: Routledge.

Harding, Geoffrey. 1988. *Opiate Addiction, Morality and Medicine.* New York: St Martin's Press.

Harman, P. M. 1982. *Energy, Force, and Matter: The Conceptual Development of Nineteenth-Century Physics.* Cambridge: Cambridge University Press.

Harris, Augustus. 1889. 'Polyglot Opera'. *The Spectator.* 4 May, 605.

Heidenhain, Rudolf. 1880. *Animal Magnetism: Physiological Observations.* London: Kegan Paul.

Bibliography

Heidenreich, Jacob Breder. 1850. 'Bericht über die Leistungen in der Ohrenheilkunde'. In *Jahresbericht über die Fortschritte in der gesammten Medicin ...*, ed. Gottfried Eisenmann, 1:150–63. Erlangen: Ferdinand Enke.

Heller, M. P. 1930. *Die Musik als Geschenk der Natur.* Berlin: Richard Birnbach.

Helmholtz, Hermann von. [1857] 1884. 'Ueber die physiologischen Ursachen der musikalischen Harmonie'. In *Vorträge und Reden.* 2 vols. 1:119–55. Braunschweig: Vieweg und Sohn.

1859. 'Ueber die Klangfarbe der Vocale'. *Annalen der Physik und Chemie* 108, 280–90

1863. *Die Lehre von den Tonempfindungen.* Braunschweig: Vieweg und Sohn.

[1868] 1884. 'Die neueren Fortschritte in der Theorie des Sehens'. In *Vorträge und Reden.* 2 vols. 1:265–365. Braunschweig: Vieweg und Sohn.

1883. 'On the Physiological Causes of Harmony in Music'. In *Popular Lectures on Scientific Subjects*, trans. E. Atkinson, 53–93. New York: D. Appleton and Co.

1954. *On the Sensations of Tone as a Physiological Basis for the Theory of Music*, trans. A. Ellis. 4th edn. New York: Dover.

Henderson, William James. 1894. 'The Downfall of Bayreuth'. *Saturday Review of Politics, Literature, Science, and Art.* 25 August, 207–08.

1895. 'A Week's Musical Topics'. *New York Times.* 1 December, 13.

1896. '"Lohengrin" at the Opera: An Excellent Performance in German of Wagner's Lyric Drama'. *New York Times.* 28 November, 8.

1901a. 'Among Musicians: End of the Season at the Metropolitan Opera House'. *New York Times.* 31 March, 20.

1901b. 'Return of Jean de Reszke'. *New York Times.* 1 January, 6.

Henrich, Dieter. 1993. *Selbstverhältnisse: Gedanken und Auslegungen zu den Grundlagen der klassischen deutschen Philosophie.* Stuttgart: Reclam.

Henseler, Theodor Anton. 1959. *Das musikalische Bonn im 19. Jahrhundert.* Bonn: Universitäts-Buchdruckerei.

Henson, Karen. 2007. 'Verdi versus Victor Maurel on Falstaff: Twelve New Verdi Letters and Other Operatic and Musical Theater Sources'. *19th-Century Music* 31/2, 113–30.

2015. *Opera Acts: Singers and Performance in the Late Nineteenth Century.* Cambridge: Cambridge University Press.

ed. 2016. *Technology and the Diva: Sopranos, Opera, and Media from Romanticism to the Digital Age.* Cambridge: Cambridge University Press.

Hentschel, Frank. 2006. *Bürgerliche Ideologie und Musik.* Frankfurt: Campus.

Hepokoski, James. 2002. 'Back and Forth from Egmont: Beethoven, Mozart, and the Nonresolving Recapitulation'. *19th-Century Music* 25/2–3, 127–54.

Herrmann, Hans-Christian von. 2007. '"Induction psycho-motrice" – Zur technischen Widerkehr der Kunst in Hysterie und Hypnose'. In *Electric Laokoon: Zeichen und Medien von der Lochkarte zur Grammatologie*, ed. Michael Franz, Wolfgang Schäffner, Bernhard Siegert and Robert Stockhammer, 82–96. Berlin: Akademie Verlag.

Herschel, John. 1831. *A Preliminary Discourse on the Study of Natural Philosophy*. London: Longman et al.

Herz, Markus. 1798. 'Etwas Psychologisch-Medizinisches; Moriz Krankengeschichte'. *Journal der practischen Arzneykunde* 5/2, 321–39.

Heyse, Paul. 1984. 'Kinder der Welt'. In *Gesammelte Werke*. 15 vols. Hildesheim: Georg Olms.

Hibberd, Sarah. 2013. '*Le Naufrage de la Méduse* and Operatic Spectacle in 1830s Paris'. *19th-Century Music* 36/3, 248–63.

Hills, Richard L. 1993. *Power from Steam: A History of the Stationary Steam Engine*. Cambridge: Cambridge University Press.

Hirjak, Dusan, Thiemo Breyer, Philipp Arthur Thomann and Thomas Fuchs. 2013. 'Disturbance of Intentionality: A Phenomenological Study of Body-Affecting First-Rank Symptoms in Schizophrenia'. *PLOS ONE* 8/9, www.ncbi.nlm.nih.gov/pmc/articles/PMC3760919.

Hoffmann, E. T. A. 1963. 'Der Dichter und der Komponist'. In *Musikalischen Novellen und Schriften*, ed. P. F. Scherber. Munich: Goldmann.

  1982. 'Der Sandmann' [1816]. In *Tales of Hoffmann*, trans. R. J. Hollingdale, 85–126. London: Penguin Books.

  1989. *E. T. A. Hoffmann's Musical Writings*, trans. Martyn Clarke, ed. David Charlton. Cambridge: Cambridge University Press.

Holmes, Gordon. 1879. *A Treatise on Vocal Physiology and Hygiene with Especial Reference to the Cultivation and Preservation of the Voice*. London: J. Churchill.

Holmes, Richard. 2008. *The Age of Wonder: How the Romantic Generation Discovered the Beauty and Terror of Science*. New York: Pantheon Books.

Horowitz, Joseph. 1994. *Wagner Nights: An American History*. Berkeley: University of California Press.

  2005. *Classical Music in America: A History of Its Rise and Fall*. New York: W. W. Norton.

Huebner, Steven. 2003. 'After 1850 at the Paris Opéra: Institution and Repertory'. In *The Cambridge Companion to Grand Opera*, ed. David Charlton, 291–317. Cambridge: Cambridge University Press.

Hugill, Andrew. 2012. *The Digital Musician*. 2nd edn. New York: Routledge.

Huhtamo, Erkki, and Jussi Parikka. 2011. *Media Archaeology: Approaches, Applications, and Implications*. Berkeley: University of California Press.

Hui, Alexandra. 2012. *The Psychophysical Ear: Musical Experiments, Experimental Sounds 1840–1910*. Cambridge, MA: MIT Press.

Hui, Alexandra, Julia Kursell and Myles W. Jackson, eds. 2013. 'Music, Sound and the Laboratory 1750–1980'. *Osiris* 28.

Hunt, E. K., trans. 1845. *Mental Maladies: A Treatise on Insanity Volume 1*, by Étienne Esquirol. Philadelphia, PA: Lea and Blanchard.

Hunter, Mary. 1999. *The Culture of Opera Buffa in Mozart's Vienna: A Poetics of Entertainment*. Princeton, NJ: Princeton University Press.

Hustvedt, Asti. 2011. *Medical Muses: Hysteria in Nineteenth-Century Paris*. New York: W. W. Norton.

Hutcheon, Linda, and Michael Hutcheon. 1996. *Opera: Desire, Disease, Death*. Lincoln: University of Nebraska Press.

2000. *Bodily Charm: Living Opera*. Lincoln: The University of Nebraska Press.

Huysmans, Joris-Karl. 1959. *Against Nature*, trans. Robert Baldick. Harmondsworth, UK: Penguin.

Huyssen, Andreas. 1986. *After the Great Divide*. Bloomington: Indiana University Press.

Hyer, Brian. 2006. 'Parsifal hystérique'. *Opera Quarterly* 22/2, 269–320.

Hyslop, Theo. 1895. *Mental Physiology*. London: J. & A. Churchill.

Itard, Jean Marc Gaspard. 1821. *Traité des maladies d'oreille et de l'audition*. Paris: Méquignon Marvis.

Izenour, George C. 1996. *Theater Technology*. 2nd edn. New Haven, CT: Yale University Press.

Jackson, Myles W. 2006. *Harmonious Triads: Physicists, Musicians, and Instrument Makers*. Cambridge, MA: MIT Press.

2010–11. 'Measuring Musical Virtuosity: Physicists, Physiologists, and the Pianist's Touch in the Nineteenth Century'. *Journal of the American Liszt Society* 61–62, 13–40.

Jacyna, L. S. 1981. 'The Physiology of Mind, the Unity of Nature, and the Moral Order in Victorian Thought'. *The British Journal for the History of Science* 14/2, 109–32.

Jakobson, Roman. 1971. 'Linguistics and Communication Theory'. In *Selected Writings II: Word and Language*, 570–9. The Hague: Mouton & Co.

1987. *Language in Literature*, ed. Krystyna Pomorska and Stephen Rudy. Cambridge, MA: Harvard University Press.

James, Frank A. J. L., ed. 1991. *The Correspondence of Michael Faraday*. 6 vols. London: Institution of Electrical Engineers.

James, William. 1879. 'Are We Automata?' *Mind* 4, 1–22.

[1890] 2007. *Principles of Psychology*. Rpt. New York: Cosima.

Jentsch, Ernst. 1904. *Musik und Nerven*. 2 vols. Wiesbaden: J. F. Bergmann.

Joal, Joseph. 1892. 'Du mécanisme de la respiration chez les chanteurs'. *Revue de laryngologie, d'otologie et de rhinologie* 14/8 (15 April), 225–49.

Jobé, J. 1971. *The Romance of Ballooning: The Story of the Early Aeronauts*. New York: Viking Press.

Johnson, James H. 1995. *Listening in Paris: A Cultural History*. Berkeley: University of California Press.

Jordan, Peter. 2015. 'Pantalone and Il Dottore: The Old Men of Commedia'. In *The Routledge Companion to Commedia Dell'Arte*, ed. Judith Chaffee and Oliver Crick, 62–9. New York: Routledge.

Kahn, Douglas. 1999. *Noise, Water, Meat*. Cambridge, MA: MIT Press.

Kalbeck, Max. 1990. '*Salome*: Music Drama in One Act after Oscar Wilde, by Richard Strauss', trans. Susan Gillespie. In *Richard Strauss and His World*, ed. Bryan Gilliam, 336–42. Princeton, NJ: Princeton University Press.

Kämmerer, Sebastian. 1990. *Illusionismus und Anti-Illusionismus im Musiktheater*. Salzburg: Verlag Ursula Müller-Speiser.

Kane, Brian. 2014. *Sound Unseen: Acousmatic Sound in Theory and Practice*. New York: Oxford University Press.

Kane, Robert, ed. 2011. *The Oxford Handbook to Free Will*. 2nd edn. New York: Oxford University Press.

Kapp, Ernst. 1877. *Grundlinien einer Philosophie der Technik: Zur Entstehungsgeschichte der Cultur aus neuen Gesichtspunkten*. Braunschweig: Westermann.

Keen, Paul. 2006. 'The "Balloonomania": Science and Spectacle in 1780s England'. *Eighteenth-Century Studies* 39/4, 507–35.

Kennaway, James. 2005. 'The Wagner Case: Nietzsche's Use of Psychiatry in his Wagner Books'. *New German Review* 20, 84–95.

    2012a. *Bad Vibrations: The History of the Idea of Music as a Cause of Disease*. Farnham, UK: Ashgate.

    2012b. 'Musical Hypnosis: Sound and Selfhood from Mesmerism to Brainwashing'. *Social History of Medicine* 25/2, 271–89.

    2012c. 'Pathologische Musik im *Zauberberg*'. *Thomas-Mann-Studien* 49, 17–35.

Keynes, R. D., ed. 1988. *Charles Darwin's* Beagle *Diary*. Cambridge: Cambridge University Press.

Kidder, Frank Eugene. 1886. *The Architect's and Builder's Pocket-Book*. New York: John Wiley.

Kienzle, Ulrike. 1998. *Das Trauma hinter dem Traum: Franz Schrekers Oper 'Der ferne Klang' und die Wiener Moderne*. Schliengen: Edition Argos.

Kiesewetter, Raphael Georg. 1834. *Geschichte der europäisch-abendländischen oder unserer heutigen Musik*. Leipzig: Breitkopf und Härtel.

Kircher, Athanasius. [1650] 1970. *Musurgia universalis*. 2 vols. Rome: Francisci Corbelletti. Facsimile edn. Hildesheim: Olms.

Kittler, Friedrich. 1987. 'Weltatem: On Wagner's Media Technology'. In *Wagner in Retrospect: A Centennial Reappraisal*, ed. Leroy Shaw, Nancy R. Cirillo and Marion S. Miller, 203–12. Amsterdam: Rodopi.

    1999. *Gramophone, Film, Typewriter*, trans. Geoffrey Winthrop-Young and Michael Wutz. Stanford, CA: Stanford University Press.

    2002. 'Goethes Gabe'. In *Wechselwirkungen: Kunst und Wissenschaft in Berlin und Weimar im Zeichen Goethes*, ed. Ernst Osterkamp, 155–66. Bern: Peter Lang.

2006. 'Number and Numeral'. *Theory, Culture & Society* 23/7–8, 51–61.

2013. 'World Breath'. *The Truth of the Technological World*, ed. Hans Ulrich Gumbrecht, 122–37. Stanford, CA: Stanford University Press.

Kleffel, Arno. 1990. 'Ueber Konfusion in der Musik'. In *'Die Konfusion in der Musik': Felix Draesekes Kampfschrift von 1906 und die Folgen*, ed. Susanne Shigihara, 145–51. Bonn: Gudrun Schröder.

Klein, Hermann. 1903. 'Modern Musical Celebrities, IV'. *The Century Illustrated Monthly Magazine*. July. 461–71.

Knowles, Thomas, and Serena Trowbridge, eds. 2015. *Insanity and the Lunatic Asylum in the Nineteenth Century*. London: Routledge.

Kobbé, Gustav. 1901. 'The Opera Season'. *Harper's Weekly*. 13 April. 390.

Koch, Heinrich Christoph. 1782–93. *Versuch einer Anleitung zur Komposition*. 2 vols. Rudolstadt: Adam F. Böhme.

Kolb, Fabian. 2016. 'Das Orchester als Klangraum: Hector Berlioz' Le Chef d'orchestre und seine Überlegungen zu Raumakustik und Orchesteraufstellung'. In *Maestro! Dirigieren im 19. Jahrhundert*, ed. Alessandro Di Profio and Arnold Jacobshagen, 109–51. Würzburg: Königshausen und Neumann.

Kolb, Katherine. 2009. 'Flying Leaves: Between Berlioz and Wagner'. *19th-Century Music* 33/1, 25–61.

Koller, Oswald. 1901. 'Die Musik im Lichte der Darwinschen Theorie'. *Jahrbuch der Musikbibliothek Peters* 7, 35–50.

Kracauer, Siegfried. 1927. 'Ornament der Masse' (Parts 1 and 2). *Frankfurter Zeitung*. 9 June.

1963. 'Die Laden Mädchen gehen ins Kino'. In *Das Ornament der Masse: Essays*, 279–95. Frankfurt: Suhrkamp.

1995. *The Mass Ornament: Weimar Essays*, trans. Thomas Y. Levin. Cambridge, MA: Harvard University Press.

2002. *Jacques Offenbach and the Paris of his Time*, trans. Gwenda David and Eric Mosbacher. New York: Zone Books.

Krafft-Ebing, Richard von. 1903. *Über gesunde und kranke Nerven*. Tübingen: n.p.

Kramer, Wilhelm. 1861. *Die Ohrenheilkunde der Gegenwart*. Berlin: August Hirschwald.

1867. *Handbuch der Ohrenheilkunde*. Berlin: August Hirschwald.

Krause, Karl Chr. Fr. 1839. *Anfangsgründe der allgemeinen Theorie der Musik nach Grundsätzen der Wesenslehre*, ed. Victor Strauss. Göttingen: Ditterichsche Buchhandlung.

Kregor, Jonathan. 2015. *Program Music*. Cambridge: Cambridge University Press.

Krehbiel, Henry Edward. 1908. *Chapters of Opera*. 2nd edn. New York: Henry Holt and Company.

Kreuzer, Gundula. 2011. 'Wagner-Dampf: Steam in Der Ring Des Nibelungen and Operatic Production'. *The Opera Quarterly* 27/2–3, 179–218.

Kroger, William S., ed. 2008. *Clinical and Experimental Hypnosis in Medicine, Dentistry, and Psychology*. 2nd edn. Philadelphia, PA: Lippincott Williams & Wilkins.

Kursell, Julia. 2018. *Epistemologie des Hörens: Helmholtz' physiologische Grundlegung der Musiktheorie*. Paderborn: Fink.

Kurth, Ernst. 1920. *Romantische Harmonik und ihre Krise in Wagners 'Tristan'*. Berlin: Max Hesse.

l'Isle-Adam, A. Villiers de. 1986. 'La Séance du Docteur Muller'. *Oeuvres complètes*, ed. Allan Raitt and Pierre-Georges Castex, 913. Paris: Gallimard.

Labouïsse, Jean-Pierre-Jacques-Auguste de. 1827. *Voyage à Saint-Léger: campagne de M. le chevalier de Boufflers suivi, du Voyage à Charenton*. Paris: Trouvé.

Laffey, Paul. 2003. 'Psychiatric Treatment in Georgian Britain'. *Psychological Medicine* 33/7, 1285–97.

Lafontaine, Charles. 1852. *L'Art de magnétiser: ou, le magnétisme animal considéré sous le point de vue théorique, pratique et thérapeutique*. 2nd edn. Paris: Baillière.

1866. *Mémoires d'un magnétiseur: suivis de l'examen phrénologique de l'auteur*. 2 vols. Paris: Germer-Baillière.

Lamperti, Francesco. 1864. *Guida teorico-pratica-elementare per lo studio del canto*. Milan: Ricordi.

Lampl, Erich. 1986. 'Ex Oblivione: Das Féré-Palimpsest'. *Nietzsche-Studien* 15, 225–64.

Lange, Friedrich A. [1865] 1880. *History of Materialism and Criticism of its Present Importance*. 3 vols. London: Trübner & Co.

Langford, Jeffrey. 2000. 'The Symphonies'. In *The Cambridge Companion to Berlioz*, ed. Peter Bloom, 52–68. Cambridge: Cambridge University Press.

Latour, Bruno. 1993 *Aramis, ou L'Amour des Techniques*. Paris: Editions de la Découverte. In English as *Aramis, or the Love of Technology*, trans. Catherine Porter. Cambridge, MA: Harvard University Press, 1996.

Lavater, Johann Kaspar. 1778. *Physiognomische Fragmente zur Beförderung der Menschenkenntnis und Menschenliebe*. Leipzig & Winterthur: Weidmanns Erben & Reich, Steiner.

Lawtoo, Nidesh. 2008. 'Nietzsche and the Psychology of Mimesis: From Plato to the Führer'. In *Nietzsche, Power and Politics*, ed. Herman. W. Siemens and Vasti Roodt, 667–93. Berlin: Walter de Gruyter.

Le Guin, Elisabeth. 2002. '"One Says That One Weeps, but One Does Not Weep": *Sensible*, Grotesque, and Mechanical Embodiments in Boccherini's Chamber Music'. *Journal of the American Musicological Society* 55/2, 207–54.

Le Trioux, O. 1875. 'L'inauguration du Nouvel Opéra'. *Chronique musicale* 38 (15 January), 74–8.

Lehmann, Lilli. 1902. *How to Sing*, trans. Richard Aldrich. New York: Macmillan.

Lehrer, Jonah. 2007. *Proust was a Neuroscientist*. Boston, MA: Houghton Mifflin Harcourt.

Lenoir, Timothy. 1986. 'Models and Instruments in the Development of Electricity, 1845–1912'. *Historical Studies in the Physical and Biological Sciences* 17/1, 1–54.

Letellier, Robert Ignatius. 2012. 'Introduction'. In *Romualdo Marenco: Excelsior and Sport*, ed. Robert Ignatius Letellier. Newcastle upon Tyne: Cambridge Scholars.

Levitin, Daniel. 2006. *This is Your Brain on Music: The Science of a Human Obsession*. Harmondsworth, UK: Penguin Plume.

Lewis, Peter. 2005. 'Original Nonsense: Art and Genius in Kant's Aesthetics'. In *Kant and his Influence*, ed. George MacDonald Ross and Tony McWalter, 126–44. London: Continuum.

Leydi, Roberto, and Renata Mezzanotte Leydi. 1958. *Marionette e burattini*. Milan: Collana del Gallo Grande.

Lichtenberg, Georg. 1789. 'Artikel über die "Riesen-Wetterharfe" des Hauptmann Haas in Basel'. *Göttinger Taschenkalender*, 129–34.

Lichtenthal, Peter. 1807. *Der musikalische Arzt, oder: Abhandlung von dem Einflusse der Musik auf den Körper*. Vienna: Wappler und Beck.

1831. *Estetica, ossia, Dottrina del bello e delle arti belle*. Milan: Giovanni Pirotta.

Lightman, Bernard. 2007. 'Lecturing in the Spatial Economy of Science'. In *Science in the Marketplace: Nineteenth-Century Sites and Experiences*, ed. Aileen Fyfe and Bernard Lightman, 97–132. Chicago, IL: University of Chicago Press.

Liszt, Franz. 1851. *Lohengrin et Tannhäuser de Richard Wagner*. Leipzig: F. A. Brockhaus.

Lo Iacono, Concetta. 1987. 'Manzotti e Marenco: Il diritto di due autori'. *Nuova rivista musicale italiana* 21/3, 421–46.

Lockhart, Ellen. 2016. 'Transparent Music: Sound–Light Analogies ca. 1800'. In *Sound Knowledge: Music and Science in London, 1789–1861*, ed. Ellen Lockhart and James Davies, 77–100. Chicago, IL: University of Chicago Press.

2017. *Animation, Plasticity, and Music in Italy, 1770–1830*. Oakland: University of California Press.

Lodge, Paul. 2004. *Leibniz and his Correspondents*. Cambridge: Cambridge University Press.

Lombroso, Cesare. 1864. *Genio e follia*. Turin: Bocca.

1894. *Genio e degenerazione*. Milan: Sandron.

2006. *Criminal Man*, trans. Mary Gibson and Nicole Hahn Rafter. Durham, NC: Duke University Press.

Lopez, Guido. 1981. *Esposizione nazionale di Milano, 1881: documenti e immagini 100 anni dopo*. Milan: Ripartizione cultura e spettacolo.

Loughridge, Deirdre. 2016. *Haydn's Sunrise, Beethoven's Shadow: Audiovisual Culture and the Emergence of Musical Romanticism*. Chicago, IL: University of Chicago Press.

Löwe, Ludwig. 1884. *Lehrbuch der Ohrenheilkunde*. Berlin: G. Hempel.

Lunn, Charles. [1874] 1900. *The Philosophy of Voice: Showing the Right and Wrong Action of Voice in Speech and Song, with Laws for Self-Culture*. 9th edn. London: Baillière, Tindall, and Cox.

Macdonald, Hugh. 2002. *Berlioz's Orchestration Treatise: A Translation and Commentary*. Cambridge: Cambridge University Press.

2008. *Beethoven's Century: Essays on Composers and Themes*. Rochester, NY: University of Rochester Press.

Macfarren, G. A. 1838. *The Devil's Opera. In Two Acts*. London: Chapman and Hall.

Mackenzie, Morell. [1886] 1891. *The Hygiene of the Vocal Organs: A Practical Handbook for Singers and Speakers*. 7th edn. New York: Edgar S. Werner.

Mackinlay, Malcolm Sterling. 1908. *García the Centenarian and His Times, Being a Memoir of Manuel García's Life Labours for the Advancement of Music and Science*. New York: D. Appleton and Company.

Magendie, François. 1816–17. *Précis élémentaire de physiologie*. 2 vols. Paris: Méquignon-Marvis.

1822. 'Expériences sur les fonctions des racines des nerfs rachidiens'. *Journal de physiologie expérimentale* 2, 276–9, 366–71.

Magnin, Émile. [1906]. *L'art et l'hypnose. Interprétation plastique d'œuvres littéraires et musicales par Émile Magnin, professeur à l'école de magnétisme de Paris*. Paris: Félix Alcan.

Maillet, Arnaud. 2012. 'Kaleidoscopic Imagination', trans. Phoebe Prioleau and Elaine Briggs. *Grey Room* 48, 36–55.

Mantegazza, Paolo. 1891. *Epikur: Physiologie des Schönen*. Jena: H. Costenobel.

Manzotti, Luigi. 1881. *Excelsior: Azione coreografica, storica, allegorica, fantastica in 6 parti ed 11 quadri*. Milan: Ricordi.

Marchesi, Blanche. 1932. *The Singer's Catechism and Creed*. London: Dent.

Marchetti, Arnaldo, with Vittorio Giuliani, ed. 1973. *Puccini com'era*. Milan: Curci.

Marenco, Romualdo. 1881a. 'I fattorini del telegrafo: nuovo galop per pianoforte a 4 mani', arr. L. Rivetta. Milan: Ricordi.

1881b. 'Il Risorgimento: gran valzer e galop (Quadro 2)', arr. Michele Saladino. Milan: Ricordi.

Marshall, Jonathan. 2008. 'Dynamic Medicine and Theatrical Form at the Fin de Siècle: A Formal Analysis of Dr Jean-Martin Charcot's Pedagogy, 1862–1893'. *Modernism/Modernity* 15/1, 131–53.

Marx, Adolf Bernhard. 1884. *Das Leben Ludwig van Beethovens*. 4th edn. Berlin: Otto Janker.

Marx, Karl. 1904. *A Contribution to the Critique of Political Economy*, trans. N. I. Stone. Chicago, IL: Charles H. Kerr & Co.

1993. *Grundrisse: Foundations of the Critique of Political Economy*, trans. Martin Nicolaus. London: Penguin.

Marx, Leo. 2010. 'Technology: The Emergence of a Hazardous Concept'. *Technology and Culture* 51/3, 561–77.

Mathew, Nicholas, and Mary Ann Smart. 2015. 'Elephants in the Music Room: The Future of Quirk Historicism'. *Representations* 132/1, 61–78.

Matteucci, Carlo. 1851. *Manuale di telegrafia elettrica*. Pisa: Mistri.

Maudsley, Henry. 1883. *Body and Will*. London: Kegan Paul, Trench & Co.

Bibliography

Maurel, Berty. [1923?]. *Victor Maurel: ses idées, son art*. Paris: Imprimerie de la Bourse de Commerce.

Maurel, Victor. 1892. *Le Chant rénové par la science*. Paris: A. Quinzard.

1897. *Dix ans de carrière, avec une préface de Léon Kerst et des portraits*. Paris: V. Villerelle.

1904. *Conférence d'ouverture du Cours d'esthétique vocale et scénique professé par M. Victor Maurel à l'École des Hautes Études Sociales*. Paris: Maison rapide.

Mawson, Harry P. 1891. 'Grand Opera in French and Italian'. *Harper's Weekly* 11/21 (21 November), 917.

Mayer, Hans. 1978. '*Tannhäuser* und die künstlichen Paradiese'. In *Richard Wagner: Mitwelt und Nachwelt*, 191–200. Stuttgart: Belser Verlag.

Mays, Thomas J. 1887. 'An Experimental Inquiry into the Chest Movements of the Indian Female'. *The Therapeutic Gazette* 3/5 (16 May), 297–9.

McCarren, Felicia. 2003. *Dancing Machines: Choreographies of the Age of Mechanical Reproduction*. Stanford, CA: Stanford University Press.

McClary, Susan. 1997. 'The Impromptu that Trod on a Loaf: Or How Music Tells Stories'. *Narrative* 5/1, 20–35.

McClatchie, Stephen. 1998. *Analyzing Wagner's Operas: Alfred Lorenz and German Nationalist Ideology*. Rochester, NY: University of Rochester Press.

McConnell, Anita. 2004. 'Papin, Denis (1647–1712?)'. *Oxford Dictionary of National Biography* 42:597–9. Oxford: Oxford University Press.

Mead, Christopher Curtis. 1991. *Charles Garnier's Paris Opéra: Architectural Empathy and the Renaissance of French Classicism*. Cambridge, MA: MIT Press.

Meeuwis, Michael. 2012. '"The Theatre Royal Back Drawing-Room": Professionalizing Domestic Entertainment in Victorian Acting Manuals'. *Victorian Studies* 54/3 (Spring), 427–37.

Ménière, Prosper. 1861. 'Mémoire sur des lésions de l'oreille interne donnant lieu à des symptômes de congestion cérébrale apoplectiforme'. *Gazette médicale de Paris* 16, 88–9, 239–40, 379–80, 597–601.

Merz, John Theodore. 1903–14. *A History of European Thought in the Nineteenth Century*. 4 vols. Edinburgh: William Blackwood and Sons.

Messmer, Franzpeter, ed. 1989. *Kritiken zu den Uraufführungen der Bühnenwerke Richard Strauss*. Pfaffenhofen: W. Ludwig.

Meulders, Michel. 2010. *Helmholtz: From Enlightenment to Neuroscience*. Cambridge, MA: MIT Press.

Micale, Mark S. 1985. 'The Salpêtrière in the Age of Charcot: An Institutional Perspective on Medical History in the Late Nineteenth Century'. *Journal of Contemporary History* 20/4, 703–31.

Moffatt, William. 1896. 'A Note on Lohengrin'. *The Looker-On*. July. 31–5.

Moll, Christian Hieronymus von. 1773. *Die ländlichen Hochzeitfeste in 5 Aufzügen*. Vienna: n.p.

Moltzor, Charles Henry. 1902. 'De Reszke on Americans: Great Tenor tells Charles Henry Moltzor'. *Los Angeles Times*. 13 September. 3.

Monroe, Lewis B. 1869. *A Manual of Physical and Vocal Training*. Philadelphia, PA: Cowperthwait.

Montgomery, L. H. 1884. 'Chicago Medical Society'. *Journal of the American Medical Association* 3/2, 50–4.

Monti Colla, Eugenio. n.d. 'La poesia della danza meccanica: Il balletto e il teatro di marionette'. www.ateatro.it.

Moreau, Jacques Joseph. 1859. *La Psychologie morbide dans ses rapports avec la philosophie de l'histoire*. Paris: V. Masson.

Morel, Benedict. 1857. *Traité des degenerescences Physiques, intellectuelles et morales de l'espèce humaine et des causes qui produisant ces variétés maladives*. Paris: J. H. Bailliére.

Morini, Mario. 1979. 'Un omaggio di Puccini a Volta'. *Rassegna musicale Curci* 32 (August), 9–14.

Mosconi, Elena. 2006. *L'impressione del film: contributi per una storia culturale del cinema italiano, 1895–1945*. Milan: V&P.

Mosse, George. 1996. *The Image of Man*. Oxford: Oxford University Press.

Motte-Haber, Helga de la. 2012. 'Impulses towards a Cognitive Theory of Musical Evolution'. In Carl Stumpf, *The Origins of Music*, ed. and trans. David Trippett, 3–16. Oxford: Oxford University Press.

Moynet, Georges. 1893. *La Machinerie théâtrale: Trucs et Décors*. Paris: À la Librairie Illustrée.

Moynet, Jean-Pierre. [1873] 1976. *L'Envers du Théâtre: Machines et Décorations*. Paris: Hachette. In English as *French Theatrical Production in the Nineteenth Century*, trans. and augmented by Allan S. Jackson with M. Glen Wilson. Binghamton, NY: Max Reinhardt Foundation with the Center for Modern Theater Research.

Mudry, Albert. 2000. 'The Role of Adam Politzer (1835–1920) in the History of Otology'. *American Journal of Otology* 21/5, 753–63.

Müller, Adam. 1996. 'On the Art of Listening'. In *German Essays on Science in the 19th Century*, ed. Wolfgang Schirmacher, 130–40. New York: Continuum.

Müller, Georg Elias. 1873. *Zur Theorie der sinnlichen Aufmerksamkeit*. Leipzig: A. Edelmann.

Müller, Johannes. 1826a. *Über die phantastischen Gesichtserscheinungen: Eine physiologische Untersuchung mit einer physiologischen Urkunde des Aristoteles über den Traum*. Coblenz: Hölscher.

    1826b. *Zur vergleichenden Physiologie des Gesichtssinnes des Menschen und der Thiere: Nebst einem Versuch über die Bewegungen der Augen und über den menschlichen Blick*. Leipzig: Cnobloch.

    1835–40. *Handbuch der Physiologie des Menschen*. 2 vols. Coblenz: J. Hölscher.

    1843. *Elements of Physiology*. Philadelphia, PA: Lea and Blanchard.

Munthe, Axel. 2004. *The Story of San Michele* [1929]. London: John Murray.

Bibliography

Murat, Laure. 2014. *The Man Who Thought He Was Napoleon: Toward a Political History of Madness*, trans. Deke Dusinberre. Chicago: University of Chicago Press, 2014.

Myer, Edmund. 1891. *Vocal Reinforcement.* New York: American Publishing Co.

Nancy, Jean-Luc. 2008. 'Foreword: Ascoltando'. In Peter Szendy, *Listen: A History of Our Ears*, x–xi. New York: Fordham University Press.

Nansouty, Max de. 1884. 'Machinerie Théâtrale. La Manœuvre du vaisseau de "L'Africaine" à l'Opéra de Paris'. *Le Génie civil* 4/14 (2 February), 221–5.

Nattiez, Jean-Jacques. 1990. 'Can One Speak of Narrativity in Music?', trans. Katharine Ellis. *Journal of the Royal Musical Association* 115/2, 240–57.

Newcomb, Anthony. 1995. 'New Light(s) on Weber's Wolf's Glen Scene'. In *Opera and the Enlightenment*, ed. Thomas Bauman and Marita Petzoldt McClymonds, 61–90. Cambridge: Cambridge University Press.

Nicolas, Serge. 2005. *Théodule Ribot philosophe breton, fondateur de la psychologie française.* Paris: L'Harmattan.

Niemann, Walter. 1913. *Die Musik seit Richard Wagner.* Berlin: Schuster & Loeffler.

Nietzsche, Friedrich. 1968. 'The Case of Wagner: A Musicians' Problem', trans. Walter Kaufmann, available at http://users.compaqnet.be/cn127103/Nietzsche_various/the_case_of_wagner.htm.

1969. *Nietzsche Werke*, ed. Giorgio Colli and Mazzini Montinari. 30 vols. Berlin: De Gruyter.

1994. *On the Genealogy of Morality* [1887], ed. Keith Ansell-Pearson, trans. Carol Diethe. Cambridge: Cambridge University Press.

Norbury, Frank Parsons. 1896. 'Nervousness in Young Women: Its Mechanism and Some of its Causes'. *The Medical Fortnightly* 9–10, 112–13.

Nordau, Max. 1895. *Degeneration.* New York: Appleton.

North, Michael. 1994. *The Dialect of Modernism: Race, Language, and Twentieth-Century Literature.* Oxford: Oxford University Press.

Nostitz und Jänkendorf, Gottlob Adolf Ernst von. 1829. *Beschreibung der königl. Sächsischen Heil- und Verpflegungsanstalt Sonnenstein: mit Bemerkungen über Anstalten für Herstellung oder Verwahrung der Geisteskranken.* Dresden: Walther.

Novalis [Friedrich von Hardenberg]. 1967. *Gesammelte Werke*, ed. Hildburg and Werner Kohlschmidt. Gütersloh: S. Mohn.

Nuitter, Charles. 1875. *Le Nouvel Opéra.* Paris: Hachette.

Offenbach, Jacques. 1955. *New Version of Les Contes d'Hoffmann (The Tales of Hoffmann): Opera in a Prologue, Three Acts and an Epilogue. Music by J. Offenbach, Libretto by Jules Barbier, English Text by John Gutman.* New York: Fred Rullman, Inc.

Orde-Hume, Arthur. 1986. *Harmonium: The History of the Reed Organ and Its Makers.* London: David & Charles.

Osterhammel, Jürgen. 2014. *The Transformation of the World: A Global History of the Nineteenth Century*, trans. Patrick Camiller. Princeton, NJ: Princeton University Press.

Otis, Laura. 2001. *Networking: Communicating with Bodies and Machines in the Nineteenth Century*. Ann Arbor: University of Michigan Press.

2007. *Müller's Lab*. New York: Oxford University Press.

n.d. 'Johannes Müller'. In *The Virtual Laboratory: Essays and Resources on the Experimentalization of Life*. http://vlp.mpiwg-berlin.mpg.de/essays/data/enc22.

Painter, Karen. 1995. 'The Sensuality of Timbre'. *19th-Century Music* 18/3, 236–56.

Pantalony, David. 2009. *Altered Sensations: Rudolph Koenig's Acoustical Workshop in Nineteenth-Century Paris*. Dordrecht: Springer.

Pappacena, Flavia. 1998. *Excelsior: Documenti e saggi*. Rome: Di Giacomo.

Pappas, Dennis G. 1996. 'Otology through the Ages'. *Otolaryngology – Head and Neck Surgery* 114/2 (February), 173–96.

Pappenheim, Samuel. 1840. *Die specielle Gewebelehre des Gehörorganes*. Breslau: Georg Philipp Aderholz.

Pasquali, Luigi. 1827. *Istituzioni di estetica*. Padova: Seminario.

Patel, Aniruddh. 2006. *Music, Language and the Brain*. Oxford: Oxford University Press.

Patissier, Philippe. 1822. *Traité des maladies des artisans …* Paris: J.-B. Baillière.

Patureau, Frédérique. 1991. *Le Palais Garnier dans la société parisienne, 1875–1914*. Liège: P. Mardaga.

Pepper, John Henry. 1866. *The Boy's Playbook of Science*. 2nd edn. London: George Routledge & Sons.

Pera, Marcello. 1992. *The Ambiguous Frog: The Galvani–Volta Controversy in Animal Electricity*, trans. Jonathan Mandelbaum. Princeton, NJ: Princeton University Press.

Peretz, Isabelle, and Robert Zatorre. 2003. *The Cognitive Neuroscience of Music*. Oxford: Oxford University Press.

Perinet, Joachim. 1792. *Der Fagottist, oder: die Zauberzither*. Vienna: Mathias Andreas Schmidt.

Pesic, Peter. 2013. 'Thomas Young's Musical Optics'. *Osiris* 28/1 *Music, Sound, and the Laboratory from 1750–1980*, ed. Alexandra Hui, Julia Kursell and Myles W. Jackson, 15–39.

2014. *Music and the Making of Modern Science*. Cambridge, MA: MIT Press.

Pfister, Manfred. 1988. *The Theory and Analysis of Drama*, trans. John Halliday. Cambridge: Cambridge University Press.

Pfitzner, Hans. 1926. *Futuristengefahr* [1917], reprinted in *Gesammelte Schriften* 1:185–223. Augsburg: Filser.

Pfitzner, Paul. 1905. 'Richard Strauss' Salome'. *Musikalisches Wochenblatt* 36, 901–3.

Pfohl, Ferdinand. 1889. 'Nachklänge an Bayreuth'. In *Der Salon für Literatur, Kunst und Gesellschaft*. 2 vols. 1:139–55. Leipzig: A. H. Payne.

Pick, Daniel. 1989. *Faces of Degeneration*. Cambridge: Cambridge University Press.

Pierron, Ed. 1885. 'Le Nouvel Opéra de Buda-Pesth: Aménagement de la scène d'après le système "Asphaleïa"'. *Le Génie Civil* 7 (31 October), 421–5.

Pinel, Philippe. 1806. *A Treatise on Insanity*, trans. D. D. Davis. Sheffield: W. Todd.

Pinon, Pierre. 1989. *The Charenton Hospital: Temple of Reason or Archaeological Folly*, trans. Murray Wylie. Liège: Pierre Mardaga.

Pitres, Albert. 1884. *Clinique médicale de l'hôpital Saint-André. Des suggestions hypnotiques*. Bordeaux: Féret et fils.

Pizzi, Katia, ed. 2012. *Pinocchio, Puppets, and Modernity: The Mechanical Body*. New York: Routledge.

Platt, Walter B. 1888. 'Injurious Influences of City Life'. *Popular Science Monthly* 33, 484–9.

Poe, Edgar Allan. 1998. 'A Tale of the Ragged Mountains' [1850]. In *Selected Tales*, ed. David Van Leer, 239–48. Oxford: Oxford University Press.

Poggi, Stefano, and Mauritio Bossi, eds. 1993. *Romanticism in Science: Science in Europe, 1790–1840*. Dordrecht: Springer.

Politzer, Adam. 1878/82. *Lehrbuch der Ohrenheilkunde*. 2 vols. Stuttgart: Ferdinand Enke.

  1883. *Politzer's Text-book of the Diseases of the Ear and Adjacent Organs*, trans. James Patterson Cassells. London: Ballière, Tindall and Cox.

  1907/13. *Geschichte der Ohrenheilkunde*. 2 vols. Stuttgart: Ferdinand Enke.

Polzonetti, Pierpaolo. 2011. *Italian Opera in the Age of the American Revolution*. Cambridge: Cambridge University Press.

Porges, Heinrich. 1983. *Wagner Rehearsing the Ring: An Eye-Witness Account of the Stage Rehearsals of the First Bayreuth Festival*. Cambridge: Cambridge University Press.

Porter, Roy. 1993. 'The Body and the Mind, the Doctor and the Patient. Negotiating Hysteria'. In *Hysteria beyond Freud*, ed. Sander L. Gilman, Helen King, Roy Porter et al., 225–66. Berkeley: University of California Press.

  2003. 'Introduction'. In *Eighteenth-Century Science*, ed. Roy Porter, 1–20. Cambridge: Cambridge University Press.

Preyer, William T. 1890. *Der Hypnotismus*. Vienna: Urban & Schwarzenberg.

Price, Kathy Kessler. 2011. 'Emma Seiler: A Pioneering Woman in the Art and Science of Teaching Voice'. *Journal of Singing* 68/1 (September–October), 9–22.

Prochasson, Christophe. 1985. 'Sur l'environnement intellectuel de Georges Sorel: l'École des Hautes Études Sociales (1899–1911)'. *Cahiers Georges Sorel* 3/1, 16–38.

Prodger, Phillip. 1998. 'Illustration as Strategy in Charles Darwin's "The Expression of the Emotions in Man and Animals"'. In *Inscribing Science: Scientific Texts and the Materiality of Communication*, ed. Timothy Lenoir, 140–81. Stanford, CA: Stanford University Press.

Propokovych, Markian. 2008. 'Die Produktion von Excelsior in Budapest 1887: Modernität, Erotik und die Bestätigung der politischen Ordnung'. In *Bühnen der Politik. Die Oper in europäischen Gesellschaften im 19. und 20. Jahrhundert*, ed. Jutta Toelle and Sven Oliver Müller, 39–53. Vienna: Oldenburg.

Protano-Biggs, Laura. 2013. '"Mille e mille calme fiamelle": Illuminating the Teatro alla Scala at the *fine secolo*'. *Studi verdiani* 23, 146–67.

Puccini, Giacomo. 2008. *Scossa elettrica di Giacomo Puccini: Marcetta Brillante*, ed. and transcribed by Fulvio Creux. Pescina: Accademia Edizione Musicale.

Puffett, Derek. 1989. *Richard Strauss: Salome*. Cambridge: Cambridge University Press.

Puschmann, Theodor. 1872. *Richard Wagner: Eine psychiatrische Studie*. Berlin: B. Behr.

Quéruel, Auguste. 1869. 'Séance du 10 décembre 1869', *Bulletin de la société d'encouragement pour l'industrie nationale* 16 (December), 736–40.

  1871. 'A propos du nouvel Opéra et des erreurs de son architecte'. *Gazette des architects et du bâtiment* 7, 329–34.

  1874a. 'Comparaison des différents projets présentés pour le nouvel Opéra'. In *Mémoires et compte rendu des travaux de la société des ingénieurs civils*, 652–69. Paris: n.p.

  1874b. 'Séance du 20 février 1874'. In *Mémoires et compte rendu des travaux de la société des ingénieurs civils*, 94–100. Paris: n.p.

R. 1883. 'Analyses'. *Annales des maladies de l'oreille, du larynx, du nez et du pharynx* 9 (November), 305–10.

Raff, Joachim. 1854. *Die Wagnerfrage*. Braunschweig: Friedrich Vieweg.

Rancière, Jacques. 2011. *Staging the People: The Proletarian and His Double*, trans. David Fernbach. New York: Verso.

Rapp, Friedrich. 1981. *Analytical Philosophy of Technology*. Dordrecht: D. Reidel.

Rayleigh, John William Strutt, Baron. 1875. 'On Our Perception of the Direction of a Source of Sound', *Proceedings of the Musical Association* 2/1, 75–84.

Raz, Carmel. 2014. '"The Expressive Organ within Us": Ether, Ethereality, and Early Romantic Ideas about Music and the Nerves'. *19th-Century Music* 38/2, 115–44.

  2017. 'Music, Theater, and the Moral Treatment: The *Casa Dei Matti* of Aversa and Palermo'. *Laboratoire italien* 20.

Regaldi, Giuseppe. 1855. *Telegrafo elettrico: Canto*. Turin: Sebastiano Franco.

Regnard, Paul. 1887. *Les Maladies épidémiques de l'esprit*. Paris: Plon-Nourrit.

Rehding, Alexander. 2006. 'Magic Boxes and Volksempfänger'. In *Music, Theater and Politics in Germany: 1848 to the Third Reich*, ed. Nikolaus Bacht, 255–72. Aldershot, UK: Ashgate.

Reich, Eduard. 1868. *System der Hygiene*. Erlangen: Ferdinand Enke.

Reichert, C[arl] von. 1884a. 'Versuch einer Richard Wagner-Studie'. *Deutsches Archiv für Geschichte der Medicin und medicinische Geographie* 7, 16–43.

  1884b. *Versuch einer Richard Wagner-Studie*. Munich: G. Franz.

Reil, Johann Christian. 1803. *Rhapsodien über die Anwendung der psychischen Kurmethode auf Geisteszerrüttungen*. Halle: Curtsch.

Restle, Conny. 2002. "' … als strahle von dort ein mystischer Zauber": Zur Geschichte des Harmoniums'. In *'In aller Munde': Mundharmonika, Handharmonika, Harmonium. Eine 200-jährige Erfolgsgeschichte*, ed. Conny Restle, 7–19. Catalogue to the exhibition in the Museum of Musical Instruments Berlin SIMPK, 2 October–7 November 2002. Berlin: n.p.

Ribot, Théodule. 1883. *Les Maladies de la Volonté*. Paris: Bailliere.

    1894. *The Diseases of the Will*, trans. Merwin-Marie Snell. Chicago, IL, and London: The Open Court Publishing Company.

    1906. *Essay on the Creative Imagination*, trans. Albert H. N. Baron. Chicago, IL: The Open Court Publishing Company.

    1911. *The Psychology of the Emotions*. London: Walter Scott.

Richards, Denise. 2012. *Acolytes of Nature: Defining Natural Science in Germany 1770–1850*. Chicago, IL: University of Chicago Press.

Richardson, Benjamin Ward. 1882. *Diseases of Modern Life*. New York: Birmingham & Co.

Richer, Paul. 1881. *Études cliniques sur la grande hystérie ou hystéro-épilepsie*. Paris: Adrien Delahaye & Emile Lecrosnier.

Richer, Paul, and Gilles de la Tourette. 1875. 'Hypnotisme', in *Dictionnaire encyclopédique des sciences médicales*, ed. Amédée Dechambre, 15:67–132. Paris: Typographie Lahure.

Riemann, Hugo. 1908. 'Degeneration und Regeneration in der Musik'. *Max Hesses deutscher Musikerkalender* 23, 136–8.

Ritchey, Marianna. 2010. 'Echoes of the Guillotine: Berlioz and the French Fantastic'. *19th-Century Music* 34/2, 168–85.

Rochefort-Luçay, Claude Louis Marie de Marquis. 1863. *Mémoires d'un Vaudevilliste*. Paris: Charlieu et Huillery.

Roller, Christan Friedrich Wilhelm. 1831. *Die Irrenanstalt nach allen ihren Beziehungen dargestellt*. Karlsruhe: Müller.

Roosa, Daniel Bennett St John. 1883. 'The Effects of Noise upon Diseased and Healthy Ears'. *Archives of Otology* 12/2, 103–21.

    1885. *A Practical Treatise on the Diseases of the Ear*. 6th rev. edn. New York: William Wood.

Ropohl, Günter. 2009. *Allgemeine Technologie: Eine Systemtheorie der Technik*. 3rd edn. Karlsruhe: Universitätsverlag Karlsruhe.

Rose, Nikolas. 2012. *Neuro: The New Brain Sciences and the Management of the Mind*. Princeton, NJ: Princeton University Press.

Rose, Whyman. 2008. *The Stanislavsky System of Acting*. Cambridge: Cambridge University Press.

Rosenkranz, Karl. 1853. *Ästhetik des Häßlichen*. Königsberg: Bornträger.

Rothschuh, Karl E. 1968. *Physiologie: Der Wandel ihrer Konzepte, Probleme und Methoden vom 16. bis 20. Jahrhundert*. Freiburg and Munich: Alber.

Rousseau, George. 2004. *Nervous Acts*. Basingstoke, UK: Palgrave.

Rousseau, Jean-Jacques. 2009. *Essay on the Origin of Languages and Writings Related to Music*, ed. John T. Scott. Hanover, NH: Dartmouth University Press.

Rubin, Julius H. 2004. *Religious Melancholy and Protestant Experience in America*. New York: Oxford University Press.

Rushton, Julian. 1983. *The Language of Hector Berlioz*. Cambridge: Cambridge University Press.

Sachs, Edwin O. 1896–8 *Modern Opera Houses and Theatres*, 3 vols. London: B. T. Batsford.

Sacks, Oliver. 2008. *Musicophilia: Tales of Music and the Brain*. London: Picador.

Saissy, Jean Antoine. 1827. *Essai sur les maladies de l'oreille interne*. Paris: Baillière.

Samson, Adelaide L. 1900. 'Grand Opera in English'. *Metropolitan Magazine*. June. 593–602.

Sandlands, John Poole. 1886. *How to Develop General Vocal Power and Cure Stammering and Defective Speech*. London: Sampson, Low and Co.

Sarasin, Philip. 2007. 'The Body as Medium: Nineteenth-Century European Hygiene Discourse'. *Grey Room* 29, 48–65.

Sarthe, Jacques-Louis Moreau de la, ed. 1806. 'Discours préliminaire'. In Gaspard Lavater, *L'Art de Connaître les Hommes par la Physionomie*, 1–74. Paris: L. Prudhomme and Levrault, Schoell et cie.

Sasportes, José. 1987. 'Virtuosismo e spettacolarità: le risposte italiane alla decadenza del balletto romantico'. In *Tornando a Stiffelio: Popolarità, rifacimenti, messinscena, effettismo e altre 'cure' nella drammaturgia del Verdi romantico*, ed. Giovanni Morelli. Florence: Olschki.

   2011. *Storia della danza italiana dalle origini ai giorni nostri*. Turin: EDT.

Saunders, John Cunningham. 1806. *The Anatomy of the Human Ear*. London: E. Cox and Son.

Scarpa, Antonia. 1789. *Anatomicae disquisitiones de auditu et olfactu*. Pavia: Petrus Galeatius.

Schaeffer, Julius. 1877. *Seb. Bachs Kantata 'Sie werden aus Saba alle kommen'*. Leipzig: F. E. C. Leuckert.

Schäfer, Armin. 2011. 'Goethes naturwissenschaftliche Kunstauffassung'. In *Goethe-Handbuch. Supplemente*, ed. Andreas Beyer and Ernst Osterkamp. 4 vols. 3:291–314. Stuttgart: Metzler.

Schelhous, Rosalie. 1991. 'Fétis' Tonality as a Metaphysical Principle: Hypothesis for a New Science'. *Music Theory Spectrum* 13, 219–40.

Schering, Arnold. [1935] 1941. 'Musikalische Symbolkunde'. In *Das Symbol in der Musik*, ed. Willibald Gurlitt, 117–45. Leipzig: Koehler & Amelang.

Schickore, Jutta. 2007. *The Eye and the Microscope*. Chicago, IL: University of Chicago Press.

Schilling, Gustav. 1834. *Universal-Lexicon der Tonkunst*. Stuttgart: Köhler.

Schmalz, Karl. 1990. 'Annus Confusionis. Eine Trilogie'. In *'Die Konfusion in der Musik': Felix Draesekes Kampfschrift von 1906 und die Folgen*, ed. Susanne Shigihara, 259–98. Bonn: Gudrun Schröder.

Schmidgen, Henning. 2006. 'Sciences of Falling Down: Time, Body, and the Machine, 1750–1900'. In *Conference: The Shape of Experiment*, Preprint of the Max Planck Institute for the History of Science 318, 79–93. Berlin: Max Planck Institute for the History of Science.

Schmidt, Jochen. 1985. *Geschichte des Genie-Gedankens in der deutschen Literatur, Philosophie und Politik 1750–1945*. Darmstadt: Wissenschaftliche Buchgesellschaft.

Schneider, Peter Joseph. 1835. *System einer medizinischen Musik: Ein unentbehrliches Handbuch für Medizin-Beflissene, Vorsteher der Irren-Heilanstalten, praktische Aerzte und unmusikalische Lehrer verschiedener Disziplinen*. 2 vols. Bonn: Carl Giorgi.

Scholl, Tim. 2007. 'Il crepuscolo degli dei: *Excelsior* in Russia'. In *Romualdo Marenco: prospettive di ricerca; scelta di saggi dai convegni del Festival Marenco di Novi Ligure, 2002–2006*, ed. Elena Grillo, 161–8. Novi Ligure: Joker.

Schopenhauer, Arthur. 2004. *Essays and Aphorisms*, trans. R. Hollingdale. London: Penguin.

Schreger, Christian Heinrich Theodor. 1823. *Handbuch der Pastoral-Medicin für christliche Seelsorger*. Halle: Hemmerde und Schwetschke.

Schulte, Christoph. 1997. *Psychopathologie der Fin de Siecle – Der Kulturkritiker, Arzt und Zionist Max Nordau*. Frankfurt: Fischer Verlag.

Schweigger, August Friedrich. 1809. *Über Kranken- und Armen-Anstalten zu Paris*. Bayreuth: Erben.

Sconce, Jeffrey. 2000. *Haunted Media: Electronic Presence from Telegraphy to Television*. Durham, NC: Duke University Press.

Scott, Derek. 2003. *From the Erotic to the Demonic: On Critical Musicology*. Oxford: Oxford University Press.

Scrivner, Lee. 2014. *Becoming Insomniac: How Sleeplessness Alarmed Modernity*. London: Palgrave Macmillan.

Scruton, Roger. 2001. 'Programme Music', *Grove Music Online, Oxford Music Online*. www.oxfordmusiconline.com/grovemusic/view/10.1093/gmo/9781561 592630.001.0001/omo-9781561592630-e-0000022394.

Scull, Andrew. 2005. *The Most Solitary of Afflictions: Madness and Society in Britain, 1700–1900*. New Haven, CT: Yale University Press.

Seiler, Carl. 1883. *Handbook of the Diagnosis and Treatment of Diseases of the Throat, Nose, and Naso-pharynx*. 2nd edn. Philadelphia, PA: Henry C. Lea's Son and Co.

Seiler, Emma. 1865. 'Ueber Gesangskunst'. *Neue Zeitschrift für Musik* 61 (10 February), 53–4; (17 February), 61–2; (24 February); 69–71 (3 March), 81–2.

1875. *The Voice in Speaking*, trans. W. H. Furness. Philadelphia, PA: J. B. Lippincott & Co.

1884. *The Voice in Singing*, trans. W. H. Furness. Rev. edn. Philadelphia, PA: J. B. Lippincott & Co. Originally published as *Altes und Neues über die Ausbildung des Gesangorganes mit besonderer Rücksicht auf die Frauenstimme*. Leipzig: L. Voss, 1861.

Sennett, Richard. 2003. *The Fall of Public Man*. London: Penguin.

Shakespeare, William. 1898. 'The Management of the Breath'. *Werner's Magazine* 21/6 (August), 515–19.

Shaw, Alexander, ed. 1847. *On Sir Charles Bell's Researches on the Nervous System*. London: John Murray.

Shigihara, Susanne, ed. 1990. *'Die Konfusion in der Musik': Felix Draesekes Kampfschrift von 1906 und die Folgen*. Bonn: Gudrun Schröder.

Sieg, Christian. 2010. 'Beyond Realism: Kracauer and the Ornaments of the Ordinary'. *New German Critique* 37/1, 99–118.

Silliman, Benjamin. 1840. 'Phrenology'. *The American Journal of Science and Arts* 39 (October), 65–88.

Singleton, Esther. 1901. 'The Opera Season of 1900–1901'. *The Bookman; a Review of Books and Life* 13/3 (May), 252–9.

Slonimsky, Nicolas. 1953. 'Non-Acceptance of the Unfamiliar'. *The Lexicon of Musical Invective: Critical Assaults on Composers since Beethoven's Time*, 3–33. New York: Coleman-Ross.

Sloterdijk, Peter. 2002. *Luftbeben: an den Quellen des Terrors*. Frankfurt: Suhrkamp.

Smart, Mary Ann. 1992. 'The Silencing of Lucia'. *Cambridge Opera Journal* 4, 119–41.

2004. *Mimomania: Music and Gesture in Nineteenth-Century Opera*. Berkeley: University of California Press.

Smilor, Raymond W. 1979. 'Personal Boundaries in the Urban Environment: The Legal Attack on Noise 1865–1930'. *Environmental Review* 3/3, 24–36.

Smith, Matthew Wilson. 2007. 'Laughing at the Redeemer: Kundry and the Paradox of Parsifal'. *Modernist Culture* 3/1, 5–25.

Smith, Roger. 1992. *Inhibition: History and Meaning in the Sciences of Mind and Brain*. Berkeley: University of California Press.

Smocovitis, Vassiloki. 2009. 'Singing His Praises: Darwin and His Theory in Song and Musical Production'. *Isis* 100, 590–614.

Spencer, Herbert. 'Opera'. 1902. *Facts and Comments*. New York: D. Appleton & Co.

Spitzer, Daniel. 1877. 'Die Prater Ausstellung'. In *Wiener Spaziergänge*, 32–8. 2nd edn. Vienna: L. Rosner.

1880. *Verliebte Wagnerianer*. Vienna: Julius Klinkhardt.

1906. *Richard Wagners Briefe an eine Putzmacherin*. Vienna: Carl Konegen [Ernst Stülpnagel].

Sponheuer, Bernd. 1987. *Musik als Kunst und Nichtkunst*. Kassel: Bärenreiter.

Spotts, Frederic. 1994. *Bayreuth: A History of the Wagner Festival*. New Haven, CT: Yale University Press.

Srocke, Martina. 1988. *Richard Wagner als Regisseur*. Munich: Musikverlag Emil Katzbichler.

Stark, James A. 1999. *Bel Canto: A History of Vocal Pedagogy*. Toronto: University of Toronto Press.

Steege, Benjamin. 2012. *Helmholtz and the Modern Listener*. Cambridge: Cambridge University Press.

Steinle, Friedrich. 2001. '"Das Nächste ans Nächste reihen" – Goethe, Newton und das Experiment'. *Philosophia naturalis* 39/1, 141–72.

   2016. *Exploratory Experiments: Ampère, Faraday and the Origins of Electrodynamics*, trans. Alex Levine. Pittsburgh, PA: University of Pittsburgh Press.

Stengers, Isabelle. 2002. *L'Hypnose entre magie et science*. Paris: Les Empêcheurs de penser en rond.

Sterne, Jonathan. 2003. *The Audible Past: Cultural Origins of Sound Reproduction*. Durham, NC: Duke University Press.

   2014. '"What Do We Want?" "Materiality!" "When Do We Want It?" "Now!"'. In *Media Technologies: Essays on Communication, Materiality, and Society*, ed. Tarleton Gillespie, Pablo J. Boczkowski and Kirsten A. Foot, 119–28. Cambridge, MA: MIT Press.

   2016. 'Afterword: Opera, Media, Technicity'. In *Technology and the Diva*, ed. Karen Henson, 159–64. Cambridge: Cambridge University Press.

Steward, Jill. 2002. 'The Culture of Water Cure in Nineteenth-Century Austria, 1800–1914'. In *Water, Leisure and Culture: European Historical Perspectives*, ed. Susan C. Anderson and Bruce Tabbs, 23–35. Oxford: Berg.

Stoepel, Franz. 1821. *Grundzüge der Geschichte der modernen Musik*. Berlin: Duncker und Humblot.

Strauss, Richard. 2009. *Salome*. New York: Dover.

Stumpf, Carl. 1883–90. *Tonpsychologie*. 2 vols. Leipzig: Hirzel.

Sully, James. 1879. 'Civilisation and Noise'. *The Eclectic Magazine of Foreign Literature, Science and Art* 29, 225–36.

Sulzer, Johann Georg. 1771–4. *Allgemeine Theorie der schönen Künste*. 3 vols. Leipzig: M. G. Weidmanns Erben und Reich.

Sydow, Eckhart von. 1921. *Die Kultur der Dekadenz*. Dresden: Sibyllen-Verlag.

Talansier, Charles. 1886. 'Machinerie théâtrale: La Manutention des décors à l'Opéra de Paris'. *Le Génie civil* 9 (5 June), 81–5.

Talia, Giambattista. 1822. *Saggio di estetica*. Venice: Alvisopoli.

Tan, Su Lian. 1997. 'Hector Berlioz, *Symphonie Fantastique*, Op. 14: An Exploration of Musical Timbre'. PhD diss., Princeton University.

Tappert, Wilhelm. 1873. 'Musikbrief: Berlin'. *Musikalisches Wochenblatt* 4/48, 672–3.

   1877. *Ein Wagner-Lexikon: Wörterbuch der Unhöflichkeit*. Leipzig: Fritsch.

Taylor, Charles. 1989. *Sources of the Self.* Cambridge, MA: Harvard University Press.

Thompson, Emily. 2004. *The Soundscape of Modernity: Architectural Acoustics and the Culture of Listening in America, 1900–1933.* Cambridge, MA: MIT Press.

Thompson, Oscar. 1938. 'On Hearing Jean de Reszke Today: Like a Dream, a Faint Voice on Wax that Propounds a Problem for Science'. *New York Sun.* 23 April. 28.

Thwing, Edward. 1876. *Drill Book in Vocal Culture and Gesture.* New York: A. S. Barnes and Co.

Tierney, John, and Roy Baumeister. 2012. *Willpower: Rediscovering Our Greatest Strength.* Harmondsworth, UK: Penguin.

Tissandier, Gaston. 1875. 'La Science au Nouvel Opéra. III. La Lumière électrique'. *La Nature: Revue des sciences de leurs applications aux arts et à l'industrie* 3/1, 150–4.

Todorov, Tzvetan. 1975. *The Fantastic: A Structural Approach to a Literary Genre.* Ithaca, NY: Cornell University Press.

Toelle, Jutta. 2009. *Bühne der Stadt: Mailand und das Teatro alla Scala zwischen Risorgimento und* Fin de Siècle. Vienna: Böhlau.

Tolstoy, Leo. 1904. *What is Art?* New York: Funk and Wagnalls.

Tourette, Gilles de la. 1887. *L'Hypnotisme et les états analogues au point de vue médico-légal: les états hypnotiques et les états analogues, les suggestions criminelles, cabinets de somnambules et sociétés de magnétisme et de spiritisme, l'hypnotisme devant la loi.* Paris: E. Plon, Nourrit et Cie.

Tovey, Donald Francis. [1911] 1944. *Musical Articles from the Encyclopaedia Britannica.* London: Oxford University Press.

Toynbee, Joseph. 1860. *The Diseases of the Ear: Their Nature, Diagnosis, and Treatment.* London: John Churchill.

Tresch, John. 2011. 'The Prophet and the Pendulum: Sensational Science and Audiovisual Phantasmagoria around 1848'. *Grey Room* 43, 16–41.

  2012. *The Romantic Machine: Utopian Science and Technology after Napoleon.* Chicago: University of Chicago Press.

Trippett, David. 2013. *Wagner's Melodies: Aesthetics and Materialism in German Musical Identity.* Cambridge: Cambridge University Press.

Tröltsch, Anton von. 1862. *Die Krankheiten des Ohres, ihre Erkenntniss und Behandlung: Ein Lehrbuch der Ohrenheilkunde.* Würzburg: Stahel.

Trower, Shelley. 2012. *Senses of Vibration: A History of the Pleasure and Pain of Sound.* London: Continuum.

Tuchman, Arleen Marcia. 1993. *Science, Medicine, and the State in Germany: The Case of Baden, 1815–1871.* Oxford: Oxford University Press.

Tucker, Kathryn M. 2007. 'Theatre as Asylum, Asylum as Theatre: Cross-channel Institutional Intersections from 1780 to 1830'. PhD diss., University College of Los Angeles.

Tuckey, Charles Lloyd. 1893. 'Quelques exemples de troubles nerveux observés chez des musiciens'. *Revue de l'Hypnotisme* 8, 85–8.

Tunbridge, Laura. 2016. 'Opera and Materiality', *Cambridge Opera Journal* 26, 289–99.

Turnbull, Laurence. 1865. 'On Disease of the Internal Ear'. *Medical and Surgical Reporter* 13, 88–90.

Twain, Mark. 1917. 'At the Shrine at Saint Wagner'. *The Complete Works of Mark Twain*, 209–27. New York: Harper and Brothers.

Tyndall, John. 1867. *Sound: A Course of Eight Lectures delivered at the Royal Institution of Great Britain*. London: Longmans, Green, and Co.

Tyson, Brian, ed. 1991. *Bernard Shaw's Book Reviews: Originally Published in the Pall Mall Gazette from 1885 to 1888*. University Park: Pennsylvania State University Press, 1991.

Urling, George. 1857. *Vocal Gymnastics: Or A Guide for Stammerers and for Public Speakers and Others*. London: J. Churchill.

Vaulabelle, Alfred de, and Charles Hémardinquer. 1908. *La Science au théâtre: Étude sur les procédés scientifiques en usage dans le théâtre moderne*. Paris: Henry Paulin.

Venanzio, Girolamo. 1830. *Della callofilia, ossia dottrina del bello nelle lettere e nelle arti contenente i principii fondamentali della estetica*. Padua: Minerva.

Vitoux, Georges. 1903. *Le Théâtre de l'Avenir: Aménagement général, mise en scène, trucs, machinerie, etc*. Paris: Schleicher frères.

Vizentini, Albert. 1868. *Derrière la toile (foyer, coulisses et comédiens): Petites physiologies des théâtres parisiens*. Paris: Achille Faure.

Vogl, Joseph. 2007. 'Der Weg der Farbe'. In *Räume der Romantik*, ed. Inka Mülder-Bach and Gerhard Neumann, 157–68. Würzburg: Königshausen & Neumann, 2007. Published in English as *Conference: The Shape of Experiment*, ed. Henning Schmidgen and Julia Kursell, 225–31. Preprint Max Planck Institute for the History of Science 368. Berlin: Max Planck Institute for the History of Science, 2008.

Voskuhl, Adelheid. 2007. 'Motions and Passions: Music-Playing Women Automata and the Culture of Affect in Late Eighteenth-century Germany'. In *Genesis Redux: Essays in the History and Philosophy of Artificial Life*, ed. Jessica Riskin, 293–320. Chicago, IL: University of Chicago Press.

   2013. *Androids in the Enlightenment: Mechanics, Artisans, and Cultures of the Self*. Chicago: University of Chicago Press.

W. 1925. 'A Lesson with the Master'. *Music & Letters* 6/3, 209–13.

Wagner, Richard. 1852. *Oper und Drama*. Leipzig: J. J. Weber.

   1882. Parsifal. Libretto (full text in German and English): http://www.operafolio.com/libretto.asp?n=Parsifal&translation=UK.

   1895. *Prose Works: The Art-work of the Future*, trans. William Ashton Ellis. London: Kegan Paul, Trench, Trübner & Co.

   1911–14. *Sämtliche Schriften und Dichtungen*. 16 vols. Volks-Ausgabe. Leipzig: Breitkopf & Härtel and C. F. W. Siegel [R. Linnemann].

Walter, Friedrich. 1899. *Archiv und Bibliothek des Grossh. Hof- und Nationaltheaters in Mannheim, 1779–1839*. Leipzig: Hirzel.

1909. 'Eine Operettendichtung Schillers?' *Mannheimer Geschichtablätter* 10/11 (November), 230–5.

Walter, Michael. 2016. *Oper. Geschichte einer Institution.* Heidelberg: Springer.

Walton, Benjamin. 2007. *Rossini in Restoration Paris: The Sound of Modern Life.* Cambridge: Cambridge University Press.

2018. 'L'italiana in Calcutta'. In *Operatic Geographies*, ed. Suzanne Aspden. Chicago, IL: University of Chicago Press, 119–32

Watkins, Holly. 2011. *Metaphors of Depth in German Music.* Cambridge: Cambridge University Press.

Watkins, Holly, and Melina Esse. 2015. 'Down with Disembodiment; or, Musicology and the Material Turn'. *Women & Music* 19, 160–8.

Weber, Ernst Heinrich. 1834. *De pulsu, resorptione, auditu et tactu. Anatationes anatomicae et physiologicae.* Leipzig: Koehler.

Weiner, Dora B. 1979. 'The Apprenticeship of Philippe Pinel: A New Document: "Observations of Citizen Pussin on the Insane"'. *The American Journal of Psychiatry* 136/9, 1128–34.

Westheim, Paul. 1908. 'Plakate aus der deutschen Vergangenheit'. *Zeitschrift für Bücherfreunde* 12/8 (November), 299–314.

Wheatstone, Charles. 2011a. 'Experiments in Audition' [1827]. In *The Scientific Papers of Sir Charles Wheatstone*, 30–5. Rpt. Cambridge: Cambridge University Press, 2011.

2011b. 'New Experiments on Sound' [1823]. In *The Scientific Papers of Sir Charles Wheatstone*, 1–13. Rpt. Cambridge: Cambridge University Press, 2011.

Whytt, Robert. 1768. *The Works of Robert Whytt.* Edinburgh: Balfour, Auld and Smellie.

Wieland, Christoph Martin, ed. 1789. *Dschinnistan, oder auserlesen Feen- und Geister-Mährchen.* Winterthur: Heinrich Steiner und Compagnie.

Williams, Alistair. 1997. 'Technology of the Archaic: Wish Image and Phantasmagoria in Wagner'. *Cambridge Opera Journal* 9/1, 73–87.

Williams, Raymond. 1989. 'Metropolitan Perceptions and the Emergence of Modernism'. In *The Politics of Modernism: Against the New Conformists*, 37–48. London: Verso.

2005. 'Means of Communication as Means of Production'. In *Culture and Materialism: Selected Essays*, 50–66. London: Verso.

Williams, Simon. 2003. 'The Spectacle of the Past in Grand Opera'. In *The Cambridge Companion to Grand Opera*, ed. David Charlton, 58–75. Cambridge: Cambridge University Press.

Willson, Flora. 2016. 'Hearing Things: Musical Objects at the 1851 Exposition'. In *Sound Knowledge: Music and Science in London, 1789–1851*, ed. James Q. Davies and Ellen Lockhart, 227–46. Chicago, IL: University of Chicago Press.

Winslow, W. H. 1882. *The Human Ear and Its Diseases: A Practical Treatise upon the Examination, Recognition and Treatment of Affections of the Ear and Associate Parts*. New York: Boericke & Tafel.

Winter, Alison. 1998. *Mesmerized: Powers of Mind in Victorian Britain*. Chicago: University of Chicago Press.

Wise, M. Norton. 2007. 'The Gender of Automata in Victorian England'. In *Genesis Redux: Essays in the History and Philosophy of Artificial Life*, ed. Jessica Riskin, 163–95. Chicago, IL: University of Chicago Press.

Wittje, Roland. 2013. 'The Electrical Imagination: Sound Analogies, Equivalent Circuits, and the Rise of Electroacoustics, 1863–1939'. *Osiris* 28/1 *Music, Sound, and the Laboratory from 1750–1980*, ed. Alexandra Hui, Julia Kursell and Myles W. Jackson, 40–63.

Wolff, Cécile. 2009. 'Aux origines de l'inconscient, une esthétique de la contemplation', in *Hypnos. Esthétique, littérature et inconscients en Europe (1900–1968)*, ed. Frédérique Toudoire-Surlapierre and Nicolas Surlapierre, 153–67. Paris: L'Improviste.

Woolf, Penelope. 1988. 'Symbol of the Second Empire: Cultural Politics and the Paris Opera House'. In *The Iconography of Landscape: Essays on the Symbolic Representation, Design and Use of Past Environments*, ed. Denis Cosgrove and Stephen Daniels, 214–35. Cambridge: Cambridge University Press.

Wosk, Julie. 2001. *Women and the Machine: Representations from the Spinning Wheel to the Electronic Age*. Baltimore, MD: Johns Hopkins University Press.

Young, Zachary. 2011. 'The Noise Goes On Forever: A History Of New Orleans Noise Ordinances'. *Offbeat Magazine*. 1 January. www.offbeat.com/articles/the-noise-goes-on-forever-a-history-of-new-orleans-noise-ordinances/.

Zacks, Jeffrey. 2014. *Flicker: Your Brain on Movies*. Oxford: Oxford University Press.

Zoglauer, Thomas. 2002. 'Einleitung'. In *Technikphilosophie* ed. Thomas Zoglauer. Freiburg & München: Karl Alber.

Index

Abbate, Carolyn, 7, 8, 199, 200, 226
acoustics, 1, 2, 5, 55, 126, 139, 219, 234, 241, 292, *see also sound*
acting, 100–4
Adler, Guido, 2, 308, 315, 333
Adorno, Theodor W., 7, 8, 31, 138, 287, 289, 290, 301, 303
Aeolian harp, 78–9, 144–7, 149, 150–3
aeolodicon, 71, 77, 78, 79
aesthetics, 2
    autonomy, 306, 310
    Idealist, 317–19
    kalokagathia, 322, 325
    music as effect, 234–5, 237–8
    musical, 232–4
affects. *See emotions*
Africaine, L' (Meyerbeer), 9
Aida (Verdi), 26, 32, 348
Aladin ou La Lampe merveilleuse (Isouard), 8
Ambros, August Wilhelm, 237, 320
ammoniaphone, 44–9, 59
analyseur du timbre d'un son, 126
anatomy, 49, 51, 112, 141, 233, 273, 274–6, 277
    glottis. *See voice*
    of the ear, 113, 141, 163
Andrée, Carl, 67
androids, 269–70, 272, *see also automata*
    cyborgs, 251, 262, 267
    Olympia, 17, 141, 269–70, 278, 286
anémocorde, 6
Appia, Adolphe, 200
Arthur, Timothy Shay, 162
asylums. *See Besançon; Charenton; Salpêtrière*
    theatrical productions, 15, 63–9
Attali, Jacques, 157
Attila (Verdi), 8
aurality, 134, 154
automata, 7, 17, 89, 98, 267, 269, 270, 272, 286, *see also androids*
    medical patients as, 17, 278–80, 286
automatic organ, 6
autonomy
    and self-control, 299

    as rational, 289, 292
    of the subject, 92, 280, 289, 291, 293, 297, 299, 300, *see also willpower*

ballet, 242–8, 251–6, 260–2, 266, 267, *see also choreography; gesture*
ballooning, 16, 185–6, *see also flying machines*
Bals (Schneider), 72–3, 79–80
Balzac, Honoré de, 5, 6, 7
Barbieri, Angelo, 6
Barr, Thomas, 159, 164
Barraqué, Jean, 127
Barthes, Roland, 18, 153
Bayreuth, 8, 281, 287–96, 300, 301
Bell, Charles, 17, 116, 274–6, 277
Benjamin, Walter, 136, 281
Bérard, Jean-Baptiste, 37
Berlioz, Hector, 1, 5, 15, 109–10, 114–33, 309, 366
Bernheim, Hippolyte, 288, 295
Besançon (asylum), 65
Bispham, David, 21, 30
Björnström, Fredrik Johan, 102
Blanchard, J.-F., 186, 188, 193, 194, 196
Blanche [Marie Wittman], 278–9
Boenninghaus, Georg, 171, 172
Boerhaave, Hermann, 37
Bois, Jules, 84, 87, 89, 91, 92
Boulez, Pierre, 109, 123, 131
Bouveret, Leon, 290
Brabant (machinist), 210, 211, 215, 219, 224
breathing. *See also techniques; voice*
    airlessness, 22, 32
    appoggio, 32, 33
    breath control, 32–9
    costal vs. abdominal, 22, 35–7
    inspiration, 47
    Sbriglia belt, 38
    tacial pneumotypes, 36–7
Bretzner, Christoph Friedrich, 186–92, 196
Brewster, David, 258
Busoni, Ferruccio, 306, 318, 319

Calvé, Emma, 37, 40, 93, 104
Cambon, Charles-Antoine, 210, 211
Camper, Petrus, 273, 274
Canguilhem, Georges, 115
Cardaillac, Etienne de, 210
Carpani, Giuseppe, 3
catalepsy, 279, 294, *see also hysteria*
Cather, Willa, 30
Cavaillé-Coll, Aristide, 130
Chamberlayne, Elizabeth, 37
Charcot, Jean-Martin, 278–80, 281–6, 288, 294, 295, 296
Charenton (asylum), 63, 66–8
Chladni, Ernst, 6, 139
choreography, 17, 244, 247, 253–6, 260–5, 266
  of workers, 265, 266, 267
  proto-robotic, 17, 251
Cid, Le (Massenet), 24
circuit, electric, 13, 227
  audience as, 238–40, 243–4, 245
  telegraph as, 244–5, 246
cochlea. *See ear*
Cogan, Thomas, 273
Comerio, Luca, 262
commedia dell'arte, 176
componium, 6
Comte, August, 140
Connor, Steven, 47
Contes d'Hoffmann, Les (Offenbach), 17, 286
Corvée, Flore, 66
Coulmier, François de, 66, 67
Courmelles, François-Victor Foveau de, 89, 279
Crary, Jonathan, 111, 114, 116, 258
Curtis, Henry Holbrook, 34, 37–41
Czermak, Johann N., 144
Czolbe, Heinrich, 141, 142

Dabney, Robert, 138
Daly, César, 203, 205
dance, 263–5
  Tiller Girls, 266
Dance of the Telegraph Operators (*Excelsior*), 17, 246–8
Danesi, Luigi, 242–6, 247, 248
Darwin, Charles, 3, 13, 274, 277, 327, 369
Dauriac, Lionel, 88, 101
David, Félicien, 8
De Rochas, Albert, 95
De Valenti, Ernst, 74, 75, 80, 81, 83
De' Filippi, Giuseppe, 232, 233
degeneracy
  and evolution, 322–5

and sexuality, 317–19
atavism, 325, 326
cultural, 282, 290, 298, 300, 304–5, 322
Degeneration (Nordau), 287, 305
musical, 17, 290, 303–4, 309, 310, 311–12, 316, 318, 320–1, 322, 330, 333–4
of taste, 321–2
Della Valle, Cesare, 236, 237, 247
Désert, Le (David), 8
Despléchin, Édouard, 210, 211
Devil's Opera, The (Macfarren), 9
Diderot, Denis, 101
Dincklage, Emmy von, 157
Dircks, Henry, 12
disalteration, 329–30, *see also Kurth*
Don Carlos (Verdi), 140
Donato [Alfred Édouard D'Hont], 89
Draeseke, Felix, 303, 317, 330, 331
Dreher, Eugen, 5
Du Bois-Reymond, Émil, 4, 141, 148
Duchenne [de Boulogne], Guillaume-Benjamin-Amand, 17, 276, 277, 278, 283, 284
Duval, Mathias, 37

ear. *See also anatomy*
  as instrument, 140, 144, 147, 150, 153, 234
  boilermaker's, 163
  diseases. *See hyperacusis; otology*
  mental ear, 136, 147
École des Hautes Études Sociales, 86, 88, 104
Edgerton, David, 202
Edison Home Phonograph, 21
eidophone, 41
electricity, 227–8, 232, 234–6, 255, *see also circuit, electric*
Ellis, Alexander, 6
emotions
  expression, 272–6
  medical experiments, 276–8
  on music, 270–2
Erhard, Julius, 162
Esquirol, Étienne, 63, 68
evolution, 319–21, 322–4, *see also degeneracy*
Excelsior (Manzotti), 13, 17, 232, 245–8, 251, 252–8, 260–5, 266, 267–8

fanciulla del West, La (Puccini), 227
fantastic, the, 110, 114, 115, 119, 121, 191, 193, 194, 196, 242
Faraday, Michael, 1, 12, 354
Feaster, Patrick, 29
Ferkel, Lina de, 84, 88, 90–5

Index 377

ferne Klang, Der (Schreker), 9, 150–3, 154
Fétis, François-Joseph, 232, 308–9
Filosofi immaginari, I (Paisiello), 178
fliegende Holländer, Der (Wagner), 12
Flugwerk. See flying machines
flying machines. *See technology, aeronautic*
Fodéré, François, 68
fonica, 227
Fontenelle, Bernard le Bovier de, 177
Fra Diavolo (Auber), 70, 73, 76
Fränzl, Ferdinand, 186–92, 197
Freischütz, Der (Weber), 12
Freud, Sigmund, 197, 278, 288

galop, 228, 236, 246, 247, 248, 263, *see also dance*
Galuppi, Baldassare, 179, 180
Galvani, Luigi, 235, 363
García, Manuel, 14, 34, 35, 38, 52–5, 56, 57, 58–60
Garnier, Charles, 2, 16, 200, 201–26, 363, *see also Palais Garnier*
Gattoni, Giulio Cesare, 146
genius, 309–11, 332–3
  relationship to insanity, 332, 333
Gerhard, Anselm, 8
Gesamtkunstwerk, 287
  and willpower, 296–300
  as hypnosis, 288, 291–2, 294–6, *see also hypnosis*
gesture, 89–93, 102–4, 266, 270, 277, *see also acting; dance*
ghosts, 9, 12, 110, 121–31, 132
Gill, André, 169, 171
Gillmore, Quincy Adams, 157
Gioberti, Vincenzo, 233, 236
glass harmonica, 6, 78, 88
Glyn, Margaret, 313
Goethe, Johann Wolfgang von, 111, 113, 185, 188
Goldoni, Carlo, 175, 176, 178–85, 192
Görgen, Bruno, 68
Gould, Steven Jay, 325
Gounod, Charles, 24, 42, 93
Grandville, J. J., 319, 320, 323
Grenié, Gabriel-Joseph, 77
Guislain, Joseph, 68

Haeckel, Ernst, 313, 316, 322
Haller, Albrecht von, 37, 277
hallucination, 9, 114, 119, 283, 284
Hanslick, Eduard, 237, 238, 287, 292, 298, 327
Haraway, Donna, 251, 260, 262

harmonium, 71, 76, 78, 79, 129
Harris, Augustus, 24
Haydn, Franz Joseph, 179–85
hearing, 122, 234
  loss of, 16, 155–9, 163, 167
  spatial, 126–31, 131–3, *see also perception*
  subject position, 116
Heidegger, Martin, 23
Heidenhain, Rudolf, 294
Helmholtz, Hermann von, 4, 6, 51, 52, 57, 60, 61, 136, 139, 140, 141, 143, 147, 148–9, 153, 160, 164, 171
Henderson, William James, 24, 25, 28
Herschel, John, 1, 3
Hoffmann, E. T. A., 2, 141, 269, 270, 278, 286
Huguenots, Les (Meyerbeer), 121
Huneker, James, 295
Hutchinson, John, 37
hygiene, 47, 297
  mental, 289, 296–300
  moral, 299
hyperacusis, 162, *see also otology*
Hyperæsthesia acoustica. See noise
hypnosis, 15, 84–7, 98–9, 294–6
  affective contagion, 288, 290
  as artistic method, 100, 102–4, 105
  as treatment, 278–80, 284
  cinema as, 289
  imagination, 101–2, 103
  manipulation, 293–4, 301–2
  musical, 88–9, 93, 288
  objectivation, 100–1
  opera, 93–8, 99
  sexual fantasy, 89–93
hysteria, 83, 278–80, 281, 282–6, 294

illusion, 7, 9, 12, 13, 181, 201, 219
  aesthetics of, 292–3, 300
imagination, 101–2, 103
  moral, 44
  operatic, 83
insanity. *See mental illness*
Isouard, Nicolas, 8

James, William, 153, 288
Joal, Joseph, 35–8
Johnson, James, 111, 114

kaleidoscope, 256–8
Kant, Immanuel, 310, 311
Kapp, Ernst, 147–9, 150
Kaspar der Faggotist, oder Die Zauberzither (Müller), 193

378 *Index*

Kellogg, John Harvey, 36
Kempelen, Wolfgang von, 12, 59
Kiesewetter, Raphael Georg, 308–9
Kittler, Friedrich, 7, 8, 146, 289, 291
Koch, Heinrich Christoph, 271
Koenig, Rudolph, 126
Koller, Oswald, 307, 328
Kracauer, Siegfried, 252, 266, 267
Krafft-Ebing, Richard von, 290
Kramer, Wilhelm, 159, 160, 163
Krause, Karl Christian Friedrich, 306, 307, 313
Kurth, Ernst, 313, 326, 329, 330, 331
Küss, Emile, 37

La Scala, 17, 96, 245, 251, 255, 256, 257–8, 260, 267
Labouïsse, Jean de, 67
Lafontaine, Charles, 88
Lamperti, Francesco, 32, 34, 37
Lange, Friedrich Albert, 142
laryngoscope, 13, 14, 34, 49, 51, 52–61
  autolaryngoscopy, 54–5
laryngoscopy. *See laryngoscope; techniques of observation*
Latour, Bruno, 203, 225
Lavater, Johann Kaspar, 273, 274, 322
Le Brun, Charles, 273
Lehmann, Lilli, 39
Leibniz, Gottfried Wilhelm, 177
Lessing, Theodor, 155, 156, 171
Lichtenthal, Peter, 82, 233, 240
lighting, 2, 7, 8–9, 77, 207, 214, 219, 227, 239, 242, 255, 257, 284, 292–3, 300
  magic lantern shows, 9, 256
  panorama, 9
Lina (Schneider), 69–72, 73, 74, 76–9
listening, 117–19, 135–9, 140, 147, 150–3, 160
  acts of, 15, 156
  automatic audition, 16, 144, 148, 150, 153
  collective, 134, 239
  conscious automaton-theory and, 153
  diegesis and, 121, 123, 135–7, 140
  listener-response theory, 138
  pathological, 327
  subjectivity, 111, 114–15
Lohengrin (Wagner), 9, 21, 22, 24, 25, 32, 37, 134, 139, 150, 154, 168, 295, 299
  Reszke as Lohengrin, 28–33
Lombroso, Cesare, 99, 305, 324, 332, 333
Longet, François-Achille, 37
Louvet, Victor, 208, 210
Löwe, Ludwig, 169
Lucia di Lammermoor (Donizetti), 6

Luftbälle, oder der Liebhaber à la Montgolfier, Die (Bretzner), 175, 186–92
lute of 3,000 strings. *See Aeolian harp*
Lütgendorf, Baron von, 186, 194

Macfarren, George A., 9
Magdeleine G. [Madeleine Guipet], 91, 93, 95, 103
Magendie, François, 112–13, 116, 131, 132, 337
magic, 2, 30, 38, 176, 193, 283, 349
magic lantern shows. *See lighting*
Magnin, Émile, 91, 93, 103
Mälzel, Johann Nepomuk, 6
Mandl, Louis, 35, 36, 38, 39
Mantegazza, Paolo, 321
Manzotti, Luigi, 13, 17, 245–8, 252–8, 260–5, 267–8
Mapleson, Lionel, 21, 22, 29, 30, 31, 43
Marchesi, Blanche, 34
Marenco, Romualdo, 13, 245, 265, 268, 349
Marquis de Sade, 64, 66, 67
Marx, A. B., 313
mass ornament (Kracauer), 252, 266–8
Massenet, Jules, 24
materialism, 141–2, 149, 153, 163, 165, 171, 279
Matteucci, Carlo, 235, 244, 245
Maurel, Victor, 15, 84–9, 95, 96, 99–105
Maurice Grau Opera Company, 27
Mays, Thomas Jefferson, 36
mechanics
  of the voice, 50–2, 54–5
mechanism
  body as, 140, 153, 270, 278–80
  machines and, 201–26, 240, 247
  sympathetic resonance, 38, 140, 144
Meistersinger, Die (Wagner), 9, 28
Melba, Nellie, 28
mental illness, 64–83, 297
  neurasthenia, 289, 290
Mesmer, Franz Anton, 78, 88, 294
Mesmerism, 294, *see also hypnosis*
Metropolitan Opera House, 25
Mettrie, Julien Offray de la, 140, 279
Meyerbeer, Giacomo, 1, 7, 8, 9, 13, 63, 121, 200
Milan National Exposition (1881), 256, 258–60, 265, 267
Moffat, Carter, 44, 49, 60
mondo della luna, Il (Galuppi), 179
mondo della luna, Il (Goldoni), 175, 178–85
mondo della luna, Il (Haydn), 179–85
mondo della luna, Il (Paisiello), 181–5
moral therapy, 297

Morel, Bénédict, 289, 305
Mucha, Alfons, 90, 91
Mueller, Adam, 138
Muette de Portici, La (Auber), 70, 76, 77
Mühlmann, Adolph, 21
Müller, Georg Elias, 143
Müller, Johannes, 4, 113–14, 116, 275, 296
Müller, Wenzel, 193
multimedia, 262, 287, 289, 291, 298
Munthe, Axel, 295
music
  and evolution, 312–17, 319–21
  and machines, 246, 247, 251–2, 265
  as degenerate, 303–12, 317–19, 320–1
  as narcotic, 18, 292, 293, 298, 301, *see also*
    willpower
  as pathological, 63, 64, 326–7
  as therapeutic, 64–9, 76–80
  effects on the mentally ill, 69–73
  effects on the nerves, 63, 76–80, 287–90,
    296–302, *see also* Gesamtkunstwerk
  electric effects, 232–9
  ghostly effects, 121–31
  health effects, 63, 69, 73–83
  moral effects, 290
  spatial effects, 125–31, 131–3

Nadar (photographer), 90
narrative
  in music, 115
  of industry, 258–60
  of progress, 17, 200, 220, 225, 241, 253, 310
nerves, 17, 116, 148, 149, 155, 158, 162, 235,
    270, 274–6, 277, 287, 312, 327
  auditory, 113, 132, 140, 142, 144, 162, 164,
    167, 293, 294
Nietzsche, Friedrich, 31, 103, 281, 282, 287,
    289, 295, 296, 297, 298, 299, 301, 305,
    319, 332
noise, 155–9
  environmental, 162–3
  health and, 157–8
    auditory pathologies, 161
  Hyperæsthesia acoustica, 164
  injury through, 16, 160, 161–4
    metaphors for, 165–6, 167
    music and, 164–72
    volume, 164
    Wagner and, 16, 168–72
  ordinances, 156–7
noise legislation. *See noise, ordinances*
Nolau, François, 210
Nollet, Abbé, 236, 238

Norbury, Frank Parsons, 299
Nordau, Max, 282, 287, 289, 290, 292, 295, 298,
    299, 300, 305, 324, 333
Nordica, Lillian, 24, 25, 30
Nostitz und Jänkendorf, Gottlob von, 68

occult, the, 9, 97, 288, 294
Offenbach, Jacques, 17, 269–70, 281, 286
opera
  acoustic effects, 9, 292
  effects, 291–2
  material history of, 200, 201–26
  polyglot, 24–5
  scenic effects, 5, 13, 255
  technology and, 7, 8–9, 126, 200, 202, 223,
    226, 257–8, 287–96, 300
orchestration, 31–2, 126–31
  and sensuality, 326, 328–9
  and the fantastic, 180
  degeneracy, 329
  degeneracy through, 317
  imitation of nature through, 180
  lunar soundscape, 180–3
  timbre, 127, 130, 317, 326
Organ of Corti. *See also ear*
  as instrument, 144, 149, 150
organicism, 312–17, 331
orgue mélodium, 129
Otello (Verdi), 86, 95, 96–9
otology, 156–72

Paisiello, Giovanni, 178, 180, 181–5, 271
Palais Garnier, 199, 200, 201–26
panharmonicon, 6
panorama. *See lighting*
Parade (Satie), 17, 246, 267
Parsifal (Wagner), 9, 200, 270, 281, 282–6
Pasta, Giuditta, 232, 239
Patissier, Philippe, 159
Pepper, John Henry, 12, 13
perception, 50–2, 60, 111–12, 115
  aural, 15, 110, 112–14, 122, *see also*
    physiology
  of space, 126–31, 133
  of the voice, 50–2, *see also laryngoscope*
Perrin, Émile, 209, 210, 211, 217, 219, 220
Pfitzner, Hans, 306, 307
phantasmagoria, 9, 256, 290, 298, 301, *see also*
    fantastic; *illusion*
Phillips, Denise, 4
phonautogram, 21
physiognomy
  and criminality, 322–5

physiology, 51, 111–13, 139–44, 234, *see also Helmholtz, Hermann von*
  of the ear, 139, 140, 141, 160, 171
  psychic automatism, 142
Pinel, Philippe, 65, 81, 82
Pisco, Franz Josef, 144
pneumograph, 36, 37, *see also breathing*
Politzer, Adam, 160, 162, 164
Porges, Heinrich, 292
Porpora, Nicola, 48, 50
possession. *See autonomy; hypnosis; trance state*
Prophète, Le (Meyerbeer), 8, 200
prosthesis, 147–53, *see also Kapp; technology*
psychiatry, 15, 63, 64, 69, 115, 288, 301, *see also mental illness*
Puccini, Giacomo, 16, 227–32, 241, 247, 248
pulvérisateur, 35
Purkyně, Jan Evangelista, 111, 113
Puschmann, Theodor, 167, 290, 295

Quantz, Johann Joachim, 272
Quéruel, Auguste, 214–20, 223–5

Regnault, Victor, 210
Reich, Eduard, 299
Reichert, Carl von, 168, 169
Reil, Johann Christian, 65, 81
Reszke, Édouard de, 21, 24, 26, 34, 40
Reszke, Jean de, 21–6, 27–35, 37–9, 41–3
Ribot, Théodule, 101, 288, 297
Richardson, Benjamin Ward, 158
Richer, Paul, 278, 279, 294
Richet, Charles, 100, 295
Riemann, Hugo, 304
Robert le Diable (Meyerbeer), 7, 200
Rochefort, Claude de, 66
Roller, Christian, 69
Roosa, Daniel Bennett St John, 160, 162, 163, 168
Rosenkranz, Karl, 164
Rousseau, Jean-Jacques, 313
Royer-Collard, Antoine-Athanase, 67–8
Rozier, Pilâtre de, 185, 192

Sacré, Jean-Joseph, 210, 211, 213, 214, 215, 216, 217, 219, 220, 224
Saint-Aubin, Jeanne-Charlotte, 66
Saissy, Jean Antoine, 159
Salome (Strauss), 18, 303–4, 312–13, 317–19, 326, 330–2, 333
Salpêtrière (asylum), 18, 270, 278, 281–2, 286, 288, 294–5

Sarthe, Jacques-Louis Moreau de la, 274
Sbriglia belt. *See breathing*
Scarpa, Antonio, 113
Schelling, Friedrich, 313
Schilling, Gustav, 78
Schneider, Peter, 64, 69–83
Schnell, Johann Jakob, 6
Schopenhauer, Arthur, 3, 103
Schreker, Franz, 9, 150–3
Schubart, Christian, 77
Schumann-Heink, Ernestine, 21
Schweigger, Auguste, 67
Scossa elettrica (Puccini), 16, 228–30, 242, 248
séance, 9, 17, 238–40, 293, *see also occult*
Seiler, Emma, 14, 49–54, 56–61
self-mastery. *See willpower*
Sensationalism, 141
sentiment. *See emotions*
sentimentality, 270–2
Shaw, George Bernard, 47–8, 61
Slonimsky, Nicholas, 165
Smart, Mary Ann, 121, 252
sound. *See also acoustics; music; noise*
  ethereality, 71, 76, 78, 79, 81
  intensity, 15, 110, 113–14, 122, 129, 130, 164
soundscape
  industrial, 155, 156, 159, 226
  urban, 155, 156, 157, 158, 164, 165, 167, 168, 171
Spencer, Herbert, 1, 328
Spitzer, Daniel, 167
stage machinery, 65, 200, 201–26, 257–8, 292
staging, 8, 255, 287–96, 300
Stanislavsky, Constantin, 101
Sterne, Jonathan, 158, 159, 199, 200, 202
Stoepel, Franz, 308
Strauss, Johann I, 229, 238
Strauss, Johann II, 229
Strauss, Richard, 18, 165, 281, 303–4, 312, 317, 318, 319, 326, 328, 329, 331, 332
Stumpf, Carl, 139, 149
subject position
  extra-diegetic, 116, 119, 124
  intra-diegetic, 116, 119, 121, 124
subjectivity, 111–12
Sully, James, 157
Sully-Prudhomme [René François Armand], 95
Sulzer, Johann Georg, 271, 272
Symphonie fantastique (Berlioz), 5, 15, 110, 115–19, 130

Talia, Giambattista, 233, 234
Tannhäuser (Wagner), 166, 168
Tappert, Wilhelm, 165, 166, 167
  Ein Wagner-Lexikon, 165–6
techniques
  acting, 100–4
  experimental, 36–7, 49–54, 116, 139–41,
    276–8, 294
  for visualising data, 39–41, 278
  of observation, 50–2
  orchestration. *See orchestration*
  vocal, 14, 22, 23–4, 33–5
technology, 23, 202, 242, 246, 291
  aeronautic, 175, 185, 191, *see also ballooning*
    cloud chariot, 193
    flying machines, 193–7
  as theme, 251, 253, 256, 258
  battery, 228, 229, 238, 241, 242, 243, 244,
    246, 247, 248
  body as, 143, 147–9, 150–2
  connectivity, 243, 248
  fairy-tale, 197–8
  medical, 44–9, 52–61
  philosophy of, 147
  recording, 21–2, 23, 29, 158, *see also
    phonautogram*
  techné, 147
  telegraph, 231, 238, 242, 243–5, 255
telegrafo elettrico, Il (Danesi), 232, 242–8
telegraph. *See technology*
Ternina, Milka, 21, 29
Tissandier, Gaston, 2
Todorov, Tzvetan, 115
Tolstoy, Leo, 293, 305
tonograph, 40, 41
Tovey, Donald, 313–16, 320
trance state, 18, 88, 283, 287, 291, 293, 294, 295,
  296, *see also hypnosis*
Tresca, Henri, 210, 214–17, 219, 220, 223, 224
Tresch, John, 7, 8, 200, 201
Tristan und Isolde (Wagner), 24, 166, 291
  Tristan chord, 313–16
Tröltsch, Anton von, 160
Troyens, Les (Berlioz), 15, 110, 121–9, 130
Tudor, Frederic, 27
Twain, Mark, 22, 293
Tyndall, John, 6, 140, 143, 145, 146

ventilation systems, 27
Verdi, Giuseppe, 8, 32, 37, 86, 95, 96–7, 99, 104,
  140
vitalism, 141, 304
voice
  autolaryngoscopy, 54–6
  castrato, 50
  glottis, 34, 39, 52, 54, 55, 57,
    59
  instruction manuals, 47, 54, *see also voice,
    pedagogy*
  location of, 41–3, *see also hearing, spatial*
  metaphorical manipulation, 56
  pedagogy, 56
  perception of, 54–9
  resonance, 23, 33, 38, *see also breathing*
  speaking machines, 59
  technique
    La Voix écrasée, 33
    La Voix étoufée, 33
  timbre, 34, 38, 55
  visualising the, 39–41
  vocal health, 29, 49–50, 57–8
  vocal self, the, 44, 47, 61
  Voix blanches, 25
Volta, Alessandro, 228, 241–5, 246, 255
Voskuhl, Adelheid, 271, 272

Wagner, Richard, 8, 134, 139, 149, 150, 156,
  162, 165–72, 270, 281–2, 284–6, 287,
  288, 289–93, 295–6, 297–302, 304, 305,
  316, 320, 334
Walküre, Die (Wagner), 166, 168
Watts-Hughes, Margaret, 41
weather harp, 146, *see also Aeolian harp*
Weber, Ernst Heinrich, 141
Wheatstone, Charles, 1, 6, 11, 12, 138, 139,
  146
willpower, 17, 18, 288, 289, 291, 296–300, 301,
  see automata; hypnosis
Winkel, Dietrich Niklaus, 6
Winslow, William Henry, 144, 150
Work Gallery. *See Milan National Exposition
  (1881)*

Zauberflöte, Die (Mozart), 8, 82, 176, 190,
  193–7

Printed in the United States
by Baker & Taylor Publisher Services